ATHENS

From the Classical Period
to the Present Day
(5th century B.C. – A.D. 2000)

*We are most grateful to the following
for their co-operation and their generosity
in allowing material to be used for the illustrations:*

First Ephorate of Byzantine Antiquities ❖ First Ephorate
of Prehistoric and Classical Antiquities ❖ Ninth Ephorate
of Prehistoric and Classical Antiquities ❖ Byzantine and
Christian Museum ❖ National Archaeological Museum ❖
National Historical Museum ❖ Epigraphic Museum ❖
Vouros-Eftaxias Museum (Museum of the City of
Athens) ❖ Benaki Museum ❖ German Archaeological Institute ❖ Archives of the Committee for the Conservation
of the Acropolis Monuments ❖ ELIA (Hellenic Literary
and Historical Archives Society) ❖ Petraki Monastery ❖
Hirmer Verlag ❖ Ny Carlsberg Glyptotek ❖ Stadt Frankfurt am Main ❖ Studio KONTOS/Photostock ❖ Mr. Dimitrios Condominas ❖ Mr. Efstathios Finopoulos

Chapters I, II, III, V, VI, VII, VIII, X, XI, XII, XVI and
XVII translated by Timothy Cullen
Chapters IV translated by Christopher Scott
Chapters IX translated by Alexandra Doumas
Chapters XIII, XIV and XV translated by Pat Tsekoura

ATHENS

From the Classical Period
to the Present Day
(5th century B.C. – A.D. 2000)

Contributors

MANOLIS KORRES
ANGELOS DELIVORRIAS
MICHAEL B. SAKELLARIOU
LINOS G. BENAKIS
CHARALAMBOS BOURAS
ALKISTIS SPETSIERI-CHOREMI
MARIA KAZANAKI-LAPPA
NANO CHATZIDAKI

FANI-MARIA TSIGAKOU
FANI MALLOUCHOU-TUFANO
MARTIN KREEB
MANOS BIRIS
GEORGIOS PANETSOS
PANAYOTIS TOURNIKIOTIS
DIMITRIS PHILIPPIDIS
NIKOS VATOPOULOS

Editorial Committee

CHARALAMBOS BOURAS
MICHAEL B. SAKELLARIOU

KONSTANTINOS S. STAIKOS
EVI TOULOUPA

English translation supervised by Timothy Cullen

KOTINOS
OAK KNOLL PRESS
2003

First Edition, 2003

Published by **Oak Knoll Press**
310 Delaware Street, New Castle, Delaware, USA
Web: http://www.oakknoll.com
and **Kotinos, Athens, Greece**
Panou Aravantinou 10, Athens GR-106 74, tel.: +3010.72.41.933, fax: +3010.72.32.754
e-mail: kotinos@libraries.gr

ISBN: 1-58456-091-6

Title: Athens: From the Classical Period to the Present Day
Authors: Collective Work
Editors: Charalambos Bouras, Michael B. Sakellariou, Konstantinos Sp. Staikos, Evi Touloupa
Typography: M. Toumbis S.A.
Publishing Director: J. Lewis von Hoelle

Library of Congress Cataloging-in-Publication Data

Athens: from the Classical period to the present day (5th century B.C.-A.D. 2000) / contributors, Manolis Korres, Angelos Delivorrias, Michael B. Sakellariou, Linos G. Benakis, Charalambos Bouras, Alkistis Spetsieri-Choremi, Maria Kazanaki-Lappa, Nano Chatzidaki, Fani-Maria Tsigakou, Fani Mallouchou-Tufano, Martin Kreeb, Manos Biris, Georgios Panetsos, Panayotis Tournikiotis, Dimitris Philippidis, Nikos Vatopoulos; editorial committee, Ch. Bouras, M. B. Sakellariou, K. Sp. Staikos, E. Touloupa; English translation supervised by Timothy Cullen.
1533 pp., 24x31 cm.
Includes bibliographical references and index.
ISBN 1-58456-091-6
1. Architecture - Greece - Athens. 2. Athens (Greece) - Civilization. I. Korres, Manolis II. Bouras, Charalambos.

NA1100.A845 2002
949.5'12-dc21

2002030712

This work was printed in Athens, Greece on Zanders Mega matt 150 gsm archival,
acid-free paper meeting the requirements of the American Standard for
Permanence of Paper for Printed Library Materials.

Preface
to the English Language Edition

In commemoration of the 2004 Summer Olympics in Athens, twenty outstanding scholars have set out to celebrate, with prose and illustration, 2,500 years of Greece's most famous city. This unique work, with its collection of rare drawings and photographs, explores historical Athens from its Classical beginnings to the city's rebirth as the bustling, modern capital of the Greek nation.

The reader is invited to view many beautiful illustrations that capture Athens' timeless architecture, mosaics, wall-paintings and sculpture that have fascinated both ancient and modern travelers. Each scholar/author shares with us their special insight into the many facets of the city's long history. In the opening chapters we are treated to the details of the Parthenon and the other temples of the Acropolis as the city of Perikles, Socrates and Plato comes alive. Chapter by chapter we follow as silent witnesses the turbulent centuries of Roman, Byzantine and Ottoman rule and their effects on the proud city. We also witness the renaissance of Athens in the 19th century with Greek independence from Turkish control.

The text of this work is presented in seventeen well-written chapters that focus on the city's architecture, art, culture, monuments, landscape, history and urban development. These essays allow the reader to form a multi-dimensional understanding of this birthplace of Democracy and origin of Western Thought and Civilization.

As publishers, we are very proud to bring this exceptionally well illustrated and researched work to the English reading public. And should this book inspire you to visit the glories of Athens, I promise you an experience you will never forget.

John Lewis von Hoelle
New Castle, Delaware

i

Introduction

The end of the twentieth century and the dawn of the new millennium were celebrated in the Western world mainly with events relating either to Christological matters and the progress of Christianity generally or to the history of the repositories of Christian civilization. This collective work entitled *ATHENS: From the Classical Period to the Present Day (5th century B.C. – A.D. 2000)* comes under the latter heading: it contains articles covering not only the planning and architecture of the city of Athens from the fifth century B.C. to our own time but also the great achievements of its citizens, especially in the Classical period, such as the establishment of democracy and the birth of philosophy as a branch of learning. Other subjects discussed in these pages include the sculpture of the age of Pheidias, religious art in the Byzantine and Post-Byzantine periods and the works of art produced by the many travellers who visited Athens during and after the Renaissance.

Athens remains to this day a point of reference for Western civilization, as its democratic system of government and its extremely high level of achievement in the arts and sciences during the Classical period represent the ideal for every well-governed state. In reaching this level of cultural attainment a crucial part was played by the archons (officers of state) and the Demos (Citizens' Assembly) when they took the decision to give the city new lustre by building monuments worthy of its people. Those monumental marble edifices, notable for their perfect proportions, their incomparable technique and their harmonious – one might almost say symbiotic – congruence with their superb sculptural ornamentation, are still a model of rational thinking, with overtones of and allusions to the relationship of the human race to its immediate natural environment. The visible side of this phenomenon is apparent in the fact that architects are constantly drawing on classical forms as irreplaceable sources of inspiration for their designs.

A vital part of the monumental architecture of Classical Greece is the sculpture that was an integral element in the design of many sanctuaries. And so, as man was regarded as the measure of all things at that time, sculptors set out on a quest for the ideal human form. Characteristics common to all those sculptures are naturalism and an emphasis on the energizing force of nature, in other words movement. The tendency to pursue the greatest possible realism is clearly apparent from the period of the so-called 'Severe Style': a time that presaged the thirty-year High Classical period (460-430 B.C.), a time when a galaxy of sculptors – poets of chisel and stone – led by Pheidias, the sculptor of the Parthenon, gave free rein to their own distinctive talents in response to Perikles's summons to beautify the city. Their work, unsurpassed for expressive artistry, conveys a sense of religious feeling, community service and transcendent personal artistic exploration.

The system of government and social organization in the city of Athens in the period known as the Golden Age was democratic. Introduced in 508 B.C. and lasting until 322 B.C., democracy was the city's outstanding political achievement: indeed, ancient Athenian democracy has never ceased to be a model for any constitution designed to ensure unrestricted participation in public affairs and equal treatment in the eyes of the law for every citizen. In this type of democracy the citizens were the sole source of power, which prompted Aristotle to define the citizen of a fully-fledged democracy, such as Athens, as 'an officer of state for life'.

However, the glory of Athens was not limited to the architectural and artistic achievements of its citizens, nor to their initiative in establishing a democratic system of government: through the cultivation of literary and scholarly writing, the Athenians finally defined the branches of learning that particularly interested them: poetry, historiography, rhetoric and philosophy, which they elevated to the level of the consummate exercise of the human intellect. The jewels in Athens' crown from the early fourth century B.C. were its schools of philosophy, which survived until the sixth century A.D. And so, while the sculptors, the visionary architects and the potters and vase-painters were busy adorning the Acropolis and the monuments of the Agora, Socrates and Plato were beginning to lay the foundations of an anthropocentric philosophy that has never ceased to exercise the human mind. The centripetal force exerted by Athens led the outstanding exponents of the First Sophistic to congregate in Athens to impart to their students the achievements of the 'schools' and philosophical circles in Ionia and Lower Italy, thus creating a philosophical environment that has left an indelible imprint not merely on the whole of the Greek world but on human thought everywhere.

On the death of Alexander the Great (323 B.C.) and the gradual emergence of the new cities founded by him and his successors (especially Alexandria, Pergamon and Antioch) as the cultural centres of the Greek world, Athens started losing its hegemony in this sphere. Yet it never lost its cultural prestige: its philosophy schools and art studios and workshops were not silenced, and generous benefactors such as Attalos I and Eumenes II (who endowed the stoas named after them) continued to beautify Athens with monumental buildings in order to perpetuate their own name. Moreover, during the Hellenistic period, when it became general practice to adorn public places with monumental sculpture, pedestals were built for the erection of chariots in honour of the rulers of Greek kingdoms in Asia Minor and the Near East.

The high prestige of Athens in the Hellenistic period – with its magnificent monuments, its gymnasia and gardens, its splendid villas, imposing public places and Long Walls – lasted until the city was taken by the Roman general Sulla in 86 B.C., when the walls of Athens and Piraeus were demolished, numerous buildings and monuments destroyed and many outstanding works of art taken back to Rome as booty. Among the casualties of Sulla's depredations was a part of Aristotle's private library containing the philosopher's own authentic manuscripts. Yet the sack of Athens did not destroy the aura attached to its name, and it was not long before pro-Athenians in all walks of life – private individuals, civic dignitaries and even kings – started spending large sums of money, sometimes on repairs to the ruined monuments and the restoration of public utilities and sometimes on the construction of splendid new buildings, with the object of restoring the city to its former glory.

After the death of Augustus in A.D. 14 there was a lull in building activity in Athens, but it did not last very long, because the accession of Hadrian brought the first philhellene emperor on to the Roman throne. It was in Hadrian's reign that, among other things, one of the greatest libraries in the ancient world was built near the Roman Agora in Athens. In recognition of all he had done for their city, in A.D. 135 the Athenians dedicated to him the arch that bears his name, which separated the new city from the old.

Athens' intellectual standing gradually declined with the spread of Christianity, and the probability that its philosophy schools would be closed on the Emperor Justinian orders in 529 dealt it a further blow. Thereafter the city sank into obscurity and, although some of the aura of its ancient greatness still lingered on, chiefly on account of its philosophy schools, the ancient buildings and monuments were left to the mercy of time and the elements. Although there are large gaps in our knowledge of the history of ancient cities during the Byzantine period, it seems that Athens was never abandoned by its inhabitants. When Emperor Basil II ('the Bulgar-Slayer') came to Greece in 1018, he made a point of going to pray in the Church of the Panagia Athiniótissa, which was none other than the Parthenon, and by doing so he linked his own victorious campaigns with Greek history.

Athens in the Byzantine period was a typical Byzantine provincial town, with its citadel (the walled Acropolis) and the Late Roman wall protecting the commercial and administrative centre and the homes of the ruling class. The rest of the town, with residential neighbourhoods, churches and small workshops, lay outside the wall. Most of the Byzantine monuments still standing are religious buildings, churches in fact, though we cannot be sure which of them were small monastery churches and which were private chapels. Be that as it may, in 1830, when Athens was liberated from the Turks, there were 120 Byzantine and Post-Byzantine churches in the town, attesting both to the Athenians' piety and devotion to the Christian way of life and to the character of the architectural activity at the time.

The examples of Byzantine and Post-Byzantine fine arts that have come down to us consist mainly of wall-paintings in churches and the celebrated mosaics of Dhafní Monastery. The oldest surviving examples belong to the painted decoration of the Panagia Athiniótissa, dating from the twelfth century. More typical than these are the wall-paintings of the Frankish period, such as those in the churches of Hagios Ioánnis Theológos in the Pláka and Hagia Marína near the 'Theseion': their most noticeable characteristics are their vivid colours and the lack of perspective in the figure drawing. Outstanding among the churches in the environs of Athens are Kaisarianí Monastery and the Ómorfi Ekklisía in Galátsi: the latter is adorned with interesting examples of Palaiologian art dating from about 1300. Kaisarianí Monastery, which is associated with the Benizelos family, one of the oldest and most influential families in Athens, still has its wall-paintings by Ioannes Ypatos, a seventeenth-century artist from the Peloponnese.

Western Europeans first came into contact with the monuments of Athens at the time of the Italian Renaissance, in the fifteenth century, and thereafter their visits became steadily more frequent. By the late eighteenth and early nineteenth centuries, when they were engaging in systematic excavations which gave their researches a strictly archaeological character, they were beginning to discover the monuments' real identity. Early references to Athens were limited to the intellectual achievements of the leading lights of its philosophy schools, with the emphasis on Plato and Aristotle. However, as the humanists started founding academies and schools modelled on ancient gymnasia in their efforts to bring the Classical period back to life in Italian centres of learning, they kindled widespread interest in the ancient world: not only in the great works of literature and learning but in the buildings and monuments too. In the course of their research the travellers began making systematic records of ancient inscriptions and sketching the ruined monuments in their journals. A notable case in point is Ciriaco d'Ancona, who travelled in the Mediterranean countries between 1425 and 1448 and twice visited Athens, where he drew the Parthenon, the Monument of Philopappos and other antiquities; while there he stayed on the Acropolis itself, in the palazzo of the Acciaiuoli, the Florentine dukes of Athens.

Ciriaco's initiative was not followed up as one might have expected, because the Turkish conquest of most of Greece in 1456 made it much more difficult to travel to Athens. Consequently, in one of the earliest illustrated educational books to appear in the West – Hartmann Schedel's *Liber Chronicarum* (1493), containing descriptions and woodcuts of the most famous cities and towns –

the illustration of Athens is a mere figment of the imagination, resembling nothing so much as a typical walled town in Germany. The earliest town plan giving the locations and names of the principal monuments was a sketch map drawn by the Capuchin friars in the seventeenth century. Visits to Greece became more frequent from then on, and Athens was never left off the itinerary. With the founding of the London-based Society of Dilettanti, rudimentary surveys and drawings of the monuments of Athens were superseded by serious and reliable scientific records of the antiquities, most notably the superb drawings and paintings by the architects and painters James Stuart and Nicholas Revett, which they published in four large-format volumes entitled *The Antiquities of Athens*.

In the early years of the nineteenth century this romantically-motivated practice of making detailed notes and drawings of the monuments of Athens took on a different form, for by this time a knowledge and study of Greek antiquities had become an essential part of every architect's training, with the result that architects intent on research flocked to Athens, hoping against hope to discover some hitherto unknown aspect of monumental architecture. Their researches led to the first unofficial excavations – and also to the widespread looting of Athenian antiquities, culminating in the seizure of the Parthenon sculptures by Lord Elgin. At the same time, however, the romantic movement for the rediscovery of Athens and the recording of its ancient monuments was a source of inspiration for some outstanding landscape paintings. Most of them are panoramic views of the city, from any and every angle, with the Acropolis as the focal point. The Acropolis, dominated by the Parthenon, was immortalized in a riot of colour conveying an impression of the natural environment as it was at the time, with conspicuous features such as the Temple of Olympian Zeus, the 'Theseion' and the Monument of Philopappos round about.

The other element in the discovery of the ancient monuments' real identity was the initiation of systematic excavations, which were incorporated into the earliest city plans of the new Athens after it had been declared the capital of the newly-established kingdom. It was clear from the first plans proposed by Stamatios Kleanthis and Eduart Schaubert that there was no intention of building the new city on top of the deeply stratified remains of the old, and also that in order to forge the city's identity it was essential to give prominence to its ancient Greek roots, especially that symbol of Greek nationhood and eternal emblem of Athens' ancient glory and beauty: the Acropolis.

The first systematic excavations around the Acropolis were put in hand in the two decades following King Otho's abdication (1862), the period that saw the mobilization of the Athens Archaeological Society, which became the official guardian of the country's antiquities. In the early twentieth century the excavations were extended and the Kerameikos quarter, including the Sacred Gate, the Dipylon Gate, the Pompeion and the Themistoklean wall, was brought to light. The idyllic appearance which these excavations gave to the natural landscape round the Acropolis and the margins of Hadrian's 'new city', with the Olympieion standing out boldly against Ardhitós Hill, changed abruptly after 1922. The population explosion, the rapid and unplanned expansion of the city and the height of the new buildings altered the historic landscape for ever – something that had not been achieved by centuries of periodic barbarian invasions, nor even by the passage of time.

The urban renewal of Athens dates from 1834, when the city was designated 'capital city and seat of the monarchy' and the architects Kleanthis and Schaubert were commissioned to prepare a new master plan for the new Athens. Unfortunately, their plan was not put into effect as it stood and its underlying philosophy was sacrificed to various practical constraints; but the centrality of the royal palace as envisaged by the Kleanthis-Schaubert plan was retained and the palace building, in its new guise as the Parliament, still offers the magnificent view of the Acropolis that its architects intended, over the 'Garden of the People'. Leo von Klenze, the famous pioneer of classicism in Munich, was commissioned to design a new city plan.

By the time King George I came to the throne in 1863, the population of Athens had passed the figure of 40,000 foreseen in the Kleanthis-Schaubert plan; within two decades it rose to 60,000, and by the turn of the century it had exactly doubled to 120,000. In the 1880s the city limits were greatly extended until they reached from Kolonós in the north-west to Ambelókipi in the east and from Patíssia in the north to Kinóssaryes in the south-east. Since then the authorities have had no qualms about periodically including all illegal or unauthorized housing within city limits, and we are still faced with the consequences of that thoughtless policy to this day.

Neoclassical Athens came into being within the urban structure envisaged by Kleanthis and Schaubert, and its construction certainly presented a challenge. Since the city had regained its former glory in the eyes of Western Europe through the re-emergence of its superb ancient monuments, the quest for an architectural style consonant with its ancient tradition led those architects along historic paths. In the romantic climate of the age, the creation of an architectural style that would blend the early examples of Neoclassicism with the ancient Greek architectural tradition, actually in the birthplace of that tradition, had philosophical overtones as well as being aesthetically appropriate. The vision of an Athens cast in that mould was not betrayed by Kleanthis, Kaftandzoglou, Kalkos or Metaxas, nor by the foreign architects Schaubert, Hansen, Ziller and Schinkel, nor by later generations.

It was in this heady atmosphere and in the knowledge that splendid buildings were needed in Athens, not only to accommodate government offices and public institutions but also for wealthy Athenians and Greeks returning from the diaspora, that construction work started on the University (1839). Thereafter the typology of the so-called 'Athenian School' of Neoclassicism started to take shape in fine buildings that were truly worthy of the Athenian architectural tradition, in terms of their well-judged proportion as well as their aesthetic effect.

Modern trends in European architecture started to make an impact in Athens in the late 1920s, at a time when historic events in Greece were causing abrupt changes to the Athenian landscape. In spite of that, a great many admirable examples of the modernist school of architecture were built, some of them winning international acclaim: not only a considerable number of multi-storey apartment blocks and other buildings in the private sector (mostly places of entertainment) but public buildings as well. The latter – hospitals and thousands of schools – were built as part of a modernization programme to cater for the influx into Athens of hundreds of thousands of refugees from the Asia Minor disaster (1922), which almost doubled the city's population overnight. This gave rise to an unprecedented political sensitivity to social welfare, health and education. The architectural criteria for these public works projects were not limited to purely functional and technical considerations: every effort was made to create designs that would express the latest thinking in European 'modern architecture'.

The period of contemporary Athenian architecture, roughly from the Second World War to the present day, has had a dire effect on the Attic landscape. In the first place, all pretence of controlling building construction in accordance with a master plan has been abandoned as more and more areas of illegally built housing are legalized retrospectively, and secondly the expansion of the city limits of Athens and the surrounding municipalities is leading to the creation of a continuous built-up area stretching from Pérama to Sounion. The natural environment is being further defaced by the steady rise of suburban houses up the slopes of Mount Pendéli and Mount Imitós (Hymettos), dramatically reducing the area of forest land in Attica, already decimated by a succession of forest fires.

All in all, the present state of Athens' urban development bears no resemblance to the picture presented by the city in the early 1950s, when the new urban framework started to take shape with the construction of new arterial roads, the broadening of existing ones and the creation of large city blocks. Although the face of Athens was not irreparably ruined then, since the historic centre was left almost intact, the fact remains that for at least thirty years after 1950 we witnessed the implementation of a 'demolition policy' which in the long run has eroded the cultural awareness of most Athenians.

Anyone setting out to describe the architectural typology of the thirty years from 1950 to 1980, even briefly, finds himself faced with the most appalling anarchy: buildings and designs by brilliant creative architects and leaders of the quest for a contemporary style of Athenian architecture – some of them still possessing their original, distinctive character – have been crowded out by structures whose whole design 'philosophy' was conceived by building contractors interested only in redevelopment for a quick profit.

The scope of this book, which deals mainly with the evolution of Athens' urban structure and its architecture through the ages, is not limited to a discussion of the urgent problems created by the thoughtless expansion of Athens, nor is its object merely to excoriate. The aim has been to focus attention on the city's human face, as shaped by the citizens of Periklean Athens and subsequently respected or disfigured by later generations and, more particularly, by conquering armies. And although every reader will soon discover how much the environment of the plain of Athens has changed in the last fifty years, the city has not lost its charm.

The Acropolis and its monuments are still clearly visible from most parts of Athens, as they always have been, while the archaeological excavations around it and the unification of archaeological sites are gradually reconstructing the historic landscape. The old town – the Pláka district – is being remodelled, pedestrianized and restored to its original form. Old neighbourhoods such as Psirrí, Keramikós and the area round the disused gasworks ('the Gázi') are acquiring new style and a fresh vitality, so that they are becoming more like the Pláka. The historic squares are being redesigned and beautified with contemporary sculptures which set off those architectural monuments that are still standing. Numerous pedestrian zones are being created, attractive street lights are being installed and there is now visible evidence of a will to maintain and enlarge public gardens. As you walk down from the top of Likavitós to Kolonáki, you look across to Ardhitós Hill and the Panathenaic Stadium nestling at its foot: both appear to be unaffected by the passage of time, and they epitomize the Attic landscape. Continue towards the Stadium and turn right, and you will find yourself looking at the Acropolis through the columns of the Temple of Olympian Zeus – the very same view that was immortalized by travellers centuries ago. Walk on and you come to the top of the Hill of Philopappos, leaving the Odeion of Herodes Atticus and the Pnyx to your right: looking southwards from this vantage point, you can clearly see the sea, with Aigina in the distance. You are left with the impression that the Attic sky and the unique Attic light still dominate the landscape, inspiring poets and creative artists, as well as the people of Athens, to see the beautiful things of everyday life in terms of everlasting ideals and human values.

For the Editorial Committee
K.S. Staikos

CONTENTS

CHAPTERS
I-XVII

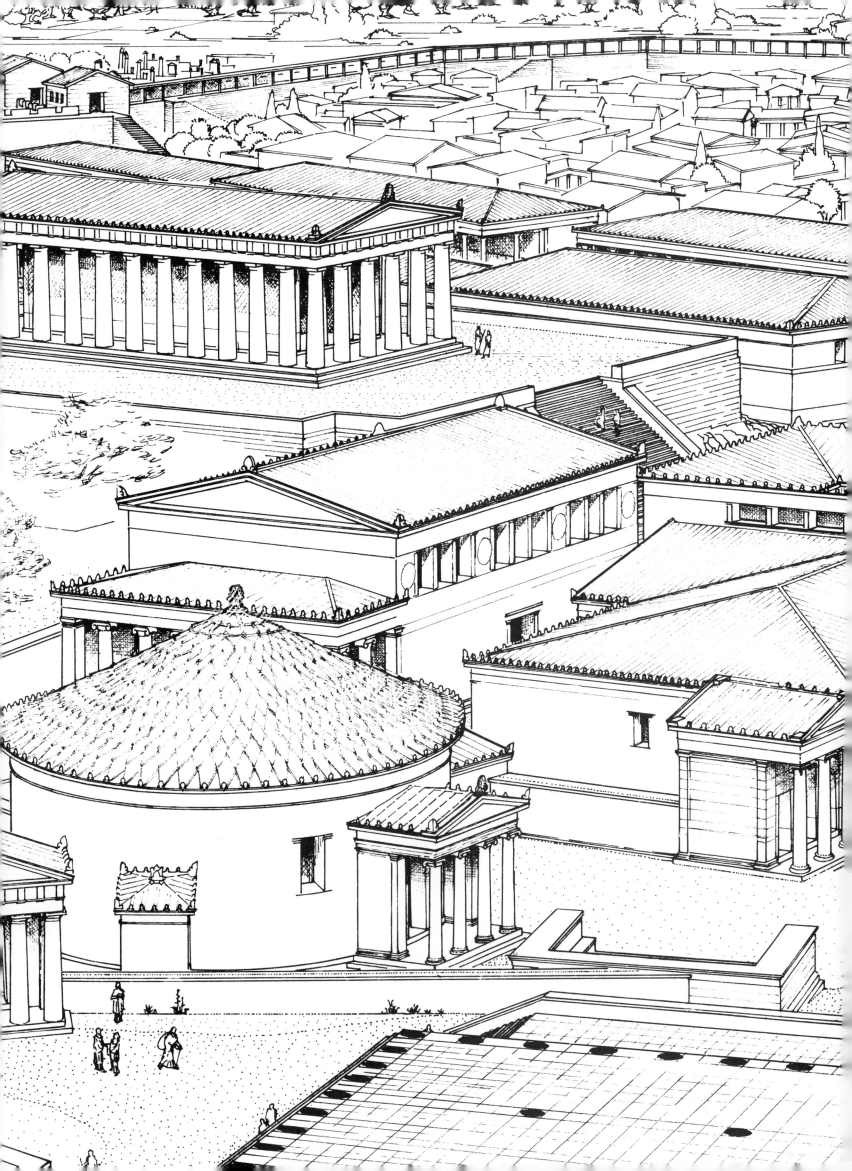

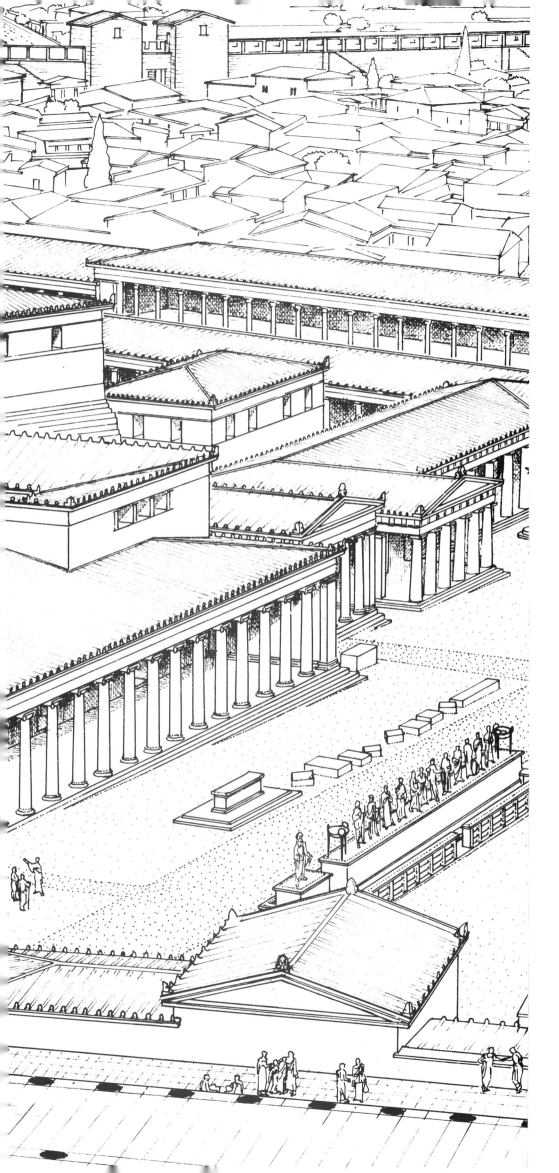

CHAPTER I

*Athenian
Classical
Architecture*

M. KORRES

2. The pronaos of the Parthenon. Reconstruction drawing. (M. Korres, 1987)

1. The Athens Agora in the second century B.C. (M. Korres, 1972)

Athenian Classical Architecture

The unrivalled works of Athenian classical architecture are the most visible aspect of a wider historical phenomenon which has had a universal and lasting impact. Other aspects of the same phenomenon, perhaps more important but less obviously visible, were literary endeavour, the birth and evolution of drama as an elevated form of creative art, the systematization of philosophy and the development of political systems and institutions. Consequently the best way to understand Athenian architecture is to consider it as just one part of the whole; and it is likewise easier to understand the way it developed if we look at it in the context of the historical and artistic background from the late seventh or early sixth century B.C. However, space does not permit more than a selective survey of the subject: this chapter covers the main types of temples and other buildings, and also certain topics relating to innovation, evolution and influences.

Before the sixth century B.C. the Acropolis still contained within its Cyclopean walls some buildings that had survived from the Mycenaean period. In the middle was the sanctuary of Athena with a large altar and a brick temple (of the Late Geometric period) with wooden columns in the sekos and pronaos. Some scant remains of it were found in 1885 a few metres south of the Erechtheion. It remained in use until 530 B.C., perhaps with a new roof, and at some point it came to be known as the *Old Temple* of Athena; later, however, that name was applied to the temple built on the same site under the Peisistrateidai.

Before monumental architecture

The Asty ('City'), a maze of winding streets teeming with life, was in early antiquity a dense huddle of buildings occupying a belt about five hundred feet wide all round the Acropolis as well as the hill of the Areopagus (Areios Pagos) and its lower slopes – an area bounded roughly by modern Polygnótou, Lysíou, Tripódhon, Vákhou, Dhionisíou Areopayítou and Apostólou Pávlou Streets. The Agora or civic centre was to the north of the Church of Hagios Nikólaos Rangavás. Bordering it, just outside the boundaries of the Asty (in the area of modern Kirrístou Street), was the area set aside for official Panathenaic religious festivals and festivals of games, which were the foundations of the Athenians' social and cultural identity. The great landowners controlled political affairs while another up-and-coming class, that of the artisans and merchant shipowners, dominated the city's commercial life and pushed steadily to acquire an equally influential role in politics. These two classes had both the means and the will to impose their taste on the development and beautification of public places in Athens, especially the religious sanctuaries, and such work kept all sorts

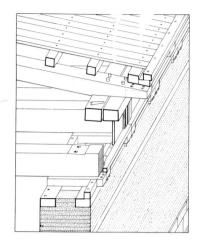
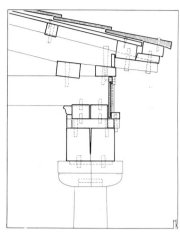

3. *Doric architecture in wood, late 7th cent. b.c. Reconstruction drawing. (M. Korres, 1992)*

4. *The first peripteral Parthenon, c. 580-566 B.C., NE corner. Reconstruction drawing. (M. Korres, 1992)*

of artists and craftsmen in almost continuous employment: potters, painters, tilers, sculptors, metalworkers, braziers and others. The kinds of project on which they worked remained unchanged during several periods: sundry types of funerary monuments, sundry types of votive tripods, sumptuous lustral basins, ritual tables, altars, sundry types of statues and so on, but the modes of artistic expression varied and were constantly evolving.

Before the middle of the seventh century, as a result of a long succession of achievements (e.g. in ironworking and writing) and social progress in all fields, aided by favourable geopolitical conditions (friendly relations and commercial dealings with Egypt), the whole of Greece experienced an unprecedented surge of economic, demographic and cultural development. In building construction, the first appearance of tiles brought about a revolution in architecture: the steeply-pitched roofs covered with thick vegetation became a thing of the past, together with the buildings they had covered. The new roofs sloped very gently, to prevent the tiles from slipping, yet they were completely waterproof thanks to the size and perfect fit of their component parts. The shape and size of tiles were highly standardized, which meant that the design of the whole building had to conform to stricter specifications, and that in turn led to the crystallization of the forms and proportions of a new style of architecture, the Doric order, which first took shape in wooden buildings (Fig. 3) but was very soon adapted for use with stone. Even then, however, stylized imitations of the components that had been devised as structural elements in wooden buildings and had become established as architectural motifs persisted as features of the Doric style. The all-wooden phase of Doric architecture appears to have been extremely short-lived and confined to what was probably its birthplace, the Argive Heraion. Evidently the process of its evolution as a medium for building in stone was very rapid, which means that Doric architecture was already being used in stone structures (or at least in buildings that were only partly of wood) by the time it started spreading to the rest of the Greek world towards the end of the seventh century, not more than thirty or forty years after its birth in wood.

Monumental stone buildings in the Doric style first appeared in Athens early in the sixth century – perhaps even in Solon's time, or hardly later than in the cradle of Doric architecture in the Peloponnese. At almost the highest point on the Acropolis, thirty metres south of the hallowed *Old Temple*, there arose a temple dedicated to Athena Parthenos (the Virgin Athena), known to archaeologists as the 'Ur-Parthenon' (Figs. 4, 7a), which was the first ever to have a peristyle (outer colonnade) on all four sides. It was a Doric hexastyle temple, probably with fourteen columns along each side, with intercolumniations of *c.* 3.80 m. and overall dimensions of *c.* 20.8 × 46 m., making it one of the biggest temples of its period, comparable with the slightly earlier Temple of Hera at Olympia (*c.* 18.75 × 50 m.). It was adorned with sculptured marble metopes (a quadriga viewed from the front, leopards, etc.), pedimental statuary of poros limestone (Herakles and Triton, huge lions, the 'three-bodied daimon', etc.), a marble sima (gutter) along all four sides of the roof and perhaps marble roof tiles. The construction of the Ur-Parthenon must have been an unusually expensive project calling for excellent administrative organization and full utilization of the available manpower. Huge blocks of stone had to be taken up to the Acropolis for the first time since the Mycenaean walls were built, necessitating the construction of a ramp of monumental dimensions at the west end of the Acropolis, perhaps on the same site as an earlier Mycenaean ramp. The temple was probably inaugurated in 566 B.C., the year when Peisistratos reorganized the Panathenaia festival. Some forty years later the Peisistratidai initiated a wide-ranging building programme that included the famous Peisistratid aqueduct as well as a gigantic dipteral Doric temple of poros limestone in the sanctuary of Olympian Zeus (on the site of an unfinished smaller temple started under Solon) and another hexastyle peripteral temple on the Acropolis (Fig. 5) on the site of the *Old Temple*, whose name it inherited. This was also Doric and was made of poros from Piraeus, with a low krepis, tall columns with stout capitals, a heavy entablature

Towards Classical architecture

5. *The Old Temple, c. 530-520 B.C., partial view of the S side. Reconstruction drawing. (F. Krischen)*

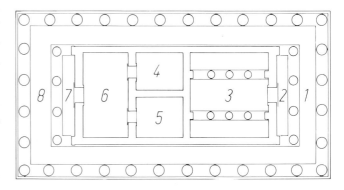

6. *The Old Temple, c. 530-520 B.C., floor plan.*

with plain metopes of Hymettos marble, marble roof tiles with a richly-decorated sima (painted Ionic ornamental motifs, animal-head spouts at the corners) and pediments of Parian marble with superb statuary (battle of Gods and Giants, lions, etc.) of the same stone. The interior layout of the sekos was unusual, for it consisted of a three-aisled sanctuary of Athena at the east end and a closed three-roomed opisthodomos at the west, with a separate entrance (Fig. 6). With only twelve columns along each side of the temple, the ratio of length to breadth was exceptionally low, and this deviation from the norm has often puzzled scholars. The explanation seems to be that the new 'Old Temple' was designed to be much broader than its predecessor, but it was not possible for the length to be increased in proportion: the west side had to be in line with the west side of the Parthenon, and a similar restriction applied to the other end so that the east façade would be at a certain specified distance from the great altar. Greater breadth was wanted for two reasons: to make the interior more spacious, especially in the opisthodomos with its two transverse rooms,

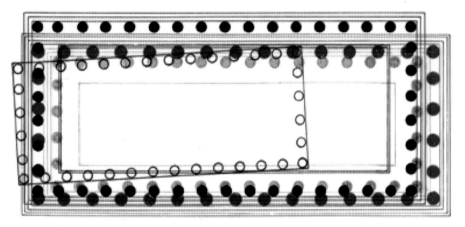

7. *Parthenon, successive phases. (a) First limestone peripteral temple, c. 580-566 B.C., (b) Second limestone peripteral temple, c. 500 B.C. (never built), (c) First marble temple, c. 490-485 B.C., (d) Second marble temple, c. 447-438 B.C. (M. Korres)*

and secondly to create wider pediments with room for bigger sculptures. The design of the Peisistratid Old Temple is a splendid example of the selective satisfaction of functional needs without being tied to universal standards of mass and proportion. This kind of approach is generally recognized in the Periklean Parthenon (the Erechtheion, not being a normal temple, is not counted), but careful observation shows that the same spirit was present, and evolving steadily, in several much older Athenian buildings.

All round the Old Temple and along the main walks were countless votive offerings standing in long rows and dense clusters: lofty tripods of the early sixth century with a stone core, wooden frame and metal surface; sumptuous marble lustral basins with Ionic volutes and figural ornamentation, imported from Naxos at about the same time; statues of horses and horsemen of Parian marble, dating from the time of Peisistratos; other statues and reliefs of Hymettos marble, and so on. Many, many more were added later, outstanding among them being the famous *korai* of Parian marble, now in the Acropolis Museum. The great construction programmes put in hand by the 'tyrants' certainly prove that Athens was going through a period of unprecedented prosperity, though the buildings were not as large and grand as those being erected in the great Greek cities in Asia Minor, southern Italy and Sicily.

After 508 the newly-installed democratic régime reviewed nearly all the building programmes initiated by the 'tyrants'. The gigantic project under way in the sanctuary of Olympian Zeus, which in Aristotle's opinion must have been a very heavy burden on the people, was abandoned, but the flourishing quarries in Piraeus continued to turn out large quantities of building stone for a huge new temple (named 'Parthenon I' by Dörpfeld, Fig. 7b) to replace the Parthenon built under Solon and Peisistratos. Nearly ten thousand blocks of stone, weighing on average at least two tons, were brought up from Piraeus and used in the stereobate of the new temple (*c.* 77 x 31.4 m.). The design provided for a peristyle with six columns at each end and fifteen along each side. The columns would have had a diameter of *c.* 2.30 m. and a height of *c.* 11.50 m., while each architrave block at the east and west ends would have been about 5.30 m. long!

This ambitious project was shelved when the Persian menace loomed shortly before 490. What followed was to be the most critical and even-tually the most glorious episode in the history of Athens, and by extension of Greece: the gruelling ordeal and final triumph of the Athenians at Marathon. The ordeal was one that threatened the Athenians' very existence, not to mention their lib-erty and the survival of their fledgling political sys-tem, while the final outcome was a triumph for audacity, spirited collective action and the new method of organization. That episode, which actual-ly lasted only a few days, lived on for decades as the inspiration for a surge of activity in every field, which led the Athenians into unparalleled historical experi-ences – from the intoxication of superpower status to the agony of self-destruction – and matchless achievements in the realm of scholarship, literature and the arts – from philosophy and the theatre to architecture and sculpture.

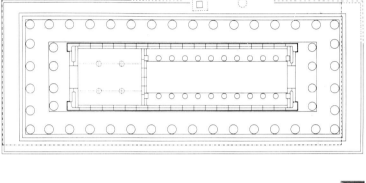

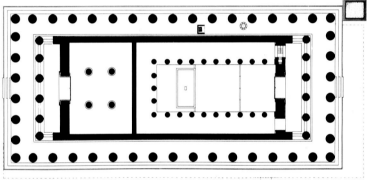

8. The first marble Parthenon, c. 490-485 B.C., and the second, c. 447-438 B.C. Comparison of floor plans. (M. Korres, 1985)

Yet another new era in architecture was inaugurated on the Acropolis with the construction of the new Parthenon. The stereobate built for 'Parthenon I' was already in place and was now used for the new tem-ple, but the design of the temple was different. For the first time in history a Doric temple ('Parthenon II', Figs. 7c, 8) was to be built entirely of marble, and for this purpose the first marble quarries on Mt. Pentelikon went into operation.

The marble Parthenon

Marble had been used by the 'tyrants', but in the Pre-Parthenon it was Hymet-tos marble for the roof tiles and metopes only, in the Old Temple it was Parian marble for the pediments only, and in the Temple of Apollo at Delphi it was Parian marble for the east front of the building only. The new Parthenon, a product of democracy and a monument to Victory, was built by the Athenians using their own material. Pentelic marble was more valuable than any other building stone, heavier than Piraeus limestone and available in abundance, but so fissured that it was difficult to find pieces large enough to make extremely long architrave blocks. For this reason the new temple was designed with shorter intercolumniations, and therefore more columns, than 'Parthenon I'. Nevertheless the fifteen intercolumniations along each side would not have covered the whole length of the huge platform put in place for the earlier, unbuilt temple. The columns would have had a diameter of *c.* 1.90 m.; their intended height is not known, but it is estimated at *c.* 9.57 m. The design of the sekos is surprising for a Doric temple, for the two end façades are prostyle instead of the usual distyle *in antis*, and the socle has a boldly-profiled moulding rather than the usual plain vertical face. These features betray an Ionian, or rather Cycladic, influence that has not been seen before.

Unfortunately that Parthenon, like its immediate predecessor, remained unfinished. Construction work on it, which had progressed to the height of the second or third column drums, was probably halted in about 485, when the threat of a full-scale Persian invasion loomed and work was begun on Themistokles' programme of strengthening the fortifications and building a large fleet. Another ambitious plan, for the construction of a magnificent marble Propylon on the site of the Propylaia that we see today, was abandoned at the same time.

In 480/479 B.C. the Persians captured the Acropolis and sacked it. Flames destroyed the roof of the Old Temple and the heavy timber scaffolding of the Parthenon and the Propylon, making the columns and walls so badly cracked and flaked that the Old Temple was unusable and it was impossible to continue with the construction of the other two buildings.

For about thirty years after the sack of the Acropolis no structural repair or maintenance work was done apart from what was absolutely necessary for the sanctuaries to function. That it took so long before rebuilding started was partly because a higher priority was given, quite rightly, to other projects connected with the reconstruction of the economy and the machinery of state, and partly because of the 'Plataian oath', whereby the Greeks undertook to leave the ruins untouched for thirty years as a symbolic reminder of the horrors of war. Thirty years after the battle of Plataiai (Plataea) a peace treaty was signed with Persia and two years after that, on the signing of a thirty-year peace treaty with Sparta, work started under Perikles on the rebuilding of the Parthenon on the massive substructure built for the abandoned Parthenon I started under Kleisthenes and Aristeides. The architects in charge of the project were Iktinos and Kallikrates.

The design of the Periklean Parthenon ('Parthenon III', Figs. 7d, 8) was more or less predetermined by that of Parthenon II. Not only are its columns of the same diameter and made of stone intended for the columns of Parthenon II, but its interior is divided into two rooms of exactly the same length as the east and west rooms of the unfinished temple. The innovation in the Periklean Parthenon is its greater breadth, necessitating the addition of two more columns to the normal hexastyle façade of a Doric temple (Fig. 8). However, an octastyle façade would be too wide in relation to its height, according to the accepted norm. The architect circumvented this problem by adding one more drum to each column, reducing the space between columns and narrowing the corner intercolumniations twice as much as was necessary to cope with the perennial problem of the corner triglyph. In addition, the pteroma was narrowed still more (usually the side walls are exactly in line with the axis of the penultimate column at each end of the façade) so that the sekos occupies a greater proportion of the overall width than usual. Because the closer spacing of the columns would reduce the overall length, with the result that the sekos

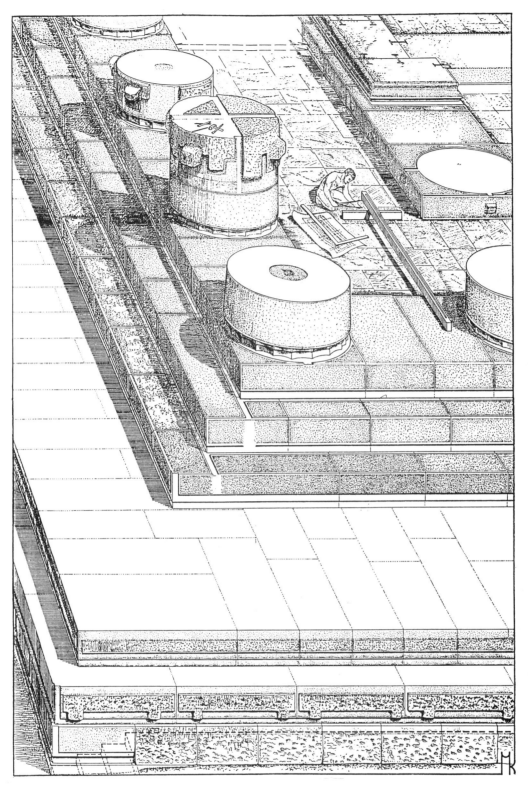

9. The first marble Parthenon, c. 490-485 B.C., SE corner. Reconstruction drawing. (M. Korres, 1982)

could not be as long as he wanted (and had originally been planned), the architect increased the number of columns from sixteen to seventeen. This extension more than made up for the total shortening caused by the narrower intercolumniation: in fact it added about 2.5 metres to the length, but part of that gain was lost because the thickness of the end walls had to be increased from 1.77 to 2.05 metres. Most of the remaining surplus was added to the depth of the pronaos and opisthodomos, to preserve their proportions in spite of the much greater width. The huge increase in the width of the temple, necessitated by the special requirement of showing up the statue of Athena Parthenos to the best effect, made possible – and perhaps provided the inspiration for – an improvement in the interior design of the sekos: the inner colonnades were

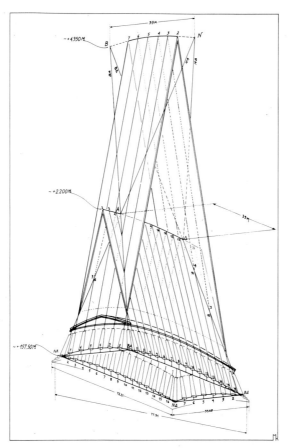

10. The optical refinements of the Parthenon. (M. Korres)

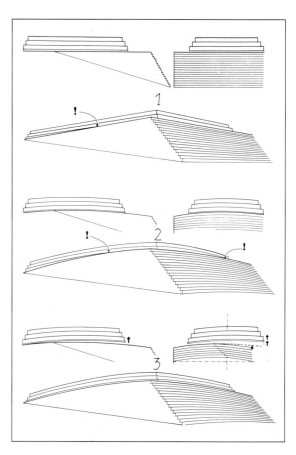

11. Refinements of refinements: subtle modifications of the curvature of the Parthenon's horizontal surfaces. (M. Korres)

supplemented with a transverse one, creating an ambulatory round the central space, and a window was therefore inserted on either side of the door to illuminate the ambulatory.

It would appear that Iktinos was not responsible for most of the innovations that make the design of the Periklean Parthenon so unusual. In the first place, although the two-roomed type of temple was very rare elsewhere, on the Acropolis it was the general rule: cf. the Pre-Parthenon,

Old Temple, Erechtheion. Secondly, the narrowness of the pteroma, the pronaos and the opisthodomos (so useful as a way of increasing the inner space), though contrary to the general practice in Greek temples, was also a common feature on the Acropolis, as exemplified in the same three temples. Lastly, the exceptional width of the temple was absolutely necessary to meet the requirements of Pheidias' statue of Athena Parthenos, while the two extra columns at each end were added so that the building could be made wider without wasting the column drums already roughed out for the exterior of the unfinished temple burnt by the Persians. That being so, how much of the design was the work of Iktinos himself? In my opinion, the following features are attributable to him. (1) The highly original approach to problems of composition for which the solutions were not imposed on him by the political leadership or the architectural tradition of the Acropolis. Among the design elements resulting from this were: the novel type of two-tier colonnade, Π-shaped in plan; the windows; the design of the coffered ceilings (Fig. 2); the use of a feature borrowed from the Pre-Parthenon, namely the four Ionic columns in the west room, but perhaps with capitals of a new type foreshadowing the Corinthian; and the abandonment of a conspicuous Ionic feature of the Pre-Parthenon, namely the bold moulding at the foot of the walls. Normally with such a moulding one would expect the architraves of the pronaos and opisthodomos to be decorated with an Ionic moulding, as in the Hephaisteion, but those of the Parthenon are Doric, and the frieze was originally to have been Doric too. Its replacement with the existing Ionic frieze – the outcome of weighty decisions by the political leadership on finding bold ways of conveying or giving prominence to certain important messages having little connection with religion – resulted in a number of minor alterations which cumulatively made a great difference to Iktinos' brilliant original design, especially in the matter of precise arithmetical and geometrical ratios. (2) The

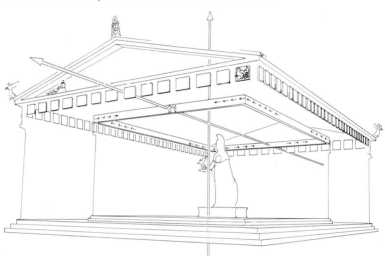

12. Grading of the thematic content of the Parthenon's sculptures according to height and orientation. (M. Korres)

breathtaking perfection and harmony in the design and composition of architectural forms and ornaments. (3) The brilliant design solutions found for all sorts of structural details. (4) The unbelievable perfectionism with which the optical refinements have been worked out and modified to suit the different parts of the building (Fig. 10). These modifications, aptly termed 'refinements of refinements', include: the precisely calculated elevation of the NW and SW corners of the building by 2.5 and 5 cm. respectively, resulting in a slight asymmetry of the curves which, in combination with a reverse asymmetry of the curves on the west side of the temple terrace (of which the curtailed stepped part survives), remedied some real optical problems (Fig. 11); the gradual reduction in the height of the sekos from the SW corner; the diminution in the curvature above the orthostates; and the steeper inclination of the entablature on the south side.

The use of statues to adorn Doric temples is fairly typical, but the Parthenon is a special case in several respects. Its statuary is quite exceptional, not only in terms of quality but of quantity as well (Fig. 12). Most temples had only a limited number of sculptured metopes, but in the Parthenon – which had far more metopes than most Doric temples – all of them were sculptured, and in such high relief that they almost look like statues in the round. Another unique feature was the Ionic frieze along all four sides of the sekos. It was rare for a Doric temple to have an Ionic frieze at all, and when there was one (mostly in Athenian temples) it was usually only on the two end façades or somewhere in the interior.

It is interesting to note how the thematic content of the sculptures is graded according to their height from the ground and their orientation. The subjects depicted in the Ionic frieze are earthly, those on the metopes are taken from mythology and those in the pediments are concerned with the gods. In the Doric frieze, gods and goddesses appear on none of the metopes on the west and south sides, on some of those on the north side and on all at the east end; the Ionic frieze has gods at the east end only; the figures depicted in the west pediment are mainly heroes, with only two Olympian deities, while the east pediment has mainly Olympian gods and goddesses, including Zeus, and no heroes. The compositions follow principles which, among other things, serve to use the architectural settings to the best advantage. The square shape of the metopes calls for self-contained subjects, the oblongs of the Ionic frieze are well suited to a sequence of scenes on a single theme, and the triangular frame of the pediments imposes strict limits on the height of the figures, which varies according to their importance. At the four corners of the building, above the pediments, were huge winged Victories facing boldly outwards (Fig. 13).

The special importance the Athenians attached to their historic past and their indigenous origins found its best expression in their local myths and age-old cults, which retained their following even after the cult of the Olympian gods had become the official religion. The coexistence of the two traditions is superbly illustrated in the west pediment. The theme of the Ionic frieze is the Panathenaia festival. Most of its length is taken up with the Panathenaic procession on the two long sides, starting from a point on the west façade that is probably intended to represent the saddling, harnessing and mustering ground, i.e. the Pompeion (in the Kerameikos district), and ending on the east side at the Acropolis, in the middle of which we see the presentation of the ceremonial peplos (robe) to Athena. The presence of these sculptures and the combination of architectural styles make the Parthenon a sort of mon-

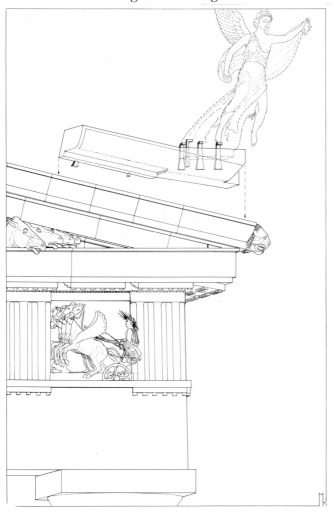

13. Parthenon, NE corner: architectural form and sculptural ornamentation. (M. Korres)

ument to coexistence: local Athenian deities together with Olympian gods, allusions in the Ionic frieze to both the old and new systems of government, Doric architectural forms and ornaments with an admixture of Ionic (the interior columns, egg-and-dart and heart-and-dart mouldings, anthemia, meanders, etc.), Doric forms with Ionic proportions (the Doric columns and, more noticeably, the architrave blocks of the sekos). At the same time the temple is also a monument to the concept of contention or competition, for on most of the metopes and the west pediment the subject is a contest of one sort or another. However, the focus of interest is not the victory of one side (the gods, the Lapiths or the Greeks, for example) nor the defeat of the other (the giants, the centaurs, the Trojans). When one looks at the metopes, where victory sometimes seems to be going to one side and sometimes to the other, it is hard to tell which side is finally going to come out on top: both seem to have an equal chance of victory. And so, since the outcome is left uncertain, the central theme is contention as a concept, in other words the eter-

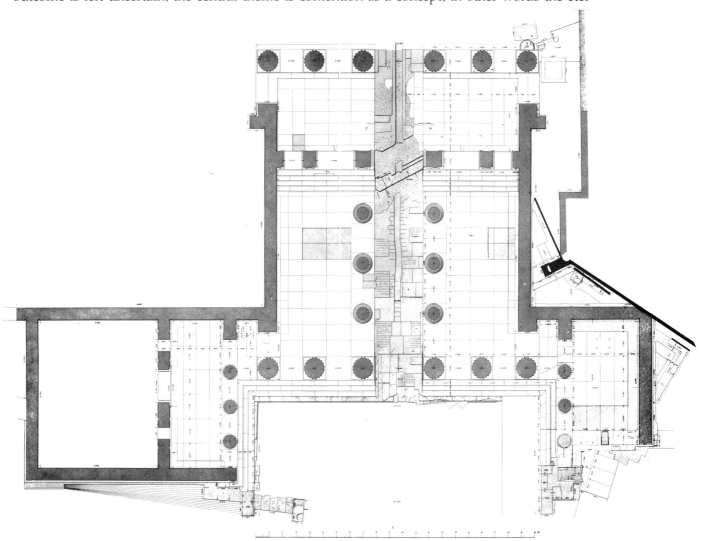

14. Propylaia: floor plan. (R. Bohn, 'Die Propyläen der Akropolis zu Athen', Berlin 1882)

16

nal relationship of opposing forces, whether supernatural or natural, historical or social or even
– why not? – personal, ideological or psychological (the centaurs).

As a testament to Athenian political thinking, the Parthenon conveys a number of messages and covert allusions concerning the values and aspirations of the Athenian republic. It goes without saying that this great monument is open to a variety of interpretations, including some that may not have been in the minds of its creators.

When all the structural work on the Parthenon had been completed (in 438) and the sculptors were busy with its pedimental statuary, construction work started on the Propylaia and the Erechtheion.

The Propylaia

The Propylaia (Fig. 14), though never completed and lacking sculptural ornamentation, is a work of great complexity, significance and originality. It was designed by Mnesikles as a synthesis of five different structural masses on a symmetrical plan built around intersecting axes. the site is sloping, in places quite precipitously, and there are five different floor levels. An integral part of the whole architectural plan is a sloping entrance courtyard of unusual design, with side porticoes and flights

of steps. The roofs were of three different types at four different heights, and close inspection of the roof tiles reveals any number of ingenious details designed specifically for this building. The Propylaia combines two different architectural orders in three compositions of different sizes, and it has doors of four different sizes. It incorporates nearly all the optical refinements found in the Parthenon, and the unfinished surfaces of the walls and floors have a great variety of projections at three different levels. The sixty architectural ornaments (not counting those on the doors and door frames) are of nine different kinds. What is more, the building fulfilled four different functions, including that of a roadway.

The present, distinctly asymmetrical, form of the Propylaia is due partly to the fact that construction work was abandoned before the building was finished and partly to the modifications that had to be

15. Propylaia, W side: perspective drawing. (K. Dekavallas, 1945)

made to an initial design which would theoretically have been symmetrical. The basic
elements of the original design are as follows: a large Doric hexastyle amphiprostyle
propylon (the Propylaia proper) with two
large Doric wings (neither of them ever built)
to north and south, perpendicular to the axis
of the propylon, and two smaller wings on
the west side (the north-west wing, or
Pinakotheke, and the south-west wing) on
an axis perpendicular to that of the large
wings. The smaller wings have porticoes of
three columns *in antis* facing the entrance
courtyard to the west of the central hall.

The most distinctive feature of the pedimented hexastyle porticoes of the central
building (Fig. 15) is that the middle interaxial is half as wide again as the other four
to allow the passage of vehicles, the additional width being filled by one extra
triglyph and one extra metope above the
middle block of the architrave. This results
in the central intercolumniation being almost
doubled (from *c.* 2.05 m. to *c.* 3.85 m.).

The central building is divided into two
unequal halls by the portal wall, which lies
much closer to the east side than to the west.
The spacious west hall or vestibule is *c.* 15.30
m. deep and has a double colonnade of three
Ionic columns (10.29 m. high) flanking the
central roadway. The depth of the east chamber is only about 7 m. Both chambers had flat
coffered ceilings. The portal wall is pierced by
five doorways, the middle one being huge
and the two end ones relatively small.
Because the central building was on sloping
ground, with a height difference of about 4 m.
in its length of about 25 m., it had to be
designed in such a way that the roadway
through the middle of it was a sloping ramp.
This problem Mnesikles solved in the follow-

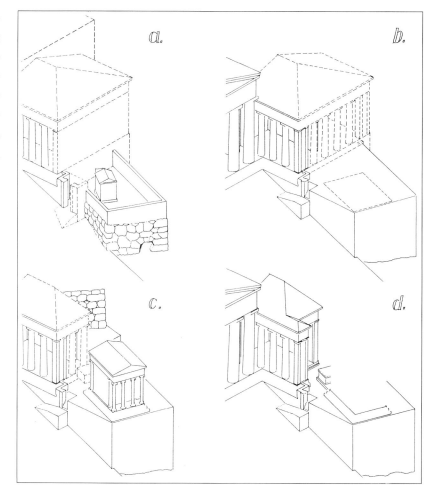

*16. Propylaia, SW wing: successive revisions of the plan. (M.
Korres)*

17. Ornamentation of the beams of the Propylaia.

ing way: at the west end he raised both the entrance courtyard and the krepidoma; in the interior he made the floor of the east hall about 1.43 m. higher than that of the vestibule; and at the east end there is no krepidoma and the rock has been cut away.

A special problem that Greek architects had never had to cope with before, because this was the first building to be laid out with its component parts on perpendicular axes, was to find the best way of draining the rainwater from the roofs. Mnesikles found a solution whereby a quarter of the roof of the central building, a quarter of the roof of the north wing (90 sq.m.) and a fifth of the roof of the Pinakotheke (total 270 sq.m.) should drain off into the narrow but much-frequented space between the central hall and the Pinakotheke. Over this space he therefore put a huge, specially-made tile measuring 2.07 x 4.50 m., which rested on the cornice of the Pinakotheke and a short extension of that cornice along the wall of the north wing and was supported by an invisible metal bar embedded in the NW column of the central building. This arrangement is exactly paralleled over the narrow space between the central building and the SW wing. The complex form of the Propylaia is the result of a design solution that looks forward to the future, though the functional considerations that led to it were rooted in the past: the central hall occupied the site of the old propylon; the Pinakotheke was approximately on the site of 'Building B' (an apsidal building of poros with a south-facing portico of three columns *in antis*); north of the central hall there had stood the unfinished 'North-West Building'; and on the site of the SW wing there had been an unroofed or partly-roofed terrace with tiers

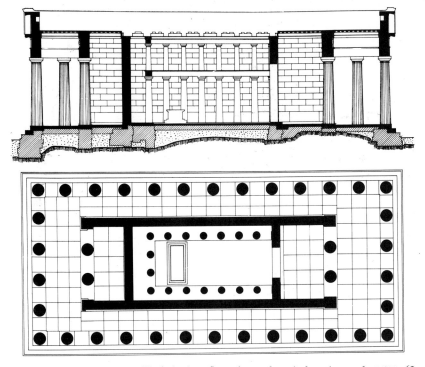

18. *Hephaisteion: floor plan and vertical section, scale 1:500. (J. Travlos)*

of seats, orthostates, etc. All those old buildings had been fairly close together, but each one stood at a different level and differed in design and orientation. New ideas now being tried out led to the decision not merely to replace the old propylon with a bigger, grander one worthy of the new Parthenon but also to replace the other buildings in the immediate vicinity with others worthy of the new era, that is to say taller, more spacious and built of marble. The architect had the idea of joining them all into a single complex the like of which had never been seen before; and for the sake of unity its main axis was aligned with that of the Parthenon. The autonomy of the old buildings had to be sacrificed to the creation of an innovative combination of multiaxial structural masses and open spaces in an integrated architectural design. And that was the origin of the earliest quadrangular building consisting of a central block, two symmetrical wings forming a Π-shape and an integrated courtyard.

Mnesikles' skill as an architect is evident in the modifications he had to make to his original plans. In the SW wing, the design of which had to be repeatedly revised and curtailed (Fig. 16), he moved the whole west side except the corner anta nearly three metres further in and gave the wing its present form by putting a slender monolithic pillar in the middle, an exceptionally thin architrave ornamented with a continuous row of guttae, a plain Ionic frieze and a plain cornice. This most unusual design, necessarily unconventional and very abstract, was admired in later times for its lightness and originality and was replicated in the façade of the famous choregic monument of Thrasyllos. The latter was first published by James Stuart and Nicholas Revett before the Propylaia had been published at all, and it provided inspiration for architects in Western Europe, especially Britain, from an early date. The Propylaia itself had its imitators even in antiquity: well-known ancient and modern copies of it include the Great Propylaia at Eleusis, the Brandenburg Gate in Berlin and the Propyläen in Munich.

In contrast to the daring originality of the architectural design, the architectural forms of the Propylaia are notable only for the technical excellence of their execution. The Doric columns are copies of those in the Parthenon, the wall cornice in the interior of the central hall is identical with that of the Parthenon in spite of the difference of scale between the two buildings, and the insertion of a cyma reversa beneath the Doric cornice – a feature that greatly influenced later architects – is actually a throwback to a stylistic element in use in the Archaic period. The sima, similar to that of the Parthenon, was decorated with painted eggs, and the spaces between them were pierces to make outlets for the rainwater (the same solution was used later in the sima of the Porch of the Caryatids in the Erechtheion). Owing to the shortage of space, the Ionic column bases were of smaller diameter than usual, with a corresponding reduction in their height. To compensate for that, flat round bosses were left projecting from the upper surface of the stylobate in the appropriate places (a similar expedient was adopted along the east and south sides of the Erechtheion). The exquisite Ionic capitals, similar to those in the Temple of Athena Nike, the Ilissos Temple and some other buildings, may well be the earliest of their kind, unless they were copied from similar capitals in the Parthenon's west chamber (unfortunately lost and nowhere recorded). The space between the volutes was filled with a rich variety of plant motifs wrought in metal, and on the cushions there were painted acanthus leaves on either side of the relief bands. The roof

19. Hephaisteion: the E wing of the pteroma and the pronaos. (H. Koch, 'Studien zum Theseustempel in Athen', Berlin 1955)

beams were like those of the Parthenon, having their vertical sides completely covered with painted designs of spiral whorls, lotus flowers and palmettes (Fig. 17): the same system of decoration is found in the Hephaisteion. The coffers of the ceiling were similar to those of the Parthenon, but smaller and less elaborate.

Mnesikles made use of almost as many optical refinements as the architects of the Parthenon.

One particularly tricky problem that had never arisen before was the juxtaposition of taller and shorter columns on the west side, which would normally have to stand on krepidomata of different heights. However, Mnesikles decided to use the same krepidoma for all the columns, with steps of uniform height on all three sides of the entrance courtyard. This krepidoma he made the right height to go with the tall columns, but he divided it into four instead of three steps and then disguised the bottom step in the places where the shorter columns stood by using black Eleusinian stone instead of white marble, with the result that the shorter columns look as if they are standing on a krepidoma of three white steps only. This ingenious device solved the problem of creating the necessary visual differentiation without using steps of different heights. The division of the krepidoma into four steps instead of three was also preferable because it made the steps easier to negotiate. In fact the use of black stone, in such startling contrast to the rest of the building, was not superficial ornamentation nor an affectation in pursuit of originality but simply an essential element of the architectural design.

Mnesikles also used black stone for specific visual effects in the orthostates of the west chamber, the benches along the walls of the west chamber and the NW and SW wings and in some places in the front wall of the Pinakotheke. This marks the beginning of trend towards the gradual replacement of polychrome painted ornamentation with blocks of coloured marble or other stone.

Mnesikles took more care over visual impressions than almost any other architect in history. What is astonishing is that he managed to find such brilliant visual solutions while simultaneously solving practical problems to do with the functions of the building and the convenience of visitors.

The Hephaisteion. The work of rebuilding temples in the Asty (the city of Athens) and the rest of Attica got under way in the mid fifth century, as it did on the Acropolis. One of those was the Temple of Hephaistos, or Hephaisteion, on the low hill of Kolonos Agoraios, west of the Agora. This was a Doric peripteral temple built of Pentelic marble with six columns at each end and thirteen along each side (Fig. 18). The sekos has distyle porticoes *in antis* and an interior colonnade. The pteroma (the ambulatory between the peristyle and the sekos wall) is narrow on both the long sides, deeper at the west end and deeper still at the east end, so much so that the east pteroma feels almost like a separate room. This is mainly because the east façade of the sekos is

Hexastyle peripteral temples

20. Temple of Athena, Pallene: perspective reconstruction. (M. Korres, 1996)

exactly in line with the third columns from the end, which makes it possible for the architrave of the sekos to be joined to the architrave of the peristyle at those two points, so forming an unbroken rectangular frame above the columns (Fig. 19). The ceiling of the east pteroma, also made of marble, has the longest beams. The feeling of separateness is accentuated on the exterior by the fact that the only sculptured metopes are the ones above the east pteroma (4+10+4).

The architecture of the Hephaisteion follows that of the Pre-Parthenon: the bottom step of the krepidoma is not of marble and the base of the outer face of the sekos walls is in the form of a cyma reversa. Other points of interest are the substitution of a cyma reversa and other Ionic elements for the usual Doric regulae on the architrave of the sekos, and the presence of an Ionic instead of a Doric frieze higher up. In the interior a colonnade of 5x3 columns (according to Dinsmoor) or 7x4 columns (according to Stevens), added to the original design after construction had started, ran round three sides of the sekos at a short distance from the side and back walls: here we can detect the influence of the interior design of the Parthenon, which was slightly earlier. Generally speaking, it is fair to say that the Hephaisteion's architectural forms (column capitals, anta capitals, wall cornices, mouldings) follow those of the Periklean Parthenon.

Temple of Athena Pallenis, Pallene. Immediately after the Hephaisteion a similar marble Doric hexastyle temple was built in the sanctuary of Athena at Pallene in Attica (Fig. 20). Here the distinctive shape of the Hephaisteion's east pteroma is replicated twice over, at both the east and west ends. The new temple was designed with an interior colonnade from the outset and has all its ceilings made of marble, even in the interior. Its krepidoma is entirely of marble (unlike those of the Hephaisteion and the Pre-Parthenon, where the lowest step was not of marble) and so is the euthynteria (the levelling top course of the foundation). In the first century B.C., in Augus-

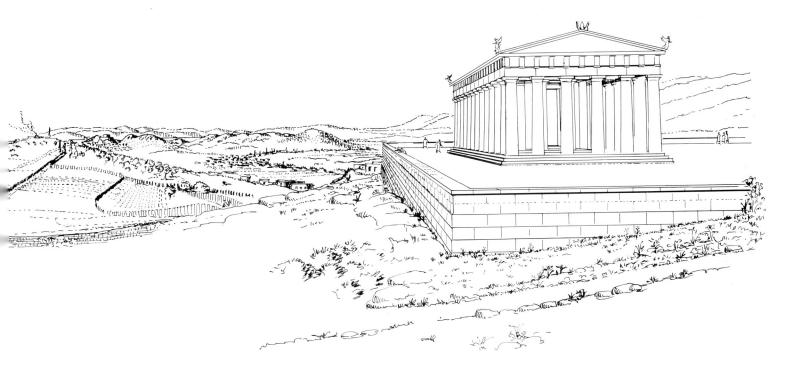

tus's reign, this temple was moved bodily to the Agora in Athens, where it was used for the cults of Ares and Aphrodite as well as Athena; Pausanias refers to it simply as the Temple of Ares.

Temple of Poseidon, Sounion. The famous Temple of Poseidon at Sounion, very similar in design to the Hephaisteion, was built *circa* 440 B.C. of very fine-grained marble from nearby Agriléza. Once again the east pteroma is deep, but here the Ionic frieze runs right round it. The west pteroma, unusually, is deeper than the east, perhaps for functional reasons. The interior has no colonnade, as was originally intended to be the case in the Hephaisteion. The columns of the Sounion temple are notable for their slender proportions and for the fact that they have only sixteen flutes instead of the usual twenty: the same number of flutes is found on some older votive colonnettes on the Acropolis, and on the massive columns of the Temple of Apollo at Syracuse. The lowest course of the walls consists of plain rectangular blocks, but not in the antae: there it takes the form of a cyma reversa, but lower than the cyma reversa in the walls and antae of the Hephaisteion, and with a somewhat flatter profile. The anta capitals are Ionic, not Doric as in the Hephaisteion. The capitals of the pronaos columns are embellished with a very narrow cyma reversa at the top of the abacus. As if to emphasize the importance of the temple and its high architectural quality, the architraves, wall cornices, sima and other parts were lavishly decorated with painted designs (Fig. 21).

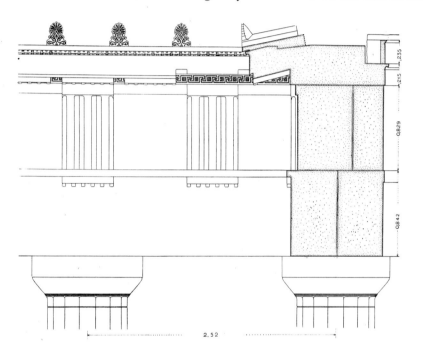

21. Temple of Poseidon, Sounion: entablature of the long sides. (A. Orlandos, 1958)

Temple of Nemesis, Rhamnous. The last of these temples to be constructed was that of Nemesis at Rhamnous. Though much smaller than those described above, it follows the same architectural design. It was built in a very short time and never actually completed: the upper part, from the akroteria to the capitals, was finished right down to the painted decoration, but below that the building is unfinished. The columns are unfluted and the surface of the krepidoma is only roughly dressed in places.

The presence of so many common features in these four Doric hexastyle temples has led some modern scholars to conclude that they were all designed by the same person, the so-called 'Theseum architect'. This hypothesis is not universally accepted. It is true that the four have certain features in common, but there are also differences between them that cannot be overlooked: where the Hephaisteion has a sculptured frieze it is only over the peristyle columns, whereas the Temple of Poseidon has one on all four sides of the pronaos. In the Hephaisteion and the Temple of Nemesis the west pteroma is shallower than the east, but in the Temple of Poseidon, unusually, it is deeper. In the Temple of Poseidon the opisthodomos and the pronaos are equal in size, in the Hephaisteion the opisthodomos is not as deep as the pronaos, while in the Temple of Nemesis it is deeper.

Temple of Apollo Delphinios. The Temple of Apollo Delphinios, south of the Olympieion in Athens, dates from the middle of the fifth century B.C. It was identical with the Hephaisteion, but here the interior colonnade was part of the design from the outset, as it was in the Temple of Athena at Pallene. It was built of poros of excellent quality; only its sima, akroteria and probably metopes were made of Parian marble.

Temple of Apollo Epikourios, Bassai. This temple in the Peloponnese (Fig. 22) follows the local traditions of temple construction, but as it was designed by Iktinos it is of interest in the context of Athenian architecture as well. It is about the same width as the Temple of Athena at Pallene, but with fifteen columns along each side it is much longer. Its interior floor plan is unique and it is exceptional in having its main façade facing north. The front and back pteromas are spacious and equal in size, as in the Pallene temple, but the entablature of the sekos is not joined to that of the peristyle. The pronaos, with two columns *in antis*, is again deep, and the opisthodomos almost equally so. In the interior, as in the Parthenon and most Athenian hexastyle temples, there is a colonnade of 5 x 3 columns (the same as in the Hephaisteion, according to one view) running round three sides of the sekos. However, the colonnade is unusual in several respects. On the east and west sides, instead of free-standing columns we have semi-columns engaged in buttresses perpendicular to the side walls, while the columns at the back are so far away from the back wall that the space behind them is virtually a separate room: this served as the adyton and could be entered through a door in the east wall. Stylistically, too, the colonnade is unique, for the semi-columns along the sides are Ionic, standing on specially-shaped bases and having square capitals with volutes on three faces, while the middle column of the back range was Corinthian. The buttresses attached to the corner semi-columns of this colonnade now lie diagonally to the side walls, but this is due to an alteration to the original design. The interior colonnade supported a continuous Ionic frieze with reliefs of mythological scenes. The ceilings of the temple rested on marble beams and had limestone coffers of different patterns. The layout and sculptural ornamentation of the temple at Bassai represent the final phase in the evolution of interior architecture, in which architectural forms from the exte-

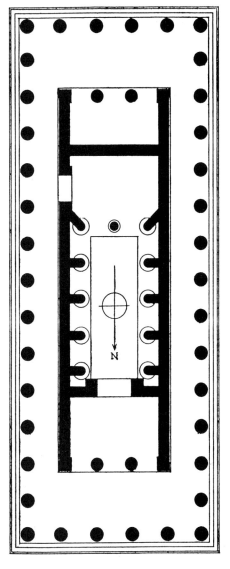

0   10   20   30   40   50 FT

22. *Temple of Apollo Epikourios, Bassai: floor plan. (W.B. Dinsmoor)*

rior were moved indoors and used in various combinations. Some of the main landmarks in this process of evolution were the interior of the Parthenon, the east pteroma of the Hephaisteion and the east pteroma of the temple at Sounion.

The Erechtheion

Whether considered as an all-marble Ionic building and work of art of complex design or as a multi-purpose temple and monument to age-old religious traditions, the Erechtheion (Fig. 25) quite outclasses all other buildings of its kind. There is no room here for even the most cursory examination of its liturgical functions, its interior layout and the historical circumstances of its construction, and those are in any case outside the scope of this article, which is concerned with architectural design. On the history of its construction there is a great deal of epigraphical evidence: this covers only the years 409 and 408, but the building was almost completed in that time. The architect is unknown, but there are many indications that Mnesikles was responsible for the overall design and partly responsible for the construction. The design of the Erechtheion was subject to strict constraints: it had to incorporate several small shrines standing at different levels to the north of the foundations of the Old Temple, without damaging any of them; it had to have four outside doors, one on each side, in predesignated positions and at predesignated heights (different in each case), each sheltered by its own porch except for the one on the west side, for communication between the inner rooms and the outdoor areas associated with them; the south porch had to serve as a heroön; any *martyria* (sacred tokens of historical and mythological traditions) had to remain visible; the architectural design of the four sides had to be adapted to the different floor levels and there should be a smooth transition from one level to the next, with no obvious stylistic break.

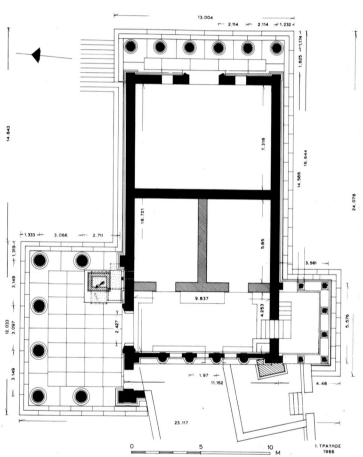

23. Erechtheion: floor plan. (J. Travlos)

To meet all these conditions, the building comprises the following parts (Fig. 23): (a) a central block measuring *c.* 23 x 12 m. and *c.* 14 m. high (up to the ridge of its pitched roof); (b) a porch *c.* 10.8 m. wide, *c.* 7 m. deep and *c.* 12 m. high, abutting on the west end of the north side; and (c) a flat-roofed porch measuring *c.* 6.2 x 4 m. and *c.* 5.9 m. high, abutting on the west end of the south side. The overall dimensions are 26.87 x 23.12 m. Adjoining it on the west is the Pandrosion, a small rectangular sanctuary with a narrow marble stoa (predating the Erechtheion) along its north side. The differences in the ground level around the

Erechtheion are as follows: the euthynteria of the south and east sides is *c*. 3.2 m. higher than that of the north side, and the euthynteria of the west side is *c*. 70 cm. higher than that of the north side (i.e. *c*. 2.5 m. lower than that of the south and east sides). Because of the differences of floor level and architectural form, the appearance of the Erechtheion is unique. From the east it looks like an ordinary hexastyle prostyle temple; from the north, a very high walled building with an unusually large tetrastyle portico attached to the right-hand end of the façade; from the south, an oblong walled building with an elaborate flat roof at the left-hand end, supported by Caryatids standing on a high wall; and from the west, a two-storey façade with a solid wall

below and a tetrastyle portico *in antis* above, flanked by the larger North Porch and the smaller South Porch (the Porch of the Caryatids).

The architectural features of the Erechtheion (Fig. 24) comprise a three-stepped krepidoma, columns, antae, walls and an entablature resting on columns or walls, the whole topped by the projecting cornice of the roof. These are found on all four sides. The columns have a tripartite base, twenty-four flutes on the shaft, a band of very rich ornamentation on the hypotrachelion at the top of the shaft and an extremely elaborate Ionic capital (Fig. 26). To match the columns, the antae have a similar tripartite base, a similar hypotrachelion and an elaborate capital composed of three successive cymatium mouldings and an abacus. And to match the antae, the walls also have a tripartite base and a coping (epikranitis) that is simply a continuation of the hypotrachelion and capital along the whole of their length. The architrave is divided into three horizontal bands crowned by cymatium mouldings, and above that there is a flat frieze of black Eleusis stone chosen to contrast strongly with the relief figures of white Parian marble that were attached to it. The cornice has a richly-carved heart-and-dart moulding along the bottom and an egg-and-dart along the top.

The tripartite bases are all of the same type, with a torus moulding at the bottom, a scotia or trochilos in the middle and another torus at the top. These triple bases are a purely Athenian invention, though the torus and scotia mould-

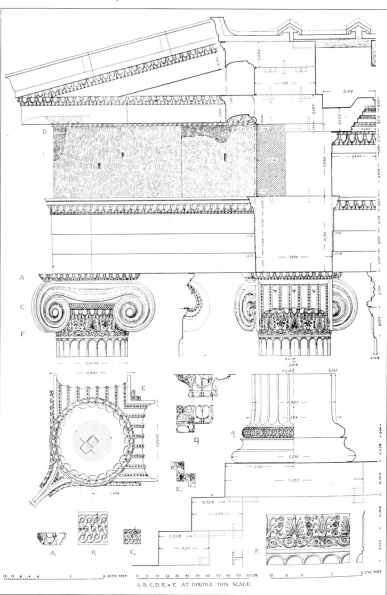

24. *Erechtheion: stylistic details of the North Porch. (G.P. Stevens)*

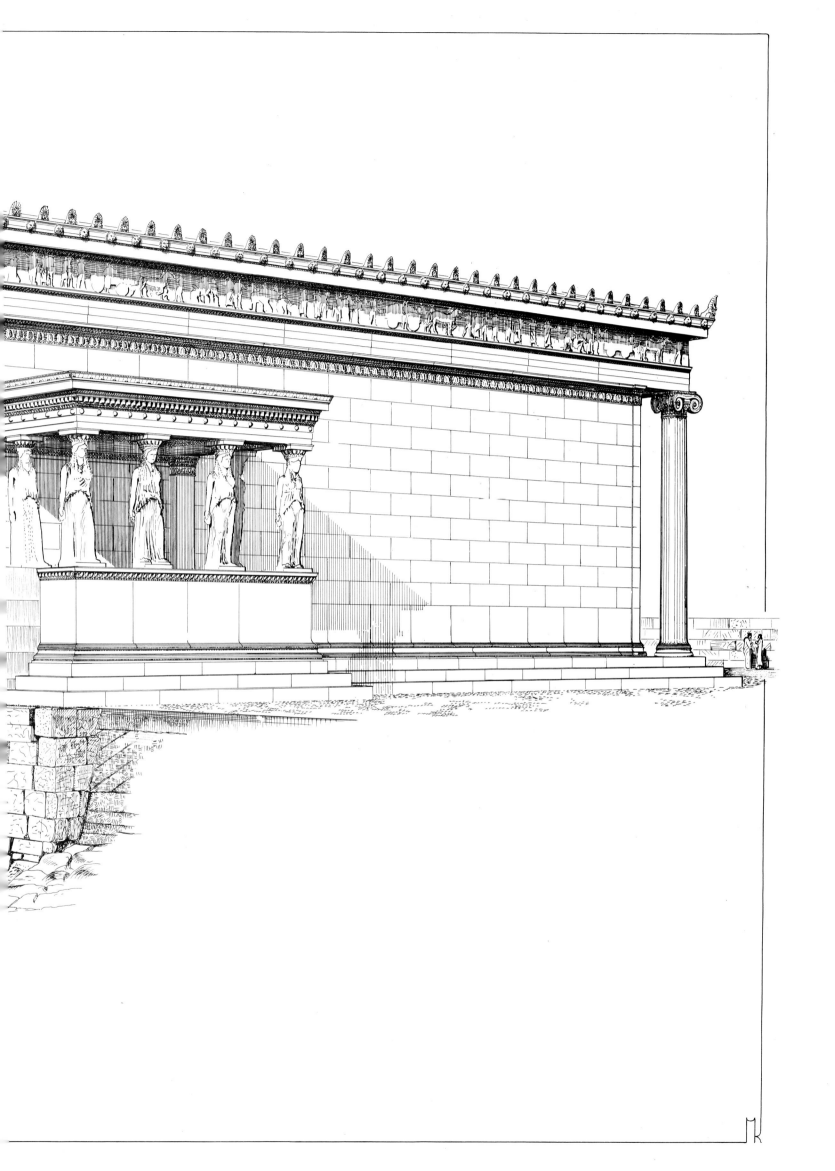

ings are common to all Ionic architecture. A point of interest in the Erechtheion is the guilloche pattern carved on the upper torus.

The origins of the Erechtheion's architecture are diverse. The East Porch is prostyle, like those of the cella of the old and new marble Parthenons and the Old Temple. The spacious North Porch shows similarities with the deep front pteromas of the Attic hexastyle peripteral Doric temples (of Hephaistos, Poseidon, Athena Pallenis or Ares, etc.). Typologically at least, and irrespective of their symbolism in this particular case, the use of the Caryatids as roof supports follows the example of the Siphnian and Knidian treasuries at Delphi. The entablature supporting the ceiling of the Porch of the Caryatids is Asiatic-type Ionic, with dentils below the cornice but without a frieze, whereas the coffers of that ceiling are of Athenian type and are in fact copied from those of the pronaos of the Parthenon. Columns with a hypotrachelion can be traced back to Samos, probably the birthplace of that particular design feature, which spread as far afield as Halikarnassos (Asia Minor), Naukratis (Egypt) and Metapontum and Locri Epizephyrii (Lower Italy). On the other hand, hypotrachelia exist on some older Athenian Ionic column capitals that do not appear to have any connection with Samos, for not only are all their parts Athenian but on one of them the surviving painted decoration of the hypotrachelion is pure Doric, consisting of a double meander (Fig. 32). In the Erechtheion the hypotrachelia are ornamented in relief with Ionic motifs: scrolls, lotus flowers and palmettes. The cushions of the capitals in the Erechtheion belong to a type otherwise unknown in Athens, for they have a series of fillets covering their whole length, as found in

26. Erechtheion: capital of the NE column of the North Porch. (M. Korres, 1980)

the Cyclades and Ionia. The scrolled parts are unique of their kind, with volutes composed of multiple fillets and grooves which enclose the 'eye' of the volute and an inlaid metal band terminating in the half-palmette.

The influence of the Erechtheion on both ancient and modern architecture has been incalculable. Its columns were copied frequently, always with some simplifications, in Athens (including the round Temple of Roma and Augustus), at Delphi, in Ionia and in Rome. Its famous marble door was copied frequently, again with simplifications, in Athens (e.g. in the Temple of Asklepios on the south slope of the Acropolis) and elsewhere. Its anta capitals were taken as models for all sorts of other structures, for example in the coping of tall pedestals for monumental chariots in the second century B.C.

🖙 *25. Erechtheion: perspective drawing from the SW. (M. Korres, 1976, 1985)*

Construction of the little Ionic amphiprostyle temple on the bastion of Athena Nike (Fig. 27) was started after 430 B.C. and completed *circa* 424/3 to a design by Kallikrates, whose hands were tied by strict constraints. Perhaps owing to Cycladic influence, the prostyle arrangement of the façades – a feature alien to tradition-al Doric temple architecture, where distyle *in antis* is the norm – had been used in the original limestone Parthenon, the Old Temple and the Pre-Parthenon and was replicated in the Periklean Parthenon and the Erechtheion.

Temple of Athena Nike and similar temples

With maximum horizontal dimensions of *c.* 9.36 × 6.60 m. and a height of *c.* 7 m. (from the surrounding paved floor to the top of the pediment), the temple is as large as it could pos-sibly have been, given the size of its site on the bas-tion (Fig. 28). Its length takes up all the available space between the west end of the bastion and the steps of the north entrance. Because it could not be made any longer and was disproportionately wide, the sekos was unusually shallow – actually wider than it was deep – and had neither an ordinary pronaos nor a front wall. Here the east pteroma has to serve as a pronaos, and instead of the front wall there are two rectangular pillars between the antae. The wider gap between the two pillars was the doorway, and there were 'windows' in the gaps between the pillars and the antae on either side. The embedded sills of these three openings and the bases of the pillars were profiled to match the wall and anta bases, which were themselves smaller-scale copies of the column bases (from the bottom upwards: astragal, scotia, torus). Similarly, the capitals of the two pillars had the same mouldings as the anta capitals (from the bottom upwards: hypotrachelion, astragal, Ionic cymatium, astragal, cyma reversa, Ionic cymatium on the abacus). It is interesting to note the likeness between the anta capitals of this temple and those of the Erechtheion, though there the decorative designs were sculptured rather than painted. The entrance door, the two 'win-dows' and the two sides of the pronaos (between the end columns and the antae) were closed off with elab-

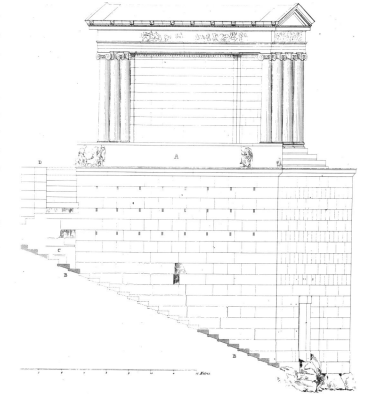

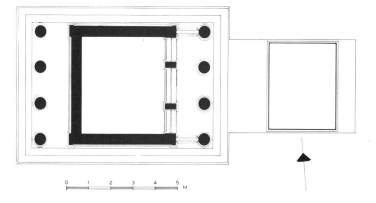

27. *Bastion and Temple of Athena Nike from the north-west. (E. Schaubert)*

28. *Temple of Athena Nike: floor plan. (J. Travlos)*

orate metal railings, each aperture having its own embedded sill profiled to match the anta bases. The longitudinal structure of these linear elements was painted, not sculptured: alternating lotus flowers and palmettes on the hypotrachelion and sima, eggs and other motifs on the Ionic mouldings, ivy-leaves on the cymae reversae and so on. The only sculptured ornaments are to be found on the column capitals: eggs on the echinos and half-palmettes.

Elsewhere, sculpture was very much in evidence. Besides the cult statue, there was a continuous frieze about 45 cm. high running right round the building (with a total length of *c.* 26 m.), pedimental statues, akroteria and the exceptionally fine reliefs of winged Victories and other figures on the three main sides of the parapet (total length *c.* 34 m.).

At about the same time as the Temple of Athena Nike, or slightly later, a similar temple was built, about ten per cent broader and higher but about fifty per cent longer. This too was tetrastyle amphiprostyle, but with a proper pronaos. It had a relief frieze of Parian marble running round all four sides. In contrast to the Temple of Athena Nike, the outer face of its architrave was flat, not composed of three separate fillets. Its column capitals were like those of the Athena Nike.

Another similar temple stood at the top of the Areopagus. Its column bases, made of Parian Marble, were not of the Attic type but closer to the Ephesian (Fig. 29). The capitals, also of Parian marble, had relief rosettes in the eyes of the volutes and in general were more richly decorated.

In the area now called Ambelókipi there was yet another similar temple of about the same size (Figs. 30-31). Its columns had only twenty flutes and their capitals had shallow volutes bounded by plain fillets instead of cable mouldings. There were also similar temples at Pallene (Yérakas), Pentele and Acharnai.

The Temple of Athena Nike represents the crystallization – or perhaps even the first appearance – of the Athenian type of Ionic tetrastyle amphiprostyle temple. This new type of temple was very widespread in Athens and Attica, perhaps because it offered great scope for sculpture. If we compare the Athena Nike with the Parthenon, which was fifty times bigger in surface area and a hundred and fifty times bigger in volume, we find that its frieze appears no smaller than that of the Parthenon because it is positioned so much lower, and moreover the view is not blocked by columns, as it is in the Parthenon. The number of figures that will fit into the frieze of the smaller temple, assum-

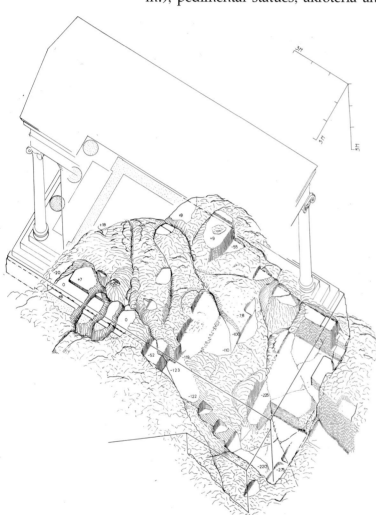

29. *Ionic temple on the Areopagus. (M. Korres)*

ing that the composition is of equal density, is no less than three-eighths of the number in the Parthenon frieze, because the length of its frieze is sixty times its height while the length of the Parthenon frieze is 160 times its height (60/160 = 3/8).

The type of temple created by Kallikrates remained popular for centuries. At least one choregic monument was an exact copy of the Temple of Athena Nike, countless features of that temple were imitated in buildings of the Roman period, and even more such imitations are to be found in the architecture of the modern era.

The first Ionic structures in Athens, predating the Temple of Athena Nike by about 150 years, were not complete buildings but either votive monuments, such as two or three early sixth-century lustral basins made of Naxian marble, or merely decorative elements of Doric temples, such

30. Ionic temple at Ambelókipi. (M. Korres, 1993)

as the great volutes on the pediments of the "Ur-Parthenon". From the same period or slightly later (*c.* 560-550 B.C.) we also have two small Ionic capitals with flat faces decorated with incised vertical volutes. From the middle of the sixth century the tendency was for the cushion of the Ionic capital to become progressively more concave, although the faces were still flat. This type

***Other Ionic
monuments***

is represented by two Ionic capitals from the Acropolis, with no echinos and with painted vertical volutes: as they are identical and fairly large, it is likely that they both come from a small distyle temple. By the last quarter of the century capitals of this type, but with horizontal volutes and a rudimentary echinos, were typical of a sort of votive column that was then very popular. It existed in two variations: one Doricizing, with a prismatic abacus and a Doric echinos (semicircular in profile, or in the form of a cyma recta) and the other Ionicizing, with an ovolo or cyma reversa in place of the abacus and an echinos with the profile of an ovolo or cyma reversa. Such columns usually supported small statues, generally korai, which necessitated a socket in the upper face of the capital. The absence of a socket in some capitals has been interpreted in various ways: the column may perhaps have carried a stable object such as a stone vase, or it may have been one of a set of columns supporting a table or something similar, or the votive monument may have consisted of a column only.

By the end of the sixth century one more step had been taken, somewhat belatedly: the volutes were sculptured and the cushions had decorative designs of their own. In the first two decades of the fifth century this process of evolution culminated in the development of a type of capital of which the most characteristic example is the one on the votive column of Kallikrates (480 B.C.). This was the first type of capital to be widely used in architecture over a long period, its earliest appearance (*c.* 478) being in the Stoa of the Athenians at Delphi (see below). By the middle of the fifth century there were already many fine examples of this type: at least one hexastyle temple in Athens on the same scale as the east cella of the Erechtheion; the typologically unique Temple of Athena Sounias; some other tetrastyle temples; three small buildings whose column capitals have a decorated hypotrachelion (Fig. 32, and compare the description of the Erechtheion above); the Ionic temple at Ambelókipi, where the capitals clearly show the

31. Ionic temple at Ambelókipi: column capital. (M. Korres, 1993)

influence of the Parthenon; the Ionic stoa in the Asklepieion on the south slope of the Acropolis, where the capitals are exactly the same size as those in the Ilissos Temple; the Pompeion; and a building which had two pairs of interior columns of unequal height (now in the Agora Museum).

The next step in the development of the Ionic capital is to be seen in the Propylaia, where the cables of the volutes and of the cushion fillets are carved in relief, as also is the echinos with its ovolo profile. This type was used again in the Temple of Athena Nike and the Ilissos Temple and reached its zenith in the peerless capitals of the Erechtheion.

All these Ionic monuments are small and, except in the case of the Erechtheion, unsophisticated in comparison with those to be found in Ionia itself. Their capitals are much less vigorous than those in Asia Minor or on Samos, yet their design is very delicate, their chiaroscuro effect is more satisfying because their component parts are concave rather than convex, and they chime better with the concave flutes of the columns than do capitals with convex profiles. This harmony is further enhanced by the insertion of flat fillets between the Ionic flutes of the columns and between the coils of the volutes.

The superb monuments on the Acropolis are followed at some distance by other works of Athenian classical architecture, also masterpieces in their own way, both in Athens and Attica and in other places such as the Panhellenic sanctuaries of Delphi and Delos. The oldest known examples are the Treasury of the Athenians at Delphi, mentioned by Pausanias – a Doric building of Cycladic marble in the form of a temple (distyle *in antis*) with sculptured metopes on all four sides, an extremely rare feature – and the little Ionic stoa (the Stoa of the Athenians) backing on

32. Ionic capital with decorated hypotrachelion. Acropolis Museum. (M. Korres, 1977)

to the massive retaining wall of the temple terrace, with its famous inscription: 'The Athenians dedicated the stoa and the weapons which they took from the enemy' (after the naval battle of Mykale in 479/8 B.C.). The stoa is an outstanding example of architectural design unfettered by strict rules: the interaxials are much wider than one would expect in proportion to the height of the columns or the depth of the stoa, but that is better suited to the purpose for which the stoa was built, namely the display of exhibits to the public.

Other buildings of the fifth century

Some thirty or forty years later Kimon's brother-in-law Peisianax built an exceptionally large and very sumptuously appointed Doric stoa on the north side of the Agora. This, the oldest truly monumental building erected in the new civic centre, with an araeostyle Ionic central colonnade, is known as the Painted Stoa (Stoa Poikile) on account of the monumental paintings on the back wall, including one of the battle of Marathon by Polygnotos.

Other notable products of this period and the years immediately following in Athens include the Prytaneion or Tholos, a rotunda with a diameter of *c.* 34 m. and a conical roof, and the Odeion of Perikles, a huge, almost square building with a forest of columns in the interior. Although neither of these buildings boasts elegant stylistic features, noteworthy architectural forms or lavish workmanship, both are among the major achievements of a new and rapidly developing trend in the design and construction of large roofed structures. The architectural origins of this new style are complex, but ultimately they can be traced back on the one hand to the large religious buildings of the early Archaic period (including the earliest phases of the Telesterion at Eleusis) where the roof was supported by row upon row of wooden posts, and on the other to the large hypostyle halls of Persian royal palaces. The fact that the masts of Persian ships were used to support the roof of the Odeion and that the building was likened to the sumptuous tent of Xerxes seems to hint at a possible Persian origin for this type of structure. On the other hand, the Odeion had a sloping roof, not the heavy flat roof of the magnificent Persian palaces, and it was designed for much more practical uses laid down by the Athenian lawgivers: it was a multi-purpose building used not only for musical performances but also for the storage and distribution of grain.

Vitruvius (VII, praef. 16) says of the Telesterion that Iktinos built a huge Doric cella with no external columns. Iktinos envisaged a hall with twenty interior columns in four rows of five, the interaxial spacing being *c.* 8.4 m. in one direction and *c.* 10 m. in the other (Fig. 33), and also a gigantic pedimented portico, probably with twelve columns, *c.* 10.5 m. deep, *c.* 54 m. wide and over 22 m. high (columns *c.* 12 m., entablature *c.* 3.8 m. and pediment *c.* 6.5 m.). His aim was to produce something to rival the greatest temples in Ionia and Sicily. The only parts of his grandiose plan that came to fruition were the walls of black Eleusinian stone with an outsized Doric entablature of poros limestone, some foundations for eight internal columns and some of the foundations of the portico. The cost of making the thirty-two massive columns would have been astronomic, and it would no doubt have been extremely difficult to find the timber for beams twelve metres in length and more than one square metre in cross-section.

The Telesterion at Eleusis

The design eventually adopted for the interior was by Koroibos and was more realistic, with six rows of seven two-tiered columns. After Koroibos's death his work was carried on by Metagenes of Xypete (the columns and metopes of the upper tier) and Xenokles of Cholargos (the huge roof with a lantern in the centre to admit light). Two or three generations later plans were drawn up for an unprecedented enlargement of the building, but the project was abandoned at an early stage of construction. The portico envisaged by Iktinos was built at this time, but to a new design by the famous architect Philo.

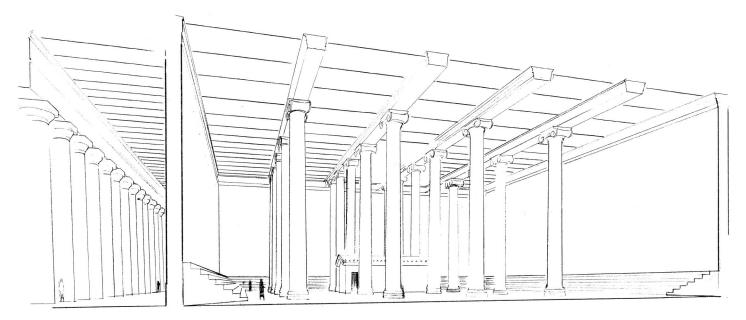

33. The Telesterion at Eleusis: interior. Conjectural reconstruction of the unrealized design by Iktinos. (M. Korres, 1978)

In spite of the hardships of the Peloponnesian War, the penultimate decade of the fifth century saw a great spate of building construction and the development of a new type of building, the stoa with rooms at the back. Among the outstanding examples were the West Stoa of the Asklepieion in Athens (421 B.C.), which was Ionic with columns of Pentelic marble, and the South Stoa of the Agora, which was Doric, about eighty metres in length with poros columns. The walls of these stoas were made of stone below and bricks above. The rooms had benches or couches on all four sides.

The Stoa at Brauron and similar buildings

The stoa in the Sanctuary of Artemis at Brauron (Figs. 34-35), built in the same period, incorporated yet another great innovation: the linear colonnade has two right-angled bends in it, forming a sort of peristyle. This means that for the first time in the history of Doric architecture, not counting the special case of the Propylaia, the unroofed area no longer surrounds the colonnade but is surrounded by it, so that it becomes an enclosed courtyard. On the west and north sides there are respectively three and six rooms opening on to the colonnaded gallery, all with beds. The gateway to the courtyard is between the second and third rooms of the west wing, and another passage between the third and fourth rooms of the north wing led into an oblong courtyard running parallel to the north wing. This smaller courtyard had a propylon at each end and a narrow colonnade supported by octagonal pillars along the north side, for votive offerings. The Doric stoa is araeostyle, with three metopes in each interaxial instead of the usual two: this system, also used in the South Stoa and the Stoa of Zeus Eleutherios in the Athens Agora, is borrowed from the central interaxial of the Propylaia.

The trend initiated in the stoa at Brauron culminated two or three decades later in the Pompeion, a building in the Kerameikos district of Athens where the participants gathered in preparation for the procession of the Panathenaia. The Pompeion consisted of a rectangular courtyard (*c.* 30 x 54 m.) with an Ionic stoa on all four sides, a grand Ionic propylon of marble on the east side and several rooms of different sizes on the north and west. The walls of the rooms and the outer walls of the courtyard were built of bricks on an imposing stone orthostate (bottom course).

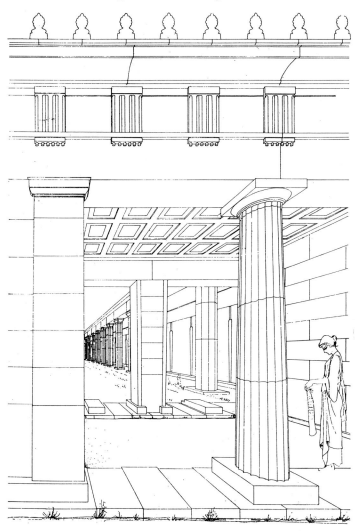

34. The stoa at Brauron. (Ch. Bouras, 1962)

With the development of the theatre and the system of *choregia*, whereby a sponsor (*choregos*) undertook the expenses of training a chorus for a drama festival, the first choregic monuments made their appearance. Initially they were simple pedestals for the commemorative tripods presented by the state to the winners of the various drama competitions, but after the middle of the fourth century they were made in a wide variety of shapes and sizes. Besides low stepped bases and somewhat higher round or triangular

Choregic monuments

pedestals, we find tall masonry pillars, often three-sided, round columns with three-sided capitals, small or medium-sized temple-shaped buildings – of which the best-known are the monuments of Thrasyllos and Nikias (Fig. 36) – and at least one with a complex and highly original design: the monument of Lysikrates (334 B.C.) in the Street of the Tripods (still called Tripódhon Street) below the east end of the Acropolis. This last (Fig. 37) consists of a very high, square, limestone podium on which there stands a marble rotunda with six Corinthian columns, an entablature of the Athenian Ionic type (like that of the Erechtheion, for example), a cornice of the Asiatic Ionic type (i.e. with dentils) and a conical roof with a triangular akroterion or finial at the apex, lavishly carved with plant motifs, to support the choregic tripod. Being 10 m. high (without the tripod) and relatively small (*c.* 3 x 3 m.) in plan, the monument is unique in its proportions and unrivalled for the ethereal lightness of its forms. Its columns are exquisite and their capitals the most superb examples of their kind. The monument of Lysikrates has had enormous influence on Neoclassical architecture. Copies of it, some excellent and some no more than mediocre, are to be found in all countries belonging to the Western architectural tradition, and selected features of it are replicated thousands of times in big cities and small cities, on grand and humble buildings, public and private monuments, furniture and utensils. In modern Athens, the marble propylon of the Záppion Hall has perhaps the grandest reproduction of its columns.

A historical survey of the architecture of the sixth and fifth centuries B.C. shows that in terms of the creation of new architectural styles the Classical period was neither more fertile nor more gifted than the Archaic period. The Archaic period produced the whole of the Doric order, from the stylobate to the mutules, and the whole of the Ionic order, while the Classical period produced only the Corinthian order; and even that was merely a by-product of the Ionic, the only difference initially being a new type of capital. Similarly, a morphological survey of the same two centuries demonstrates that the Archaic period was definitely

Aspects of the evolution of Athenian architecture

superior in its handling of architectural forms. An Archaic Doric capital, considered on its own, is much more expressive than one of the Classical period, and the same is true of every other Doric form when taken on its own. In terms of vigour of form, the Archaic Ionic capital is far superior to the Classical Ionic.

When all is said and done, a survey of the architecture of the two periods shows that the claim to fame of the Classical period lies not in its creation of new forms or perfecting of old ones, but rather in striving for and attaining the greatest possible functional and visual harmony between the various parts of a form or the various forms in a building, or between the buildings and the physical environment in a larger project. The truth is that a certain lack of harmony between the parts of a whole is all

35. The stoa at Brauron. (Ch. Bouras, 1962)

too commonly found in Archaic Doric façades, and in Archaic sculpture as well: individual architectural members or sculptural works seem to have been conceived as independent items and are not functionally or proportionately integrated into the whole. This was due in part to the initial

36. Stoa of Eumenes and choregic monument of Nikias: prespective reconstruction. (M. Korres, 1982-1985) ☞

37. Choregic monument of Lysikrates. (J. Stuart and N. Revett, 'The Antiquities of Athens', London 1762)

difficulty of adapting timber building techniques to building in stone and in part to the spirit of the age, which, although not yet ready for large-scale compositions, was marked by an insatiable urge for self-expression in single works and details. The spirit of the new age, as it matured with the passage of time and the development of the new democratic political system, called for an equilibrium governed by rules: between the individual and the community in political life, between empiricism and theory in the pursuit of knowledge, between the part and the whole in writing, the visual arts and architectural design. The capitals of the Classical Parthenon, for example, lack the exuberant vigour of those of the first Parthenon (before the middle of the sixth century), but they appear more durable because they have a more pronounced hypotrachelion and do not lessen the visual impact of the column by casting too much shadow on the shaft, as was the case in the first Parthenon. And there are even more conspicuous differences of spirit and composition between the pedimental sculptures of the Parthenon and those of the first Parthenon.

One of the most significant aspects of the evolution of Athenian architecture, the increase in the width of the interior with no corresponding increase in its length, has already been mentioned in connection with the Parthenon and the Old Temple. The same phenomenon is to be seen in the Pinakotheke (which is much wider but no longer than its predecessor on the site, Building B), the Temple of Athena Nike (where the sekos is almost the same length as the original small astylar temple but twice as wide) and the Erechtheion (where the east cella is only slightly longer but very much wider than in the previous building). This development is connected with the most unusual fact that there are windows on either side of the door in all these buildings, including the Athena Nike, and also with another structural innovation that is less well known: the raising of the ceiling to the greatest possible height beneath the roof. In the Parthenon, to make room for the statue of Athena Parthenos, the ceiling was made about 1.35 m. higher in the sekos than it was in the pteroma, pronaos and opisthodomos, by compressing the space available for the roof to the very limit.

Local typological peculiarities notwithstanding, Athenian monumental architecture is at first sight ordinary Doric imported from its original homeland, the Peloponnese. For at least a century that Doric architecture was the only style in use in Athens. Many important modifications and improvements were introduced during that time, but only as regards the proportions, decorative motifs and optical refinements, while the stylistic vocabulary remained unchanged: columns with no base (almost always); twenty flutes with sharp arrises; transition from the hypotrachelion to the abacus with no concave moulding in between; uniform, regularly-spaced triglyphs above the architrave with square metopes between them; mutules on the soffit of the cornice, arranged in position above the triglyphs and metopes. Although considerable liberties were taken with the proportions, the basics of this order remained unchanged for a further six hundred years, until the end of the Roman period!

Unlike the Doric order, the Ionic was not brought to Athens intact from its homelands of Ionia and Naxos (the Cycladic Ionic capital from Oropos in the National Archaeological Museum is an exception, as is the Aeolian capital in the Kerameikos Museum), but its initial evolution was fairly independent. Although this evolution took place several decades after the Ionic capital had reached maturity in Naxos and Ionia, it was somewhat primitive: small votive columns with no base, their capitals having flat faces with painted volutes and cylindrical cushions. The Athenian Ionic column already had one feature – the abacus – that was practically unknown in Naxian and Samian capitals, yet it was not until the third quarter of the sixth century that the echinos first appeared. At first this echinos lacked the succulent hanging carved foliage that had long been standard in Naxian and Samian capitals: instead it had a convex moulding that in the last analysis is probably related to the echinos of the Doric capital. This relationship is in no way diminished when the transition to the shaft demands inversion of the curvature of the echinos, for exactly the same inversion is to be seen in the upper part of the hypotrachelion of Doric capitals. The Athenian Ionic capital has numerous morphological features of the Doric capital, resulting in an unmistakable unity of spirit between the two (Fig. 38).

It was probably about twenty years before the end of the sixth century that capitals with carved volutes first make their appearance. Although at that time they had an echinos of the Naxos or Asia Minor type – but with the leaves painted or merely incised rather than carved in full relief – the carved volutes were not convex, as in the Asia Minor type, but concave, as in some examples from Naxos. Thereafter Athenian volutes were carved in relief and always concave and the echinos was either a cyma reversa or had the composite profile of some round capitals, consisting of two or three superimposed elements of which the lowest is a cyma reversa and the uppermost a circular impost block which sometimes resembled the abacus of a Doric capital. The earliest confirmed instance of the architectural use of this type of capital was in the Stoa of the Athenians at Delphi, built just after the repulse of the Persian invasion. In Athens itself it was probably not used in a building until about thirty years later. Only then, a century after its first beginnings, did the Athenian column capital first incorporate some features of the Asiatic type of Ionic capital that had been evolving in the meantime: cables along the volutes and the cushion fillets and a simple ovolo moulding with relief egg-and-dart enrichment in place of the earlier composite echinos. These new elements were assimilated at once, and so perfectly that their true origin is not apparent. In fact the new style was thought of as authentically Athenian, and as such it swept through Macedonia and even started infiltrating Ionia itself, supplanting the genuine Ionic architectural features of the previous period: the Temple of Athena at Priene, the new Temple of Artemis at Ephesos, the Mausoleum at Halikarnassos and countless other monumental buildings all had Athenian Ionic capitals. The same thing happened with the entablature: the Asiatic type of entablature, comprising only an architrave and a cornice with dentils, gave way to the Athenian type, in which the architrave is surmounted by a frieze of the same height and the cornice is as plain as possible, with no dentils. The new Athenian type of entablature, adopted forthwith for the stupendous Temple of Apollo at Didyma, was probably derived mostly from Doric but partly from Cycladic architecture, typical examples of which include the famous Ionic treasuries at Delphi.

The Athenian Ionic order was the basis of the variation known as Corinthian, in which the only significant difference is that the two-sided Ionic capitals is replaced by a pericentral circular capital with a square top. The new order, a genuinely Athenian invention traditionally attributed to the Athenian sculptor Kallimachos, obviated the difficulties involved in forming the corner of a colonnade, which had previously been done sometimes by bringing columns closer together (in the case of Doric columns) and sometimes by using a special asymmetrical form of capital (in an Ionic building).

It was only because the best examples of Athenian Doric, Ionic and Corinthian architecture were included in *The Antiquities of Athens* by Stuart and Revett, and because their book made such an astonishing impact in Europe, that the Athenian versions of these three orders were so widely imitated in the West from as early as 1760 or thereabouts. Consequently the Ionic columns in Neoclassical buildings in Western Europe conform to the Athenian type rather than the Samian or Ephesian, and the same can be said of the other two orders too.

Athenian architects or architects working in Athens can claim the credit for a long list of 'firsts'. They were the first to build a Doric temple entirely of marble ('Older Parthenon' or 'Parthenon II' according to Dörpfeld, *c.* 490 B.C.), the first to use a stone entablature in a colonnade (Stoa Basileios, late 6th cent. B.C.), the first to replace wooden coffered ceilings with similar ceilings made of marble (Parthenon, Hephaisteion, etc.), the first to use windows in large monumental buildings, the first to widen a Doric interaxial (Propylaia, 437 B.C., Stoa of Zeus Eleutherios, the stoa at Brauron), the first to design a stoa with a forward-projecting wing at each end (Stoa of Zeus Eleutherios), the first to design a Π-shaped stoa (Brauron), the first to build a peristyle courtyard (Pompeion), the first to unite what had been a group of separate buildings into an integrated whole (Propylaia) and the first to work out an imaginative planning scheme making it possible for a complex of multiple units built according to a set of rules to be fitted into an existing unplanned sprawl of buildings. This scheme arose out of a combination of circumstances and aspirations: in the first place, because of the hilly terrain and the great antiquity of the settlement, the city was totally unplanned and remained so even after 479 B.C., when

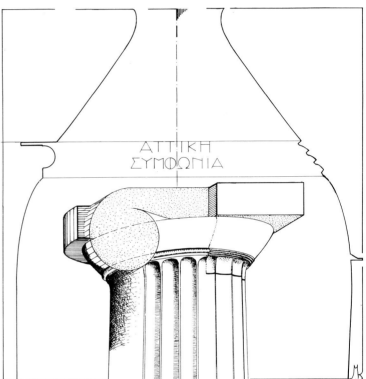

38. *Attic symphony. (M. Korres, 1983)*

the Athenians missed the opportunity of replanning as well as reconstructing it following the repulse of the Persian invasion; and secondly the great demographic, economic, political and intellectual flowering of Athens created demands (and also the right conditions) for an unprecedented building boom. This was not just a matter of putting up more buildings: first and foremost it was a qualitative improvement, and in every sector. In addition to the evolution of architectural forms, mentioned above, great progress was made with the development of building types and several completely new types came into being, such as the bouleuterion (council house), the odeion (concert hall) and the theatre. Lastly, Athenian architects worked out excellent ways of planning public spaces and the approaches to them, including the engineering of roads to cover often considerable altitude differences; they perfected the old methods of functional connection between parts; and they introduced unprecedented ways of effecting visual and conceptual linkage or separation between buildings as parts of an overall city plan (Fig. 1).

Thanks to these achievements, Athens gave the ancient world its first almost complete example of comprehensive planning capable of linking the parts and the whole on any scale, from the detail to the entire city. This example was followed as a matter of course whenever the slightest opportunity arose. The unique multiaxial design of buildings and terraces and the landscaping of the site at Pergamon in the third and second centuries B.C. is unmistakably derived from the great Athenian example of the Classical period, and the superb combination of colonnades, monumental gates and courtyards at successive levels in the Lindos acropolis is best understood as a new application of the principles first conceived by Mnesikles in his design for the Propylaia in Athens.

BIBLIOGRAPHY

Amandry, P., *La Colonne des Naxiens et le Portique des Athéniens*, Paris 1953.
Bauer, H., 'Lysikratesdenkmal, Baubestand und Rekonstruktion', *AM* 112 (1977) 197ff.
Boersma, G.S., *Athenian Building Policy...*, Groningen 1970.
Bohn, R., *Die Propyläen der Akropolis zu Athen*, Berlin 1882.
Bouras, Ch., *Η αναστήλωσις της στοάς της Βραυρῶνος*, Athens 1967.
Brouskari, M.S, *Μουσείον Ακροπόλεως*, Athens 1974.
Camp, J.M., *The Athenian Agora*, London 1986, 66-72.
Corso, A., *Monumenti periclei. Saggio critico sulla attività edilizia di Pericle*, Venice 1986.
Dinsmoor, W.B., *The Architecture of Ancient Greece*, 1950.
—, 'The Choragic Monument of Nikias', *AJA* 14 (1910) 459-484 and *AAG* (1950) 339.
—, 'Observations on the Hephaisteion', *Hesperia* 5 (1941).
Dinsmoor, W.B., Jr., *The Propylaia to the Athenian Acropolis, I: The Predecessors*, Princeton 1980.
Gruben, G., *Die Tempel der Griechen*, 3rd edn., Munich 1980, 210, 214.
Hill, B.H. , 'The Older Parthenon', *AJA* 16 (1912) 556.
—, 'The Interior Colonnade of the Hephaisteion', *Hesperia* 8 (1949) 190-208.
Hoepfner, W., 'Das Pompeion und seine Nachfolgerbauten, Kerameikos, Ergebnisse der Ausgrabungen', Band 10, Berlin 1976.
Huvitt, G.M., *The Athenian Acropolis*, Cambridge 1999.
Koch, H., *Studien zum Theseustempel in Athen*, Berlin 1955.
Korres, M., «Από τον Σταυρό στην αρχαία Αγορά», *Horos* 10-12 (1992-1998) 83-104.
—, ' The Interior Colonnade of the Hephaisteion', *Hesperia* 8 (1949) 190-208.

—, «Τοπογραφικά ζητήματα της Ακροπόλεως» in *Αρχαιολογία της πόλης των Αθηνών*, Athens (Hellenic National Research Foundation) 1996, 57-106.

Lambrinoudakis, V.K., *Οικοδομικά Προγράμματα στην αρχαία Αθήνα*, Athens 1983.

Mark, I.S., ' The Sanctuary of Athena Nike in Athens', *Hesperia* 26 (1993) 93-98.

Miller, M.C., *Athens and Persia in the fifth century BC*, Cambridge 1997.

Miller, S.G., *The Prytaneion, Its Function and Architectural Form*, Berkeley 1978.

Mylonas, Shear I., 'Kallikrates', *Hesperia* 32 (1963) 377-388.

Orlandos, A.K., *Η αρχιτεκτονική του Παρθενώνος*, Athens 1977-1978.

Papanikolaou, A., «Τα σχιστοειδούς μορφής ανοίγματα στο Ερέχθειον», *AD* 33 (1978) I 191-197.

Plommer, W.H., ' Three Attic Temples', *BSA* 45 (1950) 66-112.

Raubitschek, A., *Dedications from the Athenian Acropolis*, Cambridge Mass. 1949.

Shear, L., Jr., *Tyrants and Buildings in Archaic Athens*, Princeton 1978.

Stevens, G.P., et al., *The Erechtheum*, Cambridge Mass. 1927.

Stikas, E., «Τρίπλευρα κιονόκρανα, κορυφώματα και μνημεία», *Archaiologike Ephemeris* 1961.

Tiberi, I.C., *Mnesicle, l'architetto dei Propilei*, Rome 1964.

Touloupa, E., 'Early Bronze Sheets with Figured Scenes from the Acropolis' in *New Perspectives in Early Greek Art, a symposium, 27-28 May 1988* (Studies in the History of Art, 32), Washington 1991.

Tournikiotis, P. (ed.), *Ο Παρθενώνας και η ακτινοβολία του στα νεώτερα χρόνια*, Athens 1994, 137-161.

Travlos, J., *Bildlexikon zur Topographie des antiken Attika*, Tübingen 1988, 389, 390 (bibliography).

—, *Pictorial Dictionary of Ancient Athens*, New York 1971.

Wesenberg, *Die Propyläen der Akropolis in Athen* (Schriftenreihe der Universität Regensburg, 15), 1988, 9-57.

Wiegand, T., *Die archäische Poros-Architektur der Akropolis zu Athen*, Cassel/Leipzig 1904.

CHAPTER II

*Great Sculpture
in Fifth-Century
Athens*

ANGELOS DELIVORRIAS

2. The Tyrannicides by Kritios and Nesiotes. Roman copy. (Naples, Museo Archeologico Nazionale. Hirmer Archives)

1. A 'Caryatid' from the Porch of the Maidens in the Erechtheion. (London, British Museum)

Great Sculpture in Fifth-Century Athens

Atossa: Meanwhile, my friends, I would like to learn where
Athens is located.
Chorus: Far from here, to the west where the last rays of our
Lord the Sun set.

Aischylos, *The Persians*, 230-232

Needless to say, Athenian history – the history of an incalculable contribution to mankind – does not begin in the fifth century B.C., which was to become known as the Golden Age of Greek antiquity. Nor did Athenian sculpture begin then: it started much earlier, following remarkably closely the progress of social and intellectual evolution, that is to say the gradual transformation of the political system through the ages until finally it crystallized as an un-rivalled model for the administration of public affairs. Ever since then, this has been the yardstick by which all constitutional systems in the world have been judged.

Overture: **Adagio con spirito**, **sostenuto.** In monumental sculpture, as in every other man-ifestation of the need for self-expression, the artist's struggle to externalize his feelings is vitalized chiefly by an absolutely conscious tendency to free the dynamic of art from the shackles of materiality. This is a fundamentally important attribute of artistic creation which, while guaranteeing durability and the immutability of values, remains indifferent to the challenges of spatial relationships and the attraction exerted by untrodden paths beckoning him towards new forms – or rather the attraction exerted by the flight from the apparently real to the really apparent. In the Archaic period, during the sixth century B.C., materiality as a value and immobility as a virtue quickly reached the limits of their revela-tory powers, juxtaposing creativity with visual charm, in other words with that which is cheerful and pleasing, with a view of the beauty of things that is admittedly optimistic and positive but nonetheless purely external. However, the wonders of the world, a world in motion, naturally provoked reactions of a different kind and raised questions of a different order with ever-increasing frequency.

The end of the
Late Archaic period

Knowing that man had been posited as the measure of all things, artists soon yielded uninhibitedly to the mystical enchantment of an exploratory frame of mind that leads almost inevitably from the fascinating charm of form to the consuming excitement of its content, from its visible outer trappings to its hidden inner kernel, from the mythical dimension of its value judgments to its deeper existential meaning. In this way they discovered in movement the fundamental activating force of life, and in the anthropocentric approach to all things they discovered not only the relative contributions of individual responsibility to the conception and rendering of the world but also the potentialities of personal participation in its formulation and interpretation. In this mobile universe, respect for the pictorial elements of form and an obligation to penetrate and understand its inner meaning are kindled by the mechanisms of an unprecedented kinetic vitality, and they quickly move on from observation and admiration, optimistic acceptance and abstract generalization to active searching for its root causes. That quest in turn leads on to a dynamic remoulding of the ingredients of reality through the transference of personal characteristics on to the harmonic frequencies of a process of idealization, which, however, never transgresses the strict boundary separating the natural law from the sin of hubris. And this is a hallmark of the subsequent evolution of ancient Greek art.

3. Athena and Marsyas by Myron. A modern reproduction based on Roman copies. (Frankfurt, Museum Liebighaus)

I have no idea whether a foreigner arriving in Athens in the fifth century B.C. would have been able to realize what had gone before; whether the images of the works of art he encountered on his peregrinations would automatically have made him think of the epic struggle for self-expression, which had followed the same path in other, unexplored fields of artistic and intellectual creativity; whether he would have been able to discern the common factors that had led to the revelation of history (for example, through the realization that the responsibility for man's fate lies with man himself just as much as with God) or the birth of the theatre (where this realization is made the object of a shatteringly critical self-examination) or to the search for true knowledge through philosophy (where thought is elevated from the fundamental questions suggested by the horizons of the natural environment to the mysterious realm of human behaviour). Times had changed, of course, and democratic government had become firmly entrenched after the famous victories of Marathon (490), Salamis (480) and Plataiai (479). Following the repulse of the Persian invaders, some of the destroyed monuments of the Archaic period were used as building material for the city wall that was to protect Athens from similar harrowing experiences in the future, while others were buried devoutly under the soil of the Acropolis, where the foundations of fifth-century art were laid, as a lasting reminder of the universal significance of the conflict between the Athenians and the despotism of the East. Remembrance of the past was kept alive not by the fetishistic conservation of ruins but by a culture that strengthened character through the precepts of self-knowledge, thanks to the power of suggestion and the fact that the lessons of history were taught more tellingly through the example of mythology. From then on – and this was a characteristic of the whole gamut of Greek art throughout its dialectical continuity – exploratory trends in art were never inhibited by regret over opportunities lost in the past: on the contrary, they were encouraged by the promise held out by the present for future success in striving for an unchanging ideal.

March: Allegro marciale con anima. A lively sense of history, especially as regards the correlation of history with the preservation of memory, can be discerned in every branch of the arts, in the shape of large-scale projects

4. Roman copy of a statue of a goddess wearing a peplos. (Cherchel, Musée Archéologique)

commissioned by the state as soon as life in Athens had started returning to normal. The famous bronze monument to the Tyrannicides (Harmodios and Aristogeiton) represents the city's first honorific commemoration of its historic past, shortly before the *The Severe Style* production of Aischylos's *The Persians* at the Theatre of Dionysos in 472 B.C. (Fig. 2). This sculptural group by Kritios and Nesiotes was put up in the Agora in 477/6 to replace the Archaic version of the same theme, which had been carried off by the Persians and would never have been restored to its original home without the help of Alexander the Great nearly two centuries later. The fame of this work and good likenesses of it have been preserved by numerous Roman copies in marble, which testify to the stylistic magnificence of the original and the Romans' skill in reproducing old masterpieces to meet the ever-increasing needs of the imperial period. The vivid depiction of the tyrannicides' indomitable boldness and self-assurance and the almost naturalistic ripple of their muscles, breathing life and movement into their bodies, are still worlds away from the more advanced anatomical knowledge of Archaic sculpture. The exact relationship of the two figures in the original work and the question of which was the

5. Roman copy of a statue of a goddess wearing a chiton and himation. (Rome, Villa Albani)

front side have been the subject of interminable debate, but the message for today's viewer is one of valour, conveyed by the glorious deployment of the axial lines, which pierce – or rather which seem to be trying to break through – the obstacles to communication and the optical barriers of conventional pictorial space.

The trend towards greater realism in sculpture as a mark of respect to the natural environment is equally apparent in other works of the early fifth century B.C., the period of what art historians call the Severe Style (490-460 B.C.). Many sculptures of that time are remarkable for their bold freedom of movement, the ruggedness of their facial features and a certain despondency of expression. All those characteristics are typical of a great Boeotian sculptor working in Athens, Myron of Eleutherai, whose best-known work (made famous by Roman copies) is the bronze group of Athena and Marsyas set up on the Acropolis *circa* 450 B.C. (Fig. 3). Here the compositional relationship between the two figures possesses a unity derived from a state of mind that can now be called Classical, for it has outgrown the explosive extroversion of the Severe Style and keeps the autonomy of the figures within the bounds of a closed, unified world teeming with nuances of meaning. Myron is also credited with a number of other works that are either lost or dubiously attributed to him, including a statue of Erechtheus and one of Perseus holding Medusa's head, both on the Acropolis, and two more groups depicting Theseus in combat with the Minotaur and the bull of Marathon. Throughout the fifth century the exploits of Theseus, the Athenian hero *par excellence*, continued to provide inspiration not only for artists but also for official Athenian propaganda, as symbolizing the union of the Attic demes and the birth of democracy in Athens. The cycle of his youthful exploits, the coupling of his name with that of Herakles in the story of the Amazonomachy at Themiskyra and his two great personal triumphs in the Centauromachy and the Athens Amazonomachy, all of which served to remind the

6. Eleusinian relief of Demeter, Kore and Triptolemos. (Athens, National Archaeological Museum. Photo: K. Kontos, 2000)

Athenians of their superiority in struggles against uncivilized enemies, were retold again and again in the great public works projects of the Athenian state.

The female figures of the Severe Style are characterized by a heavier structure, greater emphasis on the weight of the garments and noticeably more restraint of movement. These basic specifications were retained until about the middle of the fifth century and are still apparent in the 'Cherchel Demeter', a statue type that appears to have no stylistic antecedents, where the gravity of the godhead is accentuated by the heaviness of the simple peplos with its few relieving folds (Fig. 4). In the 'Mocenigo Demeter', another unclassifiable type, the graceful drapery of the chiton has already begun to express the dictates of a different kind of harmony. The chiton, pleasingly combined with the tonal variations of the folds of the peplos round the body, epitomizes the aesthetic taste that was to prevail during the thirty years of the High Classical period in such works as the 'Albani Kore' (Fig. 5).

The sculptural potentialities of the peplos and of the chiton and himation are exploited together in one of the most impressive and original works of the next thirty years: the large relief of Demeter, Kore (Persephone) and Triptolemos from Eleusis, probably intended for ritual purposes and obviously carved by a very fine sculptor, whose high reputation is evidenced by the number of Roman copies of his work (Fig. 6). Other sanctuaries in Attica, too, with their splendid new temples erected on the ruins left by the Persian invaders, were adorned with an astonishing number of magnificent sculptures; and the same is even more true of the temples, sanctuaries and public places in Athens, especially the Agora, where work had already started on the sculptural ornamentation of the Temple of Hephaistos and Athena, the best-preserved Classical building in Greece. It is absolutely out of the question that the production of major sculptures in such extravagantly large numbers could have been the work of Athenian artists alone, and in any case the demand created by the acceleration of building programmes is known to have attracted a lot of experienced sculptors from other Greek cities, each working in his own aesthetic tradition. The assimilation of these different artistic approaches, with Attic workshops exerting a dominant influence and with the genius of Pheidias putting its imprint on everything, was what gave Athenian sculpture of the time of Perikles (461-429 B.C.) its special character.

Song of Praise: Allegro maestoso, vivace. Few of the attributed sculptures of the thirty-year High Classical period are mentioned in the written sources, and even fewer have survived the ravages of time. However, the existence of Roman copies that capture their essential qualities gives us a good idea of what many of them looked like and has enabled scholars to decipher the spiritual message conveyed by their mode of expression, using the Parthenon sculptures as a yardstick. For at no other time was the greatness of inspiration so faith-

7. The 'Varvakeion Athena'. Miniature replica of the chryselephantine statue of Athena Parthenos. (Athens, National Archaeological Museum. Studio KONTOS/Photostock)

fully served by inspired carving of the marble as it was in the sculptural ornamentation of
the temple erected on the Acropolis as a tribute to the city's patron goddess and her system
of government: of that there should be no doubt. Never before or since have historical facts
been epitomized with such shattering eloquence in stories from
mythology; never before or since has there been such an exciting correlation between the level of self-knowledge and the level of expressive skill, between religious feeling and social need, between individual liberty and personal commitment, between the experience of the past and the expectations of the present, between political propaganda and the ideology of a state.

In the various parts of the Parthenon's ornamentation art historians have discerned the
hands of a whole host of different artists, 'poets working with chisel and stone', each making
his own contribution to the realization of Perikles's vision and the overall design co-ordinated
by Pheidias. Plutarch expressly informs us that 'everything was managed and superintended
by Pheidias', and his reliability is not in question here. That explains the fact that it is not
just a matter of superb technical skill: the inner unity of the overall design is apparent in
every part of the decorative scheme – even in fragments of marble fragments – and in the
majestic inspiration of the guiding hand that lifts every craftsman to the peak of his potential in a chorus that is polyphonic in structure and symphonic in its organization, a chorus
in whose composition the human dimension is fused with the divine.

In the unification of the architectural design, the ornaments and the figural sculptures
an important part was played by the metopes, carved in bold relief, which ran round the
outside of the building on all four sides, subduing the upward thrust of the colonnades and
reinforcing their stability. The metopes at the east end, over the entrance to the temple, were
badly mutilated in the Early Christian period, but traces remained of the outlines of the figures and an analysis of the subject was published by Camillo Praschniker: almost certainly,
these metopes depicted Athena and other gods and goddesses in scenes from the
Gigantomachy. Also badly damaged are the metopes at the west end, which depicted the
Athenian Amazonomachy with Theseus playing a prominent part in the defence of his
homeland. Responsibility for the almost complete destruction of the north metopes with the
exception of the 32nd, which remained intact *in situ*, has to be shared between the religious
fury of the early Christians and the bombardment of the Parthenon by Morosini's Venetian
army in 1687. Yet even here archaeologists have managed to identify the subjects of some
of the panels depicting the dramatic events of the siege of Troy, giving prominence to the
feats of the Athenians and especially the participation of Theseus's two sons, who were
shown rescuing their grandmother Aithra from captivity. The metopes of the south side
showing the Centauromachy (Figs. 8-11), unlike those on the other three sides, are in very
good condition, especially since the marvellous restoration of the central section from a large
number of fragments identified and pieced together by Alexandros Mantis. Apropos of the
brutish assault on the bride and guests at Peirithoös's wedding, Theseus is once again held
up as an example of the values cherished through the ages by the Athenian political leadership. Much has been written about the symbolic implications of these mythological stories

and their connection with Athenian ideology of the Classical period: the main point here, of course, is that the conflict between the power of reason and mindless violence is to be understood as analogous to the conflict between law and order and lawless abuse, between the Greeks and the barbarians, between the Athenians and all their enemies.

An Athenian citizen would no doubt have been filled with a similar sense of pride in his country and its political system on looking at the more conspicuous sculptural groups in the pediments of the Parthenon, the birth of Athena at the east end (Figs. 12-15) and the contest between Athena and Poseidon for the patronage of Attica at the west (Figs. 16-18). Running through these highly significant compositions is a more profound train of thought and a dialectical analogy in which the patron goddess, seen as the personification of her blessed city, is the linchpin connecting a whole series of contrasting pairs of oblique allusions: in the east pediment, the peak of Mt. Olympos with the entire Hellenic pantheon welcoming the newborn goddess; in the west pediment, the flat summit of the Acropolis with the mythical founders of Athens passing judgment on the gifts offered by the competing deities. In the former, an event of the utmost theological significance projects its apocalyptic grandeur on to celestial, or rather cosmic, co-ordinates, with the rising of Helios (the sun) at one end and the setting of Selene (the moon) at the other (Figs. 13-15). In the latter, the terrestrial component of the divine nature is taken as a function of human need, with the cosmic dimension of the subject limited to the confines of Athenian territory. Here the personifications of the River Kephisos (Fig. 16), the River Ilissos and the Kallirrhoe Spring mark the outermost limits of a marvellous work of narrative sculpture which, while vindicating the Athenians' choice of the gifts offered by Athena, shows a decent generosity of spirit by giving equal honour to Poseidon – and quite properly so, in view of the Athenians' growing interest in the sea.

8-11. Metopes 28, 29, 4 and 27 from the south side of the Parthenon. (London, British Museum)

The Parthenon sculptures, or those of them that have escaped the fate of most Greek antiquities, breathe the rarefied air of an expressive range too vast to be compared with present-day values, conveying a feeling of immense freedom that knows and respects its limits; a freedom that extends its embrace in equal measure to inspiration and to execution, that goes far beyond the parameters of time and space, a freedom for which no match is to be found in the earlier or later history of sculpture. That is why they have so far withstood all attempts by art historians to explain the meaning of their forms and the significance of their subject matter. The great Greek archaeologist Christos Karouzos put his finger on the truth when he declared, in a similar context, that the dialectical miracle of the High Classical period can only be expressed in feeble oxymorons: during those thirty years in particular, he said, 'Tranquillity is a form of terrible spiritual and mental conflict, universality a form of superabundant individuality, ideality an expression of the most familiar reality.' His pithy and perceptive words come closer to the gist of the matter than anything that has been said on the subject before or since.

The only other point I should like to make about the Parthenon sculptures in particular concerns their musical tonality, that is to say their underlying rhythmic structure and their melodic values. To me it seems really remarkable that their essential quality is still expressed in musical metaphors, in spite of the gaps left by mutilation at the hands of the early Christians, destruction or damage caused by the bombardment of 1687 and systematic looting in 1800-1803, with the result that what remain of the Parthenon's sculptures are scattered in countless museums and private collections in Greece and abroad. So I would speak of a crescendo that starts at the east end – the heavenly, divine end – and grows in volume at the west. For the west end – the earthly, human end – was the first subject of the sculptural counterpoint to be seen by the pilgrim as he emerged from the Propylaia to be confronted by one of the seven wonders of the ancient world.

The rhythms of the pedimental groups, calmer and smoother at the east end, faster and more syncopated at the west, vary in intensity according to the harmonic frequencies of the reliefs in the Ionic frieze (Figs. 19-23), which crowned the walls of the temple inside the peristyle: a seemingly endless set of variations on novel thematic ideas connected with the Panathenaic procession, the intention being to draw attention to the state's achievements in improving military preparedness, fighting morale and respect for divine law, according to Jerome J. Pollitt's recent reading of the frieze in the light of Perikles's funeral oration. Scholars attempting to interpret the Parthenon's Ionic frieze owe a great debt to their many predecessors, and obviously every new 'definitive' interpretation will depend on the unforeseeable demands of future research objectives, presumably in the light of our ever-expanding knowledge of the Classical period. In any case, I am quite sure that the intellect that conceived the design and supervised the execution of the greatest composition of all time consciously chose the charismatic ambiguity of the iconography so that the work might con-

13. *The chariot of Helios (the Sun), Dionysos, Demeter with Kore, and Artemis(?), from the east pediment of the Parthenon. (London, British Museum)*

tinually be enriched by the new ideas imposed upon it – or rather wished upon it – by the art historians of future generations.

Whereas the other Parthenon sculptures are dominated by gods and heroes in more or less equal measure, the Ionic frieze is the first in the history of human civilization to glorify

 12. *Three goddesses: Hestia(?) and Dione(?) with Aphrodite, from the east pediment of the Parthenon. (London, British Museum)*

mankind, in the idealized person of the Athenian citizen (Figs. 19-20, 22). I would actually go so far as to say that it is a hymn of praise addressed to the human race rather than to the gods. The gods here are mere spectators of the humans' majestic, rhythmic ascent (Figs. 21, 23), a harmonious progression of different classes and ages, different callings and races united by the common melodic factor of a moral fibre that banishes all trace of arrogance or conceit. The artist saw to it in his wisdom that here again the scenes should unfold in an order corresponding to the subjects of the metopes and the pedimental groups. Having first heard the 'overture' at the west end, woven around themes taken from the human world, and then the glorious hymn of praise at the east, where divine affirmation is the central theme, the worshipper is spiritually and mentally prepared to accept the truth of the divine epiphany represented by the chryselephantine statue of Athena, the orchestral finale of the doxology of Athens.

The celebrated statue of Athena was made by Pheidias over a ten-year period (447-438) with the collaboration of a team of experienced craftsmen, advanced pupils, able assistants

and who knows how many others. We have a fairly clear idea of what it looked like from the detailed descriptions of it in ancient literature and the existence of a number of Roman copies. Of these, the small and somewhat frigid 'Varvakeion Athena' (Fig. 7) gives an excellent impression of the colossal scale of the original, while the warmth of Pheidias's work is conveyed better by some other replicas. The goddess is shown wearing a simple Attic peplos, the aegis over her shoulders, a spectacular Attic helmet on her head with tall plumes springing from a figure of Pegasus and two Sphinxes, costly jewellery round her neck and on her arms, and elaborate sandals on her feet with relief carvings on the soles. In her right hand, which rests on a colonnette, she proffers Victory to the Athenians; her spear rested against her left shoulder; and with her left hand she holds the edge of her shield, which rests on the ground beside her. The shield was a masterpiece of toreutics with a relief of the Athenian Amazonomachy on the outer face and a painting of the Gigantomachy on the inside. Nothing is known about the Gigantomachy scene apart from some very sketchy literary references, but the opposite is true of the Amazonomachy, thanks partly to Neo-Attic copies reproducing some of the scenes, but mainly because of modern scholars' painstaking efforts to reconstruct the original composition. The glittering figure of Athena is accompanied by the sacred snake Erysichthon, coiled up in the concave inner surface of the shield. On the pedestal there was a relief representation of the birth of Pandora, showing the gods

14. Selene (the Moon), from the east pediment of the Parthenon. (Athens, Acropolis Museum. Photo: S. Mavromatis, 2000)

bringing her their gifts while Helios and Selene (as in the east pediment) highlight the cosmic dimension of this mythical event. No more than a few traces of figures from this band of reliefs can be made out on the miniature replica from the Pnyx and the colossal copy from Pergamon. However, even if it survived intact, the interpretation of its symbolism would doubtless pose a knotty problem.

Athens in the fifth century was the centre of intellectual and artistic life in the Greek world. It was the point of intersection for all collective research projects on the senses and the intellect and for all individual researches on science and technology; and so the ground was fertile in Athens for the flowering of the High Classical, a period of some thirty years over whose terminal dates not all scholars agree. Judging by the combination of historical and artistic evidence, I would say that it covered the years from about 460 to about 430, the two crucial events being the rise of Perikles to power (461) and the outbreak of the Peloponnesian War (431), which was to be such a turning-point in Athenian history.

The dates can only be guidelines, of course, but those three decades produced the greatest achievements in formulating the fundamental principles of the constitution and in every other branch of scholarship and the arts. The same period also saw the construction of the Parthenon, a work of art far surpassing any precepts of aesthetics, suffused from within by an unprecedented and life-giving disposition towards reconciliation: something like a declaration of faith in the fellowship between the old modes of expression and the new spirit of adventurousness in visual art, between personal inquiry and general apprehension, between individual liberty and the public interest, between general expectations and particular needs, between political ideology and religious sentiment, between myth and reason, between past and present. The harmonious

15. Head of a horse from Selene's chariot, from the east pediment of the Parthenon. (London, British Museum)

intermingling of opposites holds within it the promises of guarantees for the future in an ascending scale culminating on the Acropolis, for on the steps of the Acropolis moral integrity meets beauty, emotion meets redemption, faith in human ideals meets the potentialities of democracy, the piety that is an essential protection against aberration meets the profoundest meaning of the dimensions of liberty.

If Perikles acted as the catalyst for the realization of the Athenian miracle by abruptly accelerating the rhythm of history, the presence of Pheidias was equally catalytic in terms of transcending all the established standards of artistic expression and elevating art to the level of sublime values. The different traditions represented by the sculptors who worked in Athens during the Golden Age and gave substance to Classical ideals, the different generations to which they belonged and the different personal idiosyncrasies that shaped their work: all these were tamed, or rather orchestrated polyphonically, by the prodigious personality of the supreme sculptor of all time.

Of the sculptures by Pheidias mentioned in literary sources, most stood on the Acropolis, and some have been recognized in Roman copies. However, we still do not know what his colossal Athena Promachos looked like: this bronze statue, put up *circa* 460 B.C. out of the tithe of the spoils from the battle of Marathon, was widely famed, but it has vanished without trace. The 'Kassel Apollo' (Fig. 24) – a statue type that prefigures the Classical ideal in its rendering of the anatomy and its sense of movement, and thus marks the final demise of

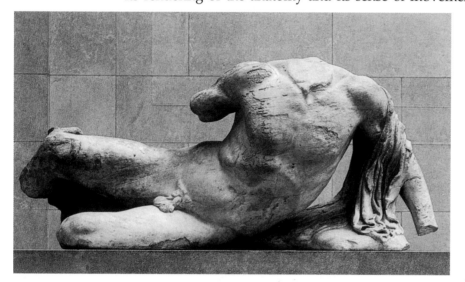

*16. The River Kephisos, from the west pediment of the Parthenon.
(London, British Museum)*

the Severe Style – has been identified by Hans Schrader as being copied from Pheidias's Apollo Parnopios. This identification has been disputed, but the fact remains that the 'Kassel Apollo' epitomizes Pheidias's way of breathing life into a man's body. The Athena Lemnia (Fig. 26), another bronze, which has been reconstructed from scattered Roman copies of the body and head through the brilliant insight of Adolf Furtwängler, shows how deftly Pheidias was able to transmute his inspirations in the years before work started on the Parthenon, i.e. just after 450 B.C. Here again we are dealing with a brilliant conception, a breadth of inspiration unclouded by any contemporary stylistic ideas about the 'androgynous' qualities of the figure depicted or the classicistic parameters of its creation. The bronze statue of the poet Anakreon, probably paired originally with Xanthippos, is mentioned by Pausanias, who does not give the sculptor's name. It was almost certainly dedicated on the Acropolis by Perikles himself in honour of his father Xanthippos, who defeated the Persians in the naval battle of Mykale (479 B.C.). Judging by the only relatively well-preserved Roman copy (Fig. 30), the statue showed the poet rapt in divine inspiration, plucking the strings of his lyre and swaying to a lilting rhythm in a way that has never been paralleled since. The original of this work is thought to have been made immediately after the Athena Parthenos was completed, or at least after the completion of work on her shield. Its identification as a copy of Pheidias's Anakreon has been staunchly championed by Ernst Buschor. Finally, the 'Doria Pamphili Aphrodite' (Fig. 27), in which the goddess's garments seem to be ruffled by a gentle breeze, may well be a copy of the marble Aphrodite Ourania from the Agora, which marked the end of Pheidias's activity in Athens just before the outbreak of the Peloponnesian War and foreshadows the trends that were to set in after he left for Olympia. Thereafter Athenian sculptors, freed from the weight of the great master's overwhelming authority and expressing themselves at last with florid demonstrativeness as well as frenetic rhythms, started standing up for a different approach to art in search of a way out of the quandaries of the troubled last quarter of the fifth century.

In the work Pheidias did in Athens, all of it between about 460 and about 430, he used his inner resources to move Athenian sculpture on from the late Severe Style to the Rich Style. However, some of his work predates his Athens period (the Delphi group and the Athena Areia at Plataiai, for example) and some was done after that (including the huge chryselephantine statue of Zeus at Olympia and the Aphrodite of Elis, also chryselephantine). All those, and many others mentioned in classical literature, together gave rise to the enormous admiration in which Pheidias has been held throughout the ages. The originals of most of his works are lost, of course, and the information to be gleaned from exhaustive archaeological research and the analysis of Roman copies yields only pale reflections of the typology and a few iconographic details of particular importance. Therefore the only Pheidian sculptures that emit the great master's aura are those of the Parthenon (Figs. 8-23), in which, ironically, what makes the most stunning impression is not so much his personal imprint as his active intervention in the overall design and conception and, most of all, the comradely care and interest he has taken in his pupils' work:

17. Kekrops and one of his daughters, from the west pediment of the Parthenon. (Athens, Acropolis Museum)

here we see a teacher giving advice and guidance, making suggestions and improvements, passing on the secrets of his genius to worthy successors.

Variations: Andante espressivo, cantabile. Of those who maintain that the great Argive sculptor Polykleitos, one of the most illustrious artists of the Classical world, was bound to have been involved in the Periklean building boom in Athens, most rely on sources of dubious reliability rather than the fact that artists have always been attracted by the prospect of working in a place where new ground is being broken. There are better arguments to be found in support of his presence in Periklean Athens: first, the noticeable influence of the Polykleitian style on the sense of movement in Athenian figural sculpture from the middle of the fifth century; secondly, the well-attested rivalry between Pheidias and Kresilas – in Athens, and probably between about 440 and 435 – when the priests of Ephesian Artemis announced their controversial competition for the statues of the Amazons. In venturing to

Athenian sculpture, 460-430 B.C.

suggest that his famous Doryphoros or Spear-Bearer, known as 'the Canon' (Fig. 25), may well have stood in Athens, I would find it hard to adduce stronger evidence than the fact that a superb bronze copy of the head bears the signature of the late Athenian sculptor Apollonios. Clearly this means that Apollonios was familiar with the original, an inference that is supported by the quality of the copy. In that case the hero represented in the statue could very well be Theseus, especially as the reasoning in support of its identification as Achilles is neither conclusive nor even convincing.

Foreign artists in Athens

A connection between the Athenian and Argive artistic traditions can be traced back to earlier periods and must have continued later, too, to judge by the sculptural group of Phrixos and the ram that Pausanias saw on the Acropolis, for a fragment of the plinth on which it stood bears the signature of the Argive sculptor Naukydes. Less is known about Deinomenes, another sculptor probably from Argos, who – again according to Pausanias –

Foreign artists in Athens

carved the statues of Io and Kallisto for the sanctuary of Zeus Polieus. Pausanias's statement would have remained unsupported had Yorgos Despinis not identified the fragments of one of these figures among the mass of broken stones on the Acropolis and recognized the statue type in Roman copies of the 'Barberini Suppliant' (Fig. 36). The other one of these two mythical heroines who had the misfortune to be loved by Zeus is perhaps to be recognized in the lovely statue of a seated figure, distinctly erotic in character, which I pieced together from many fragments years ago (Fig. 35). At that time I correctly identified it as an architectural ornament, but I misinterpreted the significance of the provenance of the fragments.

One of the foreign sculptors in fifth-century Athens who espoused Classical ideals and worked with Pheidias was Kresilas, from Kydoniai in Crete. Works by him are documented in various parts of the Greek world, but there is nothing particularly remarkable about either the quantity of his output or the quality of the copies of sculptures known to be by him. That he was highly regarded is attested by the fact that he was chosen to do the bronze statue of Perikles on the Acropolis, commissioned by the Athenians immediately after his death in 429. All that remain of this famous work are some copies of the head: nothing is

18. Iris, from the west pediment of the Parthenon. (London, British Museum)

19-20. Two slabs from the north frieze of the Parthenon: young men leading animals to be sacrificed, young men carrying pitch- ☞
ers. (Athens, Acropolis Museum. Photo: S. Mavromatis, 2000)

21-23. Three slabs from the east frieze of the Parthenon. 21: Hermes, Dionysos, Demeter and Ares. (London, British Museum).
22: The Ergastinai (weavers of the peplos). (Paris, Musée du Louvre). 23: Poseidon, Apollo, Artemis and Aphrodite. (Athens, Acropolis Museum. Photo: S. Mavromatis, 2000)

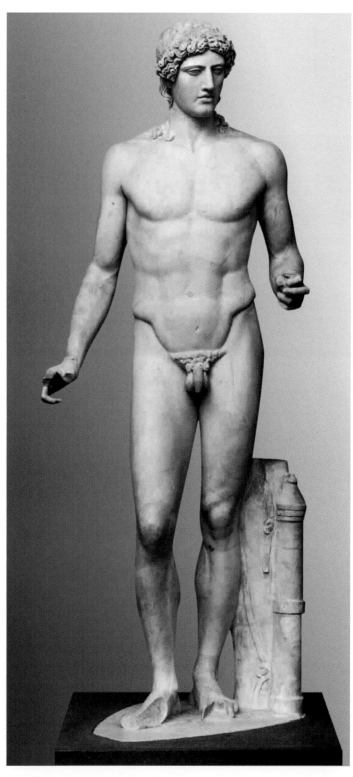

24. *Apollo. Roman copy of a statue by Pheidias. (Kassel, Staatliche Kunstsammlungen. Hirmer Archives)*

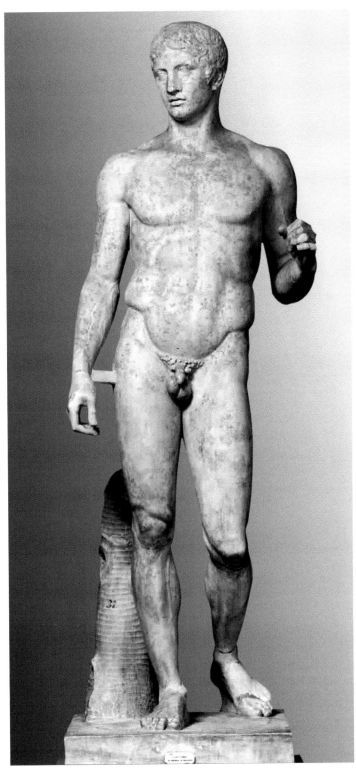

25. The Doryphoros (Spear-Bearer) by Polykleitos. Roman copy. (Naples, Museo Archeologico Nazionale. Hirmer Archives)

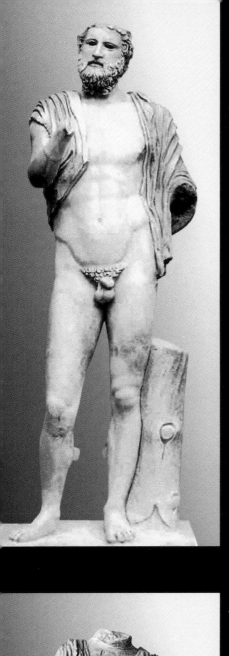

known about the posture or appearance of the body. Even this fragmentary second-hand evidence, however, conveys something of the Olympian bearing of the great statesman to whom Athens owed her Classical glory and also shows us what a strong influence the Athenian tradition exerted on artists working there. Inconsistencies cloud the evidence concerning a statue (definitely a bronze) of a wounded soldier that stood on a surviving inscribed base on the Acropolis: some time ago I suggested that it was to be identified as the original of a marble torso now in Oxford. Apropos of the portrait statue of Perikles, the bronze original of the 'Velletri Athena' statue type (Fig. 28) used to be attributed to Kresilas. According to numismatic evidence and a miniature copy of the late Classical period found by Semni Karouzou in the storerooms of the National Archaeological Museum, Athens, this impressive statue dating from *c.* 430-420 definitely belonged in Athens, but the sculptor's identity is still in dispute.

Of the numerous artists whose services were required in Athens for the ambitious projects of the fifth century, few are known to posterity by name. Some came from the islands, including Agorakritos, who was not the only one from Paros. One of his predecessors was Euphron, who had been drawn to Athens by the challenges of the open market and the promise of work. Euphron, keeping up a tradition going back to the sixth century, left his mark with the head of Hermes in the National Archaeological Museum, identified by Christos Karouzos. Agorakritos had the good fortune to be taught by Pheidias and was commissioned by the state for some of the major public projects of that time, presumably with Pheidias's backing. Among his earlier works was the cult statue of Kybele, probably a bronze, which stood in the Metroön in the Agora and seems to be quite accurately rendered in the only surviving copy at Livadhiá, identified some time ago by Ernst Langlotz. Perhaps his most famous work was the larger-than-

34. Grave stele from Aigina. (Athens, National Archaeological Museum. Studio KONTOS/Photostock)

26. *Athena Lemnia. Modern reproduction based on the copies in Dresden and Bologna. (Dresden, Staatliche Kunstsammlungen)*

27. *Aphrodite. Roman copy of a statue by Pheidias. (Rome, Palazzo Doria Pamphili)*

28. *The 'Velletri Athena'. Roman copy. (Paris, Musée du Louvre. Hirmer Archives)*

29. *The 'Farnese Athena'. Roman copy. (Naples, Museo Archeologico Nazionale)*

30. *The 'Borghese Anakreon'. Roman copy of a statue by Pheidias from the Acropolis, Athens. (Copenhagen, Ny Carlsberg Glyptotek)*

31. *Roman copy of the statue of Nemesis by Agorakritos. (Copenhagen, Ny Carlsberg Glyptotek)*

32. *Prokne and Itys by Alkamenes. (Athens, Acropolis Museum. Photo: S. Mavromatis, 2000)*

33. *'Aphrodite in the Gardens' by Alkamenes. Roman copy. (Paris, Musée du Louvre)*

life cult statue of Nemesis in her temple at Rhamnous, Attica, a figure of such Pheidian beauty that the postclassical Greeks often attributed it to the wrong sculptor. The identification of the fragments, the restoration of the statue on the basis of Roman copies that faithfully reproduce its typology (Fig. 31) and the thoughtful appreciation of its stylistic qualities by Yorgos Despinis are to be counted among the great archaeological success stories of the twentieth century. The work of restoration was carried on by Vassilis Petrakos, who pieced together the reliefs on the statue base and thus opened the way for a better understanding

35. Marble statue of a heroine. (Athens, Acropolis Museum. Photo: German Archaeological Institute, Athens)

36. The 'Barberini Suppliant'. Roman copy. (Paris, Musée du Louvre. Hirmer Archives)

of an important chapter in the history of Classical art. The discovery by Semni Karouzou of a central akroterion, which may come not from the temple at Rhamnous but from some other building in Athens, demonstrates the artist's familiarity with architectural sculpture. Little is known about the extent to which Agorakritos was involved in the great building programmes on the Acropolis, where the final result depended mainly on co-operation between many artists and craftsmen and collaboration between different workshops.

The fame of the cult monument of Athene Itonia and Zeus-Hades at Koroneia, Boiotia, leads us to suppose that Agorakritos most probably undertook commissions for other sculptural groups of this kind. Future research and the discovery of fresh evidence may well confirm the conjectural attribution to him of a cult monument of Poseidon and Athena known

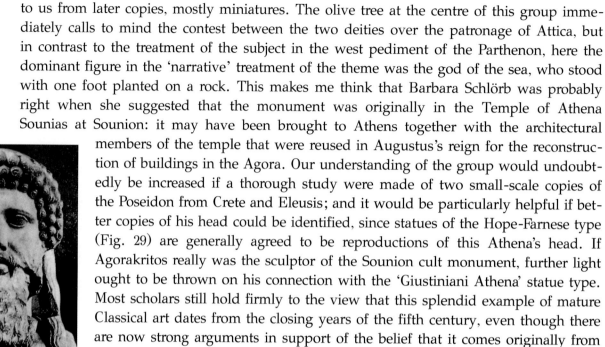

to us from later copies, mostly miniatures. The olive tree at the centre of this group immediately calls to mind the contest between the two deities over the patronage of Attica, but
in contrast to the treatment of the subject in the west pediment of the Parthenon, here the
dominant figure in the 'narrative' treatment of the theme was the god of the sea, who stood
with one foot planted on a rock. This makes me think that Barbara Schlörb was probably
right when she suggested that the monument was originally in the Temple of Athena
Sounias at Sounion: it may have been brought to Athens together with the architectural
members of the temple that were reused in Augustus's reign for the reconstruction of buildings in the Agora. Our understanding of the group would undoubtedly be increased if a thorough study were made of two small-scale copies of
the Poseidon from Crete and Eleusis; and it would be particularly helpful if better copies of his head could be identified, since statues of the Hope-Farnese type
(Fig. 29) are generally agreed to be reproductions of this Athena's head. If
Agorakritos really was the sculptor of the Sounion cult monument, further light
ought to be thrown on his connection with the 'Giustiniani Athena' statue type.
Most scholars still hold firmly to the view that this splendid example of mature
Classical art dates from the closing years of the fifth century, even though there
are now strong arguments in support of the belief that it comes originally from
the Temple of Athena Sounias. Research also needs to be done on the contribution of Agorakritos's workshop to the prolific output of 'unofficial' Athenian
sculpture: all those luminous works of art imbued with an astonishing feeling
of human warmth, such as the grave relief from Aigina depicting a stunningly
handsome young man, his grieving servant boy, a cat and a bird (Fig. 34).

Also in Athens at that time and caught up in the unprecedented artistic fer-
ment of the Classical period were a number of older Athenian sculptors who had
long been faithful followers of the Attic tradition. One of the oldest was Kalamis,
the sculptor of a bronze Apollo Alexikakos ('Averter of Evil') that stood in the
Agora and has sometimes been identified with the 'Omphalos Apollo'. One of
the pieces on which José Dörig focused in his attempt to throw light on Kalamis's
elusive stylistic idiom was the unique copy of a woman's head in the Hermitage
Museum: with the expressive darkness of her unkempt tresses and a hint of
chthonian melancholy suffusing her beautiful features, she could be an imitation
of one of the Furies from the Areopagus. And, if Evelyn B. Harrison's attractive
line of argument is right, the 'Albani Kore' statue type may well be a rendering
of the enigmatic Aphrodite Sosandra found on the Acropolis (Fig. 5).

Faulty identifications of Classical sculpture occur all too frequently, owing
to the ambiguity of the ancient sources, the damaged state of the works them-

37. Hermes Propylaios by Alkamenes. Copy from Pergamon. (Istanbul, Archaeological Museum. Photo: German Archaeological Institute, Athens)

38. The 'Borghese Ares'. Roman copy. (Paris, Musée du Louvre. Hirmer Archives)

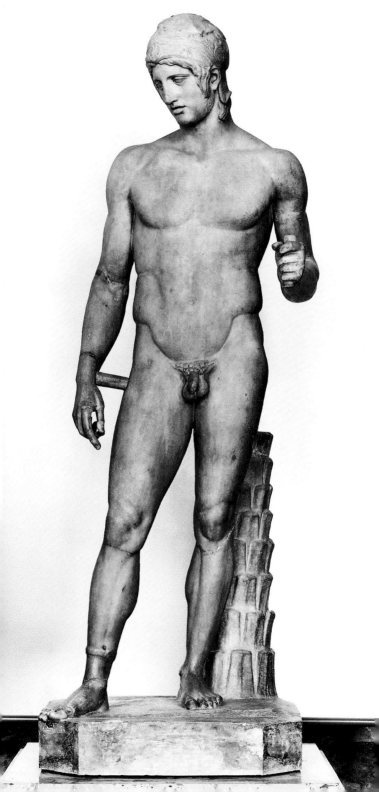

39. Boreas abducting Oreithyia. The central akroterion from the east pediment of the Temple of the Athenians, Delos. (Delos, Archaeological Museum. Photo: German Archaeological Institute, Athens)

40. Torso of a statue of Athena. (Athens, Agora Museum. Photo: S. Mavromatis, 2000)

selves and the corruption of ancient literary texts. Sometimes, too, researchers fail to recognize the affinities and the differences between well-preserved copies and the extremely rare instances of original works, which are usually in a bad state of preservation. A case in point is the so-called Aphrodite-Olympias, a statue type well known from several later copies, which has been variously misinterpreted without good reason. This masterpiece of the mid fifth century has been wrongly identified as a copy of a Pheidian Aphrodite in Rome and also as a copy of Alkamenes's 'Aphrodite in the Gardens' in Athens, equally exhaustive arguments being advanced for both points of view. Since a fragment of the marble original has been discovered on the Acropolis, since there is little or no chance of even a small piece of an original work by Pheidias having survived to the present day, and most of all since Alkamenes's Aphrodite statue type has been identified beyond doubt, it is hardly surprising that researchers have been looking in the wrong directions. Be that as it may, the identification of Aphrodite-Olympias with the Aphrodite by Kalamis, commissioned by Kallias, has been ruled out (at least for the time being) by the most recent theory that it is actually a statue of Hygieia, the goddess of health. Thus a final answer to this question will have to await the discovery of new fragments, or perhaps the more highly-developed critical acumen of future generations.

A dominant figure among the Athenian sculptors of the Classical period is Alkamenes, to judge by Pliny's references to his prolific output and Pausanias's descriptions of many of his sculptures. His early pieces, certainly done before the start of work on the Parthenon, include the Hermes Propylaios from the

Acropolis (Fig. 37), well known from numerous copies, and the triform Hekate Epipyrgidia (assuming that Werner Fuchs's identification of a copy in Hadrian's Roman villa proves to be correct). It must have been at about that time that Alkamenes started work on the sculptural ornamentation of the Temple of Hephaistos and Athena, which still stands intact in a commanding position overlooking the ruins of the Agora, though the work was repeatedly interrupted and he only completed it between 421/0 and 416/5 B.C., when he made the bronze cult statues, of which the Athena and some of the plinth reliefs have been positively identified in Roman copies. His contribution to the sculptural ornamentation of the Parthenon is confirmed chiefly by the stylistic affinity between some slabs of the east frieze (Fig. 23)

The post-Pheidian generation

and the famed cult statue of Aphrodite in the Gardens from the sanctuary of that name near the River Ilissos (Fig. 33), which provides us with a referent for the stylistic idiom he was using in the decade between 440 and 430. The free copy or adaptation of this work that he himself made about ten years later for the Sanctuary of Aphrodite at Dhafní not only gives us a firm basis for reconstructing the cult statues of the Hephaisteion and establishes a link between the Hephaisteion sculptures and Alkamenes's workshop: it also testifies to his dynamic intervention in the shifts of taste that characterize the Rich Style.

In the early years of the Peloponnesian War, when the Parthenon had just been completed, Alkamenes evidently designed another cult monument of Athena and Ares for the great temple which was moved to the Athens Agora in Augustus's reign. That was where it was seen by Pausanias, who attributes the figure of Athena to an unknown Parian sculptor named Lokros, in whose shadowy person some have sought to identify Agorakritos. The whole matter still raises important questions regarding the unity of the original composition, that is to say the conception of the subject matter and the organization of its component parts, bearing in mind the decisive role played by Alkamenes in the post-Pheidian artistic world and the generally accepted attribution to him of the original of the Borghese Ares (Fig. 38). The discovery in the Agora excavations of a marble torso of Athena (Fig. 40), assigned by Barbara Schlörb to the cult monument of the Temple of Athena and Ares, certainly put a different slant on the matter, and the problem has since been further complicated by the fairly recent finding of an almost undamaged cult statue of the war goddess Allat at Palmyra, which is unquestionably a copy of the Athena in the Agora. In view of its obvious stylistic affinity with the work of Alkamenes and its equally obvious compositional similarity to the Borghese Ares, this puts the question of Lokros into a different context.

Of Alkamenes's other works in Athens, our picture of the chryselephantine Dionysos has started to take shape thanks to the researches of Ernst Langlotz and Gerhard Neumann, but so far nothing is known about the marble statue of Hera in the temple at Phaleron that was destroyed by the Persians and left in ruins as a memorial to their desecration of the holy places. So the only surviving authentic sculptures by Alkamenes are the marble statue of Prokne and Itys (Fig. 32) – an underrated work of considerable originality dated not later than 430, which Pausanias was discerning enough to single out from among the innumerable votive offerings on the Acropolis – and the torso of Aphrodite from Dhafní. Besides these, however, a comparative study of the stylistic evidence suggests that he was almost certainly responsible for the most impressive funerary monument of the Classical period. As reconstructed from copies – and for the reconstruction we are again indebted to the sensitive insight of Ernst Langlotz – it consisted of a square base with reliefs of three figures on each side: Herakles and the Hesperides, Orpheus and Eurydice with Hermes (Fig. 41), Theseus with Herakles and Peirithoös in the underworld, Medea and the daughters of Pelias. The base presumably supported a large marble relief vase, either a lekythos like that of Myrrhine or a loutrophoros. The mood of the reliefs is cheerful, but with an undercurrent of sadness, and this is possibly the most moving of all the Athenian sculptures produced during the Peloponnesian War. The consensus of opinion in the past was that it was a memorial to one of the great tragedians and was to be dated to the very end of the fifth century, but that is surely wrong: it must have been in honour of some illustrious woman who died *circa* 420 B.C. The discovery of a fragment bearing the head of Herakles near the Sacred Way makes it almost certain that this was one of the official funerary monuments that lined the road leading to Eleusis.

The elements that unify Alkamenes's figures, giving them elegance and Attic grace, are the transposition of the centre of gravity beyond the vertical axes, the rhythmical swaying

41. Copy of a relief of Eurydice between Orpheus and Hermes. (Naples, Museo Archeologico Nazionale. Hirmer Archives)

42. Part of the parapet of the Temple of Athena Nike. (Athens, Acropolis Museum. Photo: S. Mavromatis, 2000)

43. *The funerary stele of Hegeso. (Athens, National Archaeological Museum. Photo: K. Kontos, 2000)*

of the bodies and a thoroughly personal philosophy, especially as regards the rendering of the temporal context. He seems to have invented the idea of suspending the action between two consecutive moments. The freshness of his work and the beneficial effect of that freshness on the homogenization of independent trends in Athenian sculpture are evident in the sense of well-being that comes across even in humbler pieces by anonymous sculptors, such as the attractive figure leaning expressively on a loutrophoros on a tombstone in the National Archaeological Museum, which conveys the feeling of the 'Aphrodite in the Gardens' (Fig. 33) with much greater immediacy than any of the surviving Roman copies.

In the last quarter of the fifth century – in fact during the first few years of that period, when the short-lived hopes of a 'happy ending' to the Peloponnesian War were fizzling out in the almost equally short-lived Peace of Nikias (421-415) – one more masterwork was added to the roll of honour of Athenian art: the Temple of Athena Nike. This little architectural gem on the bastion commanding the entrance to the Acropolis encapsulates the ideological trends of the Rich Style just as the Parthenon, a few years earlier, had expressed the theoretical underpinning of the High Classical period. Everything about it is on a different scale of magnitude, of course, and not only because the massive sturdiness of the Doric order here

44-45. Reliefs from the parapet of the Temple of Athena Nike. (Athens, Acropolis Museum). 44: Athena and Nike. 45: Nike undoing her sandal. (Photos: S. Mavromatis, 2000)

46. Copy of a statue of Aphrodite. (Paris, Musée du Louvre. Hirmer Archives)

gives way to the slender proportions of the Ionic, nor only because the uncompromising spirituality of the larger temple is replaced by a much more sensitive and fragile gracefulness. What is conveyed by the figures in the various panels of the Nike temple's frieze and parapet is not robust physical strength but human tenderness and a mysterious escapism,

The zenith of the Rich Style

kept within the bounds of untrammelled movement. Their sheer garments, caressing the curves of their bodies like a diaphanous second skin, transmute sensation into illusion and, with an evanescent hint of sensuality, emphasize their fleshly texture at the expense of the underlying anatomy of the bone structure that had been a feature of earlier sculpture (Figs. 42, 44-45).

These general characteristics are accentuated by the relative isolation of the figures, not only on the four sides of the frieze but also in the more or less contemporary relief slabs of the parapet round the edge of the bastion. Of the various subjects of the frieze, the most clearly discernible is the group of gods and goddesses surrounding Theseus at the east end. As regards the reliefs on the other three sides, which are so badly weathered as to be unrecognizable, it is reasonably certain that the south side depicts the battle of Marathon (as asserted by Evelyn B. Harrison). The north and west sides also have battle scenes, most probably mythological but unidentifiable. Adding to the temple's sculptural glory were the pedimental compositions depicting the Gigantomachy and the Amazonomachy (some fragments of which were found by Yorgos Despinis) and the figural akroteria – now lost without trace – which were made of bronze, probably gilded. The parapet reliefs on all three sides show Athena attended by Victories setting up trophies or leading bulls to be sacrificed (Figs. 42, 44-45): these may be allusions to the Oschophoria festival in honour of Theseus, or perhaps to victory celebrations in general. Thus myth meets history in the decorative scheme, with an allegorical message considerably less ambiguous than in the sculptural ornamentation of the Parthenon.

Elegy: **Adagio grazioso, con dolore.** The stylistic interpretation of the Nike temple's sculptures has long been a controversial issue. At one time or another they have been attributed to many different post-Pheidian sculptors, and strenuous efforts have been made to prove

The final decades of the fifth century

that they were by Agorakritos, Alkamenes or some other contemporary artist. However, all these arguments fail almost without a hearing, because they overlook the changes that take place in any artist's personal idiom over the years, and especially in the context of the incredibly rapid shifts of aesthetic taste from one decade of the fifth century to the next. This may perhaps explain the extraordinary discrepancies in the dating of major works of sculpture, even by eminent scholars. One late fifth-century Athenian sculptor who is very likely to have worked on the Nike temple is Kallimachos (described by Pausanias as the 'refiner of his art'), generally credited with having carved the original of a statue of

47. Copies of reliefs of dancing Maenads. (Madrid, Museo Nacional del Prado. Hirmer Archives)

Aphrodite known to us from numerous copies, the best two being in the Louvre (Fig. 46) and in Naples. *Pace* those art historians who see in it a continuation of the Polykleitian tradition, the enormous number of Roman imitations of this famous sculpture shows that it must have been admired above all others in antiquity; and, although its identification remains uncertain, it must have stood in an Athenian sanctuary, otherwise it is hard to explain the existence of the contemporary copy of its head, almost miniature in scale, which was found by Semni Karouzou in the storerooms of the National Archaeological Museum, or the stylistic individuality of a lovely funerary relief that marks the expiry of the Rich Style and the end of the artistic trends of the fifth century B.C.

In the exquisite funerary stele of Hegeso, daughter of Proxenos (Fig. 43), as in many other works from the same period, it is by no means easy to tell the art of sculpture apart from those of painting and toreutics. Given that Kallimachos made the magnificent gold lamp of Athena that burned day and night in the Erechtheion, one may reasonably wonder whether he also had a hand in the sculptural decoration of the last of the great monuments of fifth-century Athenian architecture. But in the Erechtheion, too, it is difficult to tell how much is due to the brilliance of the architectural design and how much to the skill of the sculptors and stonecutters who put it into effect. The tall and slender proportions of the Ionic order and the melodic values of its decorative elements; the delicate carvings of the frieze, in such high relief as to be almost in the round, with the individual figures energized by the noticeable use of perspective; the illusive chiaroscuro of the billowing garments; the fleshly texture of the bodies and the peerless combination of elegance and luxury: all these contend with other coexisting forces, which – in the Porch of the Maidens, for example – seem to suggest a longing for the past, or rather a nostalgia for the magnitudes of past ages (Fig. 1).

These characteristic features are already present, if less conspicuous, in the sculptural ornamentation of the Nike temple. However, the trend was widespread throughout the last quarter of the fifth century, making it hard to distinguish the personal touch of any individual artist in other important sculptures, such as the akroteria of the Temple of the Athenians on Delos, *circa* 420 B.C. (Fig. 39), or the slightly later akroteria of the Temple of Ares, which in the fourth century influenced the sculptural ornamentation of the Asklepieion at Epidauros. Other works in the same spirit include a group of architectural sculptures now divided between Vienna, Paris and Boston and the badly damaged Aphrodite of 'fiery beauty' from the Athenian Agora, which could equally well be assigned to the very late period of Agorakritos or to Kallimachos. It is generally accepted that Kallimachos was responsible for a choregic monument with reliefs of Maenads (Fig. 47), perhaps erected for the Athenian performance of *The Bacchai* in 406 B.C., after Euripides's death.

If we are to understand the struggle for self-expression that marked the subsequent development of art down to the Renaissance, not to mention many of the progressive movements since then, we need to approach the subject with equal measures of knowledge and imagination and at least an equal measure of humility. That is the only way we can hope to re-create the lost picture with the precepts of human values conveyed by the art of the fifth century, even in its last thirty years, when hopes were alternately raised and dashed by the vicissitudes of the Peloponnesian War – but always around the same unfailingly fertile nucleus of the creative urge. While the pace of evolution in fifth-century art had been meteoric, in the fourth century it reverted to a slower, more languid tempo. And where there had been a centripetal tendency bringing artists to Athens from all over Greece, in the fourth century even Athenian artists were lured away by chimerical centrifugal forces. After all, fourth-century Athens could boast neither large-scale public building programmes likely to attract an influx from abroad nor even enough smaller projects to keep her own artists at home. And since there was no longer any all-dominating figure on the artistic scene to orchestrate the mannerisms of personal inspiration, each individual was left free to record his impressions of the march of history in his own way, with more dramatic results.

BIBLIOGRAPHY

Bianchi Bandinelli, R. (ed.), *Storia e Civiltà dei Greci. 4: La Grecia nell' età di Pericle. Le arti figurative*, Milan 1979.

Boardman, J., *Greek Sculpture: The Classical Period. A Handbook*, London 1985.

Despinis, G.I., *Συμβολή στη μελέτη του έργου του Αγορακρίτου*, Athens 1971.

Fuchs, W., *Die Skulptur der Griechen*, IV, Munich 1993.

Höcker, C., and L. Schneider, *Phidias* (RoRoRo Monographie), Reinbeck bei Hamburg 1993.

La Rocca, E. (ed.), *L'esperimento della perfezione. Arte e società nell' Atene di Pericle*, Milan 1988.

Ridgway, B.S., *Fifth Century Styles in Greek Sculpture*, Princeton 1981.

Rolley, C., *La sculpture grecque. 2: La période classique*, Paris 2000.

Stewart, A., *Greek Sculpture: An Exploration*, New Haven/London 1990.

CHAPTER III

Athenian
Democracy

M. B. Sakellariou

2. Stele with the text of a decree (psephisma) enacted by the Athenians in the Citizens' Assembly (Ekklesia). The decree lays down measures designed to prevent the overthrow of the democratic régime and the reimposition of dictatorship. The epistyle relief shows the personification of Democracy placing a wreath on the personification of the Demos (the body of citizens). (American School of Classical Studies, Agora Excavations)

1. The meeting-place of the Ekklesia on the Pnyx. The speakers' platform seen here was made towards the end of the fifth century B.C.

Athenian Democracy

Athenian democracy, the form of government developed in Athens and in force there from 508 to 322 B.C., is a subject of the first importance for a book on the city's contribution to human civilization on various planes. First, it was Athens' outstanding political achievement; secondly, it was the only democratic polity in ancient Greece that proved to be functional, productive and long-lasting; and thirdly, it has been much studied and debated by the ideological and political fathers of democracy in modern times.

The drafting of the constitution

Modern democracy regards the citizens as the source of power, the actual exercise of power being entrusted to the citizens' elected representatives. In the Athenian *demokratia* – a word meaning 'the supremacy of the *demos*', i.e. of the populace – the citizens exercised power directly at meetings of the Ekklesia or sittings of the heliastic courts (people's courts). That is why Aristotle defined the citizen of a fully-fledged democracy like Athens as a 'ruler for life'.

The Ekklesia, or Citizens' Assembly (at which the participants were known as *ekklesiazontes*), was the supreme authority of the state. When not taking part in a meeting of the Ekklesia, the citizens were not rulers (*archontes*: see below, pp. 94-95) but subjects (*archomenoi*). At sessions of the heliastic courts the citizen was a 'co-ruler' (*synarchon*) for the duration of the hearing.

The citizen

Every citizen had the right to act as a voluntary prosecutor whenever he considered that the state or the constitution was in danger or that an archon, a citizen or a non-citizen was breaking the law.

The citizen as *archomenos* was the subject of a state with which he himself was identified as a ruling citizen. Consequently there was never any place for the modern idea that there is a distinction, and indeed antithesis, between the state and the citizen and that therefore the citizen needs special legal means in order to defend himself against the state. Even so, it was quite possible for an Athenian citizen to go to law when he considered that any action of an organ of government was prejudicial to his interests.

In 508 B.C. the reforms of Kleisthenes conferred civic rights on the descendants of old immigrants and reorganized the body politic. Old and new citizens were registered in the archives of the demes in which they happened to be living at the time. The demes were grouped together into a total of thirty *trittyes* (ten in the city, ten in the coastal zone and ten in the inland zone of Attica), and ten so-called 'tribes' (*phylai*) were formed, each consisting of three *trittyes* (one from each zone). The ten new *phylai* took over the roles played by the four previously existing tribes in the various departments of government business, mainly as administrative divisions for the electoral and military service rolls. The decision that each *phyle* should comprise *trittyes* from the three different geographical zones was taken for two political reasons: to limit the political influence of the aristocracy and to help newly-enfranchised citizens to become assimilated. For the same reasons all Athenians – whether noblemen or not, old citizens or new – were officially identified from that time on according to a uniform formula: given name (e.g. Neokles), father's name (e.g. Eukratous, son of Eukrates) and the name of the deme to which he belonged (e.g. Rhamnousios, of Rhamnous). This made it impossible to distinguish between aristocrats and commoners or between old and new citizens.

In 451 B.C., in a reversal of the democrats' initial policy, the body politic was made less inclusive by a law that limited civil rights to males whose parents were both Athenian citizens and disenfranchised the sons of non-Athenian mothers.

Both the broadening of the body politic in 508 B.C. and the restrictive measures of 451 B.C. were the work of radical democrats of the respective periods. In 508 their aim was to consolidate their majority in the Ekklesia and at elections of the archons (chief magistrates). In 451 the radical democrats, who were mostly poor, wanted to reduce the number of persons entitled to share in the benefits available to citizens, namely the remuneration paid to the archons and to participants in the Boule (Administrative Council) and the heliastic courts (it was only later that those attending the Ekklesia were paid a daily allowance), the grants made to the parents and daughters of men killed in battle, to the war wounded and physically incapacitated, the payments made out of the Theoric Fund and the occasional emergency distributions of grain.

All citizens over the age of twenty had the right to attend the Ekklesia and to vote in elections for the archonship. All those over the age of thirty were eligible to be drawn by lot for service as archons or members of the Boule or heliasts (jurors of the heliastic courts). In general, any post to which citizens were appointed by lot could not be held more than once, though it was possible to serve a second (but non-consecutive) term as a *bouleutes*. The heliasts held their posts for life. In the fourth century B.C. about fifty per cent of the citizens took their turn at one or other of these posts sooner or later.

The Demos, i.e. the whole body of citizens meeting in the Ekklesia, wielded total legislative and administrative power and some of the judicial power (see pp. 95-100).

The Ekklesia met ten times per annum in the early years of the republic and up to forty times in the fourth century B.C. Two of the meetings in each year were plenary sessions which were lawfully constituted only when at least six thousand citizens

The Demos

were in attendance; for the other meetings no quorum was laid down. Whether the attendance was six thousand or more, or only a few hundred, the Ekklesia was considered to represent the whole body of citizens. Every citizen had the right to speak.

At the plenary meetings, resolutions were adopted by using *psephoi* (pebbles) or *ostraka* (an ostrakon being a piece of broken pottery on which the voter wrote the name of a political figure whom he wished to be sent into temporary exile). At other meetings the vote was taken by show of hands. All resolutions of the Ekklesia, regardless of the method of voting used, were known as *psephismata* (decrees). Before long, however, decrees having a relatively wide application came to be known as *nomoi* (laws). The subject matter of ordinary *psephismata* ranged from the very important to the very trivial (petty expenditure, the offerings to be made at a sacrifice, etc.). *Psephismata* were also used by the Ekklesia to issue administrative orders to the Boule, the archons, official envoys of the state and the generals in command of military operations, to refer criminal cases to the heliastic courts and to deliver the verdicts of its own judicial hearings.

The most important law courts in democratic Athens were composed of citizens drawn by lot out of the body of six thousand heliasts. The number of heliasts remained constant, as vacancies caused by death were filled annually, the replacements being drawn by lot from among citizens over the age of thirty. New heliasts were required to swear the 'heliastic oath'. The number of jurors in the heliastic courts was usually 501 or 1,001,

**The main
courts of law**

but sometimes 1,501, 2,001 or 2,501 and occasionally 201 or 701. Regardless of its size, every heliastic court was deemed to represent the entire body of citizens: in effect, it was a meeting of the Citizens' Assembly (Ekklesia) in the exercise of its judicial authority. These courts dealt with all kinds of cases: purely private actions, private actions affecting the public interest and public actions on charges varying from the petty to the extremely serious, such as attempting to overthrow the constitution, high treason and gross impiety.

When democracy was introduced, the powers of the heliastic courts were extend-

3. A heliast's identity tag.

4. The ballot disc with a solid boss (left) is for a 'Not Guilty' vote.
The one with a hollow boss (right) is for a 'Guilty' vote.

ed at the expense of the Areopagus (*Areios Pagos*). During the period of aristocratic rule the Areopagus had been the highest power in the land. It played a decisive role in legislation, elected the archons and shared their administrative power. Its members, all former archons, held office for life. Solon (*c.* 594 B.C.) deprived the Areopagus of some of its major political powers, which he transferred to the Boule, a new body composed of commoners. Kleisthenes left the Areopagus untouched by his reforms, and during the Persian Wars (490-479) it regained some of its political influence, allying itself with the conservative forces opposed to the continuing advance of democracy. Eventually, in 461 B.C., the radical democrats succeeded in stripping the Areopagus of all its political powers, which were divided between the Boule and the heliastic courts. Thereafter its jurisdiction was limited to cases of premeditated murder, sacrilege, poisoning and arson.

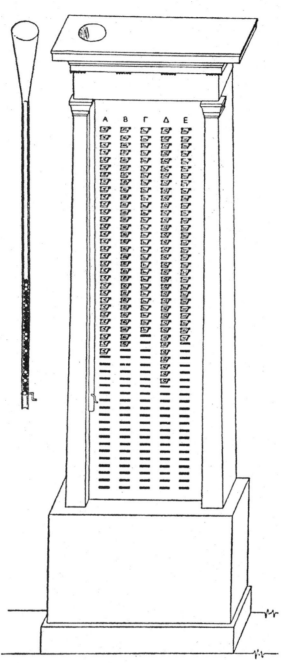

5. An allotment machine for selecting heliasts for service. (Reconstruction drawing by Sterling Dow).

Another long-established court, that of the *Ephetai*, had the same powers as it had had before the advent of democracy, namely to try cases against Athenian citizens charged with unpremeditated homicide and resident aliens (*metoikoi*, or metics) charged with any crime against life.

The functions of the Boule, a council of five hundred members (fifty from each *phyle*), were different from those of parliaments in modern democracies. In the first place, it was not a legislative body: it did not pass laws, but only worked on the drafting of proposed laws. Secondly, it was involved in the administration of the state: it super-

The Boule

vised and checked the work of all the archons, worked together with some of them and had its own areas of administrative responsibility as well; it received foreign ambassadors; and it carried out special instructions from the Ekklesia as occasion demanded. For drafting legislation and monitoring the work of the archons the Boule met in plenary session, while its administrative duties were delegated to statutory committees.

The year was divided into ten administrative periods, during which the fifty *bouleutai* from each of the ten *phylai* took it in turn to perform certain duties and were obliged to live in the Council building (the Bouleuterion) to deal with any emergencies that might arise between sunset and sunrise and on public holidays. These fifty were known as *prytaneis*, and for each day of their prytany (term of duty) one of their number, drawn by lot, served as their chairman with the title of *Epistates ton Prytaneon*. For the twenty-four hours that he held office, the *Epistates* kept the great seal and the keys of the public treasury and also chaired any plenary sessions of the Boule (and of the Ekklesia too in the fifth century).

The word *archon* means 'ruler' or 'person in authority'. In the early years of the Athenian republic they were few in number, all members of the aristocracy, and they were the chief magistrates: the Archon (or Eponymous Archon, because he gave his name to the year in which he held office), the Polemarch (Commander-in-Chief of the armed forces), the King Archon, six *Thesmothetai* (codifiers and guardians of the law) and several others of lesser importance. By the fourth century B.C. their number had risen to about seven hundred.

As time went on, more and more governmental committees of archons were formed. Most of them had ten members, a few had only five and a few had multiples of ten. Individual governmental posts were also few in number

The archons

and only two of them, both concerned with public finance, were of any real importance. The first one existed for only a few years around the middle of the fourth century, while the second was instituted after the Athenians' defeat by Philip of Macedon at Chaironeia in 338 B.C. (see below, p. 100). With a very few exceptions, all personal and collegiate archonships were open to all citizens, as no special qualifications were required and appointments were made by lot. The posts for which proven ability was an essential prerequisite – these included the ten *Strategoi* (generals) and a few financial officers – were always elective.

Responsibility for the administration of the state was shared out among all these committees and officers. The duties of the three great archons of the early days (the Archon, the Polemarch and the King Archon) were now limited to organizing certain state festivals, ministering at some official sacrifices and handling private lawsuits affecting the public interest. In military affairs, it was not long before the ten *Strategoi* took over the duties of the Polemarch. In the fiscal sector there were several ten-man governmental committees charged with handling public revenue and expenditure, arranging public auction sales, managing special accounts and keeping the official reserves. Five ten-man committees shared the responsibility for organizing official sacrifices to the gods; other committees dealt with the settlement of minor private disputes; and there were separate committees handling the work of other government departments: Comptrollers, Sanctuary Maintenance Engineers, Road-builders, Superintendents of Public Fountains, Police, Market Inspectors, Controllers of Weights and Measures, Corn Inspectors, Superintendents of Trade.

All the archons were closely supervised by the Boule and the Ekklesia. Public auction sales and other financial transactions were handled by the archons concerned under the supervision of *bouleutai*. Nine times in each administrative year the Ekklesia audited the accounts of all archons with financial responsibilities and disbarred any who were guilty of irregularities, and at the end of each administrative year all the archons had their work scrutinized by the Boule. Furthermore, every citizen had the right to bring an indictment against an archon, either during or after his term of office, for illegal acts or omissions: such cases were heard by a heliastic court.

Branches of government

Throughout the existence of democracy, legislative initiative belonged to every citizen individually, legislative power was exercised by the Ekklesia and proposed laws were drafted by the Boule. In the course of the centuries, however, a number of changes were made at various levels of the legislative process. Only the most significant of those will be mentioned here.

Quite soon after the introduction of democracy it was realized that the *psephismata* (decrees) of the Ekklesia covered matters of varying degrees of importance and that it would be sensible to use a different term at least for the basic ones. These came to be known as *nomoi* (laws), a word already used to denote the rules of law enacted by the great lawgivers of old (Drakon, Solon and Kleisthenes in the case of Athens). Once it had been accepted that decrees classified as *nomoi* ranked above ordinary *psephismata*, it stood to reason that no ordinary *psephisma* should run contrary to a *nomos*. Provision was therefore made for a legal process known as *graphe paranomon* ('indictment of illegal decrees') as a means of rescinding an unlawful decree and punishing the citizen who had proposed it.

The legislature

Before long, however, it was found that the *graphe paranomon* had some undesirable consequences, for it provided no way of repealing or amending laws that had become obsolete or had turned out to be deficient or even harmful. To deal with situations of that kind, a procedure was devised whereby: any citizen could propose an amendment to a law after first obtaining the approval of the Ekklesia. However, this system was too elementary and inefficient for a systematic review of all the laws in force.

In 410 B.C. the Ekklesia set up a committee to compile a list of all the pre-republican laws that had never been expressly repealed. The task was completed in 403, whereupon the Ekklesia voted through a procedure for the immediate overhaul of the republican laws. A commission of five hundred citizens wrote out all the laws it considered to be due for repeal or revision, together with its own proposals, on wooden boards which were put up in a busy part of the city to be read by the rest of the citizens. Then a second commission, composed of five hundred members drawn by lot from among the heliasts, debated each law separately and considered the proposals put forward by the first commission. The debates were open to the public and citizens were free to express their own opinions.

In the fourth century B.C. the Ekklesia instituted a new procedure for reviewing laws once a year and another procedure designed to bypass the *graphe paranomon*, so making it possible for the Ekklesia itself to repeal or amend laws.

The principal stages in the first of these two new procedures (known as *epicheirotonia nomon*, i.e. confirming laws by show of hands) were as follows. The motion had to be listed on the agenda for the first session of the Ekklesia in the first prytany of the administrative year, for which the quorum was six thousand: separate votes were taken on the retention, repeal or amendment of each of the laws on the agenda. In the next stage, any citizen with an opinion on the matter could set down his views in writing on a wooden board which was then put up at a designated public place in the city centre. Then the motion was debated at a later meeting of the Ekklesia, which decided whether or not to refer the matter to a commission of *Nomothetai* ('legislators'). If so, the members of the commission (either 501 or 1,001 in number) were drawn by lot from among the heliasts. The commission of *Nomothetai* functioned in the same way as a heliastic court, taking into

6. Institutions of Athenian Democracy.

INSTITUTIONS OF ATHENIAN DEMOCRACY

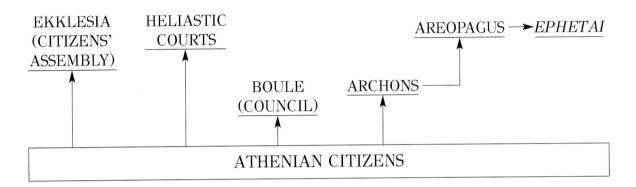

ATHENIAN CITIZENS.

All adult male Athenians, whether born of Athenian parents or naturalized, were Athenian citizens. All citizens were equal. They were divided into ten artificial 'tribes' (*phylai*), all of which were geographically fragmented. Thus the *phyle* was merely an administrative division, roughly corresponding to a modern parliamentary constituency. Each tribe sent fifty members to the Boule or Administrative Council, making a total of five hundred *bouleutai*, and had one or two or more of its members serving as archons.

EKKLESIA (CITIZENS' ASSEMBLY).

All Athenian citizens had the right to attend meetings of the Assembly and to speak, propose laws and vote for or against any proposed decree. Every meeting of the Ekklesia was considered to represent the whole body of citizens. It was empowered to legislate on all matters, to grant citizenship by naturalization, to grant amnesties, to sit as a special court of law, to monitor the performance of the Boule and the archons and to check on the legality of the actions of every *bouleutes* and every archon. Some of the Ekklesia's *psephismata* were approximately what we would now call constitutional laws, some were rules of procedure, some were like ordinary acts of parliament, some like royal or presidential decrees, some were acts of administrative law.

HELIASTIC COURTS.

The heliastic courts derived their authority from the people and represented the people. The jurors, or dicasts, were drawn by lot from among the six thousand heliasts. The heliasts were drawn by lot from among citizens over the age of thirty and held office for life. Every heliastic court was composed of several hundred jurors (201 or 501 or 1,001 or 1,501 or more). The courts were constituted at dawn and sat for one day only, each court hearing three cases. If there were more than three cases to be heard in one day, more than one court was constituted. The cases to be heard were apportioned by lot among the day's courts. These courts dealt with cases concerning the legality of *psephismata*, state security, the integrity of the constitution, impiety, acts prejudicial to the public interest, breaches of martial law and also private disputes. The heliastic courts had the power to impose the death sentence and all their verdicts were final.

THE BOULE (ADMINISTRATIVE COUNCIL).

All citizens were eligible to be members of the Boule. The *bouleutai* were drawn by lot, fifty from each *phyle*, and served for a year. This council of five hundred worked on the drafting of legislative bills passed by the Ekklesia, supervised the work of the administrative authorities and had its own areas of administrative responsibility as well. Its judicial powers were limited and appeal from its verdicts lay to the heliastic courts.

THE ARCHONS.

Most organs of government were committees of ten, but some had five, twenty, thirty or forty members. Individual archon's posts were few. Most archons (government officials) were appointed by lot. The posts for which professional competence was essential, such as the *Strategoi* (generals) and a few financial officers, were elective. Most of the archons performed administrative duties within a limited field under the direct supervision of the Boule or the indirect supervision of the Ekklesia. The archons played a part in the judicial process: they received lawsuits within the jurisdiction of their departments, they gathered evidence, referred cases to the *Thesmothetai* and served as non-voting chairmen of the judicial tribunals (heliastic courts, the Areopagus, the *Ephetai* or tribunals composed of annual archons with judicial powers) hearing the cases they had dealt with before trial. The Court of Eleven had both administrative and judicial responsibilities: in their administrative capacity they formed the governing board of the prison, while as judicial officers they tried common criminals and had the power to impose the death sentence. Some archons had judicial duties only: they tried petty civil actions and petty offences, and appeal from their verdicts lay to the heliastic courts.

THE AREOPAGUS (*AREIOS PAGOS*).

The judges of the Areopagus, all of whom had served as one of the 'nine archons', held office for life. This court tried cases of murder, arson, poisoning and sacrilege. It could impose the death sentence and its verdicts were final.

THE *EPHETAI*.

Courts of *Ephetai*, composed of judges of the Areopagus, were set up as and when required. They tried cases of murder with extenuating circumstances and their verdicts were final.

consideration the citizens' written personal submissions in favour of retaining or revising the law and listening to the speeches of the 'counsel for the defence' appointed by the Ekklesia.

The procedure for repealing, amending or replacing a specific law started with a proposal from a citizen who, when speaking at a meeting of the Ekklesia, stated his belief that the issue under discussion could not be resolved unless a change was made in the existing legislation. The proposer had to have with him a draft of his proposed amendment with his recommendation that the matter should be referred to a commission of *Nomothetai*. The Ekklesia either adopted or rejected his motion without waiting for a draft from the Boule. It was then sent on to the commission of *Nomothetai* drawn by lot for that particular case, who either approved the bill adopted by the Ekklesia as it stood or else rejected it.

The expansion and consolidation of democratic institutions and the concurrent rise of Athens to the status of a 'great power' led to rapid and drastic changes, qualitative as well as quantitative. In the first place, the scope of government was enlarged; secondly, the powers of the administration were extended and strengthened; and thirdly, the number of offices with executive and administrative responsibilities was greatly increased.

The executive

The government departments were: public finance, official religious festivals, armaments and war, foreign policy, the administration of justice, public order, victualling, the provision of public assistance for needy citizens, public works, monumental buildings and theatrical festivals. To meet all these needs on the scale and in the depth required by the statism of Athenian democracy and the imperialism of the poor and the businessmen who made up the majority in the Ekklesia, the machinery of state needed more and more manpower. This was provided by the five hundred members of the Boule, the archons (whose number had risen to about seven hundred by the fourth century B.C.) and just a few dozen secretaries and scribes.

All government offices were equal and self-sufficient and all members of governmental committees had joint and equal responsibilities. The democratic administration suffered from the total absence of a hierarchical structure and the almost total lack of co-ordination between the offices involved in the two crucial branches of administration: defence and public finance.

One of the serious flaws in the system was that the senior officers in the defence department – ten *Strategoi*, ten Taxiarchs, two Hipparchs and ten Phylarchs – had no specialized officer training, nor were they even promoted from one rank to the next. What set them apart from the civil officials was that they were elected, not drawn by lot, and they were eligible for re-election for years on end: in that way they gained experience. Secondly, the ten *Strategoi* all had equal status. Thirdly, two or more of them would be appointed by the Ekklesia to command a campaign jointly. Fourthly, the Ekklesia rarely allowed any of the *Strategoi* complete autonomy: usually it took care to keep the supreme command of a campaign in its own hands, even though that meant that it had to rely on late and sometimes inaccurate information. Athenian democracy never took steps to remedy these deficiencies. It merely took advantage of the fact

7. The Agora at the end of the democratic era. (After the plan by J. Travlos)

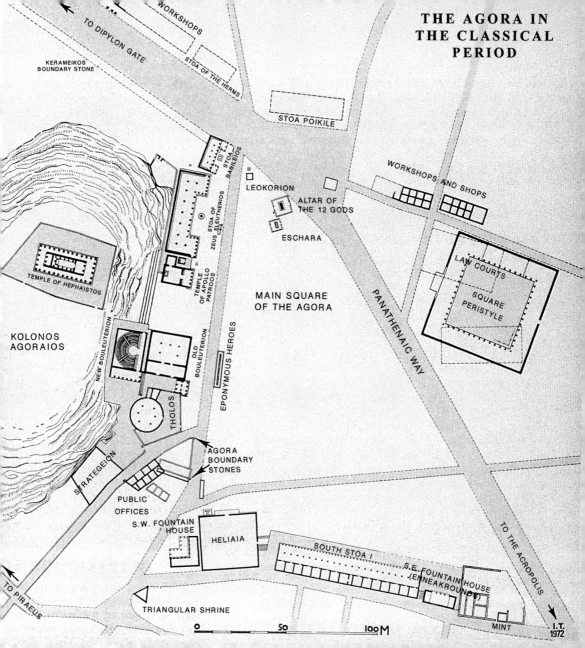

THE AGORA IN THE CLASSICAL PERIOD

TO DIPLYON GATE

WORKSHOPS

STOA OF THE HERMS

KERAMEIKOS BOUNDARY STONE

STOA POIKILE

WORKSHOPS AND SHOPS

LEOKORION

STOA BASILEIOS

STOA OF ZEUS ELEUTHERIOS

ALTAR OF THE 12 GODS

ESCHARA

TEMPLE OF APOLLO PATROOS

TEMPLE OF HEPHAISTOS

LAW COURTS

SQUARE PERISTYLE

KOLONOS AGORAIOS

MAIN SQUARE OF THE AGORA

PANATHENAIC WAY

NEW BOULEUTERION

OLD BOULEUTERION

EPONYMOUS HEROES

THOLOS

STRATEGEION

AGORA BOUNDARY STONES

PUBLIC OFFICES

S.W. FOUNTAIN HOUSE

HELIAIA

SOUTH STOA I

S.E. FOUNTAIN HOUSE (ENNEAKROUNOS)

TO THE ACROPOLIS

TO PIRAEUS

TRIANGULAR SHRINE

MINT

0   50   100 M

I.T. 1972

that a number of able self-taught military commanders emerged in the fourth century, and that some of them made considerable improvements in weaponry and tactics.

The public finance sector was extremely large and complex, as it handled huge sums in revenue from foreign countries and Athenian allies and huge disbursements on armaments, very costly wars, sumptuous monumental buildings, the daily honoraria paid to jurors, archons and members of the Boule, the wages paid to workers on public works projects and social welfare benefits. All the instructions came from the Ekklesia, which reserved to itself the right to decide on even the smallest detail, and were carried out by archons, whose duties overlapped in some places and left gaps uncovered elsewhere. Every item of expenditure was charged against one particular source of revenue. The result was that when interrelated items of revenue and expenditure fluctuated at different rates there would be a deficit in one place and a surplus somewhere else. The flaws in this archaic and elementary fiscal system had no serious consequences in the fifth century B.C., because the coffers of the exchequer were then full. The first time the Athenians made any improvement in their fiscal system was in 403/2 B.C., when there was a shortage of funds: the Ekklesia ceased to have the final say on every item of expenditure: that power was transferred to the Boule, while the Ekklesia adopted certain technical improvements. Several more fiscal reforms of a technical nature were enacted in the ensuing decades, culminating in two that necessitated a change in the democrats' mentality. In 354 B.C., following the Athenians' failure to prevent some of their allies from defecting, the citizens elected Euboulos as Treasurer of the Theoric Fund for a four-year period and gave him free rein to co-ordinate the work of the other financial officers, because he was so successful in increasing the revenue of the Theoric Fund that it had ample surpluses for the financing of major public works projects. In 338 or 334, after the defeat at Chaironeia, the Athenians set up a centralized finance office and appointed Lykourgos to be Treasurer-General: he too secured sufficiently large surpluses to fund large-scale rearmament and public works projects.

The administration of justice was in the hands of a number of law courts, which differed from each other in several respects.

In the first place, they differed in their composition. In this respect they can be divided into three categories, the first of which comprises those courts made up of the sovereign people: the Ekklesia, the heliastic courts and the Boule. In the second category we have the courts composed of men drawn from one specific section of the population, holding office for life: the Areopagus and the court of *Ephetai*. Thirdly, there were courts composed of archons during their year in office, which were of two kinds: those that functioned only as courts of law and those that had other powers as well.

The judiciary

The second difference lay in whether or not the court's verdict was open to appeal. The verdicts of the Ekklesia, the heliastic courts, the Areopagus and the *Ephetai* were final. The verdicts of the tribunal known as the Court of Eleven, composed of magistrates drawn by lot for a one-year term, were final in the case of criminals who pleaded guilty but were open to appeal in other cases. Appeals could be brought to the heliastic courts against the verdicts of all the other courts, including even the Boule.

The third difference between the various courts concerns their level of competence in criminal cases. The Ekklesia, the heliastic courts, the Areopagus, the *Ephetai* and the Court of Eleven had the power to inflict sentences of death, confiscation of property, exile and deprivation of civil rights, whereas all the other tribunals (even the Boule) could only impose fines.

Yet another difference between the various courts lay in the extent of their discretionary powers. The Ekklesia and the heliastic courts could vary their sentences widely according to the circumstances. The Areopagus, the *Ephetai* and the Court of Eleven were obliged to impose

very heavy sentences under the terms of the laws that bound them, while some other courts were similarly obliged to impose very light sentences.

The Areopagus and the *Ephetai*, which were survivals from the period of aristocratic rule, followed an archaic procedure in their hearings and were made up of members – who held office for life – drawn from one specific category of citizens: the Areopagus received a new intake every year, consisting of men who had just completed their term of office as one of the nine archons, while the *Ephetai* were appointed from among the Areopagites to form a separate court.

The heliastic courts (*dikasteria*) developed out of the Heliaia, a people's court instituted by Solon early in the sixth century. In effect, the Heliaia was a meeting of the Ekklesia in the exercise of its judicial authority, for which a quorum of six thousand was required. The heliastic courts were composed of a very large number of jurors drawn from the ranks of the heliasts (see above, p. 93). The sole function of Solon's Heliaia was to hear appeals by citizens against judicial verdicts handed down by the archons. Under the democratic constitution the heliastic courts were empowered to try cases of all kinds except those that came under the jurisdiction of the Areopagus, the *Ephetai* and the Court of Eleven (see above) and petty disputes. In the fifth and early fourth centuries the body of heliasts was divided by lot into ten sections for a year at a time, but subsequently a new method of constituting heliastic courts and allotting cases to them was introduced. The composition of the courts was decided at dawn on each working day. The number of courts in session varied according to the number and nature of the cases listed by the *Thesmothetai* for hearing that day. The dicasts, or jurors as they are usually called nowadays, were drawn by lot from among the heliasts, who gathered each morn-

8. Bust of Perikles.
Roman copy of a lost sculpture by Kresilas.
(London, British Museum)

ing outside the Heliaia. Once the courts had been constituted for the day, the cases to be heard were apportioned between them by lot.

Of the courts composed of magistrates drawn by lot for a one-year term, the Court of Eleven dated from the pre-democratic period. The rest were created by the democratic régime in the fourth century to provide a quick way of settling financial disputes.

Similarities and differences between ancient Athenian and modern democracy

The democratic principles of the sovereignty of the people, the separation of powers between the three branches of government, and human rights, are new. Those were the principles that formed the basis of the U.S. constitution, the first French republic and other republics since, and it is according to those same principles that the democratic credentials of modern systems of government is judged. In ancient Athens the radical democrats succeeded in their aim of bringing about the sovereignty of the people and the complete equality of all citizens in the matter of civil and individual rights, as well as equal opportunities for all citizens to enjoy their

Democratic principles and Athenian democracy

rights. Ancient political commentators, politicians, poets, essayists and philosophers distinguished between democracy on the one hand and oligarchy and absolute rule (whether monarchy or dictatorship) on the other, on the basis of the citizens' liberty and equality and the political supremacy of 'the many' (*hoi polloi*, meaning the common people, the underprivileged). To the ancient Greeks, the concept of the liberty of the citizen meant a combination of two things, namely that a political community should not be dependent on a home-grown despot and that every citizen should enjoy individual liberty; and the concept of the individual liberty of every citizen included the concept of the citizen's individual rights. The concept of equality among citizens meant that all citizens were equal in the eyes of the law and the same laws applied to all citizens. Before the word *isotes* (equality) became standard, the terms *isonomia* (isonomy), *isegoria* (equal freedom of speech) and *isokratia* (isocracy) were used: they were introduced by Kleisthenes and his associates, at once as political slogans and as words to describe the new system of government. Later, perhaps *circa* 462 B.C., the word *demokratia* was coined: this meant 'the supremacy of the *demos*', i.e. of the populace, and it too was originally a slogan that later came to be used to describe the radical system of government introduced at that time.

Some modern critics of Athenian democracy have found fault with it because it did not treat women on an equal footing with men, it never enfranchised the resident aliens *en masse* and it never abolished slavery. They forget how long it was before the United States abolished slavery, how long it took for all modern democracies to give women equal rights with men and, most of all, how long it has taken them to enfranchise immigrants in large numbers. What is more, an ancient Athenian would not recognize as democracy a system in which the citizens do not exercise their sovereign rights directly but delegates those rights to a handful of deputies, and in which the common man is not the dominant political force.

Yet popular sovereignty became a reality automatically from the moment in 508 B.C. when the Ekklesia passed the very first of Kleisthenes's legislative proposals, inasmuch as those proposals were concerned with what we should now call constitutional reforms. This was a revolutionary step, because until then the Citizens' Assembly had had nothing to do with constitutional reforms. One of Kleisthenes's proposals that was passed into law in 508 laid down that the Demos, in other words the body of citizens meeting in the Ekklesia, was the sole competent authority on all matters. Thus was the sovereignty of the people entrenched in the constitution. Neither then nor at any time before the end of the fifth century did the Ekklesia cede any legislative powers to elected representatives of the people. The Boule was not elected (its members were drawn by lot), nor did it enact laws (see p. 94). A truly representative body came into being in the fourth century: this was the commission of *Nomothetai* ('legislators'), which really did have legislative powers. However, the commission of *Nomothetai* was not elected but drawn by lot; it was not a permanent body but depended on the Ekklesia for its existence at any given time; and it did not initiate legislation (see pp. 96-98). So in democratic Athens – unlike republics of the modern era, where the people wield power indirectly through representatives – democracy was exercised directly throughout the republic's existence. The ordinary people were direct and active participants not only in the enacting of legislation but also in the exercise of government and most of the administration of justice (see pp. 92-93, 98-101).

9. Tetradrachm, c. 440-420 B.C. (Athens, Numismatic Museum)

The Athenian republic was also the first to achieve the equality of all citizens. This came about not through Kleisthenes's legislation but as a result of a series of measures enacted at various between then and the middle of the fifth century. It was during this process that the *thetai* (the poorest class of citizens) at last acquired the ultimate right that had previously been denied to them: that of holding office as one of the 'nine archons'.

A further series of measures gave the citizens equal opportunities to exercise the rights that belonged to them. In the first place, members of the Boule, archons (except those in charge of the armed forces) and heliasts were not elected but drawn by lot, which meant that nobody could try to canvass his fellow-citizens in the hope of being elected. Secondly, members of the Boule, archons, heliasts when in session and even citizens attending the Ekklesia received an honorarium approximately equal to an unskilled worker's daily wage for each day that they were exercising their rights, and so those who depended on their work for a living were not excluded from public life. The result was that the poor were in the majority at meetings of the Ekklesia, which was both a legislative and a governing body, and in the heliastic courts, which heard (among other things) cases with political implications.

In addition to their unlimited civil rights, all Athenian citizens, by virtue of their citizenship, also enjoyed what we now call human rights. Some of those, such as the principle of non-retroactive law, the application of the law of precedent and the ban on the imposition of sentences not provided for by the law, applied to all sections of the population. Resident aliens enjoyed equal rights with citizens as regards individual liberty, freedom to work and to own movable (but not real) property, the right of association, freedom of speech, the right to seek legal redress against anybody including the archons and freedom to practise their own religion; nor did they have to put up with xenophobia or chauvinistic snobbery. Slaves were denied civil liberties, were liable to be thrashed by their owners, were tortured when called to testify in a legal action, and many of them made to work in the mines and quarries. However, they were protected against personal abuse, some were allowed to own small sums of money and they could be raised to the status of free men either by being emancipated by their owners or by buying their freedom.

Athenian democracy never kept the three branches of government separate. The Ekklesia enacted legislation, reserved to itself the right to try cases involving serious charges, governed the country and controlled the officials with posts in the administration. The Boule played a part in the legislative process, in its capacity as the drafter of laws, and it also supervised all the executive and administrative officials and worked in close collaboration with them on anything relating to naval stores, public auction sales, revenue collection and disbursements, the organization of religious ceremonies and various other matters; besides which, it also had some judicial powers. The main archons had administrative or military duties but were also involved in the judicial process, for they received lawsuits, acted as investigating magistrates, referred cases to the courts competent to try them and chaired the sessions of all judicial tribunals, though without a vote. There were also some archons who had judicial authority only: they tried petty private disputes. Every tribunal was autonomous and subject to its own rules. The verdicts of the great courts of law – the heliastic courts, the Areopagus and the *Ephetai* – were final.

In modern democracies we have the administration on one side and the subjects, or users of the administration, on the other. In the Athenian democracy there were no dividing lines between the administration and the governed. Every citizen, from the time he came of age until his death, was one of the supreme rulers of the state in his capacity as a member of the Ekklesia of the Demos (Citizens' Assembly) and stood a good chance of serving once in his life as a member of the Boule (Administrative Council) or an archon.

Other points of comparison

In modern democracies most citizens are ill-informed and uninterested in public affairs, but Athenian citizens were personally involved. In the fourth century B.C. there were at any given time 1,200 citizens who spent a whole year working daily on the affairs of state, either as *bouleutai* or as archons. In the course of the year there would be anything up to forty ordinary meetings of the Ekklesia, where the citizens *en masse* exercised their sovereign authority and every one of them had the right to speak and even to propose a new law. Each of the six thousand heliasts could expect his name to be drawn several times a year to take part in a heliastic court. Every citizen had the right to act as public prosecutor. All in all, the picture of the Athenians presented by the sources is of a body of active, vigilant citizens.

Modern democracy differs from that of ancient Athens in many other respects, too, but it would take far too long to describe those differences with all their nuances and overtones and to define them precisely.

Generally speaking, Athenian democracy was in some ways more conservative than the modern variety (and less thoroughgoing, when compared with the achievements and aspirations of modern democracy) and in other ways more advanced (and truer to the idea implicit in the term *democracy*, namely the political ascendancy of the *demos*, the populace, as opposed to the citizens who owe their status to their lineage or wealth).

The Athenian form of democracy came into being and worked well at a time when economic, social, political and cultural conditions were very different from those surrounding the birth, evolution and present functioning of the modern variety. They are two distinct and non-alternative forms of democracy.

BIBLIOGRAPHY

General works

Bleicken, J., *Die athenische Demokratie*, 2nd edn., 1992.
Sakellariou, M.B., *Η αθηναϊκή δημοκρατία*, 1999, 2nd edn. 2000.
Stockton, D., *The Classical Athenian Democracy*, 1990.

Selected monographs or volumes of essays

Connor, W.R., M.H. Hansen, K.M. Raaflaub and R.S. Svann, *Aspects of Athenian Democracy*, 1990.
Eder, W. (ed.), *Die athenische Demokratie im 4. Jahrhundert v. Chr. Vollendung oder Verfall einer Verfassungsform? Akten eines Symposiums*, 1995.
Forrest, W.G., *The Emergence of Greek Democracy: The Character of Greek Politics, 800-400 B.C.*, 1966.
Hansen, M.H., *The Athenian Democracy in the Age of Demosthenes: Structure, Principles and Ideology*, 1991.
Ober, J., *The Athenian Revolution: Essays in Ancient Greek Democracy and Political Theory*, 1996.
Sinclair, R.K., *Democracy and Participation in Athens*, 1988.

CHAPTER **IV**

*Philosophy in Athens
(from Anaxagoras
to Damascius)*

Linos G. Benakis

ϹѠΚΡΑΤΗϹ

2. *Socrates. Wall-painting from Ephesus, 1st cent. B.C. Socrates wrote no books, but according to Alkibiades in Plato's 'Symposium' (215d-e) he was the master of natural oratory, superior even to Perikles.*

1. *Imaginary reconstruction of the Garden of the Philosophers at the foot of the Acropolis (1834). Engraving from C. Frommel, 'Dreissig Ansichten Griechenlands zu den Werken griechischen Autoren', Karlsruhe 1830.*

Philosophy in Athens
(from Anaxagoras to Damascius)

Greek philosophy was born in Ionia and South Italy before the time of Socrates of Athens and the Athenian sophists. Thus the earliest period of philosophy is that of the Presocratics (Thales, Anaximandros, Anaximenes, all from Miletos; Pythagoras of Samos; Herakleitos of Ephesos; Xenophanes of Kolophon; Parmenides and Zeno the Eleatics; Empedokles of Akragas; Leukippos and Demokritos of Abdera, and others). About the last of the Presocratics was Anaxagoras, from Klazomenai near Smyrna, who taught principally in Athens.

In the Greek world the city-state of Athens was not noted for any early political or cultural ascendancy. The city did not play any part either in the great colonial expansion to east and west in the eighth century B.C. or in the creation of the Panhellenic Idea; even in the sixth century Athens was still just one among the many city-states of the Greeks. The great change came at the start of the fifth century, when the Persian Wars and the brilliant political leadership and beneficent joint rule of Themistokles and Aristeides brought about a genuine miracle: the blossoming of Athens as the political and intellectual centre of Greece. A flood of men from the Greek colonial world poured into Athens, to find there fertile ground for intellectual activity among the Athenians, thirsty as these were for learning and wisdom. We can see from the famous *Funeral Oration* of Perikles, as given by Thucydides (II.35 ff., esp. 40 ff.) the high esteem in which learning was then held, the qualities deemed essential in a cultivated man of the time, how universal this requirement was for the citizen of a well-governed state, and how important all these things were for the rising city-state of Athens.

The great glory of Athens in Classical times was unquestionably the dazzling achievement of its citizens in art and letters (poetry, historiography and rhetoric), and also the cultivation and promotion of philosophy as the universal power of the human spirit. To the great artists of the chisel and the brush – the sculptors and vase-painters of Attica – due homage is paid elsewhere in this book. Of course, Socrates, Plato and Aristotle are the greatest pride of Athenian philosophy, but together with them other eminent philosophers who worked in Athens also have their illustrious place in the universal history of philosophy.

Philosophy was first brought to Athens by Anaxagoras, when in 456 B.C. (during the archonship of Kallias) he came from Ionia, at a mature age, and stayed for many years in the 'famous city'. Although he never endeared himself to the Athenians, he became associated with many important citizens, particularly Perikles. There are many stories about his life in Athens that witness to his prominent presence in the city's affairs. Perikles depended upon his advice to help him allay the superstitious fears of his fellow-citizens: the fear, for example, of eclipses of the sun and moon, the fall of meteorites, monstrous births of animals and so on. According to Theophrastos, Anaxagoras was well versed in mathematics and astronomy. Shortly before the outbreak of the Peloponnesian War he left Athens to avoid prosecution for 'the introduction of new gods'; in reality for being a friend of Perikles. He is said to have remarked about his threatened conviction: 'For me, as for my accusers, nature has long since reached its verdict.' One much later admirer, Michael Psellos, in the eleventh century A.D., records that 'some people jokingly called him "the Mind".' It seems that the Athenians, probably to tease him, had given him the nickname 'Mind' (*Nous*), aiming most happily at the heart of his teaching: 'He first believed in a creating Mind as the shaping cause, that which brought order out of chaos,' and elsewhere: 'He first dared to introduce Mind as the shaping cause of things.'

Together with the problem of the First Cause of Things, Anaxagoras first linked the concept of Purpose with the concept of the creating Mind. Nevertheless, in the spirit of the hylozoism or panpsychism of the Presocratics, Nous remained for Anaxagoras too an extremely subtle material substance, purer than any other. Only Nous was capable of organizing and shaping everything according to a purpose. Thus, for him, the Cosmos now appeared as the creation of Nous, as a harmonious totality, a perfected object. Indeed, that is the original meaning of the word 'cosmos', which Anaxagoras was the first to use to mean the Universe.

The most eminent of the sophists, Protagoras (481-420 B.C.), also came to Athens from a foreign homeland, Abdera in Thrace, the birthplace of Demokritos too. He lived in Athens, on and off, over many years, developing his ideas and gaining the friendship of Perikles and Euripides. He certainly influenced the great Athenian tragedian, as can be seen from the dialogues in Euripides's plays.

Only a few fragments of Protagoras's own extremely rich body of writings have survived, but Plato's dialogues *Protagoras* and *Theaitetos* give us a good insight into his personality and doctrines. In 420 he was accused of atheism by certain Athenian citizens and forced to flee from Athens for Sicily. He lost his life somewhere on that journey.

The purpose of his lessons, Protagoras maintained, was to teach virtue (*arete*) and manliness of spirit, with which the possessor may rise above others and lead them wherever he wishes. He was the first to charge high fees for teaching his pupils the art of persuasive oratory through rhetorical devices and seemingly valid arguments. He thus succeeded in making 'the worse appear the better case'. The heart of Protagoras's book on Truth, according to Plato's *Theaitetos*, was his famous dictum: 'Man is the measure of all things, both of beings that they are, and of non-beings that they are not.' This dictum represents the doctrine of 'subjective truth', the basis of that triumphant advocacy that persuades even one's opponent of the truth of what a short while before had seemed to him false. In the field of ethics the contemporary and later opponents of the sophists contested Protagoras's dangerous assertion that 'any given act may be either just or unjust, brave or cowardly, according to the circumstances in which a man performs it.'

Among the many pupils of Protagoras, Prodikos of Keos, Hippias of Elis and the Athenian Antiphon (late fifth century) all gained great fame. Antiphon, in his book *Truth*, develops more broadly than the other sophists the concept of natural justice as opposed to man-made law, and also the idea of human equality. In his work *On Concord* great importance is given to education, especially the upbringing of young men. With his 'consolatory art', as it was called, Antiphon undertook to liberate the Athenians from the cares of this life. Only a few fragments of his work survive.

After Protagoras the most important sophist is Gorgias (483-376 B.C.), from Leontini in Sicily, who came to Athens for the first time in 427 B.C. as ambassador for his home city. For what is known of his writing we are indebted, again, to Plato, whose dialogues *Gorgias* and *Menon* – like the corresponding dialogues in which Protagoras is the central figure – present those two leading sophists with the respect due to their originality, while at the same time Plato's dialectic genius delivers a powerful attack upon the negative side of their teaching.

Of the followers of Gorgias, the outstanding theoretician of extreme sophistry ('The measure of justice is physical power,' or 'Might is right') is the Athenian Kritias, Plato's uncle, who studied for a time with Socrates and subsequently became one of the Thirty Tyrants: indeed, he is described as 'the most arrant thief and the most violent of them all'.

The first native Athenian philosopher is Socrates (470/69-399 B.C.). He was the son of the sculptor Sophroniskos and the midwife Phainarete; interestingly, in Plato's *Theaitetos* Socrates likens his teaching method to his mother's profession, for he calls it 'maieutics' ('the midwife's art'). He was born in the deme of Alopeke (the present district of Ambelókipi) in the archonship of Demotion, and while still very young he began to work at his father's trade. It was then that Kriton first met him, was charmed by 'the beauty of his soul' and secured him the means of education. A different tradition has Archelaos in place of Kriton, impressed by the young artisan's rhetorical power in a discussion with his workmates on the question of their wages. More important is the tradition of Socrates's 'daimon' or 'divine guide', which early in his life possessed his soul and mind and put him under the protection of Apollo Agoraios and the Muses (see Plato, *Apology* 31d, *Republic* 496c). Socrates married Xanthippe, by whom he had three sons, Lamprokles, Sophroniskos and Menexenos. In Plato's *Phaidon* Xanthippe is described as sitting close to Socrates but giving his

3. Socrates. Inscribed herm. (Naples, Museo Nazionale)

companions a hostile reception. Aristotle mentions a second wife, Myrto, and there are many tales from ancient times about Socrates's private life, most of them poking fun at him. As for the lives of his sons, they are most often mentioned in order to make the point that great men's sons do not always live up to the stature of their parents, as in the cases of Perikles and Socrates.

All the descriptions of Socrates's personal appearance speak of an ugly man who looked much like a Silenos: bald, with a thick neck, a snub nose, a wide mouth with thick lips and a pot-belly. He certainly did not have what was considered the ideal figure for a man of his time, and his looks in no way mirrored 'the beauty of his soul'. His features are represented on two inscribed herms, one (in which Socrates is paired with Seneca) now in the Pergamon Museum, Berlin, and the other in Naples. There are many copies from Roman times, as for example a bust in the Vatican Museum (fourth century A.D.) and one in the Museo Nazionale, Rome.

Iconographic tradition All of these are modelled on one of two Greek originals, the first of which must have been taken from life; it shows Socrates, despite the Silenic shape of his head, engaged in thought, and it seems to breathe wisdom and inner strength. The second was evidently made after his death, and it represents an attempt to rehabilitate the condemned philosopher, giving him a more handsome face with noble features. Diogenes Laertius and others attribute this bust to the famous sculptor Lysippos. In the British Museum there is a statuette of Socrates standing in an attitude well known to the Athenians, as if about to greet someone in the Agora with whom he wished to speak. Lastly, in Naples, there is a bronze relief from Pompeii showing Aspasia (Perikles's second wife, whom he married in 449) with Socrates listening to her. In the background there is a little Cupid, signifying that they were talking about love.

Like every other able-bodied adult Athenian man, Socrates served his city in the army, and indeed he repeatedly showed exceptional courage. In Plato's *Symposium* Alkibiades relates how Socrates saved his life at the battle of Potidaia (432 B.C.) and then managed to get the young Alkibiades honoured for heroism rather than himself. At the battle of Delion (424), inspired by his daimon, he chose an unexpected escape route, thus saving Laches and Alkibiades for a second time. Finally, for his active participation in the battle of Amphipolis (422) our witness is Xenophon, who, however, is deliberately silent about his teacher's bravery.

Socrates's contribution to the planting and flowering of Classical philosophy in Athens can be noted here only in headings covering its principal elements. A perfected, finished version of Socratic teaching does not exist, still less a philosophic system set out in writing by Socrates himself. As appears from the work of his pupils, especially Plato, his contribution is embodied in the manner in which he probed the understanding of his fellow-citizens, mostly as an enquiry into the areas of 'the good' and 'virtue' (*arete*), i.e. right behaviour. His method is to use the *aporia* or perplexing question as his principal weapon, seen in action in the famous 'Socratic dialogues' which, through their enquiring and argumentative form, lead to knowledge (*episteme*), which is the search for the true content of every concept. That is why the philosopher is so called: simply the friend (*philos*) of wisdom (*sophia*).

4. Bust of Socrates. Roman copy. (Vatican Museum)

At the heart of Socrates's teaching lies the unity of doctrine, action and life. The Socratic ethic is founded upon the inseparability of the knowledge of moral principles and practical morality. Since right behaviour is teachable, whoever is acquainted with the good must act accordingly. The highest good is the knowledge of good. It is of particular importance for an understanding of Socrates's place in Greek philosophy to recognize his relationship with the city: the organized state and its institutions, its citizens, and its political authority. Equally important is his – and Plato's – clash with the sophists, and his rejection of their doctrines and way of life.

Socrates came into conflict with the state power twice before the great confrontation that resulted in his death sentence. The first was when, as Chairman of the *prytaneis* (see p. 94), he refused to vote for a sentence of death upon the admirals after the defeat at Arginousai (406 B.C.) on the grounds that the verdict was the result of mob hysteria and not of due judicial process. On the second occasion he gave up his seat as a *prytanis* when the Thirty Tyrants demanded the execution of one Leon of Salamis without any trial. Xenophon links the 'vote' for a law banning the teaching of rhetoric with the Thirty Tyrants' hatred of Socrates.

Our chief sources for the facts of the trial and conviction of Socrates are: Plato's *Apology* and his dialogues *Menon*, *Gorgias*, *Theaitetos* and *Phaidon*; *The Clouds* of Aristophanes; Xenophon; the speech-writer Polykrates, who drafted an indictment against the Socratics; and Lysias, who defended Socrates at his trial. The gist of the charge against Socrates must have been something like this: 'Socrates has offended against the law, in that on the one hand he does not recognize the gods that the city recognizes and on the other he has introduced new deities and taught these to young men, thus corrupting our youth. Punishment: death.' On paper, his accusers were Anytos and Meletos, and a guilty verdict was brought against him by 281 votes to 220. Three hundred of the 501 jurors then voted for the death sentence, which was carried out thirty days later with a lethal dose of hemlock, in 399 B.C. The scale of the trial and the severity of the sentence place the blame squarely on the whole city and its leaders, and reveal the sad state of affairs behind the scenes and the tragic political situation in Athens at that time. History, however, has always been strongly supportive of the philosopher's moral stature in the face of

5. Until a few decades ago the head on this herm, which actually represents Socrates, was mistakenly identified as a portrait of Xenophon. It was not until 1940 that an inscribed head was found in Alexandria, on the strength of which many other copies of the bust of Xenophon were identified. The original was most probably a bust set up in Xenophon's honour in 367 B.C., when he returned to Athens from exile.

his persecution and condemnation. His attitude stems from the principle that 'not even the just philosopher can defend himself against a corrupt and unjust state,' which also accounts for his refusal to accept the help offered by his devoted pupils to escape his death.

The best-known of Socrates's Athenian pupils are *Xenophon* (430-354), the son of Gryllos and Diodora, from Erchia (the modern Spata), a deme of the Aigis tribe in the Mesogeia plain of Attica; Antisthenes (450-365), the son of an Athenian man and a female Thracian slave; and Aischines (first half of the fourth century).

Xenophon, author of the *Cyropaedia*, the *Anabasis*, the *Symposium*, *Hieron* or *On Tyranny*, the *Oikonomikos* and other works, wrote his *Apology of Socrates* thirty years after his teacher's death, when he had been exiled to Skillous near Olympia for his pro-Spartan sympathies. A statue of Xenophon was erected there.

Antisthenes was originally a pupil of Gorgias, but soon became a passionate member of the circle of Socrates's pupils. He took a brilliant part in the discussions in the Kynosarges gymnasium, principally on matters of practical morality. Because of his insistence on upright conduct, his advocacy of effort as a means of strengthening moral fibre, and his restriction of the Socratic approach to ethics and not to nature or other fields of knowledge, he is considered to be the founder of the Cynic school.

More representative of the Cynics is Diogenes of Sinope in Paphlagonia (412-323), a pupil of Antisthenes. In Athens he was nicknamed 'the Dog' (*Kyon*), hence the name of *Kynikoi* given to the adherents of his school of philosophy. His eccentricity and ascetic life became a byword throughout the ancient world: the best-known anecdote is of his request to Alexander the Great: 'Just move a little way out of my sunlight!'

6. Two portraits of Antisthenes have come down to us: a herm from Tibur (Vatican Museum) and a terracotta from Pompeii (Naples, Museo Nazionale) which is attributed to Phyromachos, a well-known craftsman from Pergamon.

Although neither Xenophon nor Aischines holds an important place in Classical philosophy, the opposite is true of the very important contributions made by two other disciples of Socrates: one was Eukleides of Megara, the founder of the Megarian school, known from Plato's *Phaidon*, who was present at the death of Socrates and gave refuge to his fellow-pupils at Megara after 399; the other was Aristippos of Cyrene, representative of the Cyrenaic school in the Socratic tradition.

But it is with Plato (427-347), who founded the Academy in 387, and Aristotle (384-322), who founded the Lykeion or Lyceum in 335, that Athenian philosophy attained its highest glory.

Plato was born in Athens in 427 B.C., a year after Anaxagoras died and two years after

7. *The Socratic philosopher Aristippos of Cyrene. (Rome, Palazzo Spada)*

the death of the great statesman Perikles. He was the youngest of the four children of the aristocratic Ariston and Periktione. His mother was the sister of Charmides, a public figure, and her cousin was Kritias, the leader of the Thirty Tyrants. In these family surroundings the young man – first called Aristokles, and later Plato (on account of his very broad chest, according to Olympiodoros, *Life of Plato* 1.32) – received a very sound general education as well as training in the art of war, with a view to entering politics. However, he also became a pupil of the philosopher Kratylos, a follower of the Presocratic Herakleitos. Later on, Plato honoured all these men and others by naming his dialogues after them (*Charmides, Kritias, Kratylos, Alkibiades*, etc.).

In his youth Plato lived through memorable events in Athens: the rise and fall of Alkibiades, the disastrous Syracuse expedition, the destruction of the Athenian navy and demolition of the city walls, defeat in the war against Sparta, the imposition of the rule of the Thirty Tyrants and the restoration of democracy. These events, especially the arbitrary and corrupt rule of the Thirty, served to keep Plato well out of politics. In any case, Socratic philosophy had planted deep roots in him and persuaded him that what his country need-ed was a moral renaissance in its citizens and its political leadership.

The most exciting moment in Plato's life must have been his meeting with Socrates, when he was twenty and Socrates in his sixties. Of the sophists, later to become his most violent opponents, Plato had already heard Gorgias, but it was Kratylos who introduced him to Socrates. Plato himself, through the mouth of Alkibiades in the *Symposium* (215a), pro-vides us with the best account of the first impression that Socrates made on his young pupil; and in other dialogues Plato describes the acuity and moral grandeur of this man, Socrates, misunderstood and persecuted by his Athenian fellow-citizens. With his stimulating 'gad-fly' approach, and the dialectic that is developed in all of Plato's teaching, Socrates becomes the central figure in all the dialogues. Plato sat at his feet for eight creative years, from 407 until the execution of his master in 399.

For Plato the blow was terrible. At first he sought refuge in Megara, together with oth-ers of Socrates's pupils, and then for twelve whole years he journeyed for his studies in Cyrene, Egypt, South Italy and Sicily. He returned to Athens in 387, and in the same year he set up the Academy in the little grove beside the Kephisos where the hero Akademos was venerated (see the reconstruction by J. Travlos, showing the position of the school in relation to the Demosion Sema (public burial ground) and the interesting detail of a road directly linking the Academy with the Lykeion).

Plato spent the rest of his life directing and developing the Academy. In *Gorgias*, with its important content and unparalleled Platonic atmosphere, he gives us an authentic picture of the climate of the school, and indeed of its fruitful rivalry with the rhetorical school of Isokrates. Plutarch in his *Dion* describes the life of the Academy: daily philosophical semi-nars and lectures, with a monthly symposium for his closest circle of disciples; it is note-worthy that the ancients believed that Plato 'learnt Greek from his many interlocutors'. Plato's main purpose was to create a group of young Athenians having such a moral and political education that they would be able to uphold a state of justice and to pass on to others the ideal of the *kalokagathos*, the noble and good man, which leads to *eudaimonia*, the state of having an objectively desirable life – that condition that the truly noble person will acquire through the grace of his personal daimon, genius or divine guide.

Throughout the forty years during which Plato directed the Academy, he was absent for only two short periods in 367 and 361, when at the invitation of his friend Dion of Syracuse he travelled to Sicily, evidently never having quite given up his desire for political activity. Dion wanted a Platonic education for his young nephew and heir, Dionysios, and it was a sad blow and disappointment to Plato when Dion himself, after residing several years in Athens as a faithful member of the Academy, was murdered in 353 after his campaign to recapture the throne of Syracuse. Six years later Plato died, at the age of eighty.

Our desire to know what such an important philosopher actually looked like is very understandable. During the Renaissance he was portrayed with an idealized beauty, based nonetheless on information from ancient sources, as in Raphael's famous fresco in the Vatican, 'The School of Athens' (1509); this shows an imaginary gathering of all the most important Greek philosophers, with the figures of Plato and Aristotle in the centre. Of the ancient busts, one

Iconographic tradition

that seems to be an authentic portrait of Plato is a herm with the inscription ΠΛΑΤΩΝ, originally from the Castellani collection in Rome but since 1884 in the Altes Museum, Berlin. This is a Roman copy of a portrait bust that must have been carved by the famous sculptor Silanion in 340 B.C., after the philosopher's death. (Diogenes Laertius says it was dedicated by a Persian named Mithradates.) Other busts found earlier, perhaps of better quality, and said to have been portraits of Plato, puzzled the experts as they did not correspond to the idealized features as sketched, for example, by Goethe – though the great Wilamowitz was not disconcerted by this inconsistency. Another portrait before which we may still stand in awe today, besides the fine bust in Basel, is the fragmentary head of the philosopher in the Pergamon Museum, Berlin (inv. no. 107). This is a Roman copy from the first century A.D., made of Pentelic marble and taken from a Greek original of the fourth century B.C. (it has been in Berlin since 1932, having come from a private collection in Vienna). This portrait, despite the ravages of time, impresses with the clear line of the whole piece, its gentle balanced form and the concentration expressed in its features. The face is nobly framed by a long, thick beard, while the relatively small mouth, compressed lips and taut eyebrows emphasize the intellectual concentration and the decisiveness of the features.

There is an interesting postwar find from Greece. Underwater excavation at Kenchreai (modern Kekhriés), near Corinth, has uncovered a mosaic, probably in a place of worship, in which Plato is depicted facing Homer, in a clearly idealized form: noble, benevolent, with folded arms and crossed legs. It dates from the third century A.D., a period when under the influence of Neoplatonism the actual historical face of the living philosopher gives way to the ideal form of the Philosopher of All Time. Finally, life in Plato's Academy is pictured

8. Bust of Plato. Roman copy, 1st cent. (Berlin, Archaeological Museum)

in an impressive mosaic floor from the first century A.D., discovered at Pompeii and now in the Museo Nazionale, Naples.

Plato's extensive writings, in the unsurpassed literary form of the dialogue, were assembled and classified in nine tetralogies during the lifetime of Tiberius (42 B.C. – A.D. 37). Chronologically, the Platonic works fall into the following categories:

1. The early dialogues: the *Apology* (Plato's version of the defence put up by Socrates in his trial), *Krito* (Socrates as law-abiding citizen), *Ion* (the true poet and the genuine philosopher), *Euthyphro* (the essence of piety, and an account of the political climate in Athens), *Laches* (the essence of courage, knowledge and will-power), *Charmides* (moderation and self-control in the light of Socratic morality), *Lysis* (friendship), *Hippias Minor* and *Hippias Major* (sophist philosophy) and *Protagoras* (the Socratic theory of knowledge versus the false wisdom of the sophists).

2. The dialogues in which the Platonic philosophy is worked out: *Gorgias* (a polemic against barren traditional rhetoric, a course book from the time of the founding of the Academy), *Menexenos* (valuable testimony to the philosopher's love of his country), *Euthydemos* (an ironical attack on the sophists' sophistries), *Kratylos* (Plato's philosophy of language – are names arbitrarily assigned to things, or naturally connected? – his rejection of the sophists' theory) and *Menon* (the teaching of right behaviour, knowledge as reminiscence).

3. The great dialogues of Plato's maturity: the *Symposium* (true love as philosophical motive power; the first appearance of the Theory of Forms [*eide*]), *Phaidon* (the immortality of the soul; complete development of the Theory of Forms – Socrates's discussion with his disciples on the very day when he was about to drink the hemlock), *Theaitetos* (the essence of knowledge; the concept of *episteme* – a dialogue dedicated to the memory of a young Athenian pupil who fell in the battle of Corinth), *Parmenides* (the participation of specific sensations in Forms; 'not-being').

4. The very important dialogues of his old age: *Phaidros* (the Theory of Forms; the tripartite division of the soul), the *Sophist* (against the essence of sophist philosophy; what is 'not-being'?), the *Statesman* (*Politikos*) (definition of the true political man), *Philebos* (doctrine of the good), *Timaios* (Plato's cosmology; the origin of the cosmos), *Kritias* (the origin of the human race; the creation of Athens; the legend of Atlantis), *Laws* (the lawful polity).

The ten books of Plato's masterpiece, the *Republic*, belong to many periods of his working life and cover the vital subjects of justice and a proper system of government, but also include other major themes related to the theory of knowledge, psychology, ethics, metaphysics and so on. Finally the so-called *Seventh Letter*, the only one of his epistles that is unquestionably authentic, consists of autobiography of the highest quality, written after the assassination of Dion of Syracuse.

The huge achievement of Platonic philosophy can only be briefly summarized here: the Theory of Forms and approach to the problem of essence; the theory of *methexis* or 'participation' (contact or communication between the perceptible world and the world of Forms), upon which rests Platonic dualism; the tripartite division of the growth of knowledge, as an

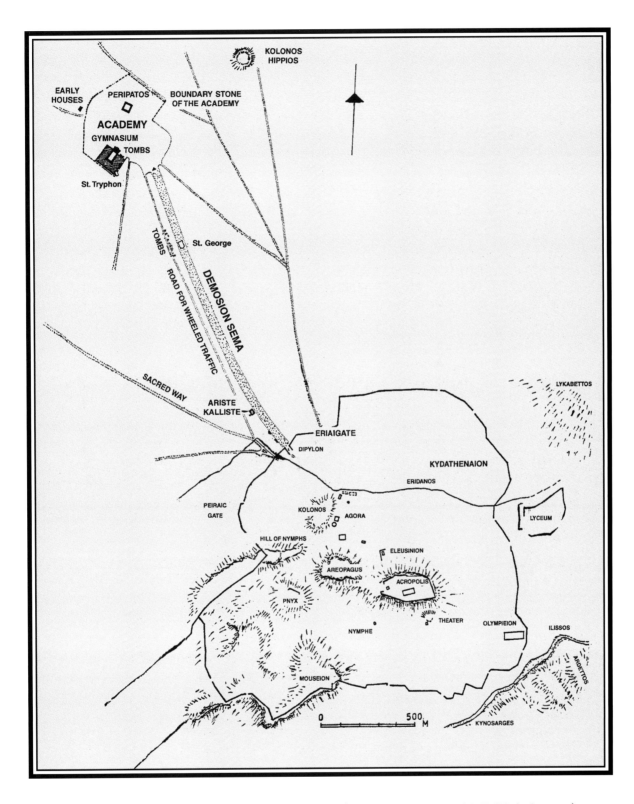

9. Plan of ancient Athens showing the position of Plato's Academy. (After J. Travlos, 1971, and R.E. Wycherley, 1978)

answer to the problem of the validity of knowledge; love and the paramount idea of the good; concepts; the sensible world; perception and knowledge; the three powers of the soul; reminiscence; the immortality of the soul; the foundations of ethics; his teaching on pleasure; his ideas on the cosmos and its divine creator, and on the soul of the world; the mathematical and geometrical model of the cosmos; matter, time, and always, of course, the part played by Forms; the operation of mathematics; and above all his political theory of personal and political virtue and the ideal Platonic republic.

Plato's philosophy has made a massive impact throughout the ages, and it would take many volumes to cover its history from Classical times to the present day. The first part would of course be about the ancient Academy after Plato's death at the age of eighty in 347, under the first of his successors, Speusippos, son of Eurymedon and Plato's sister and author of *On Pythagorean Numbers*, who directed the Academy until about 339. From then until 314 it was directed by Xenokrates, who wrote *On Indivisible Lines*. After him came Herakleides of Pontos, famous for his skill in the Platonic style of dialogue, later a pupil of Aristotle and a probable forerunner of Aristarchos in recognizing the heliocentric solar system. Herakleides was followed by Eudoxos of Knidos, an important teacher of ethics but chiefly known as a doctor and a founder of mathematical astronomy, and then by Polemon of Athens (314-270), among others. The Middle Academy, as it is called, had an important first head in the person of Karneades of Cyrene (213-129 B.C.), who had to confront the new Stoic philosophy in the work of the Stoa's founder, Chrysippos.

During the next period of the Academy's existence many important writers and public men studied there. Most notable among them are the very prolific Plutarch (A.D. 50-120), whose writings faithfully embody the Platonism of his time, and Herodes Atticus (A.D. 101-177), born at Marathon, who was a wealthy rhetorician and patron of the arts and letters in Athens. Two contemporaries at the Academy were Celsus, a declared pagan, and his Christian opponent Justin the Apologist. Finally, among the adherents of early Christian Platonism, which differs in many respects from the doctrines of the historical Plato, were two Athenian members of the Academy, Aristeides and Athenagoras.

In the person and work of Plotinus (A.D. 203-269) Platonic teaching found the last great original teacher of Hellenism. Plotinus, bringing together all the strands of the classical tradition, revived the interest of the early Christian world in the great Plato and led Greek philosophy to a new flowering, exerting great influence through the succeeding Christian centuries (Augustine, the Christian mystics, pseudo-Dionysios the Areopagite and others). This was the philosophy of Neoplatonism, which was developed by important pupils of Plotinus such as Porphyry, Iamblichus, Proklos, Marinos and the Alexandrian commentators on Aristotle, up to the closure of the Academy of Athens in A.D. 529, when the policies of the Emperor Justinian made it impossible for the Academy to survive. After the important Syrianus, Proklos (Constantinople 412 – Athens 485, pupil of Plutarch and Syrianus and head of the Academy for forty-eight years, with prolific writings to his name including commentaries on the dialogues of Plato as well as major systematic treatises), Simplicius, Priscian and Damascius (the last head of the Academy), the last representatives of the Academy were scattered throughout the East, whence the Arabs were later to become one of the sources for the West's acquaintance with Plato's work.

In Byzantium Plato was highly influential until the end of the Empire. In the persons of Georgios Gemistos Plethon and Bessarion, Plato found important students and admirers. In the Latin West, to begin with, interest was confined to Plato's *Timaios* and his cosmology. In fact all that was known of his work until the end of the fourteenth century were the dialogues *Phaidon, Menon* and *Parmenides*. When in 1429 the first manuscripts of the complete

Platonic dialogues arrived in Venice from Constantinople, Latin translations were made of them; these, together with the presence in Italy of Byzantine scholars, led to the Platonic Renaissance and the founding by the Medici of the Platonic Academy in Florence in 1459. Every year on 7th November the anniversary of the birth and death of Plato were celebrated with an official symposium, in which discussions were led by eminent members of the Florentine Academy such as Ficino, Landino and del Nero.

In modern times, it is very interesting to note the debt owed to Platonic teaching in general, and to certain Platonic ideas in particular, by such as Edmund Husserl (in his *Phänomenologie*) and his followers; also certain tendencies in the field of general concepts and mathematical logic that show Platonic influence, as well as anti-Platonic viewpoints such as that taken by Karl Popper in *The Open Society and its Enemies*. As for modern interpretative approaches to Plato's work, it is sufficient to note that the bibliography is vast and that teaching and research flourish in universities and academies worldwide. In the 1980s the International Plato Society was founded, based initially at Perugia in Italy, and has already published ten volumes in the series *International Plato Studies*. The Sixth Symposium Platonicum will be held in Jerusalem in 2001, with the *Laws* as its central theme.

10. In 1880 the base of a statue erected in honour of Karneades by King Attalos II of Pergamon was found in the Athens Agora. Roman copies giving a very expressive rendering of the face of the original statue are now to be seen in museums in Ravenna, Basel and Copenhagen.

The first critical edition of Plato's dialogues came from Henri Étienne (Henricus Stephanus) in Basel in 1578, and since then all references to Platonic texts have been made according to the pagination and columns (a-e) of that edition. The most dependable and handy edition, with innumerable reprints, is the Oxford Classical Text edited by John Burnet (5 vols., 1900 ff.), while the first volume of a new critical edition by a team of British scholars (E.A. Duke and others) appeared in 1995. Today the whole of Plato is accessible on-line in the *Thesaurus Linguae Graecae* (TLG) prepared by Irvine University,

RAPHAEL
SANTIVS
PINX

PIO SEXTO

IN AEDIBVS
VATICA
NIS

ONT. MAX.

California. All major series of classical writers published worldwide include the Platonic texts in reliable translation into the main foreign languages. Perhaps the best example is the special edition of the complete works of Plato planned for the year 2000 by the Wissenschaftliche Buchgesellschaft of Darmstadt: eight handsome volumes in 5,384 pages. The original text is that of the French Budé edition, accompanied by the classic German translation by F. Schleiermacher, with later revisions.

In Aristotle (384-322 B.C.) Greek philosophy attains its zenith. In the words of I.N. Theodorakopoulos, 'Aristotle defines the boundaries of the classical spirit.' This great philosopher was born at Stageira (a colony of Andros and Chalkis) in Chalkidike. He was the son of Nikomachos, physician to the Macedonian King Amyntas II, and of Phaistis. After the untimely death of his parents a relative, Promachos, became his guardian, and with him Aristotle spent his childhood, probably at Pella. In his most charming piece of personal writing, his will (as given by Diogenes Laertius, V.1.11-16), Aristotle orders statues to be set up of his mother, of Proxenos son of Nikanor (the intended bridegroom of his daughter Pythia) and of his brother Arimnestos, who had lived with him and died childless.

Aristotle moved to Athens in 366, when he was eighteen years old, and straight away enrolled in Plato's Academy as a student. The Academy had been in existence for twenty years, and Plato himself was sixty. When Plato returned from Sicily two years later he at once recognized the genius of his new pupil; tradition has it that Plato would often call Aristotle by the nickname 'Mind' (meaning the mind or brain of the school), just as the Athenians had once called Anaxagoras; and he would also call him 'The Reader', since he would sometimes stay away from class in order to study the Platonic dialogues better by himself.

On Plato's death in 347 B.C., Aristotle left the Academy and was warmly welcomed at Assos, on the mainland of Asia Minor opposite Lesbos. There Hermeias, the ruler of Assos and Atarneus, encouraged him to set up a sister school of Plato's Academy and to put Platonic political theory into practice, as Plato himself had wanted to do on his visits to Sicily. Aristotle's close friendship with Hermeias is shown by his marriage to Pythia, the ruler's niece, by whom he had a daughter, also called Pythia. After his first wife's death he married Herpyllis, in Athens, and had a son called Nikomachos. His daughter Pythia married the physician Metrodoros, and their son was named Aristotle after his grandfather.

The philosopher stayed three years at Assos and another three at Eressos on Lesbos, the home town of his best pupil, Theophrastos, who succeeded him at the Lykeion and was himself a considerable philosopher. In 342 Aristotle went back to Pella at the invitation of King Philip II, to undertake the education and upbringing of the King's fourteen-year-old son, Alexander, who was later to become known to all the world and all ages since as Alexander the Great. At this time Philip was planning war against the Persians, with the connivance of Hermeias of Assos, and many historians have wondered what exactly Philip's intention was in inviting Aristotle to his court. Was his purpose educational or political? What did he want

11. Raphael, 'The School of Athens'. (Rotogravure, 19th cent. Private collection)

12. Plato's Academy. Mosaic floor from Pompeii, 1st cent. A.D. (Naples, Museo Nazionale)

Aristotle to give Alexander, simply a Greek education and culture, or also a conviction that the Persians had to be punished for what they had done to the Greeks, not only in earlier times, but most recently with the murder of Hermeias after his capture and removal to Persia? Or perhaps something even more ambitious, to inspire him with the ideal of spreading Greek civilization through Asia – under the political leadership, naturally, of the Macedonians? Whatever the truth, it is a fact that the military and political genius of Alexander had the good fortune to be guided by the philosophical and scientific genius of Aristotle.

When Alexander succeeded his father as Regent on the throne of Macedonia, Aristotle withdrew for a while to Stageira, where he continued his scientific investigations with the help of Theophrastos, whom he had asked over from Lesbos. It seems that Aristotle had become

Aristotle, *Hymn to Virtue*, dedicated to Hermeias of Assos and Atarneus

Ἀρετὰ πολύμοχθε γένει βροτείῳ
θήραμα κάλλιστον βίῳ,
σᾶς πέρι, παρθένε, μορφᾶς
καὶ θανεῖν ζηλωτὸς ἐν Ἑλλάδι πότμος
καὶ πόνους τλῆναι μαλεροὺς ἀκάμαντας.
Τοῖον ἐπὶ φρένα βάλλεις
καρπὸν ἰσαθάνατον χρυσοῦ τε κρείσσω
καὶ γονέων μαλακαυγήτοιό θ᾽ ὕπνου.
Σεῦ δ᾽ ἔνεχ᾽ οἱ Διὸς Ἡρακλέης Λήδας τε κοῦροι
πόλλ᾽ ἀνέτλασαν, ἔργοις
σὰν ἀγρεύοντες δύναμιν.
σοῖς τε πόθοις Ἀχιλλεὺς Αἴας τ᾽ Ἀίδαο δόμους ἦλθον.
σᾶς δ᾽ ἕνεκεν φιλίου μορφᾶς
Ἀταρνέος ἔντροφος ἀελίου χήρωσεν αὐγάς.
τοιγὰρ ἀοίδιμον ἔργοις ἀθάνατόν τέ μιν
αὐξήσουσι Μοῦσαι Μναμοσύνας θύγατρες,
Διὸς ξενίου σέβας αὔξουσαι
φιλίας τε γέρας βεβαίου.

Virtue, Arete, you who inspire the race of men to labor,
you who are the noblest quarry in life, Maiden goddess,
it is for sake of your beauty that the fate of even death
is something to be envied in Greece, as is fierce, unstinting labor.
So great is the power you inspire in the heart,
power immortal, more precious than gold, or one's parents,
or sleep that steals softly over the eyes.
Is is for you that Herakles, the son of Zeus,
and the sons of Leda accomplished so much and endured
so many hardships in quest of your power.
In their passionate longing for you Achilles
and Ajax entered the halls of Hades.
It is for the sake of your beauty that [Hermeias], who grew up
in Atarneus lost the bright light of the sun.
Know that his deeds will be praised in song, and the Muses,
daughters of Mnemosyne, will exalt him as immortal,
as they exalt the reverence of Zeus, protector of hospitality,
and the reward for steadfast friendship.

Aristoteles, *Fragmenta* 1 (M. PIezia, Teubner 1977)..

(Translation by Diskin Clay)

estranged from the new Regent of Macedonia, having reservations over the Weltpolitik of his erstwhile pupil, and also over a sorry episode, the murder of Aristotle's kinsman Kallisthenes, accused of taking part in a plot against Alexander.

In 335 Aristotle went back to Athens, though without returning to the circle of the Academy, then headed by Xenokrates. The following year he founded his own school in the public gymnasium at the foot of Lykabettos (probably between the modern Riyíllis and Rizári Streets), where rhetoricians used to speak and sophists to teach. (See the plans of ancient Athens by J. Travlos, 1971, and R.E. Wycherley, 1978, showing the positions of the Academy and the Lykeion.) The school was called the Lykeion after the Temple of Apollo Lykeios that stood there, while later, when Theophrastos was directing it, it became known as the Peripatos

13. Aristotle. Marble herm. (Athens, National Archaeological Museum. Photo: K. Kontos, 2000)

('the Walk') from the covered colonnade that was the centre of the teaching and discussion for which the Lykeion became so famous. Indeed, because the students were in the habit of discussing matters while walking in this cloister they became known as Peripatetics ('strollers' or 'amblers'), and later the entire Aristotelian tendency in philosophy was called the Peripatetic school. It must have been Aristotle's Athenian students who provided the necessary land for the school, its large library and the buildings needed to accommodate its enormous collection of material covering all branches of knowledge, since Aristotle himself, not having Athenian citizenship, was not allowed to own property in the city. The Lykeion had something of the character of a modern research centre, more so than the Academy, as we know from Aristotle's extremely extensive writings in all fields of knowledge. Certainly what interested him most was to pass on to his students his own enquiring, systematic and synthetical spirit in research, as is testified by their own achievements in various sciences and areas of philosophy.

Aristotle worked in the Lykeion for about twelve years, perhaps the most creative in his rich life and brilliant academic career. The extent and value of the work accomplished at the Lykeion in this relatively short period of activity would today be beyond the bounds of possibility. It is from this time that his supreme works date: the *Metaphysics*, the *Nikomachean Ethics*, *On Animals*, the *Politics*. Altogether he spent over thirty years in Athens, nineteen in the Academy and the rest as founder and head of the Lykeion.

For an understanding of the evolution of Aristotle's philosophy his connexion with Plato is of the greatest importance. Unquestionably the basic principles of Aristotelian ontology comprise a reply to and further development of the Platonic Theory of Forms, and it is no surprise to find certain commentators trying to work out compromises between the respective doctrines of Plato and Aristotle in critical areas of the theory of knowledge and of ontology (e.g. general concepts, material species, etc.), nor to see the squabbles between Platonists and Aristotelians in Byzantium and the medieval West. Today, thanks to the work of major philosophical scholars and historians like Wilamowitz, Jaeger and Düring, we can understand the development over time of Aristotle's creative work much better, as well as the chronological order and interdependence of his books. The most important conclusion to have come out of these studies is that his work does not constitute a closed system, but shows the continuous endeavour of a genius constantly to recombine data in pursuit of a total philosophical interpretation

*14. Drawing of a lost bust of Aristotle.
(Vatican Library)*

of material phenomena and human behaviour. At a personal level one must stress the Stageirite's enormous respect for his great Athenian master, but also his critical attitude to him. A typical example of this is his elegy for Eudemos, who had set up an altar in honour of Plato in Athens ('... to honour the man ... who, first among mortals, showed clearly in his life and teaching that a human being can be happy in a virtuous life...'). Another tradition has Aristotle carving the epitaph on Plato's gravestone with his own hands. As to his critical attitude towards his teacher, the most authentic testimony is his own declaration in the *Nikomachean Ethics* that sums it up in the famous phrase 'A friend of Plato's, but even more a friend to truth'.

In 323 B.C. the death of Alexander the Great produced risings against Macedonian rule in all the Greek cities. Exposed to the violent attacks on him made by Demosthenes and his numerous supporters, Aristotle thought it better to remove himself to Chalkis, where he had inherited property. Biographers in later years relate that he spoke harshly of the Athenians as he left Athens: 'I do not forgive the Athenians for sinning twice against philosophy.' He describes the city of Athens, his second home, as very beautiful, but life there as very difficult ('Living in Athens is irksome'), chiefly because of the many slanderers who do so well there. The year after his removal to Chalkis, in 322, he died of a sudden illness at the age of sixty-three. The people of Stageira brought his body back to his birthplace and buried him there. He had appointed Theophrastos head of the Lykeion, and Antipater of Macedonia as the executor of his will.

The written works of Aristotle had already been classified in ancient times into two kinds. First there are the 'exoteric discourses', written for the general public, of which only fragments have survived: these are his early works, mostly in dialogue form, but different from Platonic dialogues, despite their strong Platonic spirit. We know their titles: *On Philosophy, Eudemos, or On the Soul, On Justice, On the Good, Invitation to Philosophy (Protreptikos)*, etc., and the fragments are available in critical editions by V. Rose (Berlin 1870) and W.D. Ross (Oxford 1955). Secondly we have the 'oral teachings', which comprise an astounding accumulation of human wisdom and philosophic and scientific enquiry in all fields of knowledge, the fruit of an ongoing refinement of the subjects by the philosopher and of his teaching to the students at the Lykeion (in fact Aristotle is recorded as answering Alexander, when the latter remarked that these works ought to be preserved 'in secrecy'. that they both were and were not 'published', as they could be understood only by those to whom he himself had taught them!). These books have come down to us in their entirety. The first critical edition was by Immanuel Bekker (Prussian Academy of Sciences, 1831) in two volumes of 1,462 large double-column pages, and since then reference to Aristotelian texts has been made according to the page, column and line numbering of Bekker's edition. Newer scholarly critical editions began to appear before the war from Oxford: a series in stereotype, i.e. with text only, e.g. the *Metaphysics* edited by W. Jaeger (1956), and a series of annotated editions i.e. with text only, e.g. the *Physics* edited by W.D. Ross (1936, 750 pp.).

The major categories of the Aristotelian opus are: the works on logic (six books, known as the *Organon*); the *Metaphysics* (originally entitled *The First Philosophy* or *Theology*, in fourteen books – the title *Metaphysics*, i.e. 'After the Physics', is a name given by Andronikos of Rhodes in the first century B.C., because in his cataloguing of the works it came immediately after the *Physike Akroasis* or *Physics*); the *Physics*, zoological and physiological writings (ten genuine works belonging to the main body of Aristotelian philosophy and science, as well as other non-authentic works that are nevertheless in the Aristotelian spirit); the ethical and political writings (the *Nikomachean Ethics*, the *Magna Moralia* or *Major Ethics*, the *Eudemian Ethics*, the *Politics*, *On Constitutions* (describing the constitutions of 158 cities, of which we have only the *Constitution of Athens*, from a papyrus discovered in 1890!), the *Art of Rhetoric*, the *Poetics* and the probably spurious *Economics*.

The fortunes of these works by Aristotle involved adventures that might well have cost the world the total loss of one of the most valuable achievements of our civilization. Aristotle's successor, Theophrastos, bequeathed the manuscripts to the last surviving member of the philosopher's 'inner circle' of students, Neleus of Skepsis in Asia Minor, who returned to his birthplace on the death of Theophrastos (*c.* 286 B.C.), taking with him his master's priceless manuscripts. Neleus's descendants, people with no culture or understanding of the manuscripts' value, simply packed them away in their house, where they remained 'hidden' until the beginning of the first century B.C., when the well-known Athenian bibliophile Apellikon 'discovered' them and brought them back to Athens. A little later, in 86 B.C., the Roman conqueror of Athens, Sulla, transferred the manuscripts to Rome, where one or two indifferent copies were made. Later, the original manuscripts came most fortunately into the hands of the highly cultivated Andronikos of Rhodes, to whom is owed the first authentic edition with its systematic cataloguing and establishment of the texts, which had been corrupted by interpolations from various periods of the teaching at the Lykeion.

It is to Andronikos's brilliant work that we owe the secure transmission and dissemination of Aristotle's books, leading to the later flowering of study and extensive interpretative commentary on them, chiefly by the important Alexandrian commentators of the fifth and sixth centuries A.D. (twenty-five large volumes in the incomplete edition of the Prussian Academy, 1890-1910: *Commentaria in Aristotelem Graeca*), and later by Arab, Byzantine, Post-Byzantine and Latin commentators.

To give an idea of the character and content of Aristotelian philosophy there is space here only for the titles, as even the most sketchy review of the subject would take far too many pages. It should indeed be emphasized – as in Plato's case – that the international bibliography on Aristotle, especially the contemporary and postwar items (editions, translations, interpretations of the work as a whole, thematic areas, problems, transmission and influence through the ages) is too vast to enumerate. The continuing scholarly occupation worldwide with the Aristotelian Corpus exceeds that for any other philosopher, ancient, medieval or modern. We note here a few important postwar facts: the establishment in Berlin in 1965 of the Aristoteles-Archiv for the principal purpose of collecting on microfilm all the manuscripts of Aristotle's works and of the commentaries on them, with a new survey of what is held in the hundreds of libraries in the civilized world (see the volumes entitled *Aristoteles Graecus* and the other editions in the series *Peripatoi*); the periodic meetings since 1958 of the

15. *Bust of Aristotle. Roman copy, late 4th cent. (Vienna, Kunsthistorisches Museum)*

Symposium Aristotelicum, an international symposium on specialized subjects attended by the most respected authorities on Aristotle; the organization in Thessaloníki in 1978, by the Greek government, of a World Conference on Aristotle, with exceptionally wide coverage (it was attended by 230 scholars and the *Proceedings* filled four volumes); and the decision of the Academy of Athens in 1994 to produce a new edition of Byzantine commentaries on Aristotle, under the auspices of the International Academic Union.

In order to understand Aristotelian philosophy it is most important to have a good grasp of the philosopher's generative method, his use of the *aporia*, and the enquiring, critical and pragmatic character of this philosophy. The main features of it are: the division (beyond Plato's tripartite division) into the theoretical and the practical; the establishment of logic as a dialectical skill (concepts, ten categories, judgments, categorical and inductive syllogisms, proof, etc.) and as a tool for an approach to scientific understanding; new definitions of the problem of essence, matter and form, of inherent faculties and their active exercise, the 'mover' and the 'ultimate cause', the essence of being and the first unmoved mover, the sources of knowledge (perception, experience, thought), the basic problems of physics and biology (elements, motion, space and time, the cosmos and its systems, animal and plant life), psychology (the substance and structure of the psyche, the relationship between soul and body, theoretical and practical intellect), ethics (the virtues of the theoretical and the practical life, the theory of the middle way, *eudaimonia* or happiness in having achieved an objectively desirable life), politics (the individual and the state, political power and types of constitution, the ideal polity), poetics (the concept of *mimesis* or imitation, the definition of tragedy) and many further basic subjects in philosophy.

16. Aristotle and Alexander of Aphrodisias. Bronze plaquette by Ulocrino. (London, Victoria and Albert Museum)

To trace and evaluate the influence of Aristotelian philosophy on later philosophy and science would be a major undertaking needing extensive treatment, for Aristotle was in fact the originator of many branches of science. Stoic philosophy is to a large extent a development of, or reaction against, Aristotelian theses, while Neoplatonism owes much to Aristotle's theory of knowledge in particular. The early Fathers of the Church used basic Aristotelian arguments in expounding Christian dogma on vital matters such as the orthodox doctrine of the Trinity. As for the Middle Ages in the Greek, Arab and Western worlds, the current view is that Aristotelianism was totally dominant (Byzantine scholars and commentators, Arab translators and commentators, Thomas Aquinas and the Thomists). From the Renaissance onwards serious critical reaction against Aristotle began to appear, especially in the field of natural philosophy (i.e. natural science), although he never ceased to be studied and admired, even by those who would be seen as his principal opponents, such as Galileo. At that time a serious scientific tendency developed in Padua for the study and correct understanding of the real Aristotle, no longer via the Arabs or the Scholastic translators and interpreters. This was the 'Neo-Aristotelianism' of Cremonini, which was passed on to the Greek world and prevailed there through the work of the Athenian philosopher Theophilos Korydaleus (1570-1646) and his pupils. Some of the basic elements of Aristotle's theory of knowledge, his ontology, his ethics and his political philosophy have had a positive influence on later philosophers up to the twen-

tieth century (a typical case being that of the German philosopher Nicolai Hartmann and his Critical Realism), while many eminent scholars take Aristotle as their starting-point for their studies and original publications in related areas too, like law and political science.

A particularly rich tradition in the representation of Aristotle's personal appearance has come down to us through the ages. There is an unfinished marble herm – a Roman copy of an original of the fourth century B.C. – in the National Archaeological Museum, Athens, which gives the most accurate portrayal of the philosopher's features, with a manifest expression of self-control and striking austerity. The Athens Epigraphic Museum has the base of a statue of Aristotle, dedicated by Alexander the Great to his teacher, bearing this laconic and highly characteristic inscription (which, incidentally brings together for the first time words that suggest the term 'omniscient'): 'Alexander erected [this statue of] the son of Nikomachos, the divine Aristotle, versed in all knowledge.' The original statue is lost, but there are many other portrait busts, among the best of which are: one in the Kunsthistorisches Museum, Vienna; one in the Museo Nazionale, Rome; others in museums in Copenhagen, Palermo and Paris (Louvre and Bibliothèque Mazarine); while one in the Naples museum shows the philosopher in his youth. A badly fragmented mosaic has survived from Baalbek in Lebanon (now in Beirut), showing the philosopher standing, with the inscription *APICTOTEΛHC*, probably part of a composition depicting the meeting of Aristotle with Alexander the Great.

Iconographic tradition

17. The inscription records that the statue of Aristotle which stood on this base was dedicated by Alexander. It used to be understood as referring to Alexander the Great (see, e.g., Richter II 171), but modern archaeologists (e.g. Voutyras) identify the dedicator as Alexander of Damascus. (Athens, Epigraphic Museum)

Among later representations, from medieval and more recent times, the best-known are the reliefs in the Portail Royal of Chartres cathedral (12th cent.) and in the campanile of the Duomo in Florence (by Luca della Robbia, 1399-1482), the famous fresco by Raphael in the Vatican (1509), the portrait by Pedro Berruguete and Joos van Gent (Paris, Louvre, *c.* 1500), Rembrandt's painting 'Aristotle in Thought Before the Bust of Homer' (Metropolitan Museum, New York), and various Post-Byzantine wall-paintings in Orthodox churches in Greece, the Balkans and Russia on the subject of ancient Greek sages as harbingers of the coming of Christ.

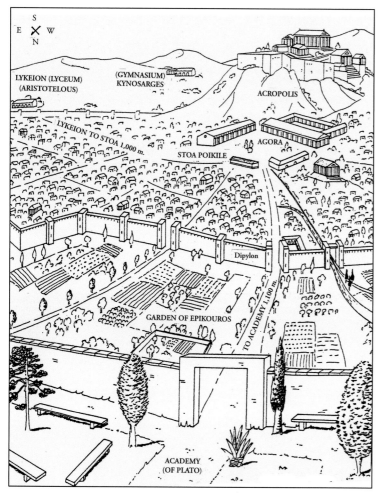

18. *For the position of the Stoa in relation to the Garden of Epicurus, the Academy and the Lykeion, see the reconstruction by C. H. Smith (1987). The Lykeion and the Academy were both about 1 kilometre away from the Stoa. In the 1980s the American School of Classical Studies discovered part of the Painted Stoa (Stoa Poikile) in an empty plot in Adhrianoú Street, more or less level with the Stoa of Attalos. (From M. Canto-Sperber, L. Brisson et al.,* La philosophie grecque, *Paris [PUF] 1997)*

Very characteristic of this last group are the full-length painting of a Byzantine-style Aristotle in the Great Lavra Monastery on Mount Athos (1530) and one in the Church of St. George at Negádhes, Ípiros (1792). Some outstanding modern representations are the busts in the Academy of Athens (by the Viennese sculptor O. Hoffner, 1879-1946) and in the Aristotelian University of Thessaloníki; the wall-paintings in the Great Halls of Athens University and the Athens City Hall; the statues in the main entrance of Freiburg University in Germany (seated, full-length) and at Stáyira (Stageira) in Greece (larger than life-size at 3.50 metres high, by the sculptor Nikolas). Lastly, very many effigies of the philosopher have appeared on Greek and foreign medallions, coins, stamps and other commemorative artefacts.

The Peripatos, the school founded by Aristotle in the Lykeion at Athens, saw a continuous succession of directors, starting with Theophrastos (372-286 B.C.), who ran the school for thirty-six years during its finest period, when it is said to have had over a thousand students. Theophrastos's long headship was exceeded only by Aristotle's third successor, Lykon of the Troad, who was head for fifty years from 275 to 225. One characteristic of this period is that all the notable pupils of Aristotle and heads of the Lykeion were foreigners working as philosophers and teachers in Athens, with the exceptions of the Athenian Demetrios of Phaleron (350-283, the well-known pro-Macedonian politician who served as head of the school and also governed Athens from 317 to 307, only to seek refuge later in Alexandria, making there a substantial contribution to the enlargement of that city's famous library) and the great comic playwright Menander.

Since the Peripatos never insisted upon a single philosophical system with binding principles, the more important of its leaders were able to develop their personal viewpoints in their own chosen fields. Those who adhered most faithfully to Aristotle's teaching were: first, Theophrastos, whose original achievements were chiefly in natural science, especially botany, of which he is considered to be the founder, basing the science upon the conceptual system of his teacher (the best-known of his many other written works, in the field of ethics, is the *Characters*); and second, Eudemos of Rhodes, who was mainly interested in trying to develop a unified approach to the problems of cosmology.

19. Zeno. Engraving from M. Meibonius, Diogenes Laertius, Amsterdam 1698.

Among the other Peripatetics one might pick out Straton of Lampsakos (head of the school 286-270), with his strong interest in natural philosophy, and Aristoxenos of Tarentum, who made important contributions in the theory of music and in his original teaching on harmony, in opposition to that of Pythagoras. Almost the last of the Peripatetics, although by his time the school had ceased to exist on an organized basis, was Andronikos of Rhodes (mid 1st cent. B.C.), who, as already mentioned, was responsible for the classification and editing of the Aristotelian texts in their definitive form. After him there came a succession of 'exegetes' with a sound knowledge of Aristotelian philosophy, chief among them being Alexander of Aphrodisias in Karia (A.D. 300), who taught principally in Athens. But most of the important commentators on Aristotle taught and wrote in Alexandria (Ammonios Hermeiou, Olympiodoros, Simplicius – who taught also in Athens – Ioannes Philoponos, David, Elias of Alexandria and others).

In 301 B.C. the Cypriot philosopher Zeno of Kition (334-261) set up his school – which was destined to acquire a high reputation and a wide following, mainly in the fields of ethics and politics – in the Painted Stoa (so named for its lavish decoration by Polygnotos) in the Athens Agora. His choice of location, so the ancients believed, was politically motivated, because he wished to purify the place where the Thirty Tyrants had executed hundreds of Athenians.

It has been correctly observed that the Stoa and Stoic philosophy sprang from the cultural and political situation in the Graeco-Roman world as it took shape from the end of the fourth century B.C., with the collapse of the ancient city-state, the increasing recognition of the supremacy of the individual beyond the arena of public affairs (the 'autarky' of virtue) and the weakening of the old religion. The Stoic philosophers saw themselves as absolutely incorporated in the Greek philosophical tradition, believing that they were giving it a radically new direction with the new world-view they taught.

Certainly, by comparison with the other new trends of the time (the philosophies of the Epicureans and the Sceptics), Stoicism is the most important and longest-lived system in Greek philosophy after Aristotle.

Despite the fact that the Stoic school had a syllabus laid down, with definite basic tenets, the philosophers who directed it over the five centuries of its active life maintained their independence and originality. Zeno's successor from 262 B.C. was Kleanthes (304-232), who arrived in Athens from the Troad as a poor workman and grew into a brilliant figure in the city's cultural life. But it is to the 700 scrolls of Chrysippos (281-208), from Soloi in Cilicia, who served for over twenty years as the third head of the school, that we owe the fullest account of Stoic dogma in all its theoretical and practical applications (logic, physics, ethics, politics). As the Athenians said later, 'Without Chrysippos there would not have been a Stoic school.'

The phase known as the Middle Stoa brings us to Panaitios of Rhodes (180-110) and the Syrian Poseidonios (130-50 B.C.), a distinguished, original and deeply learned philosopher, whom Cicero heard lecture in Rhodes. During the period of the Middle Stoa its philosophical theories became known to Roman scholars. It is strange and much to be regretted that of all the works of the Old and Middle Stoas only fragments have survived, to be found now chiefly in the writings of Cicero, Plutarch, Sextus Empiricus, Diogenes Laertius and others. The only piece to have come down to us in its entirety is Kleanthes's *Hymn to Zeus*.

Equally important figures are representative of the New Stoa of the early Christian centuries, men such as Seneca (A.D. 4-65), Epiktetos (A.D. 60-140) and the 'philosopher king', the Emperor Marcus Aurelius (121-180). His book, written in Greek and known to us as the *Meditations*, is the last achievement of Stoicism.

20. *Theophrastos. Roman copy, 2nd cent. A.D. (Rome, Villa Albani)*

Portraits of the principal Stoics, and of Epicurus, have survived, mostly in the form of bronze busts such as those of Zeno in the Museo Nazionale, Naples (2nd cent. A.D.), and at Herculaneum. They both depict the founder of the Stoic school with foreign-looking, ascetic features, 'ugly and unkempt, but with an austere air', as Diogenes Laertius describes him. The Athenians used to call him 'the Little Phoenician' in fun, as Kition had many immigrants from Phoenicia. Nevertheless, they honoured Zeno

21. *Epicurus. Marble copy, 270 B.C. (Berlin, Pergamon Museum)*

22. *Poseidonios. 1st cent. B.C. (Naples, Museo Nazionale)*

23. *Chrysippos. Copy, 2nd cent. A.D. (Paris, Louvre)*

24. *Kleanthes. Bronze statuette, 2nd cent. A.D. (London, British Museum)*

with a bronze bust in his lifetime, besides making him a freeman of the city and giving him a golden wreath and, eventually, a state funeral.

Mention is made of statues in honour of Kleanthes, but the identification of finds from his time is difficult. However, as he is said to have had a stocky body like a wrestler and therefore to have been known as 'a second Herakles among philosophers', a bust found at Ostia in 1965, first thought to be of Hippokrates, is now identified as Kleanthes. A bronze statuette of the second century A.D. in the British Museum, depicting Kleanthes seated, gives

25. Metrodoros. (Athens, National Archaeological Museum. Photo: K. Kontos, 2000)

him noble features. There was a statue by Euboulides in the Agora of Athens, said to be of Chrysippos, and the statue from the Villa Borghese depicting

Iconographic tradition

Chrysippos seated, now in the Louvre, would appear to be a Roman copy of this. His head appears on coins from Soloi – on both sides, the reverse as well as the obverse.

Three bronze busts of Epicurus have been found at Pompeii and Herculaneum, and a fourth, from the second century A.D., with the inscription *ΕΠΙΚΟΥΡΟC* on its base, is now in the Museo Nazionale, Naples. (In the same museum, and in exactly the same style, is a bronze bust of Hermarchos, Epicurus's successor as head of the school known as 'the Garden' in Athens from 271 to 240 B.C.) Diogenes Laertius mentions a bronze statue of Epicurus on Samos, and we may be sure there were also busts of him in Athens. The surviving marble busts now in Berlin (Pergamon Museum) and New York certainly reproduce Athenian busts and display a great advance in the art of representing the human face; the philosopher has been given a self-satisfied yet pleasingly modest look. Lastly, there is in a Rome Museum an inscribed herm with heads of Epicurus and his devoted pupil Metrodoros; a similar herm, but without inscriptions, is in the Louvre. The National Archaeological Museum in Athens also has a bust of Metrodoros, while the seated statue of a philosopher in Copenhagen may be of Hermarchos, since its head has been added from another find.

Epicurus (342-270 B.C.) was born on Samos of Athenian parents. His father Neokles, a teacher, arranged for his education and sent him at eighteen to do his military service in Athens, but more especially to listen to Plato's successors at the Academy. The political events of the time the death of Alexander, the conflict between the Athenians and Macedonians and so on, forced Epicurus to spend the next fifteen years at Kolophon, at

Lampsakos and finally on Lesbos with Pamphilos, a Platonist, and Nausiphanes, a disciple of Demokritos. In 310 he opened his own school on Lesbos, but in 306 he moved it to Athens, where it flourished and became known as 'the Garden', from the little plot he bought as a meeting-place for his pupils, outside the Dipylon Gate, between the city walls and the Academy (see the reconstruction by C. H. Smith, 1987). Here he lived and taught for thirty-six years before dying unmarried at the age of seventy-two.

Epicurus's school had the character of an enclosed religious community with total devotion to the teaching of its master. His philosophy originated in the atomic theory of Demokritos and its corresponding development into problems of knowledge, perception and the soul (*On Nature, Epitome of the Discourse to the Physicists*, etc.), but his greatest interest was in ethics (*On the End, On Love, Symposium*, etc.). He was opposed to Plato's teaching on virtue and held that man's first good is pleasure, against which there is only one evil, pain. This antithesis came from earlier times, when Plato had judged and rejected similar teaching by Eudoxos. However, Epicurus's position is far from that of unfettered hedonism, since he accepts and urges the dominance of man's moral sense, which guides him to a state of maximum happiness, *ataraxia*, in which he is not moved by passion and which strengthens his sound judgment.

Epicurus's teaching had a great influence on succeeding generations, as indeed did reaction against it, chiefly from Christian writers. On many subjects he agreed with the Stoics, but on others he took an opposing position.

The best-known of Epicurus's disciples, and his constant companion in Athens, was Metrodoros of Lampsakos (330-277), who even named his son after his teacher. Epicurus's successors at the Garden in Athens were Hermarchos (271-240), Polystratos (240-210), Dionysios (210-180), Basilides (180-150), who did work in mathematics, and Apollodoros of Athens (150-120), nicknamed 'the Tyrant of the Garden'. The last of these

26. Hermarchos. Roman copy, 2nd cent. A.D. (Naples, Museo Nazionale)

was the author, among many other works, of *The Dogmas Assembled*, the first history of philosophy — written, of course, from an Epicurean standpoint. Epicureanism had considerable influence in Rome, its chief representative being the great Lucretius (98-53 B.C.) in the philosophical poem *De rerum natura*.

It was Timon of Phlious, a contemporary of Kleanthes the Stoic and of Archesilaos, the head of the Academy, who brought to Athens the Sceptic teaching of Pyrrhon of Elis (360-270 B.C.). Together with Philon the Athenian and other pupils of Pyrrhon, Timon filled out and spread the original teaching, which was called Skepsis, Scepticism or Pyrrhonism. In the work of Ainesidemos of Alexandria (late 1st cent. B.C.) and especially of Sextus Empiricus (2nd half of the 2nd cent. A.D.) this late Hellenistic trend found its definitive form: a theoretical and practical withdrawal from the interpretation of phenomena, due to the virtue of indifference. Sextus, who lived and worked in Athens from time to time, is the only Sceptic of whose extensive work anything has been preserved: two books entitled *Outlines of*

27. Medallion of Aristotle designed by Vassos Falireas for the World Conference on Aristotle, Thessaloníki 1978.

Pyrrhonism and *Against the Mathematicians* (the 'mathematicians' being lovers of learning and knowledge). The main object of his teaching was to challenge the dominance of the syllogism and Stoic dogma, in favour of attainable mental power, the practical ability to grasp concepts. With Sextus Scepticism comes to an end as a presence in Greek intellectual life. In modern times its arguments have been revived and used by empirical philosophers such as John Stuart Mill (1806-1873).

The school of the Cynics, as they were called, also exerted considerable influence in the Hellenistic period. Its teaching did not confine itself to the ideal of pleasure but to a subjective *ad hoc* alignment with the circumstances of life. A pupil of the famous Diogenes of Sinope was the Theban Krates, who lived and taught in Athens (he was a member of the Academy for a short time in 269-268 B.C.), where he used to recite his short satirical poems or *paignia*. Perhaps his greatest claim to fame is that he was the first teacher of Zeno, the founder of the Stoa.

SELECT BIBLIOGRAPHY

Ιστορία του Ελληνικού Έθνους II, III, V, VI, Athens (Ekdotike Athenon) 1971-1976 (chapters by I.N. Theodorakopoulos, L.G. Benakis, E.N. Roussos).

Lanza, D., *Anassagora. Testimonianze e frammenti, traduzione e commente*, Florence 1966.

Zeppi, S., *Protagora e la filosofia del suo tempo*, Florence 1961.

Guthrie, W.K.C., *Οι Σοφιστές* (= *The Sophists*, Cambridge 1971), tr. D. Tsekourakis, Athens ²1991.

Gigon, O., *Sokrates. Sein Bild in Dichtung und Geschichte*, Basel 1947.

Fritz, K. von, 'Die Sophisten und Sokrates' in *Grundprobleme der Geschichte der antiken Wissenschaft*, Berlin 1971, 221-250.

Tatakis, B.N., *Ο Σωκράτης. Η ζωή του, η διδασκαλία του*, Athens 1970.

Guthrie, W.K.C., *Σωκράτης* (= *Socrates*), tr. Tassos Nikolaidis, Athens ²1991.

Friedländer, P., *Platon*, 3 vols., Berlin ³1960-1964.

Natorp, P., *Platons Ideenlehre*, Leipzig ²1921.

Theodorakopoulos, I.N., *Εισαγωγή στον Πλάτωνα*, Athens ⁵1970, 378 pp.

Despotopoulos, K.I., *Πολιτική Φιλοσοφία του Πλάτωνος*, Athens 1957, ²1980.

—, *Φιλοσοφία της Ιστορίας κατά Πλάτωνα*, Athens 1982.

—, *Φιλοσοφία του Πλάτωνος*, Athens 1997, 298 pp.

Taylor, A.E., *Πλάτων. Ο άνθρωπος και το έργο του* (tr. I. Arzoglou), Athens ²1992.

Kobusch, T., and B. Mojsisch, *Platon. Seine Dialoge in der Sicht neuer Forschungen*, Darmstadt 1996, 307 pp.

Wilamowitz-Moellendorf, U. von, *Aristoteles und Athen*, Berlin 1893, repr. Hildesheim 1985.

Georgoulis, K.D., *Αριστοτέλης ο Σταγιρίτης*, Thessaloníki 1962.

Ross, W.D., *Αριστοτέλης* (= *Aristotle*, ²1930), tr. M. Mitsou, Athens 1991, 478 pp.

Düring, I., *Aristoteles. Darstellung und Interpretation seines Denkens*, Heidelberg 1966.

Moraux, P. (ed.), *Aristoteles in der neueren Forschung*, Darmstadt 1968.

Adler, M.J., *Aristotle for Everybody: Difficult Thought Made Easy*, London 1978.

Cauquelin, A., *Aristote*, Paris 1994 (Greek tr. by S. Vlontakis, Athens 1996, esp. 51-115, 214-243).

Benakis, L.G., «Η νεώτερη έρευνα για τον Ανδρόνικο τον Ρόδιο και την διάσωση-έκδοση των έργων του Αριστοτέλους» in *Πρακτικά Διεθνούς Συμποσίου της Ακαδημίας Αθηνών «Πόλις της Ρόδου – 24 αιώνες»*, Athens 1995, 113-124.

Kullmann, W., *Η πολιτική σκέψη του Αριστοτέλη* (tr. A. Rengakou), Athens 1997.

Wehrli, F., *Die Schule des Aristoteles*, Basel ²1967-1969.

Krämer, H.J., *Platonismus und hellenistische Philosophie*, Berlin 1971, 396 pp.

Rist, J.M., *Stoic Philosophy*, Cambridge 1969.

Long, A.A., *Hellenistic Philosophy: Stoics, Epicureans, Sceptics*, London 1974.

Tatakis, B.N., *Panétius de Rhodes, le fondateur du moyen Stoïcisme*, Paris 1931.

Shofield, M., *Η στωϊκή ιδέα της πόλης* (tr. Chloe Balla), Athens 1997.

Bayionas, A., *Η πολιτική φιλοσοφία των Κυνικών*, Athens 1970.

Skouteropoulos, N.M., *Οι αρχαίοι Κυνικοί (Αποσπάσματα και μαρτυρίες)*, translation and commentary, Athens (Gnosi) 1998.

Siorvanes, L., *Proclus. Neo-Platonic Philosophy and Sciences*, Edinburgh 1996, 340 pp.

Athanassiadi, P., *Damascius: The Philosophical History*, Athens 1999, 403 pp.

143

Veue d'une porte et d'un
par l'Empereur Hadrien a

CHAPTER V

Planning and Architecture in Hellenistic Athens

Charalambos Bouras

2. The ruins of the Stoa of Eumenes on the south slope of the Acropolis. (Photo: S. Mavromatis, 2000)

1. The Temple of Olympian Zeus in 1672. (Drawing by J. Carrey from H. Omont, 'Athènes au XVIIe siècle', Paris 1898)

Planning and Architecture
in Hellenistic Athens

If one compares the political and cultural life of Athens at the time of the Diadochoi with that of the fifth century B.C. or even with that of large contemporary cities with a Greek population, one might be tempted to talk of a decline. However, it is not as simple as that. It is true that by the time of Alexander's death Athens had lost her hegemony and power had passed to the new cities of the East, but in Athens the institutions of public life were still functioning as before, diplomacy and foreign relations were still flourishing and constant efforts were being made to preserve the city's independence as far as possible. Most important of all, Athens' cultural and intellectual prestige remained undimmed.

The fact is that in the Hellenistic period Athens was a centre of education, chiefly in philosophy and rhetoric, and offered scholars and artists a comfortable life with little or no restriction on their work and movement. Among other things, it was a centre for the export of works of art and craft products of all kinds. The Panathenaia festival continued to be celebrated with great pomp and ceremony. Written sources and innumerable inscriptions make it possible for us to follow the city's history in some detail throughout the Hellenistic period.

Underpinning all these activities was a fairly sound economy. Athens was on excellent terms with the powerful grain-trading cities and so it developed into a major commercial centre in which a leading part was played by a middle class of entrepreneurs, merchants and artisans who maintained close relations with Delos and its cosmopolitan environment. Between 165 and 100 B.C., in particular, Athens would appear to have enjoyed economic prosperity. This was helped by the fact that large building projects were financed not out of public funds but by wealthy benefactors who wished to perpetuate their name and were attracted to Athens by its prestige.

The terminal dates of the period are rather vague. Conventionally it is deemed to start in 323 B.C., with the death of Alexander the Great, and to end in 86 B.C., when the city was sacked and very badly damaged by the Romans under Sulla during the First Mithradatic War.

Most of what we know about the planning and architecture of the Hellenistic period comes from the systematic excavations carried out by the American School of Classical Studies, and for the analysis of the archaeological evidence we are indebted chiefly to John Travlos. Other archaeologists whose writings have contributed to our understanding of the Athenian built environment and the history of the Hellenistic city include Homer Thompson, R.E. Wycherley, C. Habicht and J.M. Camp. More and more is constantly being added to our knowledge by continuing excavations, sometimes systematic (such as those of the American School in the Agora, which are reported in *Hesperia*) and sometimes rescue excavations (which take place wherever necessary in the ancient city and are reported in the *Archaiologikon Deltion*). Imperfect interpretation and problems with dating and correlating the finds make it difficult for the new evidence to be used in new books and articles in such a way as to fit Athenian architectural developments into their proper place in the history of Hellenistic architecture and city planning.

City planning

Athens never had a proper city plan in antiquity. The street plan came into being haphazard in the Archaic and Classical periods and remained basically unchanged until the end of the ancient era. Its growth was dynamic, as with all the pre-Hippodamian Greek cities, and little is known for certain about its general form. Some radial roads led out from the Acropolis and the circuit road surrounding it, passing through the ten(?) gates in the Themistoklean city walls. The most important of these was the Panathenaic Way, which ran from the Dipylon Gate through the large open Agora to the Acropolis. Although we do not know its general street plan, there are several small excavation sites that tell us a good deal about the character of the town. The streets were narrow and winding and the houses were built round internal courtyards, which meant that they were turned in on themselves. Most of them were small and packed tightly together, but references to large houses in Hellenistic Athens prove that some parts of the walled city were less densely built. Excavation suggests that there was very little interest in renewing the urban environment, as it was common practice for old houses dating from the Classical period to be repaired and kept in use for as long as possible. A well-known passage from pseudo-Dikaiarchos (2nd cent. B.C.) presents a striking picture of the huge difference between public sanctuaries and private houses, which were humble and dilapidated and had little water. Archaeological evidence also shows that the surrounding countryside suffered from extensive destruction and desecration, mainly to cemeteries and sacred groves, following the invasions of Attica by Antigonos and Philip V.

Signs of the new ideas that swept through the Greek world in the Hellenistic period are to be found in Athens in the public places, especially the Agora. Here in the cradle of democracy, where Kimon and Perikles put their grand projects into effect by means of broad, progressive planning, we now find modernization: that is to say, both the overall layout of the buildings and the architecture follow contemporary ideas concerning the built environment, based on a regular rectangular grid.

Reorganization
of public places

The systematic excavations and publications of the American School of Classical Studies enable us to study these developments chronologically. Around 180 B.C. the Agora was bisected by the so-called Middle Stoa, at nearly 150 m. the longest building

3. The Athens Agora in the late Hellenistic period. (J. Travlos, «Πολεοδομική εξέλιξις...»)

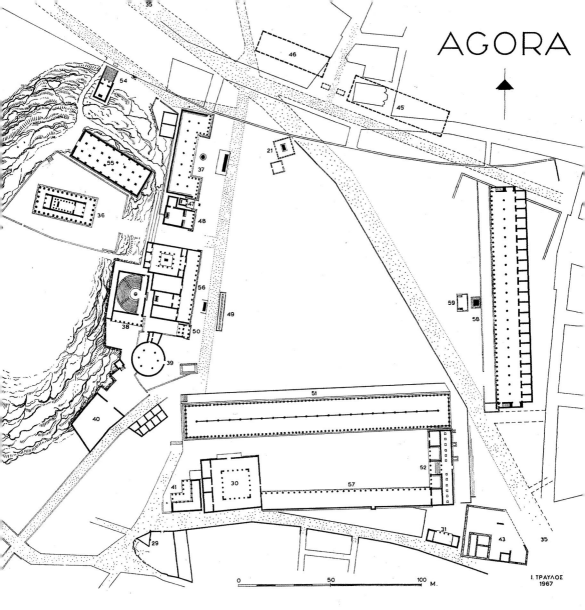

AGORA

Ι. ΤΡΑΥΛΟΣ
1967

there, cutting off the part known as the South Square. This stoa was a Doric building made of grey Aigina limestone, with no walls, which was used as a huge market shed. The Middle Stoa, aligned on an east-west axis, formed the southern limit of the main square of the Agora. The intention of creating a regular rectangular layout is attested by the demolition of the old South Stoa I and its replacement by the South Stoa II, running parallel to the Middle Stoa, and the construction twenty years later of the Stoa of Attalos, exactly perpendicular to the other two stoas. The South Stoa II, also Doric, was 93 m. long and bounded on the west by the large square Heliaia building. The erection of the Stoa of Attalos and the Metroön stoa opposite it, which completed the Hellenistic building programme, left the main square of the Agora as an almost regular rectangle with colonnaded buildings on all four sides and optical escapes between them, in keeping with the general demand for regularity of form.

With regard to two other building complexes whose layout is thought to have been redesigned in the Hellenistic period, we do not have such a clear picture as the American School's excavations have given us of the Agora. The first is the stretch of the Panathenaic Way from the Dipylon Gate to the Agora, which was commonly known simply as the Dromos ('the Road') and – according to two later writers, Himerios and Pausanias – was a broad avenue flanked by colonnaded 'shopping malls' in conformity with Hellenistic practice. Here stood the Euboulides ex-voto adorned with marble statues, and there were many other statues in front of the stoas. The stoas seen by those two writers would have been built after the sack of Athens by Sulla in 86 B.C., but the columns probably came from Hellenistic colonnaded buildings that had stood on the same spot.

The second building complex also consisted of a road lined with colonnades, this time running along the foot of the

4. A view of the Athens Agora showing the remains of the Middle Stoa. (Photo: S. Mavromatis, 2000)

5. The ruins of the Asklepieion on the south slope of the Acropolis. (Photo: S. Mavromatis, 2000)

Acropolis on the north side. The houses of the modern Pláka district have prevented excavation, and our archaeological knowledge of this stretch of road is limited to its starting-point, a three-arched monumental building almost touching the Clock of Andronikos of Kyrrhos ('Tower of the Winds'), generally known as the Agoranomeion (Market Inspectors' Office). That is a misnomer and the existing remains of the building definitely date from the Roman period; but the building most probably did mark the western end of a broad road lined with two-storey stoas similar to the Stoa of Attalos, with Doric columns on the ground floor. Few traces of these buildings have come to light, but the columns from one of the stoas were reused much later for the restoration of the interior of the Parthenon when its original columns had been badly damaged by fire.

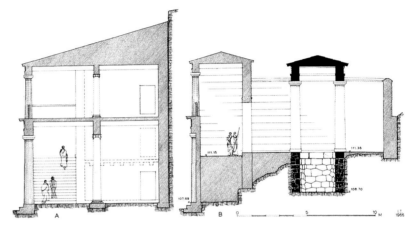

Large-scale redevelopment in the Hellenistic period also took place on the south slope of the Acropolis. A zone of housing was demolished to make way for the two-storey Stoa of Eumenes, 162 m. in length, which provided shelter and a promenade for theatregoers from the nearby Theatre of Dionysos. Behind the east end of the Stoa of Eumenes and slightly higher up the slope stood the Asklepieion, with an Ionic stoa of Classical date and a Doric one dating from 300 B.C.

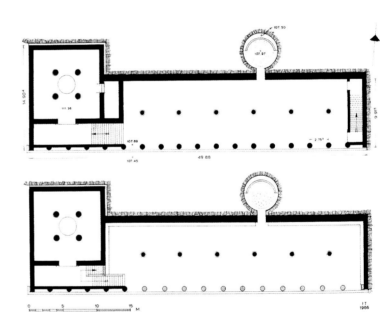

6. The Doric stoa of the Asklepieion. Reconstruction drawings: two lateral sections and plans of the two building phases. (J. Travlos, 'Pictorial Dictionary of Ancient Athens', 1980)

Big changes in the techniques of defensive warfare during the Hellenistic period did not leave Athens unaffected. The city walls rebuilt by Konon in 394 B.C. were repaired from time to time and improved by the addition of outworks and moats, and so were the walls in the Kerameikos district

Fortifications and cemeteries

and those recently unearthed in Kotziá Square, just outside the Acharnian Gate. The Long Walls between Athens and Piraeus were repaired in 306 B.C. and again during the First Mithradatic War, by which time they had long fallen into use, leaving no fortified corridor down to the sea.

One of the city's public utilities was the water supply, which were greatly improved in comparison with the Classical period by the construction of aqueducts (including one to the south of the Acropolis and one recently discovered in Vassilíssis Sofías Avenue). Evidence has also been found of the existence of numerous Hellenistic wells, reservoirs and bath-houses in the city.

The cemeteries were outside the walls. Hundreds of Hellenistic graves have been unearthed in excavations in recent years, usually on both sides of a road such as the Sacred Way, the road to Acharnai (in modern Kotziá Square) or the road from the Dipylon to the Academy. Unfortunately there are no elaborate funerary monuments above ground, partly because of the sumptuary laws enacted by Demetrios of Phaleron (317-309 B.C.) and partly because terrible devastation was done in the course of military campaigns in the country around Athens, especially during the Chremonidean War (266-262 B.C.).

7. The façade of the Temple of Olympian Zeus. (R. Tölle-Kastenbein, 'Das Olympieion in Athen', Vienna 1994)

The practice of putting up monumental sculptures in public places, which became widespread in the Hellenistic period, already had a long history in Athens, both in the Sanctuary of Athena on the Acropolis and in the Agora. Besides votive offerings, there were any number of commemorative or honorific monuments, usually with statues, known to us either from the inscriptions on their bases or from decrees. It is interesting to note that the base of the Monument of the Eponymous Heroes in the Agora was enlarged to make room for statues of the two new 'eponymous heroes', Antigonos and Demetrios, when the Athenians were particularly keen to curry favour with them. In a similar spirit, three identical tall pedestals were erected to support monumental chariots bearing the kings of Pergamon, in acknowledgement of their generous benefactions to the city. Only one of the three survives, on the approach to the Propylaia: it is known as the Monument of Agrippa, whose statue was placed there considerably later. One of the others was erected in honour of Attalos II in front of the stoa named after him, and the third was in front of the north-east corner of the Parthenon.

Monumental sculpture

More in keeping with the spirit of the age were the sculptural groups put up at various places in the city, of which the most impressive examples had some connection with Pergamon. Pergamene sculptural groups were erected during this period at Delphi (in a stoa specially built to house votive offerings from Attalos) and on the Acropolis in Athens. The great ex-voto of Attalos by the south wall of the Acropolis, erected *circa* 200 B.C., had numerous bronze statues: according to Pausanias there were representations of 'the legendary war with the giants, ... the Athenian battle with the Amazons, the engagement with the Persians at Marathon and the destruction of the Gauls in Mysia'.

Unfortunately none of these great statues have survived, but some of the statue types are known to us from Roman copies. Another work that is said to have been equally fine was the group of marble statues dedicated to the city by its sculptor, Euboulides, which extended for about 25 metres along the Panathenaic Way between the Dipylon and the Agora. What remains of this great work, which exemplifies the typically Hellenistic predilection for beautifying city streets with sculptures, is to be seen in the National Archaeological Museum, Athens. A similar instance of using sculptures as an integral part of the landscaping is recorded in the gardens of the Peripatetic school, adjoining the Lyceum, in Theophrastos's time.

The construction of the great Temple of Olympian Zeus in Athens was an event of great significance in the history of Hellenistic architecture because the Corinthian order, which until then had been used only in temple interiors or in smaller buildings, was fully developed in its exterior columns. According to the written sources, construction work started on the Temple of Zeus in 174 B.C., with funding from the Seleucid king Antiochos IV Epiphanes, on the foundations of an Archaic limestone temple which had never been completed. Thus it was in Athens that the Corinthian order, which became very popular in the Roman period, was first used in a large building. Recent research by Manolis Korres has shown that work on the temple began in the time of the orator Lykourgos, shortly before the conventionally accepted starting date of the Hellenistic period. Be that as it may, the Olympieion was not finished until several centuries later, when its completion was financed by the Emperor Hadrian.

Because little new building was done and the splendid monuments of the Classical period were still standing intact, no new temples of any importance were erected in Athens during the Hellenistic period. Not that there was any lessening of religious devotion: heroa were built in the Agora, the shrine of Aglauros was renovated, as were that of Theseus (in 165 B.C.) and some others, and new shrines were built, including those of Demos and the Graces (229 B.C.) and of Sarapis (215 B.C.). Unfortunately nothing is known about the architecture of these sanctuaries.

Unlike the Olympieion, the great stoas that changed the face of the Agora cannot be credited to Athenian architecture: they were designed by Pergamene architects and probably built by Pergamene masons. The buildings donated by the Attalid kings were functional property developments of unprecedented size and grandeur presenting imposing but impersonal façades to the city's public places, just as on the acropolis of Pergamon. The Stoa of Attalos II (reigned 159-139 B.C.) was a two-storey building nearly 120 m. in length, with a second row of columns inside the first and twenty-one good-sized shops along the back of each floor. The complete reconstruction of the stoa between 1952 and 1956, for use as the Agora Museum, allows us to appreciate its size, proportions and layout, while simultaneously serving a

8. The Acropolis, the Olympieion and the Kallirrhoe Spring. E. Dodwell, 'Views in Greece', London 1821) ☞

Planning and Architecture in Hellenistic Athens

153

Hellenistic architecture

practical purpose. The façade and interior colonnade were of Pentelic marble, with Piraeus limestone being used for the rest of the masonry and grey Hymettos marble for certain special features; the roofs and floor were of wood.

The Stoa of Attalos provided the Athenians with plenty of space for strolling about with their friends, as well as luxury shops (which the Demos presumably rented out to private shopkeepers), an excellent grandstand for watching the Panathenaic procession and a vast uncluttered backdrop for statues, memorials, inscriptions and so on. In front of the stoa, just off-centre, stood the tall pedestal surmounted by King Attalos in his chariot and a dais for speakers addressing public meetings in the Agora. It is typical of the period that one of the statue bases found in the Agora excavations should have borne a memorial to the philosopher Karneades erected by two kings, Attalos II of Pergamon and Ariarathes of Cappadocia, in acknowledgement of his services as their teacher at the Academy.

The other Pergamene stoa, donated by Eumenes II (197-159 B.C.), also had two storeys and a second colonnade in the interior. Here there were no shops because, as we have seen, the stoa served a different purpose. As in the Stoa of Attalos, the columns of the façade were Doric on the ground floor and Ionic on the upper floor, while the interior columns on the ground floor were Ionic and those on the first floor had palmate Pergamene capitals. Above and behind the stoa ran the Peripatos, as the road running round the Acropolis was called, and in front of it was a very broad paved esplanade. Today practically nothing remains of this imposing building apart from the retaining wall at the back, which consists of a row of blind arches. Recent research has shown that the white marble of which the stoa was made was not Pentelic but probably from Asia Minor: this means that most of the architectural members were brought over to Athens ready-made, or at any rate roughly dressed.

An original Hellenistic feature common to both the Pergamene stoas is the use of arches

9. The ruins of the Stoa of Attalos before reconstruction. (American School of Classical Studies)

10. The north end of the Stoa of Attalos during the Turkish period. (S. Pomardi, 'Viaggio nella Grecia', Rome 1820)

11. The façade of the Stoa of Attalos after reconstruction. (Studio KONTOS/Photostock)

made out of massive voussoirs. In the Stoa of Attalos they formed the doorways of some narrow rooms (*oikoi*) with benches round the walls, under the staircases at both ends, while in the Stoa of Eumenes there were 42 blind arches in the north retaining wall. At the entrance to the Agora excavators have found some remains of the Gate of Hippomachia, which was adorned with trophies and an equestrian statue and is also believed to have been arched. It was a triumphal monument erected to commemorate a victory of the Athenian cavalry during the siege of Athens by Kassandros (304 B.C.), and it must have been one of the oldest monuments in which a semicircular arch was used to commemorate a triumph.

The Asklepieion, a considerably older foundation (419 B.C.), also has a Doric stoa which is dated on epigraphical evidence to 300-299 B.C. or else to the time of Lykourgos. Its complex ground plan, with a roofed well at the west end, was necessitated by special functional requirements. At the back, the stoa is hemmed in by the sheer north wall of the Acropolis. The building was rebuilt in the Late Roman period and is now completely in ruins.

13. Doric cornice from the Stoa of Eumenes. (Third Ephorate of Prehistoric and Classical Antiquities)

In the course of the Hellenistic period some new public buildings were put up in the Agora and some others were redesigned. Unfortunately the excavators found all of them in a state of utter ruin and it is hardly possible to reconstruct their original design and appearance. A Hellenistic building approximately 45 m. long and 17 m. wide on the north slope of the low hill crowned by the 'Theseion' (Temple of Hephaistos and Athena) is thought to have been an arsenal. Our only evidence of its size and shape comes from the cuttings in the rock. Mention has already been made of the alterations to the Metroön, the public records office on the west side of the Agora. New additions were also made, for functional reasons, to the Archaic building of the Stoa Basileios (Royal Stoa): this had apparently been drastically repaired after part of it was destroyed by the Persian invaders in 480 B.C., and now a three-columned portico was added at each end, perhaps in imitation of the neighbouring Stoa of Zeus. Also Hellenistic were the new Bouleuterion (Council House) and the new klepsydra (a rather unsophisticated water-clock) in the Agora. For the record, it should be noted that the Clock of Andronikos of Kyrrhos (the 'Tower of the Winds', at the end of Aiólou Street), which was a much more accurate chronometer, was not built in the Hellenistic period but slightly later: Joachim von Freeden's earlier dating of the building is no longer accepted.

12. The double colonnade of the Stoa of Attalos after reconstruction. (Studio KONTOS/Photostock)

14. Reconstruction drawing of the Pergamene honorific monument in front of the Parthenon. (M. Korres)

The well-known passage in pseudo-Dikaiarchos describing Athens in the first half of the third century B.C. speaks highly of its gymnasia as well as its religious sanctuaries. A gymnasium was a large open space outside the city walls with facilities for athletic training (which were also used for military training) and buildings for theoretical instruction. The Athens gymnasia had gardens, tree-lined avenues and woodlands, which were destroyed by Sulla's army during the First Mithradatic War.

Gymnasia

The Kynosarges gymnasium was on the south bank of the River Ilissos, near the Kallirrhoe Spring to the south-east of the city. Such buildings and fixed installations that have been found and identified there have all been much later than the Hellenistic period, dating from Hadrian's reign. The Academy, where Plato taught, was out to the west. Widely renowned in antiquity for its high standard of learning, it covered an area of about 1.4 hectares (3½ acres) on a site that was occupied continuously from prehistoric times until the sixth century A.D., when Justinian closed the Athenian philosophy schools. Extensive excavations at the Academy have revealed a peristyle quadrangle of the fourth century B.C., the actual gymnasium and the palaistra (wrestling school), both late Hellenistic, as well as paved walks and a water cistern. Unfortunately nothing remains of the gymnasium and palaistra above the foundations, so we have no evidence of their architecture. Lastly, the Lykeion or Lyceum, where Aristotle taught, occupied a large site east of what is now Syntagma Square. Here too the buildings have been destroyed almost without trace: an inscription from there has been found at the Sotíra tou Likodímou Church in Filellínon Street, and recently the foundations of a large square building were discovered under the gardens between Vassilíssis Sofías Avenue and Riyíllis Street. Judging

MACEDONIAN RULE

*15. Reconstruction drawing of the Gate of Hippomachia in the Agora.
(W. B. Dinsmoor, Jr., American School of Classical Studies)*

by its ground plan, this would appear to have been a palaistra, but here again the architecture of its superstructure can only be guessed at. In any case, there is explicit literary evidence that the palaistra of the Lyceum was built under Lykourgos, shortly before the Hellenistic period.

Still standing in Syntagma Square is the *horos*, the boundary stone of the 'Garden of the Muses', which marked the limit of the garden and school started by Aristotle's pupil Theophrastos. According to literary sources the Garden of the Muses, which contained colonnades, paved walks and a shrine of the Muses, was attached to the Lyceum, but no remains have been found on the site except a few architectural members of doubtful provenance.

Athens had two more gymnasia, of whose architecture nothing is known. One was the Diogeneion, erected in honour of Diogenes, who in 287 B.C. was officially declared a benefactor of the city. Archaeological evidence of this has been found in inscriptions on stone blocks built into the Late Roman city wall in the modern Pláka district. The other was the Ptolemaion, probably built in honour of Ptolemy III of Egypt. Its location has been the subject of much debate and conjecture but remains unknown.

The question of Athenian dwelling-houses in the Hellenistic period has not been studied as a subject in its own right, owing to problems of dating, the difficulty of distinguishing clearly between the original fabric of older houses and the repairs carried out at various times thereafter, and the poor quality of construction. The areas of housing that have been studied most thoroughly are in the Koile district (the south-west part of the city) and on the north and west slopes of the Areopagus. Sporadic excavations keep bringing to light **Private** parts of houses, or even whole houses, where it is usually possible to distinguish **houses** the central courtyard and the *andron* (the main reception room, used for entertaining male guests only), which was usually square, with the floor slightly raised beneath the wooden couches round the walls. In the Hellenistic period the floor of the *andron* sometimes had a pebble mosaic (usually black and white), or else it was surfaced with mortar.

Although most Athenian houses in the Classical and Hellenistic periods were small and cheaply built, expensive and luxurious houses – such as that of Kallias – are heard of as early as the fifth century in the less crowded parts of the city. The characteristic sign of progress towards larger and more comfortable houses was the inner courtyard with a peristyle of columns or pillars. Although no complete Hellenistic house with peristyle courtyard has yet been found in Athens, the habit of holding symposia and other parties, which apparently flourished in Athens more than anywhere else, was connected with that architectural development. In the late Hellenistic period wealthy merchants such as the sons of Dies of Tyre, who became naturalized Athenian citizens, had palatial residences in Athens.

The practice of painting the interior walls of houses in imitation of ashlar masonry, known from Delos and Pella and subsequently termed the First Pompeian style, is also attested in Athens: for example, in some rooms of the Pompeion, which was repaired and redecorated *circa* 90 B.C., and in private houses too.

What we call the Hellenistic period lasted for two and half centuries, too long a period for the history of its built environment to be summed up briefly, even with reference to a city such as Athens. What can be said is that great efforts were made to modernize public buildings and other public facilities in accordance with the spirit of the age, though the existence of the heritage of great Classical monuments and the decline in the city's political power meant that large-scale construction programmes were neither necessary nor expedient. The biggest Hellenistic buildings in Athens were erected by kings from Asia Minor, partly because the Diadochoi were always vying to outdo each other in the cultural arena but mainly because of the undying intellectual lustre of Athens. The constructional activities of the Demos were limited to public buildings, educational establishments and honorific monuments to perpetuate the memory of large-scale benefactors.

And so, in spite of the eventful and sometimes turbulent history of Athens between 323 and 86 B.C., the city had evidently lost none of its cultural prestige and still held a position of pre-eminence in Greece proper in the field of architecture and planning. Even after that, when Rome had consolidated its hold on the eastern Mediterranean, Athens still retained its primacy in matters of culture, education and the civilized way of life that marks the Greeks and their imitators in the ancient world.

16. The boundary stone of the Garden of the Muses in Syntagma Square. (Photo: N. Panay-otopoulos, 2000)

SELECT BIBLIOGRAPHY

Aleshire, S.B., *The Athenian Asklepieion: The people, their dedications and the inventories*, Amsterdam 1989.

Camp. J.M., *The Athenian Agora*, Princeton 1986.

Delorme, J., *Gymnasion. Étude sur les monuments consacrés à l'éducation en Grèce*, Paris 1960, 37-49, 51-59.

Fiandra, E., 'La stoa di Attalo nell' Agora Ateniese', *Palladio* 8 (1958) 97-120.

Forsèn, B., and G. Stanton, *The Pnyx in the History of Athens*, Helsinki 1966.

Habicht, C., *Athen im hellenistischer Zeit. Gesammelte Aufsätze*, Munich 1994.

Korres, M., «Ολυμπιείον», *Ανθέμιον* 5 (1999) 27-29.

Metzger, H., 'Recherches d'architecture et de topographie à l'Asklépieion d'Athènes', *Bulletin de Correspondance Hellénique* 73 (1949) 316-350.

Thompson, A., 'The Stoa of Attalos II in Athens', *Picture Book* 2, Princeton 1959.

Thompson, H.A., «Μέση στοά», *Hesperia* 21 (1952) 86-90; 23 (1954) 50-51; 37 (1968) 61-64.

—, «Νοτία στοά II», *Hesperia* 29 (1960) 359-363.

Thompson, H.A., and R.E. Wycherley, *The Agora of Athens*, Princeton 1972.

Travlos, J., *Πολεοδομική εξέλιξις των Αθηνών*, Athens 1960, 75-92.

—, «Παλαιές πόλεις της Ελλάδος», *Ιστορία του Ελληνικού Έθνους* V, Athens 1974, 470.

—, «Το γυμνάσιον του Κυνοσάργους», *Αρχαιολογικά Ανάλεκτα εξ Αθηνών* 3 (1970) 6-14.

—, *Pictorial Dictionary of Ancient Athens*, New York 1980.

Vanderpool, E., 'The Museum and Garden of the Peripatetics', *Αρχαιολογική Εφημερίς* (1953-54.II) 126-128.

Wycherley, R.E., *The Stones of Athens*, Princeton 1978, 77 ff.

CHAPTER VI

Urban Development and Monumental Buildings in Athens under Augustus and Hadrian

ALKISTIS SPETSIERI-CHOREMI

2. *The Monument of Philopappos (A.D. 114-116). (R. Sayer, 'Ruins of Athens, with Remains and Other Valuable Antiquities in Greece', London 1759)*

1. *Model of the Acropolis in the 2nd cent. A.D. (M. Korres)*

Urban Development and Monumental Buildings in Athens under Augustus and Hadrian

Athens retained the splendours of her Classical and Hellenistic monumental buildings, gymnasia, luxury villas and gardens until 86 B.C., when the Romans under Sulla besieged, captured and sacked the city. The fortification walls of Athens and Piraeus were razed, many monuments were destroyed and many great works of art were carried off. According to the geographer Strabo, the city was reduced to 'a few houses round the port and the Sanctuary of Zeus Soter'. Nevertheless the Romans granted Athens a fair degree of autonomy and independence. The lustre of her past influenced her conquerors – who in private life were well-born and wealthy men – and also the rulers of other countries, who were soon vying with one another to spend fabulous sums of money on the rebuilding of ancient monuments, the provision of infrastructure services and the construction of splendid new buildings to restore the city to her former grandeur. Two who deserve special mention are Ariobarzanes II, king of Cappadocia, who financed the reconstruction of the Odeion of Perikles (destroyed by Sulla), and the astronomer Andronikos of Kyrrhos in Macedonia, who beautified the city by building his famous and unique clock, generally known as the Tower of the Winds.

The first person to embark on a systematic reconstruction programme was the Emperor Augustus (27 B.C. - A.D. 14), who came to power after the battle of Actium (31 B.C.). Augustus visited Athens three times and showed respect for her cultural heritage: in fact all his actions evinced admiration for the past. During his reign there was a constant interchange of ideas, artists and materials between Athens and Rome.

Athens in Augustus's reign

Public buildings and other monuments in the capital of the Roman Empire were built in imitation of Athenian models, while new ideas about planning and new architectural forms were introduced into Athens. Members of the Roman imperial family gave themselves the names and attributes of ancient Greek deities and were worshipped as such, sometimes in existing temples that were restored, sometimes in new temples that were moved bodily from various places in Attica or were built of reused blocks from other temples.

Augustus's building projects in Athens were spread about various parts of the city. Most of them were in the Agora, where there is clear evidence of the application of new planning concepts: in particular, the great civic and commercial centre of earlier antiquity was turned into a centre for emperor-worship and a showcase for the achievements of the Empire. The whole main square of the Agora which had been used for meetings of the Ekklesia (Citizens' Assembly) – the most important function of the famous Athenian democratic system – was filled with large buildings such as the Odeion of Agrippa, the Temple of Ares, the altar of Zeus Agoraios and the South-West Temple.

It was evidently thought that the existence of the Pax Augustea did away with the need for the Ekklesia, and so the most vital organ of Athenian democracy ceased to exist. Before that happened, however, the function of the Agora had already been altered when all the shops were moved to a broad, flat site about a hundred metres further east, where the Roman Agora or Agora

3. Portrait of Augustus found in the Roman Agora. (Athens, National Archaeological Museum. Photo: K. Kontos, 2000)

of Caesar and Augustus was built. This was the first building of its kind in Athens, but no reference to it is to be found anywhere in the extant literary sources. It is a mystery why Pausanias, who visited Athens in the second century A.D. and gave detailed descriptions of the Agora and even Hadrian's Library, only a few metres away, makes no mention of the Roman Agora or any of the buildings further to the east. The explanation may be that the main purpose of his *Description of Greece* was to describe older buildings connected with the history, mythology and religious cults of Athens and not secular buildings used in everyday life.

The Roman Agora (Market)

The Agora of Caesar and Augustus was a typical Roman forum. It was rectangular in plan (111×98 m. overall), with a high outer wall made of regular limestone blocks, an internal courtyard with colonnades on all four sides and shops, storerooms and offices for the market officials along the back of the colonnades. There were two monumental gateways into the forum, one on the west side and one on the east. The one on the west, a Doric propylon made of Pentelic marble, was called the Gate of Athena Archegetis because, according to the inscription on its architrave, it was dedicated to the city's patron goddess by the Athenian *demos* during the archonship of Nikias (11-10 B.C.). The east gate was Ionic, with unfluted columns of grey Hymettos marble and column bases and capitals of white Pentelic marble. Neither gate lay on the central axis of the forum: the west gate was slightly south of centre – at the end of the ancient Broad Way mentioned in inscriptions, which ran eastwards from a point just south of the Stoa of Attalos in the Agora – and the east gate still further south, presumably straddling the same road, which must have started in a south-easterly direction before curving back to the east. In the middle of the south side there was a fountain of drinking water for the use of the public, and right next to the fountain was a narrow staircase leading up to a small door that opened on to a road running along the south wall of the forum. This was an ancient road lying well above the floor level of the forum, and so the south wall also served as a retaining wall to prevent the hillside from slipping.

According to the inscription on the architrave of the west gate, the forum was built through the generosity of C. Julius Caesar and Augustus. Construction work is thought to have started in about 47 B.C., with a grant from Julius Caesar, and to have been abandoned soon afterwards owing to a shortage of funds, since the money in the Roman treasury was being spent on the civil wars between the Roman generals. It was completed much later, between 19 and 11 B.C., with funds donated by Augustus, who spent some time in Athens in 19 B.C. on his way back from Asia after defeating the Parthians. Apparently some repairs and alterations were carried out and the floor of the quadrangle was paved with marble slabs in Hadrian's reign (A.D. 117-138). It was then that a stele was set up on the north side of the central passageway through the propylon, inscribed with Hadrian's edict concerning the tax liabilities of oil producers and oil merchants. The positioning of this inscription proves that the central oil market was located in the Roman Agora.

The Roman Agora was an original building quite separate from the ancient Greek Agora, though its siting was planned to fit in both with the Agora and with the existing street plan. The main (west) façade of the forum overlooked the road running from south to north and the monumental west gate faced the end of the Broad Way, which ran eastwards from the

4. *Model of Athens in the 2nd cent. A.D. (J. Travlos)*

Agora. Dominating the Broad Way was the Gate of Athena Archegetis with an equestrian statue of Lucius Caesar, Augustus's grandson, as an akroterion at the apex of the pediment. The statue no longer exists, but travellers to Athens in early modern times saw its inscribed base and reproduced it in their engravings. A ramp led up to the central passageway of the gate, which was five metres above the level of the Broad Way.

It is not known when the Roman Agora was destroyed. What we do know is that after Athens was sacked by the Herulians in A.D. 267 and the inhabitants retreated into the safety of the Late Roman wall, the commercial and administrative centre of the city was moved to the Roman Agora and Hadrian's Library. In the Byzantine and Post-Byzantine periods the site was built over with houses and three churches that have since been demolished: the Church of the Taxiarchs (rebuilt in the nineteenth century and commonly known as the Panagia Grigoroússa), Profítis Ilías and the Sotíra tis Pazaróportas. In 1456, during the Turkish period the Fethiye Camii (Mosque of the Conqueror) in the northern part of the Roman Agora on the ruins of an Early Christian basilica.

Outside the east gate of the Roman Agora there was a broad flight of steps leading up to the so-called Agoranomeion (Market Inspectors' Office), a building erected in the mid first century A.D., which stood about 4.70 m. higher up the hillside. Part of its façade is still standing, pierced by three doors with arched lintels of grey Hymettos marble, as well as portions of the north and south walls, built of regular blocks of limestone.

Agoranomeion

Much of the 'Agoranomeion' lies buried beneath Márkou Avrilíou Street and the Goulandris-Horn Foundation. An inscription on the Pentelic marble epistyle records that this building, too, was dedicated to Athena Archegetis and the Divi Augusti. Unfortunately the beginning of the inscription, giving the name of the building, is broken off and has not been found, and so it has yet to be satisfactorily identified. Paul Graindor, who excavated it and published the first study of it, concluded that it was the Agoranomeion, while the American archaeologist M. Hoff argued that it was the Sebasteion, but neither of these identifications is now accepted.

Due north of the 'Agoranomeion' is the Clock of Andronikos of Kyrrhos or Tower of the Winds, built by the astronomer Andronikos of Kyrrhos in Macedonia, probably in the mid first century B.C. It is mentioned by Varro (writing in 37 B.C.) and by Vitruvius (in 27 B.C.), but not by Pausanias (2nd cent. A.D.). Evidently it was the first building to be erected in this area, predating the Roman Agora. J. Freeden maintains that it must have been built much earlier, perhaps in the second century B.C. It consists of an octagonal tower of Pentelic marble standing on a three-stepped base, with a pyramidal roof, a round turret attached to the south wall and two doors with porches. The roof was crowned by a bronze weather vane, now lost, and personifications of the winds are carved in relief on the eight walls, with their names incised just below the

*Tower
of the Winds*

5. *The west gate of the Roman Agora, known as the Gate of Athena Archegetis. Reconstruction drawing. (J. Stuart and N. Revett)*

Fig. 1.

cornice. They are, going clockwise from the north: Boreas (north), Kaikias, Apeliotes, Euros, Notos, Lips, Zephyros, Skiron (north-west). Incised beneath the figures of the winds are the lines of eight sundials. Inside the tower there was a hydraulic clock fed by water from the springs on the north slope of the Acropolis, so that it would still be possible to tell the time even on cloudy days and at night-time. The workings of the clock were reconstructed by J. Noble and D. De Solla Price on the basis of descriptions of other ancient water-clocks, but their conclusions have been challenged in the light of recent research by the architect H. Kienast, who is making a systematic study of the architecture of the monument and, in collaboration with astrophysicists, is trying to reconstruct the way it actually worked. The Tower of the Winds could be described as an early sort of meteorological station. It was very important for the merchants in the nearby market to know the exact time and the direction of the wind, so that they could work out roughly when goods sent by sea could be expected to arrive at their destination. In the Early Christian period (5th cent. A.D.) the Tower of the Winds was converted for use as a chapel, or possibly as the baptistery of a nearby church, and excavations have shown that the area outside its north-east door was used as a Christian cemetery. In the eighteenth century it was used as a *tekke* by Turkish dervishes and in the nineteenth as a store-room for finds from the first excavations of the Archaeological Society (1837-1846).

A few yards north-west of the Tower of the Winds were the so-called latrines of Vespasian, built in the first century A.D. for the convenience of the many shoppers in the nearby forum. They were housed in a rectangular building with a narrow vestibule on the east side, a rectangular room with a tetrastyle atrium in the middle and benches along the walls with holes at intervals for sitting on, beneath which there ran a deep sewer.

The grandest and most important of the new buildings erected in Augustus's reign was the Odeion of Agrippa (the Agrippeion) in the Agora, abutting on and perpendicular to the terrace of the Middle Stoa, which was originally intended as a concert hall. It was disproportionately large for its site and quite out of scale with the other buildings round about, and it

Odeion of Agrippa

had some purely Roman characteristics totally alien to the Attic tradition, as regards both its architectural form and its location in a dominant position right across the Agora, almost touching the Panathenaic Way. It had some similarities to the Bouleuterion at Miletos (2nd cent. B.C.) in its internal layout and external form, but it bore an even closer resemblance to the indoor theatre at Pompeii (80-75 B.C.). The Agrippeion showed clear evidence of the interaction of Eastern and Western architectural ideas and techniques.

The Odeion was endowed by Marcus Vipsanius Agrippa, Augustus's son-in-law, who visited Athens in 15 B.C. while on a tour of the East. In gratitude for his benefaction the Athenians erected a statue of him on a tall pedestal in front of the Propylaia of the Acropolis. From the ruins of the building and the architectural members that were found by the Americans in their excavations between 1934 and 1936, it is possible to reconstruct what it looked like. It was

6. The Gate of Athena Archegetis on the west side of the Roman Agora. (Photo: Studio KONTOS/Photostock)

a large rectangular building with stoas round all four sides. The core of the building contains a wide but shallow rectangular stage, an orchestra and an auditorium with curved rows of seats for a thousand spectators arranged in a quadrant of a circle. The stage was reached through a four-column portico on the north side, while the entrance to the auditorium and stoas was on the south side at a higher level (the level of the terrace of the Middle Stoa). The stage and orchestra were paved with marble flagstones in several different colours and decorated with classicizing sculptures. The central core, which rose above the lean-to roof of the stoas like a separate building, had a pitched roof with no internal supports. On three sides (north, east and west) the stoas were supported by a row of stout piers that projected from the walls both on the inside and on the outside, forming pilasters with Corinthian capitals. The auditorium was illuminated by windows between the piers and by two open colonnades at a higher level on the south front. The capitals were Corinthian with elaborately-carved acanthus leaves. Round about

7. A column capital from the Odeion of Agrippa. (Photo: S. Mavromatis, 2000)

A.D. 150 the roof fell in and the Agrippeion was rebuilt in considerably altered form. The auditorium was reduced to half its former size by the construction of a lateral partition wall, and a row of six colossal statues – three serpent-tailed Giants and three fish-tailed Tritons, copied from male figures in the pediments of the Parthenon – was added on the north façade. From then on the Agrippeion was regularly used for classes and lectures by philosophers and sophists, as attested by two passages in the work of the ancient author Philostratos. Three of the colossal statues, now to be seen in the Agora, were reused on the façade of a huge building constructed soon after 400, which covered the site of the Agrippeion and part of the Middle Stoa.

In about 15 B.C. the Temple of Ares was moved bodily to the main square of the Agora. This was a Doric temple built in the fifth century B.C., which had originally stood either in the deme of Acharnai or, according to a recent study by Manolis Korres, in the deme of Pallene.

Temple of Ares

In the first century A.D. it was dismantled piece by piece and transported to the Agora, where it was re-erected on the east-west axis of the main square in front of the north façade of the Agrippeion. The altar was set up on the point where the axes of these two buildings intersect. Their positioning in relation to each other is a clear instance of the Romans' ideas on the axial relationships between buildings. Nothing has been found of the Temple of Ares except the foundations, which are now roofed over for protection from the weather. The blocks of stone have code letters incised on them so that the workmen re-erecting the temple on its new site

8. The Clock of Andronikos of Kyrrhos or Tower of the Winds. Reconstruction drawing. (J. Stuart and N. Revett)

Fig. 1.

ΑΠΗΛΙΩΤΗΣ   ΚΑΙΚΙΑΣ   ΒΟΡΕΑΣ

ECHELLES DE

would know exactly where each one belonged. The reason why the temple was put up in such a central position in the Agora was presumably connected with emperor-worship: this, at least, is the conclusion to be drawn from the inscription on a statue base of A.D. 2 in honour of Gaius Caesar, Agrippa's son and Augustus's adopted son, who is called 'the new Ares'. Both the statue and its base were found near the temple.

Some of the other buildings of this period were also intended for emperor-worship. At the end of Augustus's reign, or shortly after his death in A.D. 14, a double temple of unusual form was built of reused blocks of stone behind the fifth-century B.C. Stoa of Zeus Eleutherios. At the same time an earlier structure in front of the Stoa was enlarged for use as the altar of the new temple.

Many new buildings of the Roman period made extensive use of material from Classical temples and shrines. One reason for that, of course, was that it saved money, but it was also very much in keeping with the Romans' classicizing and archaizing tendencies. This fact proves that the temples and sacred buildings in Attica were derelict or in ruins. Yet their reconstruction, sometimes on new sites far away, must have been part of a general programme of restoring the temples and shrines of gods and heroes, and inscriptions provide evidence of just such a programme. Doric columns from the temple at Thorikos and Ionic columns from the Temple of Athena Sounias at Sounion were reused in the rebuilding of two prostyle temples in Athens, each standing on a high podium: the South-West Temple between the Middle Stoa and the Agrippeion, facing the Tholos, and the South-East Temple in the south-east corner of the Agora, facing north over the Panathenaic Way. According to epigraphic and other evidence, the former was dedicated to Artemis Boulaia and the latter to the Eleusinian Goddesses.

Another ancient monument that was transported to the Agora in this period (1st cent. B.C. - 1st cent. A.D.) was the Altar of Zeus Agoraios, which was moved down from the Pnyx and re-erected east of the Metroön. Here again the blocks of stone are marked with code letters to facilitate their reassembly. It is significant that the altar of Zeus, who watched over and guided the ancient Athenians' political meetings, should have been moved away from the Pnyx at the very time when Augustus was reducing the powers and responsibilities of the Citizens' Assembly.

There was also a programme of renovating and enlarging existing monuments, but only on a limited scale. A propylon and an enclosure wall were added to the Tholos, the pyramidal-roofed rotunda built in 465 B.C. and used as the headquarters of the fifty *prytaneis* (the 'government': see p. 94), and a new floor was laid. A water fountain was built near the Bouleuterion for the use of the *bouleutai* and a propylon was added to the Strategeion, which evidently served a dual purpose as an administrative centre (for it was the headquarters of the ten *Strategoi* or generals, who were very important in the hierarchy of the Athenian state) and as the shrine of the 'Hero Strategos'. A colonnade was built in the middle of the north side of the Agora and a bath-house (replacing an older one) outside the south-west corner of the Agora. Besides these, some blocks of luxury housing and shops were constructed a little way below the sites of two large buildings erected in Hadrian's reign: the Basilica (an administrative building in the north-east corner of the Agora, part of which has been excavated) and Hadrian's Library eighty metres further east.

9. *Statues of Giants from the second phase of the Agrippeion (A.D. 150), used in the façade of the Gymnasium (5th cent. A.D.).*
(Photo: Studio KONTOS/Photostock)

The only new building erected on the Acropolis in this period was the Temple of Roma and Augustus. Repairs were also carried out to the Erechtheion, which was damaged by fire, and the architects working on it were so impressed by it that they imitated its style and ornamentation both elsewhere in Athens and in Rome. The little Ionic Temple of Roma and Augustus was built *circa* 19 B.C. The cult of Roma had been introduced into Athens much earlier, while the cult of Augustus is attested by the numerous inscribed altars that have been found in various parts of Athens, especially in and around the Agora. The temple was round (about 8.60 m. in diameter) and built of Pentelic marble, with nine Ionic columns. Its height is unknown. Although Pausanias does not mention it, most archaeologists agree that its site must have been exactly where Ciriaco of Ancona found its inscribed architrave and other architectural members,

***Temple of Roma
and Augustus***

some twenty metres away from the east front of the Parthenon and in line with its longitudinal axis. The axial relationship between the two temples is typical of Roman practice (cf. the Temple of Ares and the Agrippeion in the Agora). In style and ornamentation, the Temple of Roma and Augustus resembles the Erechtheion, but with differences of proportion and detail. Most probably it was built by the same architect who supervised the repairs to the Erechtheion.

Some monuments on the south slope of the Acropolis, which had been damaged by Sulla, were repaired at this time. In the Asklepieion, the sanctuary of the god of healing, founded in the fifth century B.C., the old propylon was replaced by a new one which, according to the inscription on its architrave, was dedicated to Asklepios, Hygieia and Augustus Caesar. Not long afterwards a small stoa was erected due east of the propylon and south of the temple.

Minor repairs and alterations were carried out to the Theatre of Dionysos, the oldest theatre in the world, which took shape gradually between the sixth and fourth centuries B.C. The marble thrones reserved for the priests of Augustus, Demos, the Graces and Roma date from Augustus's reign. Some years later the plain rectangular skene (scene-building) with projecting paraskenia (wings), built in the fourth century B.C., was replaced by a new two-storey building dedicated to Nero and Dionysos, as we know from an inscription on part of its architrave (A.D. 61-62). The skene was extended forwards into the orchestra, which was reduced in size, altered in shape (from a circle to a slightly extended semicircle) and repaved with marble slabs of different colours. In Hadrian's reign the proskenion (stage) was adorned with statues of kneeling Sileni. The theatre was destroyed in 267 when the Herulians sacked Athens. It was then rebuilt *circa* 400 by the archon Phaidros, who used the kneeling Sileni to adorn the projecting forestage (the bema of Phaidros) that was added at that time.

Between Augustus's death and Hadrian's accession not much building work of any consequence was done in Athens. In Claudius's reign several monuments were repaired and two monumental staircases were built, one leading up to the Propylaia on the Acropolis and the other from the main square of the Agora to the Temple of Hephaistos. Early in the second century, under Trajan, colonnades were erected to form monumental façades along the main thoroughfares, in front of the shops and other buildings. Some remains of these colonnades have been found on both sides of the Panathenaic Way and the Broad Way (which ran from the ancient Agora to the Roman Agora) and along the north wall of the Library of Pantainos. Pausanias, and Himerios after him, both mention the colonnades in their descriptions of the Panathenaic Way.

The most important monument of the period between Augustus and Hadrian is the Library of Pantainos, south of the Stoa of Attalos. This was the first properly organized library with codified regulations, which have been found inscribed on a stele. It was built in A.D. 98-102 by a wealthy Roman, Titus Flavius Pantainos, and dedicated to Athena Polias, the Emperor Trajan and the city of Athens: these and other particulars are given in an inscription on the lintel of its main door. From the two inscriptions we learn that the library was part of a larger building.

*Library of
Pantainos*

It was thanks to the large-scale building programme of the Emperor Hadrian, that great philhellene, that Athens recovered her ancient lustre. In the words of Strabo the geographer, 'Having been badly scarred by the war against the Romans, Athens flourished once more in Hadrian's reign.' The city enjoyed a period of peace, urban development and intellectual brilliance: splendid new buildings were erected and Athens became once again a major centre of scholarship and the arts, with philosophy schools to which students came from all over the Empire. Much of what we know about this 'renaissance' in Athens comes from Pausanias, whose descriptions have helped modern archaeologists to identify most of the ancient monuments.

Hadrian was a passionate admirer of Athens. He went there three times, initiated a huge building programme and turned the city into a Panhellenic centre. On his first visit in 124-125, when he spent several months in Athens, he extended the city to the east. The new city, called Hadrianopolis or Novae Athenae, covered an area of 2,200,000 sq.m. roughly corresponding to the present-day Záppion Gardens, National Gardens and Syntagma Square. It had a circuit of 1,750 metres and also included the Olympieion and a group of sanctuaries and public buildings further south. It was one of the most beautiful parts of the city, with gymnasia, bath-houses and luxury villas with elaborate mosaic floors. In the old city many of the old buildings were renovated and some large public buildings were erected, but the fortification walls were not repaired. In about 135 a grand triumphal arch ('Hadrian's Arch') was put up by the Athenians on the dividing line between the old city and the new, as a token of their gratitude to the imperial benefactor. An inscription on the west face of the arch reads 'This is old Athens, the city of Theseus,' and on the east face 'This is the city of Hadrian, not of Theseus.' The arch was built

*Athens in
Hadrian's reign*

10. Inscription with the regulations of the Library of Pantainos. (Archive of K.S. Staikos)

at the north-west corner of the Olympieion precinct, straddling the ancient road from the old city to the sanctuary. It is an unusual structure, 18 metres high. The lower part is a typical example of a Roman triumphal arch: it consists of a marble wall terminating in two pilasters with Corinthian capitals, with an opening in the middle for the arch, which is buttressed by two low pilasters also with Corinthian capitals. Flanking the arch on both faces are Corinthian columns standing on high bases: the columns were joined to the wall by a displaced entablature, a feature also found on the façade of Hadrian's Library. The upper part of the arch, which is more like a Greek propylon, has three apertures and an Ionic entablature. The middle aperture, which is pedimented, was probably blocked by a marble slab in such a way as to form two small rooms shaped like naiskoi, which were once believed to have contained statues of Theseus and Hadrian; however, research has proved that that was not the case.

11. Portrait of Hadrian. (Athens, National Archaeological Museum. Photo: K. Kontos, 2000)

The most impressive of Hadrian's projects in Athens was the completion in 131-132 of the huge Temple of Olympian Zeus (the Olympieion). The Emperor himself was identified with Zeus and was worshipped with the epithet 'Olympian', as attested by numerous inscribed altars and statue bases dedicated to Hadrian. The temple, measuring 107.70 x 42.90 m., was begun as a Doric building under the Peisistratidai (*c.* 515 B.C.) in imitation of the gigantic temples being built elsewhere at that time (the Heraion on Samos, the Temple of Artemis at Ephesos, the Didymaion at Miletos). After the fall of the 'tyrants' or absolute rulers, construction work was halted and the temple was left as it was for several centuries, presumably because the people of democratic Athens had no wish to complete a

Temple of Olympian Zeus

building so strongly associated with the 'tyranny'. Around 175 B.C. Antiochos Epiphanes, the king of Syria, had the ambitious idea of completing the temple, keeping the original dimensions but substituting the Corinthian for the Doric order, to a design by the Roman architect Cossutius. This time the work had almost been finished when it was abandoned on the death of Antiochos. Apparently some of the architrave blocks had not been laid in position: at any rate, in 86 B.C. Sulla took some of the Corinthian columns back to Rome for use in the Temple of Jupiter Capitolinus. Suetonius informs us that there was another plan to complete the building in Augustus's reign, but nothing was done about it until Hadrian finally brought the project to a successful conclusion in about 131. The sekos was roofed over and the colossal chryselephantine statue of Zeus was constructed inside it. Of the original 104 columns, sixteen now remain (fifteen standing and one fallen) to give us an idea of the immense size of the building. Besides the temple itself, Hadrian also built a buttressed wall around it to enclose a rectangular

12. Hadrian's Arch. (Photo: Studio KONTOS/Photostock)

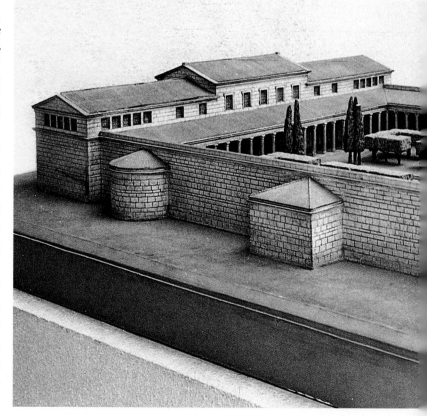

precinct with a perimeter of four stades (163 m.), according to Pausanias. Once the temple had been finished and consecrated, Hadrian founded the Panhellenic League, a confederation of all Greek cities with its headquarters in Athens and the Olympieion as its focal point. Delegates of the Panhellenic League met at the Panhellenion (Sanctuary of Zeus Panhellenios and Hera Panhellenia), which was built at the same time and has been identified by John Travlos with the ruins discovered between the great temple and the bank of the River Ilissos: it was a temple standing on a podium, with an enclosure wall round it. In Pausanias's opinion, the most sacred building erected in Hadrian's reign was the Pantheon, a joint sanctuary of all the gods and goddesses identified by some scholars with a huge building on a podium to the east of the Roman Agora and Hadrian's Library, parts of which have been excavated and are preserved at Nos. 74, 78 and 84-88, Adhrianoú Street. Another of the Emperor's major benefactions was the Gymnasium, probably situated in the Kynosarges area, where the foundations of a gymnasium have been found.

The most important cultural institution founded by Hadrian in Athens was the Library, a building of the same type, on the same orientation and of approximately the same dimensions as the Roman Agora, which stood about eighty metres east of the ancient Greek Agora and was begun in about 132, when the Emperor was on his third visit to Athens. It was a rectangular building measuring 122x82 m., with a high, blank outside wall and a large open courtyard in the middle, colonnaded on all four sides. Pausanias, in his book on Attica, refers to 'the hundred columns of Phrygian marble, with walls built of the same material as the columns, and rooms adorned with a gilded roof and with alabaster stone, as well as with statues and paintings. Books are kept in them'. The library had a single entrance, a door with a portico on the west side. The four fluted Corinthian columns of the portico were made of Phrygian pavonazetto, a white-and-purple veined marble; only the northern-most of the four is still standing *in situ*. All that remains of the façade is the north wing, built of Pentelic marble, and still standing against this white backdrop is a row of un-fluted columns of green cipollino from Karystos, standing on high bases. Above this wall was the so-called attic, which has not survived. According to M.A. Sisson, who first identified the building, there was probably a statue on the top of each projecting column, in front of the attic wall. Although the façade has some features reminiscent of the architecture of Asia Minor, it is notable for its clean surfaces and its lack of fussy ornamentation: this clearly reflects the influence of Athenian Classical architecture. The high outer wall is built of limestone in pseudo-isodomic masonry. The books (actually papyrus rolls) were stored in wooden boxes or cupboards in symmetrically arranged recesses in the walls. The central section of the east side, which was two storeys high, had a gallery all round the interior at the level of the second storey, to give access to the third (topmost) tier of recesses. The two rooms on either side of the library proper were presumably reading rooms, while the two larger corner rooms, which had curved tiers of benches, were obviously lecture rooms. On each of the long sides (the north and south) there were two apsidal structures (*exedrai*) and one rectangular recess (an *oikos*) projecting from the outer walls: these six alcoves, which were roofed but open to the cloister and courtyard, were secluded places for reading, discussions, lessons and simply relaxing, for the library was evidently used for teaching and also as a quiet place for resting during the day. The central courtyard was laid out as a garden, with a long, narrow pool in the middle (see Fig. 13). In front of the west façade there was a large outer forecourt, at least 22 m. wide, paved with rectangular slabs of marble. The overall design of the building resembles that of the Templum Pacis in Rome and the Trajaneum at Italica in Spain, the birthplace of the emperors Trajan and Hadrian. The most noticeable difference is that here there was no temple for emperor-worship, but archaeological evidence – inscribed statue bases and altars in honour of Hadrian and a recently-discovered inscribed base referring to the high priest of the Divi Augusti, who held office for life – shows that the cult of the emperor was in fact practised here. Some scholars, relying on a different interpretation of a passage in Pausanias and more particularly on comparisons between this and other library buildings in Asia Minor,

***Hadrian's
Library***

13. Model of Hadrian's Library. (Rome, Museo della Civiltà Romana. Photo: German Archaeological Institute, Rome)

believe that the rites were performed in the two-storey building in the middle of the east side and that the papyrus rolls were kept in the flanking rooms, but the general consensus of opinion is that the books were kept in the two-storey building and that the centre of the emperor cult may have been the Pantheon, which lay just a short distance to the east of the library.

In A.D. 267 Hadrian's Library was very badly damaged, especially in its western and southwestern sections, when the Herulians raided and sacked Athens. Ten years later the building was incorporated in the so-called Late Roman city wall, constructed between 276 and 286. Early in the fifth century the inner courtyard and the rooms on the east side were repaired by Herculius, the governor of Illyricum (407-412), who was commemorated by a statue in the portico, to the left of the entrance, according to an extant inscription on the wall. Some archaeologists consider that it may have been in the course of that repair work that the pool was filled in and the monumental quatrefoil building which was an Early Christian church – actually the first in Athens – was erected on top of it. Others contend that the quatrefoil building was put up later, in the second quarter of the fifth century, by the Empress Eudokia (the former Athenais), the daughter of the Athenian sophist Leontios and consort of Emperor Theodosios II. It is very likely that Eudokia did endow such a splendid building, partly to bring glory on her birthplace and partly to show that Christianity was the official religion of the Empire.

In the sixth century the quatrefoil building was destroyed and in its place a large three-aisled basilica was built in the seventh century, using materials from the ruins of the earlier church. That in turn was burnt down in the eleventh century, and in the twelfth century a simple single-nave basilica was erected on the same site: it was known as the Megáli Panagia (the Great Church of Our Lady) and was the first metropolitan church (cathedral) of Athens. Also built in the twelfth century, abutting on the portico of Hadrian's Library, was the domed cruciform church of Hagios Asómatos sta Skaliá, which belonged to the Chalkokondyles family. The latter was destroyed in the sixteenth century and restored almost immediately: the wall-painting of the Last Judgment now visible under a protective cover on the upper part of the marble wall of the façade dates from that restoration. The church itself was demolished in 1849.

Further additions, alterations and new building in the Post-Byzantine era, especially in the Turkish period, so altered the appearance of Hadrian's Library that travellers to Greece from Western Europe did not realize what it was. It was not until the early nineteenth century (1816) that Col. W.M. Leake, the well-known English traveller, recognized the ruins as being all that remained of the building with a hundred columns of Phrygian marble mentioned by Pausanias.

Besides religious sanctuaries and public buildings devoted to scholarship and the arts, Hadrian (as well as other Roman benefactors) spent money on public utilities such as water supplies, drains and roads. His greatest contribution in this field was the Aqueduct, which brought water from Mt. Pentelikon to a reservoir on the lower slopes of Lykabettos (altitude 136 m.).

14. *The middle part of the façade of Hadrian's Library. (J. Stuart and N. Revett, 'The Antiquities of Athens', II, London 1762-1787)*

15. *The Monument of Philopappos. (Photo: Studio KONTOS/Photostock)*

In places the conduit was carried high above ground on arches, elsewhere it was tunnelled through the rock. The reservoir, which was repaired again and again and was still in use until

***Hadrian's
Aqueduct***

very recently, had a monumental Ionic portico which remained standing until 1778, with four Ionic columns and a free-standing arch in the middle. Another important infrastructure project was the drainage system. Sewage was carried by a network of drains into the River Eridanos, which was turned into a sewer. Part of this vaulted main sewer was found recently near Monastiráki Square during the excavation work for the new Athens Metro.

The streets of Athens were always narrow and unsurfaced, except for a few that were grav-

Roads

elled or paved with flagstones, sometimes of marble. The paved roads included a stretch of the Panathenaic Way between the Stoa of Attalos and the Eleusinion, the Broad Way between the Stoa of Attalos and the Roman Agora and the road leading from the Monument of Lysikrates to the diazoma of the Theatre of Dionysos. Hadrian also repaired the Sacred Way and built the bridge on the approach to Eleusis.

16. The Odeion of Herodes Atticus. (Photo: Studio KONTOS/Photostock)

In the Roman period the dead were buried in the old cemeteries outside the city walls: near the Acharnian Gate and the Eriai Gate, at the western foot of Lykabettos, in the deme of Koile and on the south-east slopes of the Hill of the Muses. At the summit of that hill stands the monumental tomb of the benefactor Gaius Julius Antiochus Philopappos, built in 114-116. Philopappos, by whose name the hill is now known, was a prince of the royal family of Commagene in Syria who came to Athens in A.D. 72: he was a generous benefactor to the city and held high office under the Romans. In return for his largesse the Athenians made an exception to the rule and allowed him to be buried in this imposing tomb, not merely inside the city but in a very conspicuous position facing the Acropolis. Pausanias has a vague reference to the Monument of Philopappos. It stands on a pedestal consisting of a concave wall facing north-east, with a relief frieze in the lower part and three niches for statues above. The frieze depicts the dead man driving his chariot; the central niche contains a statue of Philopappos and is flanked by a statue of his grandfather Antiochos IV and an empty niche that used to contain a statue of Seleukos, the founder of the dynasty.

Cemeteries

No picture of Roman Athens would be complete without a description of the two great monuments endowed by the sophist and orator Herodes Atticus, another generous benefactor: the Odeion that bears his name and the ancient Panathenaic Stadium, which he rebuilt.

The Odeion of Herodes Atticus, or Herodeion, was built between 160 and 175 at the west end of the south slope of the Acropolis, in memory of Herodes' deceased wife Regilla. It was a typical Roman odeion (concert hall), semicircular in plan, with a seating capacity of 5,000. It had a three-storey façade with niches for statues and lavish ornamentation, and mosaic floors. According to the sources, the roof was made of cedar and had no internal supports. It was the third odeion to be built in Athens: it was considered necessary because the Odeion of Perikles was too small and the Agrippeion was out of use since its roof had collapsed. The Herodeion was destroyed in the Herulian raid of 267. Since its restoration in 1954 it has been used every summer for theatrical performances and concerts, mainly in the Athens Festival.

Herodeion

Between 139 and 144 Herodes paid for the complete reconstruction of the Panathenaic Stadium (originally built in 330 B.C.) just across the Ilissos from the Olympieion, in the form of a Roman stadium with a semicircular sphendone and seats for 50,000 spectators. Pausanias described it as 'a wonder to behold' and Philostratos, writing a little later, called it 'a piece of work that surpasses all other marvels'. At about the same time it would appear that the bridge over the Ilissos was also rebuilt. Through the generosity of George Averoff the Stadium was restored towards the end of the nineteenth century for the first Olympic Games of the modern era, held in 1896.

Stadium

The urban development of Athens in the Roman period is characterized by new ideas, such as the perpendicular axial orientation of large buildings (while preserving the old, unplanned street layout as far as possible), frontality and theatricality in the approaches to great monuments, a scenographic rethinking of the frontages of old buildings through the addition of uniform stoas along the main streets, and the introduction of new architectural forms (Agrippeion, Roman Agora, Hadrian's Library, Pantheon) in which traditional stylistic elements interact with others from West and East. In the construction of monumental buildings a classicizing approach is clearly discernible in the use of traditional architectural styles, building materials and techniques (the Ionic order, Pentelic and Hymettian marble and Piraeus limestone, stone-dressing methods, double-T cramp-irons) and a tendency to imitate Classical buildings, especially in the Augustan era. Under Hadrian, on the other hand, we find new architectural features, building materials and techniques being used side by side with the traditional ones: arches, barrel-vaults, *opus incertum* (rubble set in cement) in foundations and also in walls, either with an outer facing (Gymnasium, Bath-house) or in combination with bands of bricks with no outer facing (the arches of the Aqueduct). A form of brick masonry known as *opus testaceum* was also used in foundations, walls and arches (Library, Aqueduct). We also find a tendency to luxury and polychromy with the use of coloured marble (Libyan in the Gymnasium, Phrygian and Karystian in the Library), alabaster, gilding and wall-paintings (mentioned in the sources in connection with the Library). A common feature of the Hadrianic buildings in Athens is the use of rusticated masonry (large regular blocks of limestone with smooth, recessed joints and the rest of the face left rough), and another is the almost exclusive use of the Corinthian order and the practice of placing free-standing columns on bases in front of walls (with which they are connected by a displaced entablature) to heighten the monumental appearance of the building. Generally speaking, in spite of all the new morphological features, the Roman buildings of the first two centuries of the Christian era blended well with the old urban structure and cultural environment of ancient Athens and enhanced the city's prestige and lustre.

17. The Panathenaic Stadium in Athens as rebuilt by Herodes Atticus in the time of Pausanias.

SELECT BIBLIOGRAPHY

Bouras, Ch., «Η Αρχιτεκτονική στην Αθήνα στα χρόνια του Αδριανού», *Αρχαιολογικά Θέματα* 1971 160-164.

Camp, J.M., *The Athenian Agora: Excavations in the Heart of Classical Athens*, London 1986, 181-214.

Graindor, P., *Athènes sous Auguste*, Cairo 1927.

—, *Athènes sous Hadrien*, Cairo 1934.

Kienast, H., 'The Tower of the Winds in Athens: Hellenistic or Roman?' in Hoff, M.C., and S.I. Rotroff (ed.), *The Romanization of Athens* (Oxbow Monograph 94), Oxford 1997, 53-67.

Kokkou, A., «Αδριάνεια έργα εις τας Αθήνας», *Αρχαιολογικόν Δελτίον* 25 (1970) Α´ Μελέται, 150-173, Pls. 47-56.

Papachadzis, N., *Παυσανίου, Ελλάδος Περιήγησις*, I: *Αττικά*, Athens 1992.

Robinson, H.., 'The Tower of the Winds and the Roman Market Place', *AJA* 7 (1943) 291-305.

Shear, T.L., Jr., 'Athens: From City-State to Provincial Town', *Hesperia* 50 (1981) 356-377.

Sisson, M.A., 'The Stoa of Hadrian at Athens', *BSR* 11 (1929) 50-72, Pls. XVII-XXVII.

Spetsieri-Choremi, A., 'Library of Hadrian at Athens: Recent Finds', *Ostraka* (Naples) 4 (1995) 137-147.

—, *Ρωμαϊκή Αγορά. Το πρώτο εμπορικό κέντρο της Αθήνας – Αρχαιολογία της πόλης των Αθηνών – Επιστημονικές-Επιμορφωτικές Διαλέξεις*, Athens (City of Athens Cultural Centre) 1996.

Travlos, J., *Πολεοδομική Εξέλιξις των Αθηνών*, Athens 1960 (2nd edn. 1993), 93-124, Pl. V.

—, *Pictorial Dictionary of Ancient Athens*, New York 1971.

Walker, Susan, 'Athens under Augustus' in Hoff, M.C., and S.I. Rotroff (ed.), *The Romanization of Athens* (Oxbow Monograph 94), Oxford 1997, 67-80.

Willers, D., *Hadrians panhellenisches Programm*, Basel 1990.

CHAPTER VII

*Athens from
Late Antiquity
to the Turkish
Conquest*

MARIA KAZANAKI-LAPPA

2. *Early Christian gravestone. Athens, Byzantine Museum. (Photo: S. Mavromatis, 2000)*

1. *Byzantine churches in Athens: Hagii Asómati sta Skaliá. J.V. Chacaton. (Athens, Benaki Museum)*

Athens from Late Antiquity
to the Turkish Conquest

'There has been preserved the very charm of the country, the temperate climate, the fruit-ful, all-productive soil, Mount Hymettos rich in honey, quiet Piraeus, the once mysterious Eleusis, the plain of Marathon beloved by horsemen, and the Acropolis itself, on which I now seem to be standing every day on the very peak of Heaven.' In these words Michael Choni-ates, the learned Archbishop of Athens in the late twelfth century, described the beauty of the Attic landscape, which remained unaffected by the great social, cultural and religious changes that had taken place over the centuries and reduced the proud city of Classical antiquity to a Byzantine provincial town 'recognizable only by the name and the hallowed ruins'.

The history of Christian Athens begins in A.D. 53, when St. Paul preached the new religion on the Pnyx in the presence of the Areopagites, summing up the spiritual message of Christianity in the resounding sentence: 'God dwelleth not in temples made with hands, neither is worshipped with men's hands.' Paul's sermon did not make much of an im-pact on the Athenians, but a small Christian community came into being with Dionysios the Areopagite as its first *episkopos* (overseer or 'bishop'). We know from a few references in the sources to the names of its bishops that the community survived for the next two centuries, but no material ev-idence of its existence has come to light. The earliest archaeological finds – gravestones with crudely incised inscriptions (Fig. 2) and clay lamps with Christian symbols (Fig. 3) – date from the mid fourth century and the first half of the fifth: they attest to the gradual infiltration of Chris-tianity into Athens and the spread of the new religion, initially among the lower classes.

Late Roman and Early Byzantine periods

In the Late Roman period Athens enjoyed one last renaissance as the intellectual and artistic centre of the Empire. Thanks to the favour shown to it by various Roman emperors and the generous benefactions of emperors and plutocrats, splendid new buildings were erect-ed in the first and second centuries A.D. and the city doubled in size in Hadrian's reign with the construction of 'New Athens' towards the River Ilissos. Pausanias, writing in the middle of the second century, has preserved for us a picture of the city and its buildings and mon-uments at the time when it was again at its zenith. However, this period of prosperity was rudely brought to an end in 267, when Athens was sacked by the Herulians, a barbarian tribe

from the North. The Herulian raid marks the end of the classical city.

Athens survived as a shadow of its former self, occupying a small area round the foot of the Acropolis. The Agora, where the only building that remained intact was the Temple of Hephaistos (the 'Theseion'), was left deserted for more than a hundred years, and the ancient Themistoklean wall, which had been repaired by the Emperor Valerian just a few years before the Herulian raid, was also abandoned. A new city wall enclosing a much smaller area was constructed between 276 and 282 with material from the ruined buildings, to protect the Athenians against further attacks by the barbarians. This wall, known as the Late Roman wall, which was henceforth to be the city's main line of defence, started along the line of the Panathenaic Way from the north-west corner of the Acropolis, just below the Propylaia, and enclosed the area round the Roman Agora and Hadrian's Library on the north side of the Acropolis and the area from the Herodeion to the Theatre of Dionysos on the south.

Recovery from the catastrophe of 267 was not long in coming. By the middle of the fourth century Athens had already re-established itself as an important educational centre to which students from all over the Empire, inspired by the ideals of Classical learning, flocked to be taught by famous teachers. It was to Athens that Libanios came to study, and here the young Julian, who as Emperor was to institute a short-lived revival of the ancient pagan religion, met two future Fathers of the Christian Church, Basil the Great and Gregory

3. Clay lamps with representations of Athena Promachos (above) and St. Peter (below). 5th-6th cent. Athens, Agora Museum. (Photo: S. Mavromatis, 2000)

of Nazianzos. In the fifth century the Academy enjoyed one last period of glory as a school of philosophy under the direction of eminent Neoplatonists, the most important of whom was Proklos. Even so, the philosopher Synesios, a future bishop of Cyrene who visited Athens from Alexandria between 395 and 399, wrote: 'There is nothing at all august about Athens except the glorious place-names.' His strictures may seem exaggerated, but it may well be that he saw the city just after Alaric and his horde of Visigoths had invaded and devastated Attica in 396, only the Late Roman wall preventing them from sacking the city as well.

The continued growth and development of Athens despite these setbacks is attested by the rapid expansion of the urban area beyond the Late Roman wall and the resurgence of building construction. In the early part of the fifth century the Academy, Hadrian's Library, the scene building of the Theatre of Dionysos, the Tholos and the Metroön were all repaired, and many new buildings were erected: the imposing Gymnasium in the Agora, a building in honour of the emperors Arkadios and Honorios near where the Metropolis now stands, private schools on the slopes of the Areopagus and to the south of the Acropolis. Throughout this period the culture of Athens remained predominantly pagan: some institutions dating back to the Classical period and some rituals belonging to the ancient cults still survived, such as the institution of the 'eponymous archon' (which lasted until 485) and the Panathenaic procession (which continued until the very end of the fifth century). Yet, despite these survivals, it is clear that the Graeco-Roman tradition was on the wane, giving way to the rise of Chris-

4. *Clay lamps with the symbol of the cross. 5th cent. Athens, Agora Museum. (Photo: S. Mavromatis, 2000)*

tianity. This slow process is reflected in the ornamentation of the clay lamps found in the excavations of the Agora and the Kerameikos district: from about the middle of the fifth century, pagan motifs are gradually replaced by the Christian symbols of the chi-rho and the cross (Figs. 3-4).

The first Christian churches in Athens also date from the mid fifth century. The marble quatrefoil church known as the Tetraconch (Fig. 5), probably an imperial foundation, was built in the courtyard of Hadrian's Library in the administrative centre of the city; and a large three-aisled basilica with mosaic floors (Figs. 6-7), sculptural ornamentation and marble revetments was built on the islet in the Ilissos next to the burial vault of Bishop Leonides of Athens. The surviving remains of these two churches testify to the splendour of the buildings and the continuity of the Graeco-Roman tradition. Five more basilicas have been found in excavations outside the city walls, as well as a great many architectural members from other Early Christian churches, which shows that the total number of churches was greater still. The building of the first Christian churches in Athens is traditionally associated with the Empress Eudokia, originally named Athenais, a daughter of the Athenian sophist Leontios who was converted to Christianity and married the Emperor Theodosios II. The story may well contain a kernel of truth, but the fact is that the Christian building boom from the mid fifth century proves that in Athens, as in the rest of the Empire, the Christian community was now much more influential with the upper classes and had no shortage of funds.

The pagan and Christian worlds continued to coexist peacefully until in 529 Justinian, in a determined bid to impose religious unity throughout his dominions, forbade pagans to teach the young and closed the Academy, probably confiscating its property at the same time. The philosophers abandoned Athens in droves, the sophists and rhetoricians found themselves without pupils. Although education could hardly have died out altogether, Justinian's measures dealt a severe blow to Athens by depriving her of much of her income and her prestige.

In the sixth century Christianity became firmly entrenched as the religion of the Byzantine Empire, and it was doubtless then that the ancient temples – which had apparently not been used since the end of the fifth century – were converted into churches. The pagan gods had been driven out for good and it was now possible for the Christian saints to supplant them in the ancient cult centres. In the second half of the sixth century the Parthenon was consecrated as a church dedicated to Our Lady (Fig. 8), having first undergone considerable alteration to fit it for the purpose: the entrance was moved to the west end and an apse was built on at the east end. Not long afterwards, in the early seventh century, the Erechtheion was converted into a three-aisled basilica (Fig. 9), the Temple of Hephaistos in the Agora became a single-nave church and the little Temple of Artemis Agrotera by the Ilissos was also converted into a church. On the south slope of the Acropolis a three-aisled basilica was built on the site of the Asklepieion and a small mortuary chapel, basilican in form, in the east parodos of the Theatre of Dionysos. The *coup de grâce* was delivered by the Slavs and Avars, who raided Athens in 582 and caused extensive damage. Most probably it was then that most of the basilicas outside the walls and the Tetraconch in the courtyard of Hadrian's Library were destroyed.

5. The ruins of the quatrefoil building (Tetraconch) in Hadrian's Library. (Photo: N. Panayotopoulos, 2000)

6. The Ilissos Basilica. Portion of mosaic floor with a representation of a wreath. Athens, Byzantine Museum. (Photo: S. Mavromatis and N. Panayotopoulos, 2000)

In the next two centuries, the so-called Dark Ages, Athens went into a state of gradual decay like all other Byzantine cities. In Athens' case, this decline was due partly to the repeated incursions of Slavs and Arabs, as well as to the major administrative, economic and social changes that transformed the cities of late antiquity – which had been autonomous centres of government and organized urban life – into medieval fortress towns. Historians and chroniclers rarely mention Athens during this period. A valuable source of information about Athens during the Dark Ages is provided by the Parthenon graffiti, which were scratched on the columns during the Early Christian and Byzantine periods. The graffiti, mostly invocations to God or memorials to the dead, attest to the unbroken continuity of life in Athens and give indirect evidence of the

Dark Ages

7. The Ilissos Basilica. Portion of mosaic floor with a representation of a stork. Athens, Byzantine Museum. (Photo: S. Mavromatis and N. Panayotopoulos, 2000)

city's ecclesiastical and administrative organization. Similar information is provided by the lead seals used by church dignitaries and government officials. The conclusion to be drawn from this circumstantial evidence is that Athens in the Dark Ages was a minor centre of civil, military and ecclesiastical administration. Its walls, which had been repaired and reinforced with square towers by Justinian, made the city safe enough for Konstans II to spend the winter of 662-663 there with his army and his large retinue.

Archaeological excavations, which have been hampered by the presence of the modern city built on the ruins of the old, have told us little about this period. In the whole of the seventh century it would seem that the only new buildings put up in the Agora were crude dwellings and small tile-yards and olive-presses in the ruins of the Tholos, the Metroön and the Gymnasium of the Giants; but a three-aisled basilica built on the ruins of the Tetraconch is dated to the seventh century and the discovery of numerous architectural reliefs from churches suggests that building construction continued on a fairly large scale. In view of the relatively large number of coins of this period found in the Agora excavations – the most numerous being those of Konstans II, doubtless because of his long stay in Athens with his army – it would seem that the city's decline set in at about the end of the seventh century. On the basis of the fragmentary evidence referred to above, combined with what we know of the history of other Byzantine cities in the same period, it is reasonable to suppose that during the Dark Ages the city did not extend beyond the Late Roman wall, its population remained small and its economy was basically agrarian. Even then, however, there must have been a flourishing local aristocracy, since two female members of the Athenian Sarantapechos family, Irene and her niece Theophano, married Byzantine emperors.

8. Marble slab, probably from the ambo of the Parthenon basilica. Athens, Byzantine Museum. (Photo: S. Mavromatis and N. Panayotopoulos, 2000)

From about the middle of the ninth century the Byzantine Empire entered on a period of reconstruction and reorganization. The consolidation of its frontiers in Asia Minor and the Balkan peninsula and the establishment of naval supremacy in the eastern Mediterranean created favourable conditions for economic development. Meanwhile the renaissance of literature and scholarship and the restoration of peace in the Church after the internecine Iconoclastic controversy gave the Empire a chance to extend its influence over neighbouring peoples and pursue a more international policy.

Middle Byzantine period

The economic recovery and the administrative reorganization helped to breathe new life into the old cities, including Athens. For administrative purposes the district of Athens belonged to the 'theme' (province) of Hellas, which had been created at the end of the seventh century. At first the capital of the theme of Hellas was Thebes, but it was probably moved to Athens in the first half of the ninth century, to judge by a graffito on one of the columns of the Parthenon referring to Leo, *Strategos* (Governor) of Hellas, who died in Athens in 848 and was probably buried on the Acropolis: *† The servant of God Leo, called Kotzes, imperial protospatharios and Strategos of Hellas, came to the end of his labours in the month of August in the year 6[3]56, 11th indiction.* At some time in the early part of the ninth century, in the course of a reorganization of the Church in Greece, the

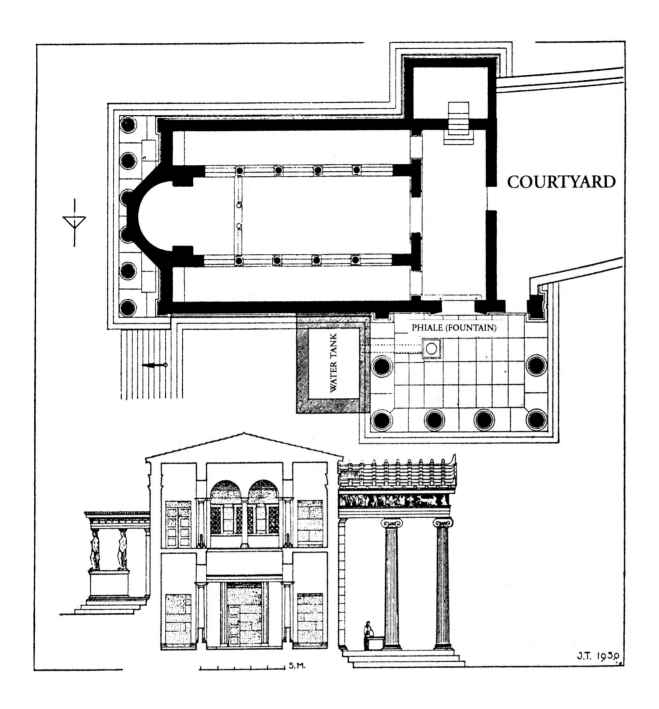

COURTYARD

PHIALE (FOUNTAIN)

WATER TANK

5.M.

J.T. 1959

9. The Erechtheion converted into a Christian church. (Drawing by J. Travlos, 1967)

bishopric of Athens was elevated to the status of an archbishopric. In an episcopal roll attributed to Emperor Leo VI 'the Wise' (886-912), giving the relative standing of the archbishoprics in the hierarchy and the number of bishoprics under their jurisdiction, Athens occupies 28th position out of 51 and has jurisdiction over ten bishoprics.

It would appear that Athens made a fairly rapid recovery, judging by the fact that the first evidence of new building construction is to be found well before the end of the ninth century. The dedicatory inscription from the Church of Hagios Ioánnis Mangoútis, a small three-aisled, wooden-roofed basilica inside the city wall on the north slope of the Acropolis, records that it was built in 871, and the oldest buildings of the Byzantine settlement in the Agora have been dated to the ninth to tenth centuries, which proves that the town had already begun to spread beyond the Late Roman wall. At about the same time the Great Church of Athens – the Parthenon in its new guise – came to be renowned throughout the Empire as a place of pilgrimage. One of its visitors was a fourteen-year-old boy named Luke who later became a hermit and whose name is now familiar from the Monastery of Ósios Loukás, founded in his honour. Another, in about 970, was Nikon Metanoites, who reconverted Crete to Christianity after the expulsion of the Arabs. In 1018 Emperor Basil II, after crushing the rebellious Bulgars, dedicated the spoils of his victory to Our Lady of Athens before returning to Constantinople.

Finds of coins afford evidence of the economic recovery. Copper *folles*, which had once been in common use but had disappeared in the eighth century, started reappearing in the ninth and had become more and more widespread by the end of the tenth. An indication of the economic growth of Athens, which reached its peak in the eleventh and twelfth centuries, is given by the large number of churches built during that period, not only inside the Late

10. Marble epistyle of an iconostasis: detail of confronted birds. Athens, Byzantine Museum. (Photo: S. Mavromatis and N. Panayotopoulos, 2000)

Roman wall and the ancient city wall but also outside the town. These churches are of the 'inscribed cross' or 'cross-in-square' type, which by this time had become standardized with certain minor variations. They are all small, gracefully proportioned buildings of compact form, and their outer walls are adorned with sawtooth bands and brickwork. The roofs are of different heights, with the cruciform core of the church standing higher than the angle-chambers, and the crossing is crowned with a slender dome adorned with arches supported on marble colonnettes. Examples of the splendid sculptural ornamentation from the interior of these churches are to be seen in the Byzantine Museum (Figs. 10-11). Some of the churches, including Hagii Apóstoli in the Agora, Kapnikaréa, Hagii Theódhori, Hagii Asómati and the Panagia Gorgoepíkoos or Little Metropolis (Fig. 13), are still standing in their original form in the city centre. Some, such as Hagios Nikólaos Rangavás, Hagía Aikateríni, the Sotíra tou Kottáki and the Metamórphosis (Fig. 14), have been much altered by subsequent rebuilding, while others, such as Profítis Ilías and the Taxiárkhes in the Roman Agora (Fig. 12) and Hagii Asómati sta Skaliá (Fig. 1), are known to us only from pictures drawn or painted by travellers long ago. A variant of the inscribed cross type, in the form of a plain octagon with a broad dome in the centre, is exemplified by the Church of the Sotíra Likodhímou, which may have been the katholikon of a monastery within the city walls. It is reasonable to suppose that many of these churches were built by members of the local aristocracy – wealthy landowners and senior government officials – who wielded great influence both economically and socially. A plaque on the wall of Hagii Theódhori bears a dedicatory inscription in verse which vividly expresses the pride of the donor, the *spatharocandidatus* Nikolaos Kalomalos, in having replaced the 'old, decaying, brick-built church' that was there before. Most probably the local aristocracy also endowed the monasteries in the countryside around Athens, the most famous of which is Dhafní, with its superb mosaics in the Constantinopolitan style.

Demographic growth followed in the train of economic prosperity. Excavations in the Agora, on the slopes of the Areopagus and the south slope of the Acropolis, in the Kerameikos district and around the Olympieion, and more recently north of the Agora and beneath Síndagma Square, have shown that those areas were densely populated and that the city had by now outgrown the Late Roman wall. The houses in question were simple dwellings built of cheap materials, often on top of the rubble of earlier buildings, with a few rooms ranged round a small internal courtyard and cellars containing large *pithoi* (storage jars) embedded in the floor for storing oil, grain and so on. They were obviously the homes of middle-class and lower-class families, and it is clear that these neighbourhoods had simply grown at random, with no sort of planning.

11. Marble slab with guilloche ornament and rosettes. 12th cent. Athens, Byzantine Museum. (Photo: S. Mavromatis and N. Panayotopoulos, 2000)

A fragmentary but extremely interesting picture of Athens in the Middle Byzantine period is given by a document of the eleventh or twelfth century, part of a register of the properties belonging to an ecclesiastical institution in Athens, probably a big monastery, and of the *paroikoi* or serfs working on those lands. Each entry lists the nature of the property (field, vineyard, etc.), the names of the neighbours, the dimensions and the area of land. The *paroikoi* are listed village by village, with their names, the number of family members and the taxable potential of each family. This precious document gives the names of forty villages or localities and over a hundred families in Attica.

Athens is listed in the register as the *kastro* or citadel, a term commonly used of Byzantine towns, which makes it clear that the main function of a town was to provide a safe refuge for the inhabitants of the surrounding country in the event of attack by enemies. The register lists thirteen large fields actually within the *kastro*, that is within the city walls, most of them bounded on one side by the 'imperial wall' and surrounded by houses and churches on the other sides. Their location is denoted by such phrases as 'in the neighbourhood of the Tzykanitzerion', 'in the locality of the Elaphos', 'below the Epano Porta' and 'below the neighbourhood of the Konchylarioi'. The 'imperial wall' is the ancient city wall, which presumably was the outer limit of the town and was probably so called because it had been repaired by Justinian. The large size of the fields and their location just inside the walls shows that much of the walled town was rural in character and that most of the agricultural land was near the perimeter. The Epano Porta or Upper Gate is probably to be identified with the ancient Dipylon Gate leading in to the Agora: at that time, according to the land register, the area near the Dipylon was woodland with some ancient buildings and Christian churches.

The town was officially divided into 'neighbourhoods'. The Tzykanitzerion district was probably in the north of the town and took its name from the ground where *tzykanion* was played: this was a form of polo which is known to have been popular with aristocrats in many Byzantine cities and towns. We know of three churches in this neighbourhood: the Pródhromos, the Church of Christ and the Church of the Panagia. The neighbourhood of the Konchylarioi (from *konchylion*, a seashell) was presumably so called because the fishers of murex shells, highly valued as a source of purple dye for silks, lived there. The Athenians are known to have engaged in the murex trade since ancient times. The discovery of deposits of such shells in earlier excavations near the Herodeion suggest that the area where the murex fishers had their workshops, and probably their homes as well, was between the Acropolis

12. *Byzantine churches in Athens: Profítis Ilías and the Taxiárkhes. From T. du Moncel, 'Vues pittoresques'. (Athens, Benaki Museum)*

13. *Byzantine churches in Athens: the Panagia Gorgoepíkoos. From T. du Moncel,* Vues pittoresques. *(Athens, Benaki Museum)* ☞

and the Hill of the Muses. In the locality of the Elaphos (Deer) we have documentary evidence of the Church of Hagía Marína, the Monastery of Hagios Dhionísios and the Church of Hagios Ísavros. This neighbourhood must have been to the north-west of the Acropolis near the Hill of the Nymphs, because we find references to 'immovable rocks' and 'the cliffs of the mountain', and also because the remains of the Monastery of Hagios Dhionísios Areopayítis and the Church of Hagía Marína have been found thereabouts.

The economy was basically agricultural, as it was in all the cities and towns of the Byzantine Empire. The produce of the surrounding countryside – grain, oil from the olive-groves covering most of the plain of Athens, resinated wine, the far-famed Hymettos honey, beeswax and a few livestock products – was barely enough to meet local demand. Archaeological evidence indicates that there was also a certain amount of manufacturing: potters' kilns for making everyday household utensils have been found in the neighbourhood of the Roman Agora

and on the Areopagus, an olive-press and a tannery near the Olympieion and a small soap factory in the Kerameikos district. Most of the manufactured products were doubtless made for the local market, but the soap and the purple dye were probably intended for the flourishing silk industry in Thebes. Athens must also have been something of a trading centre, since it was one of the towns where the Venetians were given free trade rights by a chrysobull of Alexios I in 1082 – a privilege that was renewed by other emperors in the twelfth century.

In form, Athens during this period was a typical Middle Byzantine town with its citadel (the Acropolis) and the lower town huddled round it. Three concentric fortification walls – the Acropolis ramparts, the Late Roman wall and the 'imperial wall' – divided it into three zones. This threefold division, found in other Byzantine towns as well, corresponded to separate economic and ideological functions of the town and mirrored the clear-cut social stratification of its inhabitants. Inside the citadel of the Acropolis were the metropolitan church (cathedral) of the Panagia Athiniótissa, the archbishop's residence and the offices of the archbishopric. The administrative and economic centre was within the perimeter of the Late Roman wall and so too, probably, were the homes of the upper classes, senior government officials and church dignitaries. The greater part of the town lay between the Late Roman wall and the ancient city wall: residential neighbourhoods interspersed with churches, workshops and craft centres. The main roads followed the general lines of the ancient street plan, but they were now narrower and more winding owing to the intrusion of middle-class and working-class houses. Athens was to remain divided into three zones for several hundred years, as is evident from a letter written by Symeon Kabasilas to Martin Crusius in 1578: 'In the old days Athens was a city of three zones and all of it was inhabited. Now the inner zone ... is entirely inhabited by Ishmaelites [i.e. Muslims]. The zone outside that (I mean the middle zone) is entirely inhabited by Christians. Of the outermost zone, one third is inhabited.'

In the middle of the twelfth century the Arab geographer Edrisi described Athens as a populous city surrounded by gardens and farmland. By 1182, however, when Michael Choniates arrived from Constantinople to be installed as Archbishop of Athens, things had evidently changed. Choniates had had an excellent classical education and knew all about the city's glorious past. His letters present a picture of a town that not only bore no trace of its ancient splendour but had lost all semblance of a city and the very form and condition of a city'. The fortification walls were in ruins, where there had been houses there were now fields and market gardens, the streets were deserted and the people were dressed in rags. The town was suffering from extortionate taxation and arbitrary behaviour by the

14. Byzantine churches in Athens: the Metamór- phosis. From A.M. Chenavard, 'Voyage en Grèce', Lyon 1858. (Athens, Benaki Museum)

Byzantine officials, oppression by the oligarchy of the rich, food shortages and pirate raids. The poorest inhabitants had no option but to migrate away from Athens, with the result that 'there was not a bellows-maker to be found, we had no blacksmith, no coppersmith and no knife-maker, and all these existed yesterday and the day before.' In his speeches Choniates alternated between admonishing, castigating and flattering the visiting judges from Constantinople, he wrote letters to people with political influence and even a memorandum to the emperor, but all to no avail: the situation appears to have remained essentially unchanged. Choniates was a scholarly man from the imperial capital who was getting his first taste of the realities of life in the provinces, and his descriptions of Athens may contain an element of exaggeration, but they do give us a good insight into the decadence of the civil and military administration and the dominance of the Church in provincial towns towards the close of the twelfth century.

At the beginning of 1204, when Athens was attacked by Leo the Curly-headed, the ruler of Nauplion, Choniates brought all the population up on to the Acropolis for safety and organized a successful defence of the town. However, at the end of that year he had to surrender to the army of the Fourth Crusade. He himself, after seeing 'the most blest and illustrious sanctuary in Athens desecrated and despoiled' and his library looted, and after spending a year travelling from town to town in Greece, he went to live on the island of Kea and stayed there until 1217. The last years of his life he spent at the Pródhromos Monastery at Mendhenítsa, near Thermopylai, where he died in 1222. Wall-paintings depicting Choniates in his archiepiscopal vestments (Fig. 15) in two churches, Hagios Pétros at Kalívia Kouvará (12th-13th cent.) and the Chapel of the Pendéli Cave (1233/34), both painted after his death, show that he was venerated locally by the people of Attica.

15. Portrait of Michael Choniates. Wall-painting, 12th-13th cent. Church of Hagios Pétros, Kalívia Kouvará, Attica.

For the next two hundred and fifty years after 1204, when Constantinople and much of the Empire were conquered by the armies of the Fourth Crusade, Athens was ruled by 'Franks', i.e. Western Europeans: first two French noble families, de la Roche and de Brienne (1204-1311), then by the knights of the Catalan Company (1311-1388) and finally **Frankish period**
by the Florentine Acciaiuoli family. Apart from a few years when they were ousted by the Venetians (1395-1403), the Acciaiuoli stayed in Athens until 1456, when the Turks captured the town and put an end to the period of Frankish rule.

All these Catholic rulers tried to transplant the feudal system and the precepts of medieval chivalry on to Greek soil. The first Frankish ruler, the Burgundian nobleman Otho de

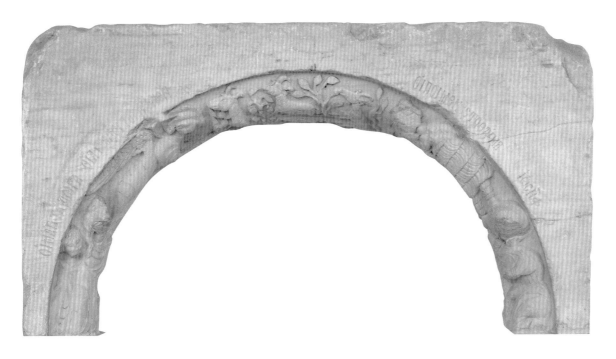

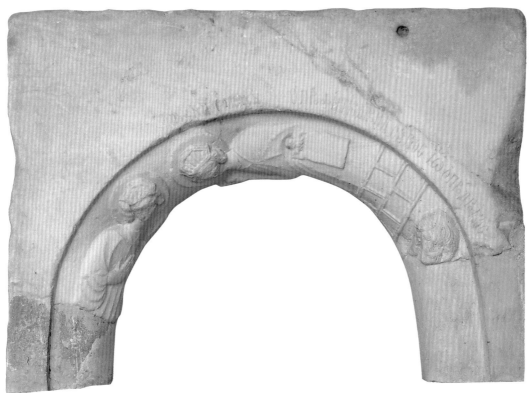

16. *Arches with reliefs of the Nativity and the Descent into Hell. 13th cent. Athens, Byzantine Museum. (Photo: S. Mavromatis and N. Panayotopoulos, 2000)*

la Roche, was awarded Athens as his fief by Boniface of Montferrat in recognition of services rendered on the Fourth Crusade, and he was given the title of Dominus Athenarum or Sire d'Athènes, which was translated in to Greek as Megas Kyres (usually rendered by English writers as Megaskyr or Grand Seigneur). In 1259 Louis IX of France conferred the title of Duke of Athens on Otho's successor, Guy I, and thereafter the territory was known as the Duchy of Athens. It comprised the whole of Attica, the Megaris and Boiotia and from time to time was enlarged to include parts of the Peloponnese and Central Greece.

One of the first concerns of the new French rulers was to strengthen the fortifications of the Castel de Setines, as Athens was now called. A new wall known as the Rizókastro was built at the foot of the Acropolis in the first half of the thirteenth century, incorporating sections of the Late Roman wall on the south slope. Around the middle of the century a stout rampart was built blocking the main entrance of the Acropolis: the way into the citadel was diverted through the gate below the bastion of the Temple of Athena Nike, which now became a fortified bastion in the proper sense of the word. The Klepsydra Spring was fortified and made accessible from the Acropolis by way of a staircase and the new north gate below the Propylaia. After all these alterations, which took some years, the Acropolis became a real medieval fortress. Inside the enceinte the Parthenon was converted into a Catholic church, the Erechtheion into the Catholic bishop's palace and the Propylaia, which had previously been the residence of the Orthodox archbishop, into the ducal palace. The Burgundians ruled their duchy wisely for more than a hundred years, during which time Athens was a relatively peaceful and safe place to live. Piracy was suppressed, Venetian and Genoese merchants settled in Athens and also in Thebes, which developed into a major centre of the silk industry. A set of marble reliefs now in the Byzantine Museum, made in Athens and dated to the second half of the thirteenth century, attests to the high standards achieved by Athenian artists as well as their borrowing of iconographic elements from Western art (Fig. 16).

The period of French rule ended when the knights of the Catalan Company, a band of roving mercenaries (called Almughavars in the Byzantine sources) who had on occasion fought on the side of the Byzantine Emperor, offered their services to the Duke of Athens but then quarrelled with him, defeated the French army at the battle of Almyros in 1311 and occupied Thebes and Athens. Wishing to legalize their régime and win international backing, the Catalans offered the suzerainty of the duchy first to the kings of Sicily and then to the kings of Aragon, who took the title of Duke of Athens and appointed regents to exercise power in their names. Thebes became the capital of the duchy, Catalan was made one of the official languages (together with Latin) and the legislation governing relations between the foreign overlords and the native population was based on the law of Barcelona. It was illegal for the local inhabitants to own real property or to make mixed marriages, and the only public office they were allowed to hold was that of notary.

The sources mention the names of two Greek notaries in Athens, Nikolaos Makris and Demetrios Rentis from whom the modern Athenian district of Hagios Ioánnis Réndis takes its name). The Catalans ruled the duchy with a ruthless and oppressive hand. According to Nikephoros Gregoras, who got his information from a man who had travelled in the duchy,

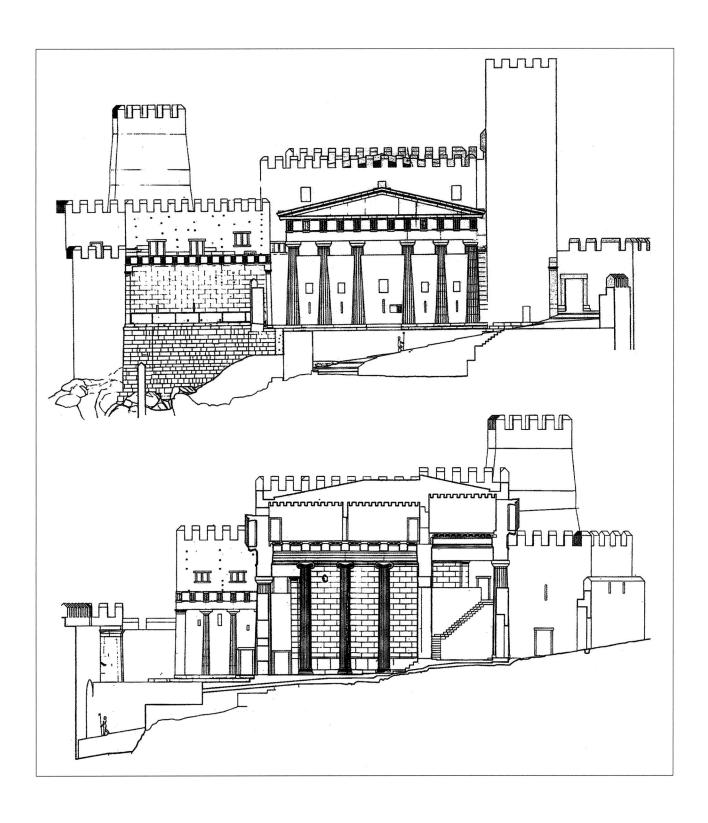

17. The Propylaia converted into a Florentine palazzo by the Acciaiuoli. (Drawings by T. Tanoulas)

by the mid fourteenth century the Athenians and Thebans had been reduced to 'the direst slavery and had exchanged their former prosperity for the life of peasants'.

In 1388 the military occupation by the Catalans gave way to the rule of the Florentine family of Acciaiuoli. The new rulers moved the capital from Thebes back to Athens, reinstated the Orthodox archbishop and made Greek the official language. Under their rule the social and economic situation took a turn for the better, living conditions improved for the local people and some Athenian families, such as the Chalkokondyles family, acquired considerable power. The first two dukes, Nerio I (1387-1395) and his son Antonio (1403-1435) converted the Propylaia into a grand Florentine palazzo (Fig. 17), beautified the Church of Santa Maria di Setines, in other words the Parthenon, restored churches and repaired the roads. It was the Acciaiuoli, too, who built the tall 'Frankish Tower' in the south wing of the Propylaia. The massive bulk of the tower, which was demolished in 1874, stands out incongruously among the Classical monuments in all the early travellers' prints and paintings and in the first photographs of the Acropolis – a relic of an alien cultural tradition and a reminder of the historical train of events that brought the 'Frankish' knights to Athens.

Throughout the Frankish period Athens remained a small town confined within the perimeter of the Late Roman wall. Its population during the period of Catalan rule has been estimated at between five and six thousand. Nicoló da Martoni, an Italian notary from Capua who visited Athens in 1395 on his way home from the Holy Land, estimated the number of houses at about a thousand. He walked all over the town, went up to the Kastro (as he called the Acropolis), admired the great Church of Santa Maria and took notes which, though naive, are not inaccurate. Another Italian traveller, Ciriaco d'Ancona, a humanist and pioneering archaeologist, made two journeys to Athens in 1436 and 1444. He admired the ancient monuments, copied out inscriptions and was the first person for several hundred years to use the ancient names of the Acropolis and 'the Temple of Pallas, a marvellous building by Pheidias'. A few years later, in 1456, the last Florentine duke surrendered the town to the Turks, an event that signalled the end of the Middle Ages in Greece and the start of a new chapter in Athens' long history.

BIBLIOGRAPHY

Bouras, Ch., «Πολεοδομικά των μεσοβυζαντινών και υστεροβυζαντινών πόλεων», *Δελτίον της Χριστιανικής Αρχαιολογικής Εταιρείας* 20 (1998-1999) 89-98.

Chatzidakis, M., *Βυζαντινή Αθήνα*, Athens 1958.

Frantz, Alison, *The Athenian Agora*, XXIV: *Late Antiquity: A.D.* 267-700, Princeton 1988.

Granstrem, E., I. Medvedev and D. Papachryssanthou, 'Fragment d'un praktikon de la région d'Athènes (avant 1204)', *Revue des études byzantines* 34 (1976) 5-43.

Gregorovius, F., and S. Lampros, *Ιστορία της πόλεως των Αθηνών κατά τους μέσους αιώνας*, I-II, Athens 1904.

Herrin, Judith, 'Realities of Byzantine Provincial Government: Hellas and Peloponnesos 1180-1205', *Dumbarton Oaks Papers* 29 (1975) 255-287.

Lampros, S., *Αι Αθήναι περί τα τέλη του δωδεκάτου αιώνος*, Athens 1878.

—, *Μιχαήλ Ακομινάτου του Χωνιάτου Τα Σωζόμενα*, I-II, Athens 1879-1880.

Makri, E., K. Tsakos and A. Vavylopoulou-Charitonidou, «Το Ριζόκαστρο, Σωζόμενα υπολείμματα: νέες παρατηρήσεις και επαναχρονολόγηση», *Δελτίον της Χριστιανικής Αρχαιολογικής Εταιρείας* 14 (1987-1988) 329-366.

Miller, W., *Ιστορία της Φραγκοκρατίας εν Ελλάδι* (= *The Latins in the Levant: A History of Frankish Greece*, London 1908, tr. with additions and improvements by S. Lampros), I-II, Athens 1909-1910.

Moschonas, N., «Η τοπογραφία της Αθήνας κατά τη βυζαντινή και μεταβυζαντινή περίοδο» in *Αρχαιολογία της πόλης των Αθηνών*, Athens 1996, 137-156.

Orlandos, A.K., and L. Vranoussis, *Τα χαράγματα του Παρθενώνος*, Athens 1973.

Setton, K., *Catalan Domination of Athens*, 1311-1388, Cambridge Mass. 1948, revised and expanded edn. London (Variorum Reprints) 1975.

—, *Athens in the Middle Ages*, London (Variorum Reprints) 1975.

Sotiriou, G., A. Xyngopoulos and A. Orlandos, *Ευρετήριο των Μεσαιωνικών Μνημείων της Ελλάδος*, I-III, Athens, 1927-1930.

Tanoulas, T., *Τα Προπύλαια της Αθηναϊκής Ακρόπολης κατά τον Μεσαίωνα*, I-II, Athens 1997.

Thompson, H.A., 'Athenian Twilight: *A.D.* 267-600', *Journal of Roman Studies* 49 (1959) 61-72.

Travlos, J., *Πολεοδομική εξέλιξις των Αθηνών από των προϊστορικών χρόνων μέχρι των αρχών του 19ου αιώνος*, Athens 1960, 75-92.

—, 'Athen' in *Reallexicon zur byzantinische Kunst*, Stuttgart 1966, I 349-389.

CHAPTER VIII

*Middle Byzantine
Athens: Planning
and Architecture*

CHARALAMBOS BOURAS

2. The ruins of the portico of Hadrian's Library and the door of the Monastery(?) of Hagii Asómati sta Skaliá in 1672. (Drawing by J. Carrey, from H. Omont, 'Athènes au XVIIᵉ siècle', Paris 1898)

1. The Church of Hagii Anáryiri in the Psirrí district of Athens before the alteration of the exterior in 1908. (T. Stademan, 'An Ort und Stelle aufgenommen und herausgegeben', Munich 1847)

Middle Byzantine Athens: Planning and Architecture

Although the political hegemony of Athens in antiquity was limited to the fifth century B.C., her cultural hegemony lasted a great deal longer – in fact until the end of the ancient era and the eventual triumph of Christianity. In the Classical, Hellenistic and Roman worlds Athens always had a reputation as a great cultural centre, acquired through a unique combination of circumstances in the fifth and fourth centuries B.C.; and that reputation was continually renewed by a host of scholars, philosophers, artists and art-lovers, collectors and foreign rulers who visited the city and were overwhelmed by the brilliance of its intellectual and cultural heritage.

Athens in the Middle Ages was just a small town, a shadow of her former self: gone was her ancient code of values; the products of her ancient civilization had been taken into the care of the imperial capital, Constantinople; and the ancient monuments still standing in Athens were neglected and in disrepair. And yet, even for the most ignorant visitor, the town still possessed an aura of departed grandeur, wisdom and elevated standards.

In the so-called Dark Ages, from the late sixth to the mid ninth century, it is notoriously difficult to trace the history of almost all Byzantine provincial towns or even to be sure whether they continued to exist. In the case of Athens, however, we have firm documentary evidence to prove that the thread of continuity was never broken, and that fact is not unconnected with the city's ancient fame and the security offered by its citadel, the Acropolis, and the excellent natural harbour of Piraeus. Even when the Byzantine Empire was at its lowest ebb, in the mid seventh century, Athens remained a small but secure centre of habitation. During Byzantium's economic, demographic and cultural revival, from 900 onwards, Athens – like other towns in Greece – was reorganized and entered a period of modest manufacturing activity.

The way was opened for Athens' rise to prosperity during the Middle Byzantine period in 961, when the future emperor Nikephoros Phokas captured Crete and rid the Aegean of the Arab menace; and conditions became still more favourable not long afterwards when Emperor Basil II ('the Bulgar-Slayer') brought the Bulgarian wars to an end. When Basil himself came to Greece in 1018 to reorganize the Empire's Greek provinces, he made a point of going to pray in the Church of the Panagia Athiniótissa, which was none other than the Parthenon: the building still retained its ancient prestige, and by this act of worship he linked his own victorious campaigns with a unique historic monument and with history itself.

Middle Byzantine Athens, then, was a country town in the Theme (province) of Hellas, far from the imperial capital, Constantinople, with a small local aristocracy of landowners. The nearest towns were Thebes (the headquarters of the military governor of Hellas) and Corinth. Athens was the seat of an archbishopric whose jurisdiction extended to Euboia, some towns in Roúmeli and some of the nearby islands. It was also the centre of an area of fairly fertile agricultural land.

Documentary records of Athens during this period are scarce and patchy. A copy of a *praktikon* (land register) of the eleventh or twelfth century, brought to light only twenty years ago, provides a certain amount of information about the various districts of the town and about medieval place-names in Athens and the surrounding country. But for the richest source of documentary material we have to turn to the writings of Michael Choniates, brother of the historian Niketas Choniates. Michael Choniates, an extremely learned scholar with a wide knowledge of ancient Greek literature, who lived in Constantinople and was Archbishop of Athens for the last twenty years of the twelfth century, yearned for the Athens of classical antiquity and was grievously disappointed in what he found: a poor, run-down town with uneducated inhabitants and its ancient monuments in ruins. We cannot be sure whether his picture of desolation and poverty is simply a rhetorical device intended to emphasize the contrast with the

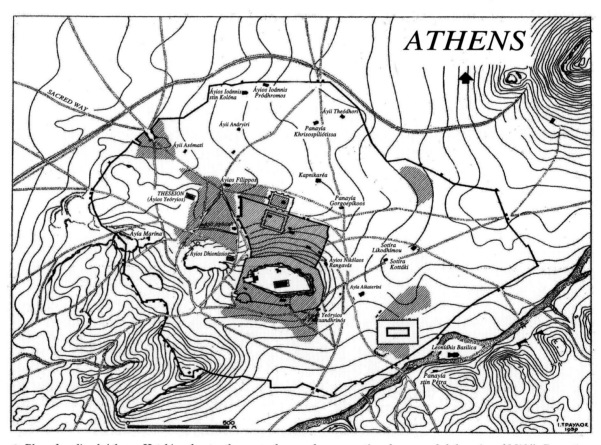

3. Plan of medieval Athens. Hatching denotes the areas where modern excavations have revealed the ruins of Middle Byzantine houses. (J. Travlos, «Πολεοδομική εξέλιξις των Αθηνών», Athens 1960, with additions)

city's glorious past or whether Athens had in fact been sacked just before Choniates arrived there, but there is no documentary evidence of any such disaster. Whatever the truth of the matter, modern historians have relied largely on his testimony in analysing the economic and political conditions prevailing in the southern half of Greece under the later Komnenos emperors and the Angelos dynasty.

The strictly historical evidence is therefore very limited, very sketchy and sometimes difficult to interpret. Much more information is provided indirectly by the material remains, which tell us that the town made continuous progress, both economically and demographically, from the middle of the tenth century until the Fourth Crusade in 1204. Athens was a tiny place by present-day standards, and not easily accessible from Constantinople, but in comparison with other Byzantine provincial towns it was by no means inconsiderable, either in size or architecturally.

The urban development and architecture of Athens in the Middle Byzantine period is a very interesting topic, but one that has been sadly neglected. The only scholarly work that has been written on this subject as a whole – the eighth chapter of John Travlos's book on the urban development of Athens – came out forty years ago. Travlos took part in the great excavations carried out by the American School of Classical Studies in the Athenian Agora, and so he had first-hand experience of the wealth of information to be obtained from systematic excavation.

Research to date

He was the first person to draw a general plan of the city showing not only the Byzantine churches and fortification walls but also the areas in which the remains of Byzantine houses had been found. On the subject of Middle Byzantine churches in Athens, Travlos gave some general facts, compiled a bibliography and listed every source of information concerning the churches that no longer exist and are known only from pictures and descriptions.

Since 1960, when Travlos's book was published, a great deal of new evidence has emerged, mostly from unscheduled rescue excavations in the city centre. However, no systematic efforts have been made as yet to reconstruct the shape of the medieval town of Athens. Any such project should be based on the following:

(a) The ancient monuments that were landmarks in the medieval town. Some of them were in a much better state of preservation in the Middle Ages than they are now.

(b) The Middle Byzantine monuments of Athens, mainly churches, including those that survive to the present day and those known only from pictures or architectural drawings. They should be studied most particularly in relation to their environment.

(c) Monuments of which nothing remains today except low walls, floors and foundations discovered in archaeological excavations.

(d) A fresh attempt to interpret Byzantine written sources directly or indirectly concerned with the topography, architecture or general appearance of the town.

The ancient heritage was undoubtedly the most striking visual element in the medieval town. The Acropolis commanded the whole scene by virtue of its height and bulk, and in the eleventh and twelfth centuries the Parthenon looked completely undamaged, at any rate from the outside. It had been converted into a Christian church in the reign of Justinian the Great and attracted pilgrims from all over the Empire, as we know from hagiographical writings. In the time of Michael Choniates and his predecessor, Nikolaos Hagiotheodorites, the Parthenon underwent some major repairs and alterations, about which several articles and studies have been written recently. The bema apse was renovated and adorned with a majuscule inscription of which fragments survive; a spiral staircase was built to the right of the main (west) entrance to the church; and two water cisterns were built, one on either side of the apse. The interior was in the form of a three-aisled basilica, but the spaces between the Doric columns of the interior peristyle had been walled up to create an ambulatory separate from the body of the church.

Ancient monuments in the medieval town

As for the second temple on the Acropolis, the Erechtheion, we have no idea what is was used for in the Middle Byzantine period, but it was definitely still in good condition. The Propylaia still had its façades and its ancient marble ceilings. Part of it had been converted for use as the residence of the Archbishop of Athens, as Michael Choniates informs us in his letters, and a small chapel – the ruins of which were removed by classical archaeologists a hundred years ago – had been built on to its north wall. Lastly, the little Temple of Athena Nike was still standing almost intact *in situ*, in front of the Propylaia and surrounded by its own wall.

Down in the town there were other conspicuous ancient monuments in a good state of preservation. The Temple of Hephaistos and Athena (the so-called 'Theseion') was being used as the Church of St. George and was in excellent condition. The Ionic Temple of Artemis Agrotera on the banks of the Ilissos was

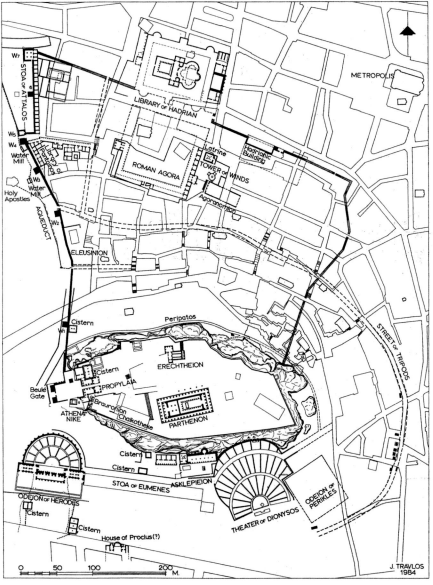

4. Plan of the centre of Athens showing the line of the Late Roman wall superimposed on the modern street plan of the Pláka. (Drawn by J. Travlos, from Alison Frantz, 'The Middle Ages in the Athenian Agora')

the Church of the Blessed Virgin, known as the Panagia stin Pétra. In the Agora, the statues from the Stoa of the Giants stood tall amid the huddle of small houses, but the Temple of Ares had been almost entirely demolished and was used as a 'quarry' for white Pentelic marble.

The same fate would seem to have befallen the gigantic Temple of Olympian Zeus in the eastern outskirts of the town: certainly eighty of its 104 Corinthian columns had collapsed by the middle of the fifteenth century, though we do not know exactly when. Hadrian's Library, which was the site of the market in medieval times, still had its four-columned portico; between two of the columns was the door of a small monastery (?) of the Middle Byzantine period. The

two theatres south of the Acropolis lay buried, but their façades were still visible above ground. The learned Michael Choniates identified the Are-opagus and the temples on the Acropolis, but he thought that the ruins of the Stoa of Attalos were the Stoa Poikile or Painted Stoa (dating from Kimon's time), which he had read about.

Besides these there were other ancient monuments of less impor-tance that were local landmarks, such as Hadrian's Arch, the west propylon of the Roman Agora and the Monu-ment of Philopappos. The quatrefoil building in the courtyard of Hadri-an's Library and the choregic monu-ment of Thrasyllos had been rebuilt as churches, both dedicated to the Blessed Virgin.

5. Reconstruction drawing of the east end of the Parthenon in the twelfth century, with water cisterns on either side of the apse. (M. Korres)

Of the buildings erected during the period under examination, those still standing include a con-siderable number of churches – certainly more than in any other town in Greece. One can fair-ly say that the ancient Athenians' love of religious architecture lasted right through to the Mid-dle Ages. It is significant that in 1830, when Athens was liberated from the Turks, there were no less than 120 Byzantine and Post-Byzantine churches in the town.

Only twenty-five of those are still standing today, plus some others that have been drastically altered by later additions and restorations. One major factor contributing to the survival of so many Byzantine **Middle Byzantine church architecture** buildings was the privilege granted to the Athenians by Mehmet the Conqueror, who decreed in 1458 that no churches in Athens except the Parthenon were to be converted into mosques.

Very little historical evidence is available concerning the Byzantine churches of Athens. We cannot be sure which of them were small monastery churches or private chapels, nor what their immediate surroundings were like at that time. Since there are hardly any surviving inscriptions, the only way of dating them is by stylistic comparison, and on that evidence it would appear that nearly all of them were built in the tenth, eleventh and twelfth centuries. Certain similarities between them as regards their architectural type, morphology and construction methods prompted Gabriel Millet to classify them together in what he called 'the Helladic school of Byzantine architecture'. None of these churches are imperial foundations and all of them are small, but they are notable for their clarity of line, well-balanced proportions and excellent construction.

A common feature of all the Middle Byzantine churches in Athens is the abundance and high quality of their marble sculptural ornamentation – iconostases, door frames, window colonnettes, icon stands, sarcophagi and other objects of carved marble. Many of these are still *in situ* in the churches for which they were made, but many others are in museums and scattered in archaeological sites in Athens. The Byzantine Museum has what is undoubtedly the biggest collection of Middle Byzantine sculpture in the world, but unfortunately not all of it has been published. This abundance of ornamental sculpture must have been mainly due to the plentiful availability of white Pentelic marble from ruined temples, as already mentioned; but there are so many items of sculptured marble from the eleventh and twelfth centuries that it is hard to believe they all come from demolished churches in Athens. Most probably many of them were pieces of decorative stonework carved in Athenian marble workshops for sale outside the town.

6. The ruins of the Temple of Artemis Agrotera by the River Ilissos, rebuilt as the Church of the Panagia stin Pétra. (J. Stuart and N. Revett, 'The Antiquities of Athens', London 1762-1830)

Architectural activity had started in Athens two or three centuries before the period under consideration, with the construction of smaller churches that have not survived. Among those built in the tenth century were the katholikon of the Asómati Monastery (known as the Moní Petráki after the family that refounded it in the seventeenth century) and the demolished Church of Profítis Ilías in the Staropázaro. Both these fine churches are of the domed cruciform type, which was then prevalent in the Byzantine Empire.

The first of the elaborate churches with the characteristic features of the 'Helladic school' were built round about the year 1000. One of them is the Hagii Apóstoli in the Agora (sometimes known by the name of the Solakis family), whose morphological features – horizontal denticulated bands and ornamental brickwork with Arabic Kufic lettering in the walls, the octagonal dome with double-light windows and arched cornices, the marble inlay in the floor, as well as the high quality of the workmanship – show a close affinity with the Church of the Panagia at Ósios Loukás Monastery in Fokás. Typologically, Hagii Apóstoli is unique: its general plan is more or less circular, with eight apses symmetrically placed round the circumference and four columns in the centre supporting four arches and the dome. All these features prove that there was a very good architect working in the provincial town of Athens at that time: an architect who was familiar with the innovative trends then emanating from Ósios Loukás and was also looking for new forms for church interiors.

Hagii Theódhori (1049?), founded by a high-ranking official in the Byzantine government, has some typological peculiarities and is adorned with relief ceramic plaques bearing decorative designs and Arabic lettering. Fragments of the marble iconostasis can be seen built into the walls of the later bell-tower. Kapnikaréa, built in the eleventh century, is notable for its beautiful proportions: it is also a domed cruciform church, with the addition of an arcaded narthex and a graceful two-columned portico at the west end. The Metamórphosis on the north slope of the Acropolis and the Hagii Asómati near the 'Theseion' are fairly similar to each other. Hagios Nikólaos Rangavás, built by the aristocratic Rangavás family, was much altered in the nineteenth century but was successfully restored about ten years ago.

Features common to all these churches include the very fine masonry of their exterior walls, the marble door frames, marble window colonnettes and octagonal domes of the type known to scholars as 'Athenian', although the archetype was the dome of the Church of the Panagia at Ósios Loukás. There were other churches with the same kind of dome in Athens, but some of them are no longer standing and others (including the Sotíra tou Kottáki, the Taxiárkhis in the Roman Agora, Hagii Asómati sta Skaliá and Hagios Geórgios Alexandhrinós) have been remodelled in modern times. Finally, the Sotíra tou Likodhímou, the biggest of the churches under consideration, is unquestionably the oldest and closest copy of the katholikon of Ósios Loukás, with its octagonal

7. *Hagii Apóstoli in the Agora, from the south-west. (Photo: S. Mavromatis, 2000)*

8. *Hagii Theódhori. (Photo: N. Panayotopoulos, 2000)*

9. *Hagios Nikólaos Rangavás: the north side. (Photo: N. Panayotopoulos, 2000)*

10. *The Ómorfi Ekklisía in Galátsi, with the slightly later single-nave chapel built on to its south side. (Photo: S. Mavromatis, 2000)*

drum supporting a broad and relatively low dome. It was probably the katholikon of a monastery. It was drastically altered after the War of Independence and is now generally known as the Russian church, as it has been the parish church of the Russian community in Athens since 1847.

The little church of Hagios Ioánnis Theológos in the quarter of the Pláka dates from the twelfth century, as does the Megáli Panagia in Hadrian's Library, now demolished, about which quite a lot is known from descriptions and pictures. The Panagia Gorgoepíkoos, also known as the Little Metropolis, was built in the late twelfth century and is made entirely of material taken from the ruins of ancient Greek, Roman, Early Christian and Byzantine buildings. Its outer walls are a unique and highly picturesque collage of assorted reliefs put together in 'sweet disorder' and saturated with evocative allusions to two thousand years of Greek history. The Gorgoepíkoos is thus at once a Byzantine church and an exhibition of ancient art of indeterminate date. Manolis Chatzidakis suggested that it was probably built by Michael Choniates in token of his love of the city's ancient past.

Within a fairly short radius of Athens, in the area now covered by suburbs, a number of cenobitic monasteries were built in the Middle Byzantine period: their katholika are of considerable architectural interest and their interiors are adorned with religious paintings. In Galátsi, north of the city centre, the twelfth-century Ómorfi Ekklisía still stands in an excellent state of preservation. Two churches on the slopes of Mt. Hymettos, Hagios Ioánnis Kynigós and the katholikon of Kaisarianí Monastery, are of the same period. The latter, a domed cruciform church, is notable for its graceful proportions and its excellent construction. Dhafní Monastery, on the road out to Mégara and the Peloponnese, was a much bigger foundation, yet contemporary written sources have nothing to say about it. Its katholikon is fairly large and of a similar type to the Sotíra tou Likodhímou: in other words, it is a copy of the katholikon of Ósios Loukás. In the twelfth century a two-storey open-fronted colonnade, made with graceful Ionic columns taken from an unidentified building of Hadrianic date, was added at the west end. In the Frankish period Dhafní Monastery was taken over by the Cistercians. It is especially famous for the magnificent mosaics in the katholikon.

11. The Panagia Gorgoepíkoos, also known as Hagios Elefthérios or the Little Metropolis. (Photo: Studio KONTOS/Photostock)

12. Four Byzantine marble closure slabs built into the walls of the Panagia Gorgoepíkoos. (Photo: Studio KONTOS/Photostock)

All these churches and religious foundations in and around Athens attest to the town's prosperity in the eleventh and twelfth centuries, the accumulation of large private fortunes by local aristocrats or civic dignitaries from Constantinople, enabling them to finance major construction projects, and also the flourishing state of monasticism.

Of all the architectural monuments whose superstructure is no longer standing, the most important are the fortification walls.

The existence of the fortifications had a significant bearing on the street plan and cityscape of any urban settlement, as they set an inflexible limit on its expansion. In Athens the matter was more complicated than elsewhere, because there were almost certainly three different lines of fortification throughout the period under consideration.

The most strongly fortified part of the town was the Acropolis, of course, which was protected by a very high wall all the way round and had only one gate at the west end. The Acropolis wall was the ancient Greek one, perhaps with some additions. According to one inscription, a new fortified tower was built somewhere on the Acropolis (its position is not specified) by a certain Leo, who held the titles of *synkellos* and *rector*. Major alterations were made to the wall by the Franks after 1205. Given that the Parthenon was the cathedral of Athens, to which the townspeople came on Sundays and major feast-days (as we know from the ceremonial orations of Michael Choniates), in those days the Acropolis could not have been a fortress closed to all except the military. And in view of the recommendations of Kekaumenos (11th cent.), who states in his *Strategikon* that a citadel kept out of bounds to civilians is an absolute necessity, there is a case for arguing that there must have been an inner fort within the Acropolis walls: but, if so, not only is there no trace of any such fort remaining, but it is not mentioned in any of the sources either.

Fortifications

13. Plan of an unidentified little church completely surrounded by houses in the medieval town. (T.L. Shear, American School of Classical Studies)

FIRST PHASE   SECOND PHASE   LATE ROMAN

Be that as it may, the Acropolis was of great strategic importance as a fortress, because it was virtually impregnable. It is likely that the entire population of Athens was accommodated there for some years before and after the Slav invasion of 582, of which grim evidence has been found by archaeologists in many parts of the town.

The second line of defence was the so-called Late Roman wall built soon after the catastrophic Herulian raid of A.D. 267, when all the public buildings in the city centre were burnt down. It enclosed a large part of what is now the Pláka district and a narrow strip of land along the south side of the Acropolis. It remained standing until the end of the Middle Ages, and in the Frankish period the fortified area was extended southwards by the construction of an extra loop of wall called the Rizókastro. Nothing is now left of the Late Roman wall except the foundations and sometimes the lower courses of a few sections (as in the Agora area), because most of it was demolished by classical archaeologists in the nineteenth century.

The third line of defence was the ancient Themistoklean wall, which also seems to have remained standing at least until the Latin conquest in 1204. Its practical defensive value was minimal, however, as the popu-

14. The Church of Hagía Triádha in the Kerameikos, now demolished. (Drawing by H.C. Stilling from M. Bendtsen, 'Sketches and Measurings: Danish Archaeologists in Greece, 1818-1862', Copenhagen 1993)

lation of Athens was never large enough to man it effectively along its entire length.

Which of the city's defences were built by Justinian the Great is a question that has yet to be resolved. Prokopios, in his book *On Buildings*, states that the fortification walls were restored because they had fallen into disrepair and no one had bothered to do anything about them, but it unclear whether he is referring to the Themistoklean or the Late Roman wall; and the matter is further complicated by the fact that in his *Secret History* Prokopios says that Justinian did nothing at all for Athens. A cubicle built on top of the architrave of the Temple of Olympian Zeus, formerly believed to have been a stylite's cell, is now thought to have been a lookout post built in the Dark Ages in connection with the town's defensive system.

Lastly, mention should be made of at least two large water cisterns on the Acropolis, which were essential to the defences. They too were demolished by classical archaeologists in the nineteenth century.

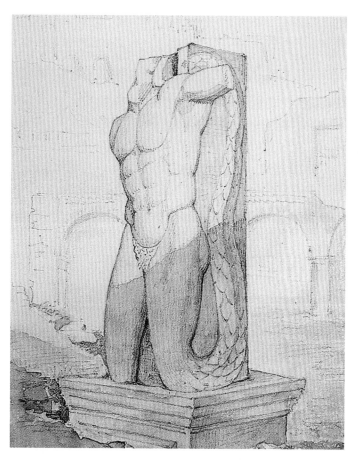

15. One of the statues of Giants from the façade of the Gymnasium in the Agora. (Drawing by H.C. Stilling from M. Bendtsen, 'Sketches and Measurings: Danish Archaeologists in Greece, 1818-1862', Copenhagen 1993)

All we know about the residential districts of Middle Byzantine Athens is derived from archaeological excavations, sometimes carried out systematically and sometimes – as already mentioned – done in haste when construction work is about to start on new buildings or the new lines of the Metro. The redevelopment of the modern city on top of the ancient remains, not only in Athens but in almost every town in Greece, has created a great many problems, and medieval archaeology has suffered particularly badly. Even when the

Archaeological remains of residential areas

excavations were systematic, especially in the nineteenth and early twentieth centuries, the archaeologists were so eager to get down to the ancient Greek strata that they destroyed much of the evidence of the Byzantine architectural legacy. These problems are compounded by the cheap construction of Middle Byzantine houses and the great difficulty of dating them. The method of dating by stylistic comparison, which works for churches, is futile for dwelling-houses: firm dating is only possible if sherds or coins are found in the rubble of the walls or floors. Because of the poor standard of construction, the only remains of houses found so far have been very low sections of wall, foundations, floors and traces of staircases. The stairs, where they existed, led down to basements or semi-basements generally containing *pithoi* (huge earthenware storage jars), which means that they were storerooms rather than living areas.

What emerges clearly from the excavations in Athens is that until well into the tenth century the town was wholly within the Late Roman wall and that expansion outside that wall

16. Two views of the ruins of the Middle Byzantine houses in the Agora before they were cleared away. (J. Travlos, «Πολεοδομική εξέλιξις...»)

started in the eleventh century and gathered pace in the twelfth. The existence of these residential areas between the Late Roman and Themistoklean walls proves, first, that the population was growing rapidly, and secondly that the people must have felt fairly confident of their safety, as the ancient wall did not provide effective protection in the event of an attack on the town.

It was normal in the Byzantine Empire for the local aristocrats and Constantinopolitan dignitaries to live in the cities and towns, but in Athens at any rate it is impossible to tell whether their houses were different from those of the ordinary people. They are thought to have lived in the old part of the town (inside the Late Roman wall) for reasons of both security and social status, but unfortunately the few traces of Middle Byzantine houses found in that area, mostly in and around the Roman Agora, were destroyed in the excavations of Koumanoudis (1890), Philadelpheus (1910) and Stavropoulos (1930) without being properly studied.

The two main residential areas during the Middle Byzantine period were in the Agora and on the south side of the Acropolis.

In the Agora everything was excavated unhurriedly and with great care by the Americans, from 1935 onwards. Most of the site was covered with the dense network of streets and houses, which had lasted from the eleventh or twelfth century to the twentieth. Only a few of the buildings would appear to have been built before 1000. Very little of all this is still to be seen today, and that is on the north side of the Agora, in the area excavated since 1980: all the rest of the Byzantine remains were cleared away to give access to the Roman and ancient Greek strata which, it is true, are of the greatest interest. Unfortunately only a few perfunctory studies of the Byzantine houses have ever been published. The two archaeologists concerned, John Travlos and Alison Frantz, are no longer alive, and their preliminary reports were brief and somewhat sketchy. Two photographs in Travlos's book, giving general views of the site, show that the whole of the Agora area was completely unplanned. Some workshops were found among the houses, as well as a large square building with rooms round the outside (found in 1935), which may have been a covered market or an inn.

The only published works that attempt to reconstruct the appearance of medieval Athens deal with the area on the north side of the Agora, which was excavated in 1980-1982 and 1989-1993. The detailed studies by Leslie Shear give us a good idea of what the residential districts of the medieval town must have looked like. In this area there was a winding street running approximately north-south with houses packed together on either side of it, the total absence of planning being a conspicuous feature. The houses consisted of small rooms surrounding a rectangular courtyard: they were usually irregular in shape and most of them had been built in two or three stages. The inner courtyards, which were floored with mortar, usually contained a well. The floors of the rooms were of compacted earth, with cavities in which to stand *pithoi* for storing provisions. In amongst the houses there were also some small shops and workshops and a few churches, also small and poorly-built.

The little we know about the ground floor of a medieval Athenian house is of no help, of course, in reconstructing the layout of the upper storey, where the living quarters were. Travlos, writing about a twelfth-century house he had studied, noted the remarkable similarity between its ground plan and that of a house of the fifth century B.C. and suggested that this was evidence of continuity in the architecture of Athenian houses. However, the eventful history of Athens during the many centuries between these two examples makes it impossible to speak of continuity: the similarity was simply due to the function of the dwelling-house, which was much the same in the Middle Ages as it had been in antiquity.

Along the south side of the Acropolis there was another residential district of the eleventh and twelfth centuries, some of it inside the Late Roman wall but most of it outside. Foundations, floors and low sections of wall have been found in excavations carried out from the mid nineteenth century to the present day in various parts of this area: in the cavea and in front of the Theatre of Dionysos, in front of the Odeion of Herodes Atticus, to the west of the Stoa of Eumenes and also further south, at the corner of what is now Kallispéri Street and in the grounds of the Acropolis offices at the corner of Makriyánni Street (two major excavations, one of them still in progress, which are of great interest).

Here again, unfortunately, very little is available in the way of published work. The general situation is similar to that in the Agora: there is no sign of overall planning, it is often impossible to tell which house the rooms belong to, the construction work is shoddy and the basements are full of earthenware or stone storage jars. The Church of Hagios Yeóryios Alexandhrinós, a gem of a building that was probably the katholikon of a small monastery, stood just to the south of the Theatre of Dionysos. The excavations at the corner of Makriyánni Street are of particular interest, because

17. A section of the Late Roman Wall in the area of the Agora. (Photo: S. Mavromatis, 2000)

that area was also inhabited in the Early Christian period. Here the stratigraphical picture is extremely clear, with a deep layer of natural fill between the destroyed Early Christian buildings and the Middle Byzantine remains. The recent excavations for the new Metro line revealed the existence of workshops in this area as well as houses. In Amalías Avenue a ruined Roman bath-house was apparently rebuilt and enlarged in the Middle Byzantine period for use as a storehouse containing deep silos. Remains of other Byzantine houses have been found in Tziraíon Street, Voulís Street and at the lower end of Adhrianoú Street (where it overlies the Panathenaic Way).

Other residential areas, most of them outside the Late Roman wall and all dating from the eleventh and twelfth centuries, present a similar picture to the Agora. Around the Olympieion the houses were less closely packed together and there may also have been some workshops. In the Kerameikos they were built on top of the ruins of the Pompeion, again with some workshops among them. And there were more on the slopes of the Areopagus, in the area of the modern Syntagma Square and on the site of Hadrian's Library, where all the Byzantine remains were destroyed by classical archaeologists 120 years ago.

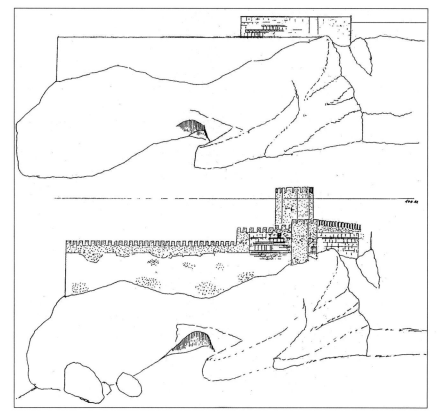

18. The east walls of the Acropolis in the Middle Byzantine period and after the strengthening of the fortifications by the Franks. (M. Korres)

It is not possible to identify these neighbourhoods with the place-names given in the *praktikon* (see p. 224) except in the case of the Koile and Kerameikos districts, which were still known by their ancient names. The Koile was to the west of Filopáppou Hill and the Kerameikos to the west of the town centre.

Excavation has also shown that in addition to the ornate, well-built churches already mentioned there were others that were smaller, cheaply constructed and so thoroughly integrated with the surrounding houses that their side walls would not have been visible: Hagios Thomás (excavated and studied by Manolis Chatzidakis), a chapel near Adhrianoú Street, Hagios Nikólaos at the north end of the Agora archaeological site, a little church in the atrium of Hadrian's Library, Hagii Theódhori in Níkis Street, Panagia Piryiótissa at one end of the façade of the Stoa of Attalos, and the Sotíra tou Dhikaíou. Nothing is left of them except low walls, but they are all immediately identifiable as churches even though they are so unpretentious. All are dated to the Middle Byzantine period on the evidence of pottery and coins, and most of them were built in two or three stages. Presumably these were either parish churches or private chapels belonging to people of modest means. Cyril Mango has conjectured that many of the surviving Byzantine churches belonged to monastic foundations: that would explain why such care was taken over the appearance of their exterior walls, as their position in the middle of the monastery precinct would have meant that they were visible from all sides. The silence of the written sources on the subject of Byzantine parish churches and the individualism of the medieval Greeks (which prompted them to found monasteries in order to boost their social standing) tend to support Mango's hypothesis.

Something has already been said about the prerequisites for a comprehensive new study of the urban structure of Middle Byzantine Athens. Any such work will have to take into consideration the results of the most recent excavations, especially on the south side of the Acropolis, and also the unpublished records of earlier excavations, which are to be found in the archives of the Greek Archaeological Service, the Athens Archaeological Society and the American School of Classical Studies in Athens. Other useful sources of information are the notebooks of Stamatios Kleanthes and Eduard Schaubert: these were used as a basis for the first accurate plan of Athens, which was drawn immediately after the end of the War of Independence and the

Continuity during the Turkish period

departure of the Turks in 1830. At that time many of the Byzantine and Post-Byzantine churches that have since been demolished were still standing and, even more important, it was still possible to trace the lines of the streets and narrow alleyways between houses, which may well have been as they were in the Byzantine period.

With regard to this last point, it is by no means certain how much of the street plan and architecture of Athens did actually remain unchanged in the six centuries or more between the Middle Byzantine period and the eighteenth and nineteenth centuries, when the first reliable town plans and the first pictures of Athenian architecture were made. During that time the town had diminished in importance and become run-down, first under the Franks and then much more so under the Catalans, in the thirteenth and fourteenth centuries. Worse was in store for it in 1687, during the Venetian-Turkish war, when the Acropolis was bombarded and very badly damaged, causing the population to flee and leave the town deserted for a time. However, the complete absence of town planning under the Turks and the extreme con-

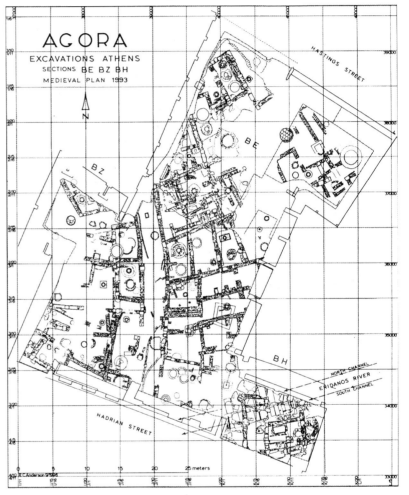

19. Plans of Middle Byzantine houses in a densely built-up area. (T.L. Shear, American School of Classical Studies)

servatism of the inhabitants – Turks as well as Greeks – make it likely that the overall shape of the town remained unchanged. Travlos came to the conclusion that the main streets followed the same lines as they had in the Middle Ages and that a low, crudely-built wall was erected in 1780 with gates in the same places as the gates of medieval Athens. Serious research is now at last under way to establish the degree of resemblance between the town as it was in the eleventh and twelfth centuries and the fragmentary picture presented by the prints and drawings of later travellers.

The two cities that symbolize the ancient world, Athens and Rome, had very different histories after the end of the ancient era. For some time in the early Middle Ages they were both mere provincial towns, but later Rome, as the home of the Holy See and the focal point of Western Christendom, developed into an ecclesiastical, political and cultural centre of international standing. In the twelfth century Athens, too, was a thriving place, but on a different scale and in different ways from Rome. For Athens, the year 1204 marked the beginning of a very long period of stagnation and decline, whereas in Rome the growth and development of the popu-

20. Pithoi (storage jars) built into the floor of a Byzantine house in the Agora. (A. Frantz, American School of Classical Studies)

lation, the built environment and social and administrative structures continued undiminished. It was not until the eighteenth century, under the influence of romantic classicism and in complete different circumstances, that these two unique cities started once again to attract the interest of people all over Europe: humanists for the sake of the 'ancient spirit' and historic values they represented, and art collectors for the sake of the treasures to be found in the monuments of their glorious distant past.

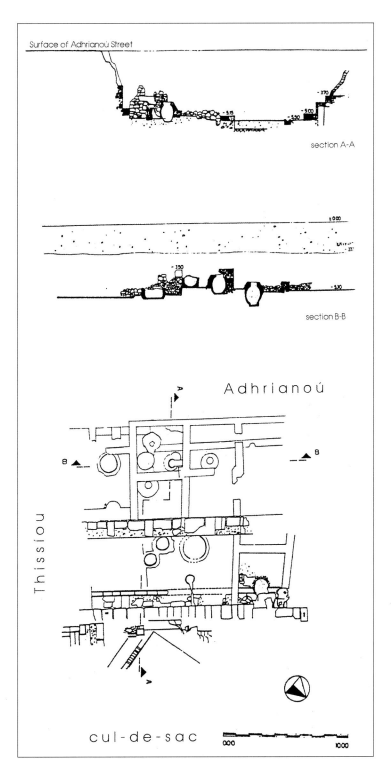

Surface of Adhrianoú Street

section A-A

section B-B

Adhrianoú

Thissíou

cul-de-sac

21. *Remains of Byzantine houses overlying the ancient Panathenaic Way.*
Plan and two sections. (Drawing by Y. Nikolopoulou, from her article
«Ανασκαφή της οδού Θησείου».

SELECT BIBLIOGRAPHY

Avramea, A., and T. Tanoulas, «Τα χαράγματα των Προπυλαίων», *Proceedings of the Ninth Symposium of the Christian Archaeological Society*, 1989, 21-22.

Bouras, Ch., 'The So-Called Cell of the Athenian Stylite' in *Architectural Studies in Memory of Richard Krautheimer*, Mainz 1996, 23-27.

—, «Πολεοδομικά των μεσοβυζαντινών και των υστεροβυζαντινών πόλεων», *Δελτίον της Χριστιανικής Αρχαιολογικής Εταιρείας* 20 (1998) 89-98.

Casanaki-Lappa, M., 'Atene' in *Enciclopedia dell'arte Medioevale* II, Rome 1991, 686-692.

Casanaki-Lappa, M., *Μεσαιωνική Αθήνα, Οικονομική Ιστορία του Βυζαντίου*, Athens (National Bank Cultural Foundation), in press.

Castrén, P. (ed.), *Post Herulian Athens: Aspects of Life and Culture in Athens, A.D. 267-529*, Helsinki 1994.

Chatzidakis, M., *Βυζαντινή Αθήνα*, Athens n.d.

—, «Η Βυζαντινή Αθήνα», *Σύναξη* 16 (1985) 13-18.

Frantz, Alison, *The Middle Ages in the Athenian Agora* ('Excavations of the Athenian Agora Picture Books', No. 7), Princeton 1971, 18, Figs. 34-35.

—, *The Athenian Agora: Late Antiquity, A.D. 267-700*, Princeton 1988.

—, *The Church of the Holy Apostles*, Princeton 1971.

Grantstrem, E., I. Medvedev and D. Papachrissanthou, 'Fragment d'un Praktikon de la région d'Athènes (avant 1204)', *Revue des Études Byzantines*, 34 (1976) 5-44, Pls. I-IV.

Hoepfner, W., *Das Pompeion und seine Nachfolgerbauten* (Kerameikos, Vol. X), Berlin 1976, 192-195 ('Byzantinische Haüser').

Janin, R., *Les églises et les monastères des grands centres byzantins*, Paris 1975, 332 ('Athènes').

Korres, M., «Χρονικά Α΄ ΕΠΚΑ (Νοτία κλιτύς Ακροπόλεως)», *Αρχαιολογικόν Δελτίον* 35 (1980), Β΄ 18-19.

Kuebler, M., *Mitteilungen aus dem Kerameikos IV*, (Athen Mitt. LVI), 1928, 169 ff., esp. 181-183.

Makri, E., K. Tsakos and A. Vavylopoulou-Charitonidou, «Το Ριζόκαστρο, Σωζόμενα υπολείμματα: Νέες παρατηρήσεις και επαναχρονολόγηση», *Δελτίον της Χριστιανικής Αρχαιολογικής Εταιρείας* 14 (1987-1988) 329-366.

Mango, C., 'The Conversion of the Parthenon into a Church: The Tübingen Theosophy', *Δελτίον της Χριστιανικής Αρχαιολογικής Εταιρείας* 18 (1995) 201-203.

Metcalf, D.M., 'The Slavonic Threat to Greece circa 580: Some evidence from Athens', *Hesperia* 31 (1962) 134-157.

Moschonas, N., «Η τοπογραφία της Αθήνας στην βυζαντινή και την μεταβυζαντινή εποχή» in *Αρχαιολογία της πόλης των Αθηνών*, Athens 1996, 137-156.

National Technical University, *Βυζαντινά μνημεία, Εκκλησίαι περιοχής Αττικής* (album of drawings), Athens 1970.

Nikolopoulou, Y., «Ανασκαφή της οδού Θησείου», *AAA* No. 1 (1971) IV, 1-9.

Orlandos, A.K., *Ανασκαφή νοτίως της Ακροπόλεως, Έργον*, 1956, 7, and *Έργον*, 1957, 7.

—, *Η Όμορφη Εκκλησιά*, Athens 1921.

Orlandos, A., and L. Vranoussis, *Τα χαράγματα του Παρθενώνος*, Athens 1973.

Setton, K., 'Athens in the Later 12th Century', *Speculum* 19 (1944) 179-208.

Shear, T.L., Jr., *The Athenian Agora: Excavations*, 1989-1993.

—, 'John Camp II, Annual Report, Athenian Agora', *Αρχαιολογικόν Δελτίον* 47 (1992) 17-20.

—, 'Athenian Agora: Middle Byzantine Houses', *Hesperia* 53 (1984) 50-57.

Sinos, S., 'Die sogenannte Kirche des Hagios Elias zu Athen', *Byzantinische Zeitschrift* 64 (1971) 359 ff.

Stikas, E., «Ο ναός των Αγίων Ασωμάτων "Θησείου"», *Δελτίον της Χριστιανικής Αρχαιολογικής Εταιρείας* 2 (1959) 115-126.

Tanoulas, T., *Τα Προπύλαια της Αθηναϊκής Ακρόπολης κατά τον Μεσαίωνα*, Athens 1997, 17-21, 280-289.

Touloupa, E., «Ο Άγιος Ασώματος "στα σκαλιά"», *Ευφρόσυνον* II, Athens 1992, 593-600.

Travlos, J., «Ανασκαφικαί έρευναι παρά το Ολυμπιείον», *Πρακτικά της Αρχαιολογικής Εταιρείας* 1949, 25-43.

—, «Ανασκαφαί εν τω Διονυσιακώ Θεάτρω», *Πρακτικά της Αρχαιολογικής Εταιρείας* 1951, 45.

—, *Πολεοδομική εξέλιξις της πόλεως των Αθηνών*, Athens 1960, 149-162.

—, 'Athen' in *Reallexikon zur byzantinische Kunst*, Stuttgart 1966, I 349-389.

Xyngopoulos, A., *Βυζαντινά και Τουρκικά Μνημεία των Αθηνών, Ευρετήριον των Μεσαιωνικών Μνημείων της Ελλάδος* 1.B, Athens 1929, 63-94.

CHAPTER IX

Mosaics and Wall-Paintings in Byzantine and Postbyzantine Churches in Athens

NANO CHATZIDAKIS

2. *The Panagia Atheniotissa in the Parthenon. Angel in supplication. 12th cent. (Photo: Byzantine Museum, Athens, B.I.E. archive)*

1. *Omorphi Ekklesia, Galatsi. View of the vaults and the dome. Late 13th cent. (Photo: K. Kontos, 2000)*

Mosaics and Wall-Paintings in Byzantine and Postbyzantine Churches in Athens

Athens never ceased to be one of the most important cities in Greece, in spite of the rise of new and more powerful administrative centres, not only in Byzantine times but also during the Ottoman period.

Many fine new churches were built in the old city during the Middle Byzantine period, but few examples of their original decoration have survived. The earliest traces are preserved in the church of the *Panaghia Atheniotissa* (fig. 2), into which the Parthenon was converted in the twelfth century, when Athens was enjoying a heyday and the episcopal see was transferred there. Michael Choniates, Metropolitan of Athens from 1182 to 1204, took up residence there and his chief concern was to embellish the church and donate valuable new furniture and liturgical vessels.

Panaghia Atheniotissa
(The Virgin of Athens)

The decoration, which is now barely visible, was preserved in fragmentary condition and was published by Andreas Xyngopoulos in 1920 (see also A. Cutler 1994). Prior to this, it had been copied by Westlake in 1885, in watercolours commissioned by the Marquis of Bute. It apparently followed the standard iconographic programme for Middle Byzantine churches, with the Virgin and Child in the sanctuary apse, while the Last Judgement and the Deesis, Christological scenes and single figures of saints were represented in the narthex. All that remains of the mosaic of the Virgin and Child, known only from descriptions (Lubinau 1588-1589), are 188 scattered gold, reddish and green tesserae, which were taken to the British Museum in 1848. At the west end of the church, in the narthex and exonarthex (corresponding to the opisthodomos of the Parthenon), traces have survived of the original design of the representations, painted directly on the marble, with no ground layer. In the exonarthex, represented beneath a painted arch, is the enthroned Virgin and Child flanked by two angels (fig. 2). Despite the damage to the central part of the composition, it is still possible to discern the figure of the Virgin, seated on a high-backed throne and holding the Christ Child in the middle of her body, as in the well-known Constantinopolitan model in the sixth-century icon of the Virgin in the monastery of St Catherine on Sinai. Either side stands a full-bodied, supplicating angel. The one on the left, in better condition, is depicted in three-quarter pose, walking towards the Virgin, with both hands extended in prayer. The deft drawing bespeaks a competent hand and familiarity with classical models, for the flowing drapery and overfolds of the angel's himation follow the movement of the body, as in ancient figures of Victories (Nikai). The subject was established for the decoration of the sanctuary apse after the Triumph of Orthodoxy in 843, the most splendid example being the Virgin and Child in the sanctuary apse of Hagia Sophia at Constantinople.

The rest of the scenes are in very poor condition. In the exonarthex (opisthodomos) there are traces of the Last Judgement, the Crucifixion (only the left arm of the Cross is discernible) and the Virgin in deesis below. Some other figures are visible: an angel from the scene of the Myrrh-Bearing Women at the Tomb and twelve full-bodied hierarchs, as well as busts of saints in medallions and decorative bands. There was also a representation of the Lamentation, which is known only from Xyngopoulos's description (1920). The wall-paintings have been compared with the mosaics in the monastery of Daphni and are dated between the late eleventh and the late twelfth century. Because of their bad state of preservation, it is impossible to date them more precisely or to draw any other conclusions concerning the style or the identity of the patron of this decoration.

The wall-paintings discovered recently in two small churches near the Acropolis and the Theseion (1st Ephorate of Byzantine Antiquities, Kounoupiotou-Manolessou 1975; Koilakou 1981) date from the Frankish period. The wall-paintings in *Hagios Ioannis o Theologos*, a small church of the eleventh-twelfth century in Erechtheos Street, can be dated to the first half of the thirteenth century and include Christ Pantocrator in the dome, the Ascension (fig. 4) on the vault and walls of the bema, and a large-scale

3. Church of Hagios Ioannis o Theologos, Erechthéos Street, the prothesis. St Helen. First half of 13th cent. (Photo: K. Kontos, 2000)

Hagios Ioannis o Theologos (St John the Theologian)

soldier saint on horseback (fig. 5), covering most of the vault of the prothesis. Only fragments remain of some other saints: the heads of Sts Constantine and Helen in the prothesis, and the head of a deacon on the north wall of the narthex. St Helen (fig. 3), next to St Constantine, reveals a more powerful spiritual presence, with her lively, sidewise gaze and the careful modelling of the flesh, with its brown underlayer and the warm reddish brown tints on her cheeks. Characteristic features of these wall-paintings are the large planes of vivid colours, dominated by brick red and deep blue, the flat modelling of the flesh, and the schematic drapery of the garments with their bold outlines. The solitary figures of the Pantocrator and the saints are appropriately static and solemn. In contrast, the rendering of the apostles participating in the scene of the Ascension, rep-

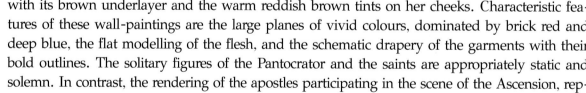

4. Church of Hagios Ioannis o Theologos, Erechthéos Street, the bema. The Ascension. First half of 13th cent. (Photo: K. Kontos, 2000)

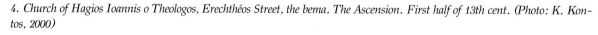

5. Church of Hagios Ioannis o Theologos, Erechthéos Street, the prothesis. Military saint on horseback. First half of 13th cent. (Photo: K. Kontos, 2000)

resented on the vault of the bema (fig. 4), is lively and expressive. The presence of some Western elements in these paintings points to a more direct influence of 'Crusader art', which developed in the Latin-held East. The equestrian military saint on the broad surface of the prothesis vault (fig. 5), an imposing figure astride his steed, is drawn with calligraphic precision and decorative disposition, in the style of thirteenth-century Crusader icons in Sinai, with no attempt to impart plasticity. This style, widely diffused in Venetian-held territories, is also found in the thirteenth-century wall-paintings in the church of the Virgin Arliotissa on Naxos, probably executed by the same workshop; St George's horse there is painted in exactly the same manner and the reins are decorated with the same Greek key pattern. The depiction of a military saint on horseback, and especially on such a scale, although unusual in the side chapels of the sanctuary, is also encountered in the same place in the Naxos church. Lastly, the marble columns supporting the dome of *Hagios Ioannis o Theologos* are coated with plaster bearing some kind of painted decoration, difficult to decipher. Marble columns decorated in this way, though rare in Greece, are known from the Eastern Mediterranean, such as those in the basilica of the Nativity at Bethlehem, which was adorned with wall-paintings in the period of Latin rule (1130-1169), and in the twelfth-century church of Christ Antiphonitis in Cyprus.

The Byzantine church of *Hagia Marina sto Theseion* is hewn out of the rock in the southeast corner of the later church and was decorated with wall-paintings in the thirteenth, seventeenth and nineteenth centuries: some of these have been detached and are now displayed in the north aisle of the church, along with other ecclesiastical treasures

Hagia Marina sto Theseio (St Marina at the Theseion)

(*keimelia*). The earliest wall-paintings, which are quite badly damaged, are in the bema, where the enthroned Virgin and Child, flanked

6. Church of Hagia Marina sto Theseio. St George, detached fresco. 13th cent. (Photo: K. Kontos, 2000)

7. Church of Hagia Marina sto Theseio, the bema apse. Angel. 13th cent. (Photo: K. Kontos, 2000)

8. Church of Hagia Marina sto Theseio, the bema apse. St Basil. 13th cent. (Photo: K. Kontos, 2000)

9. Church of Hagia Marina sto Theseio. Anonymous saint and St John the Baptist, detached fresco. 17th cent. (Photo: K. Kontos, 2000)

10. Church of Hagia Marina sto Theseio. St Mark. 17th cent. (Photo: K. Kontos, 2000)

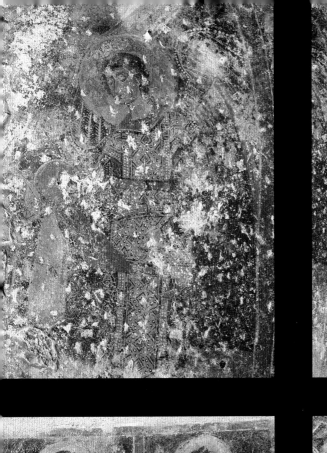

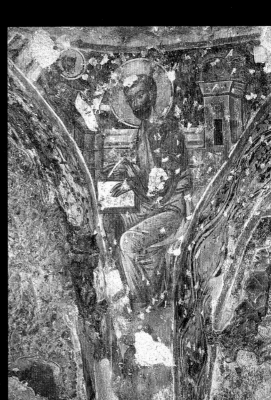

by two angels and concelebrant hierarchs, occupies the apse (figs 7-8). Recognizable in the two best-preserved figures, a venerating angel in imperial attire (fig. 7) and St Basil the Great (fig. 8), is the well known style of workshops active in Attica during the Frankish period (cf. fig. 28: St Catherine, from the Pendeli cave, 1235), the distinctive characteristics of which are the linear rendering of the faces, with the large eyes and rouging on the cheeks, and the richly decorated fabrics. Two full-bodied soldier saints painted in the thirteenth century are in bad condition. St George (fig. 6), of heroic stature and well-proportioned body, is a work of exceptional quality, suggesting an artist trained in a major centre and recalling the wall-painting of St Orestes at Episkopi in Evrytania, which too dates from the thirteenth century. The wall-paintings in the dome and on the side walls of the chapel (*parekklesion*) are later; they date from the seventeenth century and depict scenes from the Twelve Great Feasts (Dodecaorton), notably the Nativity, the Annunciation and the Transfiguration. Visible on one of the pendentives is St Mark the Evangelist (fig. 10), and below it is the inscription recording the painter's name, Demetrios, followed by the surname 'the Athenian': σοφω ... ζωγραφου χηρ Δημήτρις Ἀθην[αιος] ο γράψας. Some figures have been detached from the walls, including St Anthony, Prophet Elijah, an unnamed saint and St John the Baptist (fig. 9). Wall-paintings by 'Demetrios from Athens', with the same type of signature, are also known from Paliachora on Aegina (1609-1610) and the church of St Demetrios at Maroussi, Athens (1622). Lastly, fragments of Byzantine wall-paintings were collected from different layers during the excavation of the church of *Hagios Thomas*, behind the Stoa of Attalos in the Ancient Agora of Athens, near Evrysakiou or Vrysakiou Street (1st Ephorate of Byzantine Antiquities, M. Chatzidakis 1979).

11. Church of Hagia Marina sto Theseio. Signature of the painter, Demetrios the Athenian. 17th cent. (Photo: K. Kontos, 2000)

The wall-painting of the so-called 'Virgin of the Catalans', now in the Byzantine Museum, Athens (inv. no. T. 152), was removed from the church of *Profitis Ilias sto Staropazaro*, one of several churches in central Athens that were demolished after 1843. The representation was thus named by Dimitrios Kambouroglou, the first scholar to publish a study of the work (in 1886), who dated it to the period of the Catalan occupation of Athens (1311-1388). However, recent

Prophitis Ilias sto Staropazaro
(Prophet Elijah in the Grain Market)

research has shown that the representation is associated not with Catalan but with Genoese families settled in Athens, and that it was most probably painted in the mid-fifteenth century.

The wall-painting, which was located under an arch, combines Byzantine and Western elements. The Virgin is depicted in strictly frontal pose, according to the traditional Byzantine iconographic type of the Hodegetria, with the Christ Child in her left arm. Seated on a cushion, she has a majestic presence. The highly stylized drapery of her garments and a certain lack of harmony in the proportions of her body are closer to the Western manner, which is even more obvious in the development of the vegetation, with low stylized bushes and Western-style trees that fill the dark blue ground. Two escutcheons hang from the branches of the trees: the one on the left bears the lion rampant and the initials F.A., of the family of Franco (Francesco) Acciaiuolo (1451-1460), while that on the right has the chequered charge and the initials L.S. of the family of Lorenzo Spinola (*c.* 1453). Both families were members of the Genoese community established in the area of the Ancient Agora of Athens.

12. '*The Virgin of the Catalans' from the Church of Prophitis Ilias sto Staropazaro. 15th cent. Athens, Byzantine Museum, T. 152. (Photo: S. Mavromatis and N. Panayotopoulos, 2000)*

The most noteworthy ensemble of wall-paintings in the city of Athens in Postbyzantine times were those executed by Georgios Markou in 1719, in the eleventh-century katholikon of the *Moni Petraki* (figs 13-16, 18-20). They cover all the interior walls of the church and constitute one of the most splendid examples of the fine painter's work, which has yet to be studied. Georgios Markou, the most important painter of churches in Athens and Attica in the eighteenth century, was a native of Argos. After the Ottoman conquest of the Peloponnese in 1715, he moved to Attica, where he created a workshop with many apprentices and a prolific artistic production. Without doubt his most important work is the

Moni Petraki
(Monastery of Petrakis)

wall-paintings in the Phaneromeni church on Salamis (1735), which, together with the katholikon of the *Moni Petraki*, attest to his creative talent. Markou published the *Service [Akolouthia] for St Peter*, *Bishop of Argos and Nauplion*, printed in Venice in 1729, and so was familiar with Italian painting, from which he introduced new elements into the traditional religious iconography. Even so, his work is characterized by recourse to the conservative models of the Cretan painters, a tendency that also prevailed in other workshops in northern and central Greece during the eighteenth century.

In the dome of the katholikon of the *Moni Petraki*, the Pantocrator is surrounded by a host of angels (fig. 13), while the walls of the nave are covered with scenes. The four evangelists are depicted on the pendentives, according to the established arrangement (figs 14-15), while scenes from the life of Christ fill the vaults and full-length figures of saints and hermits cover the lower part of the walls (fig. 20). Outstanding among the many subjects are the representations in the upper part of the sanctuary, which illustrate the twenty-four stanzas of the Akathistos Hymn (figs 16, 18-19). This work is closely connected with the extended cycle of the Akathistos, painted some years later by the same artist, in the Phaneromeni church on Salamis. The Meeting of Mary and Elisabeth (fig. 18) illustrates Verse V 'The Virgin, holding God in her womb, hastened to Elisabeth ...', while Verse VI 'Joseph, a prudent man, was troubled within himself by a tumult of cares and doubts' is illustrated by the Virgin standing and listening to the reproof of Joseph, opposite her (fig. 19). Last, for Verse VII 'The shepherds heard the angels singing of the incarnate presence of Christ ...', the Nativity is depicted (fig. 16). The compositions are symmetrical and with few figures, distinguished by the dignity and restrained grace of their movements. Their models should be sought in sixteenth-century Cretan painting and are markedly conservative in character, though not without borrowings from Western art, while the setting in which the scene unfolds is an important feature of them all. The figures, tall and slender with rather small heads, are often depicted against a backdrop of composite, ornamental

13. Moni Petraki, the dome. Christ Pantocrator and angels. Georgios Markou, 1719. (Photo: K. Kontos, 2000)

14. Moni Petraki. St Mark. Georgios Markou, 1719. (Photo: K. Kontos, 2000)

15. Moni Petraki. St Luke. Georgios Markou, 1719. (Photo: K. Kontos, 2000)

16. Moni Petraki, the vault of the bema. Akathistos Hymn, Stanza VII. Georgios Markou, 1719. (Photo: K. Kontos, 2000)

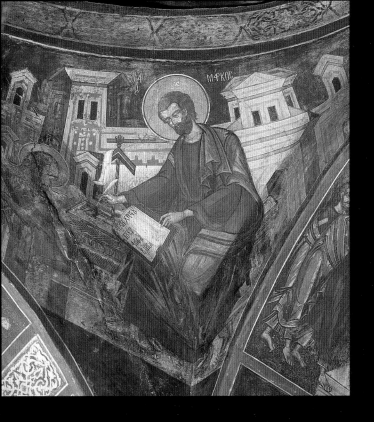 

buildings, rich versions of which can be recognized in some scenes from the Akathistos, such as the Meeting of Mary and Elisabeth (fig. 18) and the Conversation between Joseph and Mary (fig. 19). Similar buildings also frame the evangelists (figs 14-15), while the setting for the Nativity (fig. 16) is defined by the landscape with its rocky mountains in the background. Last, the single figures of saints, such as St Savvas and St Anthony (fig. 20), are shown in frontal pose and austere manner. Harmonious colours, balanced compositions and elaborate settings are some of the characteristic traits of Georgious Markou's art in the *Moni Petraki*, heralding the thematically richer decoration he painted eighteen years later in the Phaneromeni church on Salamis.

17. St Catherine from the Convent of Hagios Andreas, the community to which St Philothei belonged, which occupied the site of the present Metropolitan Cathedral in central Athens. Detached fresco. 17th cent. Athens, Byzantine Museum. (Photographic archive of the Byzantine Museum)

Wall-paintings in a number of churches are attributed to the workshop of Georgios Markou and his circle, including those in the church of St George or St Nicholas at Chostos (1727), at Karettos (Gargettos) in Attica. Those in the church of the *Koimesis tis Theotokou* (Dormition of the Virgin) at Koropi (1732) are signed by Markou's pupil Demetrios. There are some interesting wall-paintings by the workshop of Georgios Markou in the diakonikon of the monastery of Daphni too. Last, but not least, the wall-paintings in the monastery church at Kaisariani (see below) belong to the same circle.

The wall-paintings that adorned the *Moni Hagiou Andrea* (convent of St Andrew), where St Philothei was a nun (which stood on the site of the present Metropolis), can be ascribed to an analogous workshop. The church was demolished after the War of Independence, along with many other churches in central Athens, and all that remain are a few fragments of detached wall-paintings, kept in the Byzantine Museum, Athens. One fragment that is better preserved depicts St Catherine in regal raiment (fig. 17), with regular features and a noble expression, revealing a dependence on the models of the great Cretan painters.

All these wall-paintings by Georgios Markou and his workshop attest to the importance of Athens as a centre that attracted the best painters of the day and exerted a strong influence on the artistic activity of the region. They need to be studied thoroughly, in order to enhance the distinctive traits of the workshop and to extend our knowledge of its creative contribution to eighteenth-century painting.

18. Moni Petraki, the bema. Akathistos Hymn, Stanza V. Georgios Markou, 1719. (Photo: K. Kontos, 2000)

19. Moni Petraki, the bema. Akathistos Hymn, Stanza VI. Georgios Markou, 1719. (Photo: K. Kontos, 2000)

20. Moni Petraki. St Savvas and St Antony. Georgios Markou, 1719. (Photo: K. Kontos, 2000)

The surviving Byzantine decorations in the environs of the old capital are both numerous and important. Outstanding in every respect is the decoration in the *Moni Daphniou* (monastery of Daphni), a splendid monument and an excellent example of the best Constantinopolitan art of the late eleventh century (fig. 21). The luxurious marble revetment on the walls of the interior was complemented by the superb mosaics in the upper parts of the church.

Moni Daphniou
(Monastery of Daphni)

The mosaics at Daphni are characterized by a pronounced recourse to the classical models that were revived in enlightened cultural circles of the Church and Court at Constantinople, in the years following the Triumph of Orthodoxy over Iconoclasm, and especially under the Macedonian dynasty (867-1056). The continuation of this vigorous movement into the next period is enhanced in the decoration at Daphni as a whole. The mosaics, which are of outstanding artistic quality, are not only the most important work of Byzantine art in Athens and its environs, but also the last example of extant mosaic decoration that echoes the classicizing art of Constantinople in the late eleventh century.

The mosaics are preserved in fairly good condition on the uppermost surfaces of the church, in spite of the damage suffered in the earthquakes in 1889, 1894, 1981, and most recently in September 1999. Unfortunately, the marble revetment of the walls has been completely destroyed. The iconographic programme of this octagon-plan church with its large dome follows that established in Constantinopolitan churches after Iconoclasm. Christ Pantocrator in the dome is surrounded by prophets, while scenes from the Gospels occupy the squinches and the upper parts of the walls in the nave and the narthex. At Daphni the standard Christological cycle is enriched with scenes from the life of the Virgin. The Nativity of the Virgin, in the nave, corresponds to the scene of the Adoration of the Magi, while the Dormition is depicted on the west wall. In the narthex are depicted the Prayer of Joachim and Anne, the Presentation of the Virgin in the Temple, and the Blessing of the Virgin by the priests. The decoration is completed with single figures of saints.

21. Moni Daphniou. Watercolour by F. Perilla. (Daphni. Le Monastère, Thessaloniki 1928)

The imposing Pantocrator in the dome (fig. 22), in flawless technique, is outstanding for its clarity of drawing, its bold outlines and deep shadows round the eyes, which gaze sideways. Christ blesses with his right hand and holds a closed, gilt-bound gospel book in his left,

22. Moni Daphniou, the dome. Christ Pantocrator. Late 11th cent. (Photographic archive of Ekdotike Athenon S.A.)

which is drawn with analogous tension because of the unusually large distance between the forefinger and the other fingers. This stern Christ, the 'Righteous Judge', contrasts starkly with the classical style of the decoration in the drum of the dome, where the prophets are depicted in calm poses of ancient philosophers. The mosaic of the Virgin in the conch of the sanctuary, a representation that has largely been destroyed, was flanked in the two lateral conches by two archangels standing on gold-embroidered footstools and clad in sumptuous aristocratic dress.

Represented in the four squinches are scenes of the most important events preceding the Passion: the Annunciation, where the majestic figure of the archangel advances in the manner of an ancient Victory (Nike) towards the motionless figure of the Virgin, the Nativity, set in a Hellenistic landscape of variegated low hills with sheep grazing on the banks of a stream; the Baptism with its unique rendering of the naked Christ in a serene, statuesque pose (fig. 27); and the Transfiguration, where Christ stands resplendent in a mandorla, in the pose of an ancient orator, and the apostles are placed in the low hills of the landscape.

Scenes of the rest of the Twelve Great Feasts unfold on the other parts of the side walls and on the vaults. Noteworthy among them is the Adoration of the Magi (figs 23-24), this secondary episode in the Nativity cycle, which is accorded a prominent place on the east wall of the nave. It is treated with the formality of a palace scene, in which the Virgin is seated on a throne with the Child on her lap, giving audience to the three Magi, who, dressed in colourful, gold-embroidered costumes of the Orient, approach her bearing their gifts. In two other prominent positions on the east wall are mosaics illustrating the two most important doctrines of the Christian Faith: the Crucifixion, in the north transept, and the Resurrection (Anastasis), in the south transept (figs 25, 26). The Crucifixion, with the calmness of its three-figure composition, the Virgin's expression of restrained grief, the relaxed pose of St John who raises his hand towards Christ with dignity, and the harmonious proportions and

23. *Moni Daphniou. The Adoration of the Magi. Late 11th cent. (Photographic archive of Ekdotike Athenon)*

24. *One of the Magi from the Adoration. Detail of fig. 23. (Photographic archive of Ekdotike Athenon)*

25. *Moni Daphniou. The Crucifixion. Late 11th cent. (Photographic archive of Ekdotike Athenon)* ☞

26. *Moni Daphniou. The Anastasis. Late 11th cent. (Photographic archive of Ekdotike Athenon)*

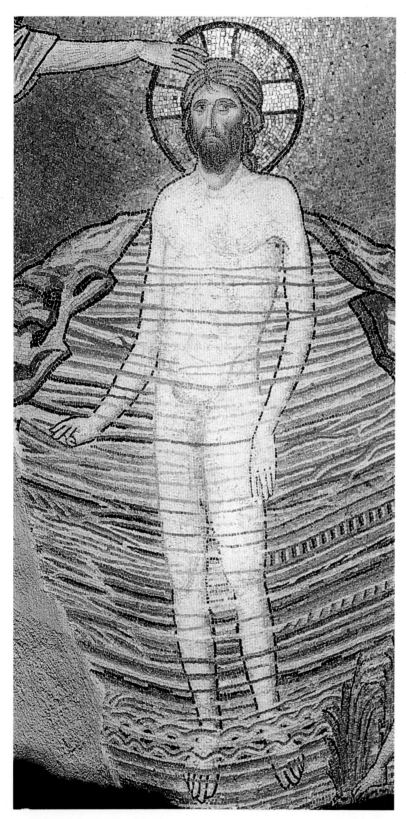

sensitive modelling of Christ's naked body, epitomize the classical style. The classical ethos is expressed in a different way in the many-figured composition of the Anastasis, where the radiant figure of Christ, wearing a chiton and a himation, densely striated with gold brushstrokes, strides vigorously towards the left, carrying the Cross, while from the obliquely placed sarcophagus at the side emerge the figures of Adam and Eve, on the left, and St John the Baptist and the Righteous, on the right. The personification of defeated Hades, in a posture similar to that of the statue of the Dying Gaul, is an outstanding testimony to deep knowledge and creative assimilation of classical models.

Other Christological scenes – the Last Supper and the Washing of the Feet (both fragmentary), and the Betrayal – together with scenes from the life of the Virgin, are placed in the narthex. Among the latter, the Prayer of St Anne, set in a verdant garden, with a fountain and trees with birds perched in the branches, and a little house in which a young maidservant draws back the curtain, again refers to scenes of everyday life in the palace.

The mosaics at Daphni, together with those in Hosios Loukas in Phocis (1011-c. 1035) and the Nea Moni on Chios (c. 1045), are among the most magnificent examples of eleventh-century Constantinopolitan art. Although nothing is known about the founder of the monastery, the high quality and markedly classical style of the interior decoration point to someone with a classical education and refined taste, whose aesthetic preferences welled from the art flourishing in the imperial milieu of Constantinople.

27. Moni Daphniou. Christ, from the Baptism. Late 11th cent.
(Photographic archive of Ekdotike Athenon)

The wall-paintings in the *cave of Pendeli*, also known as the cave of Davelis (after the notorious bandit chief in the nineteenth century), date from the Frankish period. They adorned the south and north chapels, which had been a place of worship since the Early Byzantine period, before Iconoclasm. Only fragments of these works remain *in situ*: most

The Cave of Pendeli have been detached and are now in the Byzantine Museum, Athens and the 1st Ephorate of Byzantine Antiquities. As the study of the wall-paintings has shown (Mouriki 1973-1974), the south chapel was the main church, while to the north one, which was dedicated to St Nicholas, was added later a funerary chapel of cruciform plan, in which the decoration was better preserved. The wall-paintings are precisely dated to 1233/4 by an inscription in the dome of the north chapel. Outstanding among the figures of saints in the south chapel, unfortunately in very bad condition, is a portrait of Michael Choniates, who was Metropolitan of Athens from 1182 to 1204 and died in exile, far from the city, in about 1222. His memory is honoured in another church in Attica, St Peter at Kalyvia Kouvara, where his figure is included in the decoration of the bema (see p. 214, fig. 15) and his facial features are similar.

The wall-paintings in the south chapel, which appear to be slightly earlier and are in fragmentary state, include the Virgin between two angels, concelebrant hierarchs, the Melismos and several single figures of saints. Those of the north chapel, by a more proficient painter, are in better condition. Preserved in the bema apse is St Nicholas in bust. Depicted on the masonry iconostasis is St Catherine (fig. 28), one of the best-preserved figures, in her sumptuous imperial raiment with *thorakion* and diadem, she stands tall and slender, praying in three-quarter pose, her head bowed slightly towards the sanctuary. In the

28. Cave of Pendeli, north chapel. St Catherine, 1233/34. Detached wallpainting. 1st Ephorate of Byzantine Antiquities.

dome, Christ Pantocrator (fig. 29), in a medallion, is surrounded by the Virgin and ten half-length figures (two archangels and eight prophets). In the decorative band at the base of the dome, the last three digits of the date are preserved: [ς]ΨΜΒ (6742), that is 1233/4. This system of decorating the dome of the little chapel in the cave of Pendeli, also encountered in other churches in Attica and in Cyprus from the twelfth century onwards, testifies to the wide dissemination of the innovative trends in the iconography of the dome, the symbolic character of which is enriched with references to the Incarnation and the Last Judgement.

The Pantocrator holds a closed gospel book in his left hand and raises his right slightly in blessing. His large, wide-open eyes stare to the left and his hair is painted in a calligraphic manner, falling in waves behind his right shoulder. Directly below him, the Virgin, frontal and in orant pose, is flanked by two archangels in intercession. Michael, on the left, is almost entirely destroyed. Gabriel, on the right, wears the imperial *loros*, studded with jewels. Clearly drawn, he has large, expressive eyes, his hair falls loose to his shoulders and his wings are rendered as peacock feathers. Arrayed on the rest of the surface are eight prophets, holding open scrolls with inscriptions, and pointing up to Christ Pantocrator with their right hand. Next to the two archangels stand the two prophet kings in frontal pose, Solomon on the left and David on the right, distinguished by their richly embellished imperial mantle and Byzantine crown. Daniel is further distinguished by his oriental costume, whereas all the other prophets are dressed like ancient orators, in chiton and himation. Of the rest of the painted decoration, two of the four evangelists are preserved in the pendentives, as well as a few remnants of the Nativity, apparently works by painters of a different calibre.

The wall-paintings in the chapels in the cave of Pendeli do not all belong to the same workshop. Of the extant representations, those in the dome and the figure of St Catherine in the north chapel are without doubt superior in quality. They are distinguished by the flat treatment of the figures, the clear design, the bold outlines, the highly expressive faces with their large eyes, as well as by the attention to detail in the rendering of the luxurious ornamentation of the garments, particularly striking in the case of St Catherine, the archangels and the prophets in the dome. The linear and often decorative character of these wall-paintings, with the lack of plasticity in the flesh and the drapery, reveals a conservative disposition for the time, which cleaves to the models of Comnenian painting of the twelfth century. These stylistic features are also to be found in other churches in Attica, dating from the first half of the thirteenth century, bespeaking the activity of local workshops. Among these, the wall-paintings in St Peter at Kalyvia Kouvara, dated 1235, are so closely akin in style to those in the north chapel of the Pendeli cave, that they were obviously made by the same workshop, which wanted, once more, to commemorate Michael Choniates, the banished Metropolitan of Athens in the period of Frankish rule.

Irrefutable evidence of the widespread activity of Athenian painters during this period is provided by the wall-paintings in the *Hagia Triada* (Holy Trinity) at Kranidi in the Argolid, which, according to the dedicatory inscription, are by the Athenian painter Ioannes, who decorated the church in 1244. However, these wall-paintings belong to a different workshop from those in the cave of Pendeli: they are distinguished by a greater plasticity in the rendering of the figures, livelier movements and more agitated expressions. The similarity of the Kranidi wall-paintings to those in the church at Psachna on Euboea (1245) as well as to the detached wall-paintings from the church of St George at Oropos in Attica, have led to the hypothesis that during the fourth decade of the thirteenth century, there was another flourishing local Athenian workshop, in touch with the new trends elaborated in the workshops of Constantinople.

An extremely interesting example of Palaeologan art, from around 1300, is the decoration in the *Omorphi Ekklesia* at Galatsi, where the interior of the nave, the narthex and the side chapel (*parekklesion*) are covered with wall-paintings. The iconographic programme in this twelfth-century monument is quite extensive, including not only scenes from the life of Christ (figs 1,

29. Cave of Pendeli, north chapel. The dome, 1233/34. Detached wall-painting. 1st Ephorate of Byzantine Antiquities.

30-35) and of the Virgin, but also from the Old Testament and the life of St George, to whom the church was dedicated. The imposing Pantocrator in the dome (fig. 31) was surrounded by angels, prophets and saints. Single figures of prophets (fig. 30) and saints are also depicted on the arches and side walls. The choice of scenes and their positioning in the church present some small but significant deviations from the norm; they also hint at certain advanced theological ideas suggested by the conjunction

Omorphi Ekklesia ('Beautiful Church') at Galatsi

of different subjects, such as Christ Pantocrator in the dome, Christ as the Ancient of Days on the domical vault of the northwest part of the nave, and Christ Emmanuel on the cross-vault of the southwest part. Furthermore, some elements of the decoration show direct or indirect influence from the art of the Frankish period.

The Pantocrator in the dome (fig. 31) is treated in a highly painterly manner, accentuating the figure's volume in accordance with trends prevailing in the major centres, Constantinople and Thessaloniki, during the late thirteenth century. The volume style can be seen in other representations too, and especially in the single figures of the prophets, such as Daniel in the parekklesion (fig. 30), the angels (fig. 32), and saints, which are reminiscent of but less imposing than those painted by Michael and Eutychios Astrapas in the Peribleptos church at Ochrid (1295).

The Dormition of the Virgin (fig. 34), in the nave, and the Last Supper (fig. 35), in the parekklesion, preserved in a relatively good condition, constitute variations of the compositions, in which the figures form a tight group around the central subject. In the Dormition the apostles, with anxious expression, are huddled

30. Omorphi Ekklesia, Galatsi. Prophet Daniel. Late 13th cent. (Photo: K. Kontos, 2000)

31. Omorphi Ekklesia, Galatsi, the dome. Christ Pantocrator. Late 13th cent. (Photo: K. Kontos, 2000)

32. Omorphi Ekklesia, Galatsi, cross-vault. Archangel Raphael. Late 13th cent. (Photo: K. Kontos, 2000)

round the bier, while Christ, holding the Virgin's soul, inclines towards her head to the left, following the same model as that of the two famous contemporary painters, Michael and Eutychios Astrapas, in the Peribleptos church at Ochrid. In the Last Supper, the apostles are seated in a close-knit group round the table. In the Raising of Lazarus (fig. 1) Christ is depicted walking calmly to the right, followed by the apostles. Mary Magdalene (fig. 33), prostrate at his feet, her body wrapped in her maphorion, is a figure whose movement and facial expression are full of tension: her grief is etched in her contracted facial features, while strands of hair fall freely onto her shoulders, escaping from under her headcovering.

33. Omorphi Ekklesia, Galatsi. Mary Magdalene, detail from the Raising of Lazarus (see fig. 1). Late 13th cent. (Photo: K. Kontos, 2000)

The style of the wall-paintings in the *Omorphi Ekklesia* is distinguished by the high quality planning of the compositions and the painterly rendering of the figures. Differences in the accuracy of the drawing and the balance of the compositions are due to different painters, presumably working in the same workshop. These painters followed creatively the dominant currents of the period, while their art shows their affinity with contemporary workshops in Macedonia. Their relationship with the wall-paintings in the churches of central and southern Greece, such as the Olymbiotissa at Elassona in Thessaly, and the Metropolis and Sts Theodore at Mystras, has also been noted.

In the small Byzantine churches built on the slopes of Mt Hymettos in the eleventh and twelfth centuries, which were katholika of monasteries, no trace survives of the original interior decoration. Earlier traces of wall-paintings are preserved in two monasteries. In the *Moni Kaisarianis* (monastery of Kaisariani), a female figure, a Virgin in deesis, in very bad condition and dating probably from the fourteenth century, can be seen in the chapel of St Anthony. In the monastery of *Hagios Ioannis o Kynegos* (St John the Hunter, also know as the *Moni Philosophon*, monastery of the Philosophers), conservation work has revealed traces of saints' garments, which can be dated to the thirteenth and fourteenth centuries.

Most of these monasteries were decorated with wall-paintings in the Postbyzantine period. In the katholikon of the *Moni Kaisarianis* (fig. 36), dedicated to the Presentation of the Virgin in the

34. Omorphi Ekklesia, Galatsi. The Dormition of the Virgin. Late 13th cent. (Photo: K. Kontos, 2000)

35. Omorphi Ekklesia, Galatsi. The Last Supper. Late 13th cent. (Photo: K. Kontos, 2000)

Temple, the earliest decoration is found in the narthex (figs 40-42), painted by the Peloponnesian artist Ioannes Hypatos (1682); the surfaces of the nave (figs 37-39) are covered with wall-paintings of conservative character, dated to the early eighteenth century. The wall-paintings in the narthex include a dedicatory inscription recording the circumstances of its deco-ration and the names of those who contributed to it: The narthex was decorated on 20 August 1682, at the expenses of those who had taken refuge in the monastery from the plague then afflicting Athens, and had

*Moni Kaisarianis
(Monastery
of Kaisariani)*

been saved by the grace of the Holy Trinity and the protection of the Blessed Virgin. These per-sons were the 'most learned' son of the nobleman Ioannes Benizelos, together with his mother, his sisters and their retinue. The abbot at the time was Hierotheos, 'a very wise hieromonk'.

The monastery's connection with the Benizelos family – one of the great Athenian fam-ilies, whose members held posi-tions of power and influence throughout the Ottoman period – is also apparent from a defensive tower that was built inside the monastery precinct and known to this day as the Benizelos Tower.

According to the same inscrip-tion, the wall-paintings in the narthex were executed by the Pelo-ponnesian artist Ioannes Hypatos and included subjects alluding to the historical circumstances of its decoration. The symbolic represent-ation of the Holy Trinity in the dome and the scenes from the life of the Virgin are associated with the dedication of the church and the invocation in the inscription. The parables illustrated in the south vault, including those of the Rich Fool, the Workers in the Vineyard, the Sower, and the Rich

36. The katholikon of Kaisariani Monastery. Late 11th cent. (Photographic archive of M. Toubis S.A.)

Man and Lazarus, allude to everyday life in the countryside and were probably chosen by the noble donor, a member of the Benizelos family. Finally, there are scenes from the Gospels for matins and two large symbolic representations, the Tree of Jesse and Christ as the Vine, on the north and the south wall respectively.

37. Moni Kaisarianis. The dome, early 18th cent. (Photographic archive of M. Toubis S.A.)

38. Moni Kaisarianis, the nave. The Baptism, early 18th cent. (Photographic archive of M. Toubis S.A.)

Ὁ ΠΑΝΤΟΚΡΑΤΩΡ

Η ΒΑΠΤΙCΙC ΤΟΥ ΧΥ

ΙC ΧC

All these compositions are many-figured and through details narrate the successive episodes of different scenes, that often run into each other, as in the case of the parable of the Prodigal Son (fig. 40) and the parable of the Publican and the Pharisee (fig. 41), as well as the scene of the Myrrh-Bearing Women in front of Christ's empty tomb, who are depicted together with the scene of the 'Noli Me Tangere' (fig. 42). The bright colours emerge from a dark, almost black background. The clear outlines, simple modelling and immediacy of the movements are constant traits of the work of Ioannes Hypatos, one of the painters of this period from the Peloponnese (including the Moschos brothers and Kakkavas) who followed a trend characterized by the directness of folk art.

39. Moni Kaisarianis. View of the bema apse, early 18th cent. (Photographic archive of M. Toubis S.A.)

The decoration of the nave is attributed to a different workshop and dated slightly later, to the first half of the eighteenth century, when Attica began to be repopulated by those inhabitants who had sought refuge in the Peloponnese, after the Venetian conquest. The iconographic programme follows a long-established tradition. In the dome the Pantocrator (fig. 37), and in a zone below, in the tympanum, the Virgin, St John the Baptist and angels, framing the Hetoimasia (the Preparation of the Throne). Between the windows of the drum, the prophets, and on the pendentives, the evangelists. In the conch of the sanctuary, the Virgin (fig. 39) flanked by two angels, and in a lower zone the Divine Liturgy and Communion of the Apostles. The vaults are decorated with scenes of the Twelve Great Feasts, including the Nativity, the Baptism (fig. 38), the Transfiguration, the Entry into Jerusalem, the Anastasis, the Ascension and Pentecost; the Crucifixion, the Annunciation and the Dormition of the Virgin are omitted.

The artist followed Athonite models by sixteenth-century Cretan painters, characterized by well-balanced compositions, calm movements and harmonious colours. In the Baptism (fig. 38), in front of high crags, John the Baptist, on the left, and four angels, on the right, flank the figure of Christ, who stands in frontal pose in the River Jordan and gives his blessing, while lower down emerges the personification of the Jordan, the smaller figure of an old man holding a pitcher. Other scenes include some borrowings from Western art, as well as from icons by seventeenth-century painters. This is borne out by the representation of the Vir-

gin in the sanctuary apse, which is modelled on the icon of the Virgin Enthroned by Emmanuel Tzanes (1664), that at one time adorned the church where the daughter of Angelos
Benizelos, later St Philothei, was a nun (see p. 258, fig. 17), and is now in the Byzantine Museum, Athens.

The conservative style of the decoration in the church is consistent with a more general
tendency to hark back to earlier models, that is encountered in the work of other eighteenth-
century painters too. The art of these wall-paintings, although different from that of Georgios

Markou, the most significant painter working in Attica at
the time, points to an equally good and related workshop,
while the presence of a painter called Nikolaos Benizelos
in Markou's team (*Koimesis tis Theotokou* at Koropi, 1732,
Phaneromeni church on Salamis, 1735) poses the question
of his relationship to both the same family and Ioannes
Hypatos, the other artist from the Peloponnese who was
commissioned by the Benizelos family to decorate the
narthex of the monastery of Kaisariani in 1682.

Among the smaller but interesting wall-painting en-
sembles preserved in other churches on Mt Hymettos and
as yet unpublished, are those in *Hagios Ioannis Prodromos*
(St John Baptist), a dependency (*metochi*) of Kaisariani,
which were painted in 1572 and probably belong to the
circle of the Theban artists Georgios and Frangos Kon-
daris (M. Chatzidakis 1973-1974). The best preserved of
them are scenes from the Dodecaorton and the life of John
the Baptist, including the Raising of Lazarus, Herod's
Banquet and the Beheading of St John the Baptist, as well
as figures of the evangelists and an archangel on the west
wall. A dedicatory inscription on the south wall records
the name of the patron, the monk Sophronios Stanitzas:
'This sacred and venerable church of the virtuous and
glorious prophet John the Baptist, the Precursor, / was
renovated through the contributions of the Christians
under the most holy monk Sophronios, surnamed Stanitzas, / ... in the month of March 7080 ...' (1571/2).

Some seventeenth-century wall-paintings survive in
other monasteries on Mt Hymettos, such as the *Moni
Asteriou* and the monastery of *Hagios Ioannis o Theologos*,
above the modern suburb of Papagou, where there is a
badly damaged Pantocrator surrounded by angels in the
dome. In the monastery of *Hagios Ioannis o Kynegos* (St
John the Hunter, or *Moni Philosophon*, monastery of the

*40. Moni Kaisarianis, the narthex. The parable of
the Prodigal Son. Ioannes Hypatos, 1682. (Photographic archive of M. Toubis S.A.)*

*41. Moni Kaisarianis, the narthex. The parable of
the Publican and the Pharisee. Ioannes Hypatos,
1682. (Photographic archive of M. Toubis S.A.)*

Philosophers) there are fragments remaining from successive layers of wall-paintings of the seventeenth, eighteenth and nineteenth centuries. Lastly, the previously mentioned wall-paintings by the workshop of Georgios Markou, in the church of *Hagios Demetrios* at Maroussi and in the diakonikon of the monastery of Daphni, complete the picture of the flourishing religious art in Athens and Attica during the Ottoman period.

42. *Moni Kaisarianis, the narthex. 'Noli Me Tangere' and the Myrrh-Bearing Women. Ioannes Hypatos, 1682. (Photographic archive of M. Toubis S.A.)*

Chatzidakis, N., *Byzantine Mosaics* (in the series 'Greek Art'), Athens (Ekdotike Athenon) 1994.

—, *The Monastery of Kaisariani*, Athens (Apollo) 1977.

Chatzidakis, M., *Βυζαντινή Αθήνα*, Athens 1956.

—, *Βυζαντινά μνημεία Αττικής και Βοιωτίας*, Athens 1956.

—, Aspects de la peinture murale du XIIIe siècle en Grèce, in *Symposium Sopocani*, Belgrade 1965. Reprinted in M. Chatzidakis, *Studies in Byzantine Art and Archeology*, London (Variorum Reprints) 1972.

—, Βυζαντινά και Μεσαιωνικά Μνημεία Αττικής, Πειραιώς και Νήσων, *Αρχαιολογικόν Δελτίον* 29 (1973-1974) (1979) 190-193, Pls 127γ, 133-135.

—, *Έλληνες ζωγράφοι μετά την άλωση*, I, Athens 1987.

Chatzidakis, M., and Drakopoulou, E., *Έλληνες ζωγράφοι μετά την άλωση*, II, Athens (N.H.R.F.) 1998.

Cutler, A., The Christian Wall-Paintings in the Parthenon: Interpreting a lost monument, *Δελτίον της Χριστιανικής Αρχαιολογικής Εταιρείας*, 4th ser., 18 (1993-1994) 171-180.

Kambouroglou, D., *Μελέται και Έρευναι*, Athens 1923, 5-43.

Koilakou, Ch., Θησείο-Αγία Μαρίνα, *Αρχαιολογικόν Δελτίον* 36 (1981) Β1, Χρονικά, 79.

Kounoupiotou-Manolessou, E., Αθήναι Άγιος Ιωάννης Θεολόγος, *Αρχαιολογικά Ανάλεκτα εξ Αθηνών* 8 (1975) 140-151.

Lazari, M., Οι τοιχογραφίες του ναού της Αγίας Παρασκευής στο Μαρκόπουλου Μεσογείων, *Δελτίον της Χριστιανικής Αρχαιολογικής Εταιρείας*, 4th ser., 11 (1982-1983) 191-223.

Loewenthal, L.J.A., A Note on the So-called Panaghia of the Catalans, *Αρχαιολογικά Ανάλεκτα εξ Αθηνών* 4 (1971) 89-91.

Manolessou, E., in the newspaper *Kathimerini*, 24/12/1995 (special supplement on Byzantine Athens).

Millet, G., *Le monastère de Daphni*, Paris 1899.

Mouriki, D., Οι βυζαντινές τοιχογραφίες των παρεκκλησίων της Σπηλιάς Πεντέλης, *Δελτίον της Χριστιανικής Αρχαιολογικής Εταιρείας*, 4th ser., 7 (1973-1974) 79-115.

Panselinou, N., Άγιος Πέτρος Καλυβιών Κουβαρά Αττικής, Επιγραφές – Συμπληρωματικά στοιχεία, *Δελτίον της Χριστιανικής Αρχαιολογικής Εταιρείας*, 14 (1987-1988) 173-187.

Vassilaki, A., *Οι τοιχογραφίες της Όμορφης εκκλησίας στην Αθήνα*, Athens (Christian Archaeological Society) 1971.

Xyngopoulos, A., Παρθενώνος βυζαντιναί τοιχογραφίαι, *Αρχαιολογική Εφημερίς* (1920) 36-53.

—, *Ευρετήριον των μνημείων της Ελλάδος*, II, Athens 1929.

—, *Φ. Κόντογλου, Τσίμας, Παπαχατζηδάκης, Τοιχογραφίαι εκκλησιών Υμηττού*, Athens (Hellenic Arts) 1933.

CHAPTER X

*The Rediscovery
of Athens by
Artist Travellers*

FANI-MARIA TSIGAKOU

T'is living Greece no more.

2. *View of the Acropolis, 1822. Watercolour on paper, 39 x 28 cm., by J.M.W. Turner. Signed and dated.*
(Museum of the City of Athens)

1. *View of Athens from the west, 1852. Watercolour on paper, 27 x 43.5 cm., by Eduard Hildebrandt.*
Signed. (Athens, Benaki Museum, 23037)

The Rediscovery of Athens by Artist Travellers

'Mighty indeed are the marks and monuments of our empire which we have left. Future ages will wonder at us, as the present age wonders at us now. We do not need the praises of a Homer....' In these words Perikles extolled the glories of his native Athens. Yet it was to be many centuries before the city of Pallas became a source of inspiration for the pens of poets or the brushes of artists.

To European artist travellers, Athens – and indeed the whole of Greece – was more of a vision, an ideal, than a real place. After the fall of Byzantium European humanists, despite their enthusiasm for the heritage of the ancient Greek civilization, paid very little attention to the actual country of Greece. Athens, the centre of the ancient world, was in an isolated position a long way off the main East-West trade routes, and so gradually it sank into oblivion. It is interesting to note ***Early references*** that the 'first city' of Greece rates no mention at all in many fifteenth-century illustrated books, while in most atlases it is marked as Setines (or Setine, Satines, Cetines, etc.), a corrupt form of its name. Ciriaco di Ancona, the most important antiquarian traveller in the fifteenth century, made drawings of the Parthenon in 1436 and 1444, but he did not draw the town itself, so the earliest printed picture of Athens is the woodcut in Hartman Schedel's *Liber Chronicarum* (Nürnberg, 1493). It is a general view rendered in the style characteristic of conventional 'views of cities' at the time, with the result that European readers were presented with an Athens that looked just like a typical Northern European country town without a single distinguishing feature. Equally stylized was the picture by Sebastian Münster (Fig. 3) in his *Cosmographia*, published nearly fifty years later: he, however, shows Athens as a seaside town, probably because he was thinking of Piraeus.

Seventeenth-century visitors to Athens found a useful aid in the contemporary sketch map of the town drawn by the Capuchin friars who had a house there (Fig. 4). This was the first publication to have some directions (even if only a few, and not very precise) and the names of the most important monuments marked on it. Valuable information about Athens and Attica in the mid seventeenth century is to be found in the *Travels* of the Turkish traveller Evliya Çelebi and the reports of the French consul, Jean Giraud. The latter, which were eventually published two hundred years later, were written for Louis

XIV's special envoy, Marquis François-Olivier de Nointel, who visited Athens in 1674. One of the members of the diplomat's large retinue was the painter Jacques Carrey, who made about four hundred drawings of the Parthenon's sculptural ornamentation (the 'Carrey Drawings') just a few years before the temple was destroyed by Francesco Morosini. He also painted a large canvas commemorating Nointel's visit to Athens (Fig. 6), which bears witness to his artistic maturity. This monumental composition shows Nointel and his retinue against a backdrop of Athens, in which the whole town and its immediate environs are depicted in minute detail.

'Enslaved and brought to her knees, Greece had been forgotten and expunged from the annals of nations,' we read in the Founding Charter of the Athens Archaeological Society (1838), 'and it was not until 1674 that it was discovered anew by Nointel, Spon, Wheler and their fellows.' The books published by Jacob Spon and George Wheler may be considered the first examples of a scientific approach to Greek antiquities. Although their sketch maps of Athens (especially Wheler's, Fig. 5) are ill-drawn and incomplete, their pictures of the ancient monuments were for many years the most accurate representations of Athenian antiquities ever seen in Western Europe. Spon also published a treatise on Athens written by his compatriot Abbé Jean-Paul Babin. The 'view of Athens' drawn by Babin is fairly imaginative and does not give a true picture of the town at all, but its very existence is proof of the first stirrings of interest in Athens' ancient monuments. The growth of European interest in Athens and Greek antiquity at that time was not unconnected with the Great Powers' political aspirations in the eastern Mediterranean. During the Venetian-Turkish war (1684-1697) some major geo-

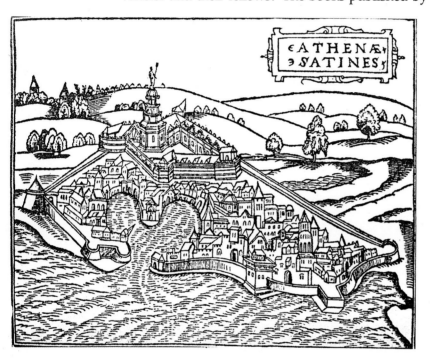

3. View of Athens, 1541. Woodcut, 9.5 x 12 cm. From S. Münster, 'Cosmographia', Basel 1541.

graphical research was carried out under the auspices of the Venetian Republic, resulting in the works of Vincenzo Coronelli (Fig. 8), among others. In addition, detailed sketch maps of battlefields and artists' impressions of military and naval engagements were drawn by engineers in the Venetian army, including a series of pictures of the catastrophic bombardment of the Parthenon by Morosini's army in 1687. Among them was a watercolour by

4. Sketch map of Athens, 1670. Coloured engraving, 20 x 39 cm. (Athens, Benaki Museum, 22955)

5. Sketch map of Athens, 1682. Engraving, 12 x 13 cm. From G. Wheler, 'A Journey into Greece', London 1682.

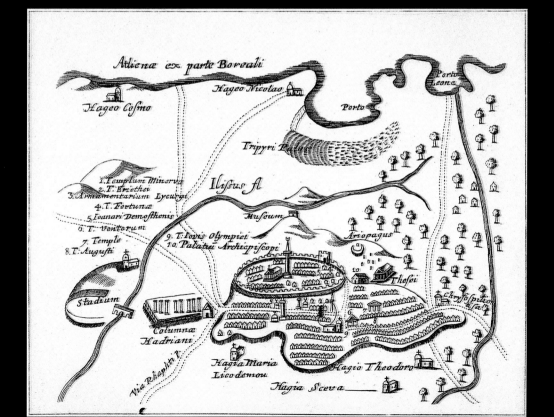

Giacomo Milheau Verneda (Fig. 13) which is one of the most accurate and detailed drawings of Athens, showing nearly all the ancient, Byzantine and Turkish monuments.

In the eighteenth century it became possible for Western Europeans to learn much more about Greek art without having to go to Greece: this was mainly due to the excavations at Herculaneum (1738) and Pompeii (1748) and the 'discovery' of the Greek temples at Paestum (Poseidonia). To promote the 'Classical Greek' style, the London-based Society of Dilettanti sent James Stuart (1713-1788) and Nicholas Revett (1720-1804), both painters and architects, to Athens in 1751 to study the ancient monuments and make systematic pictorial records of them. The product of their collaboration was a three-volume *édition de luxe* entitled *The Antiquities of Athens* (Fig. 9). While the Dilettanti were producing their monumental editions with accurate and well-drawn pictures of what remained of ancient Athenian architecture, the German scholar Johann Joachim Winckelmann was urging the people of Europe to espouse his theory that 'the sole source of models for life and learning was ancient Greece'. The process of idealizing the ancient world was now under way and Athens started broadcasting her sublime message to Europe once again. It is from this period, naturally enough, that we find the first 'View of Athens' that can be described as an adequate pictorial representation. Amateur pictures from travellers' books were superseded by paintings and drawings up to a professional standard, partly because it now became common practice for a traveller to take a competent draughtsman with him, while at the same time some leading European artists started painting views of Athens. The French ambassador, Comte de Choiseul-Gouffier, who went on a trip round the Aegean islands in 1776-1777 to hunt for ancient works of art, was the patron of two artists, Lancelot Théodore Turpin de Grissé (1782-1859) and Jean-Baptiste Hilaire, in whose pictures of Athens the ancient monuments were the centres of attention. The foreground of Hilaire's 'View of Athens' (Fig. 11) is dominated by the Temple of Olympian Zeus, with just a few houses and other buildings visible between its towering columns. In front of the columns, painted in a miniaturistic style and with skilful handling of colour, are some groups of Athenians with Choiseul-Gouffier himself among them. Visual allusions to the natural environment of the Athenian monuments are neatly sketched in *Les Ruines des plus beaux Monument de la Grèce* by the architect Julien David le Roy (Paris, 1758), while the magnificent album by Louis François Cassas contains the fullest panoramic view of the whole town inside and outside the wall of Hadji Ali Haseki (Fig. 14). These pictures, redolent of the romance of ancient ruins, completely satisfied the antiquarian interest of the general public in the Age of Enlightenment. Before the end of the eighteenth centu-

6. *View of Athens, 1674. Oil, 2.60x5.20 m., by Jacques Carrey. Athens, National Gallery of Art, on loan from the Chartres Museum, France. (Photo: S. Mavromatis, 2000)*

7. *Sketch map of Athens, 1678. Engraving, 10x15 cm. J. Spon, 'Voyage d'Italie, de Dalmatie, de Grèce et du Levant', Lyon 1678.*

8. *Sketch map of Athens, 1687. Engraving, 50x68 cm. Leaflet entitled 'Antica e moderna città d'Atene dedicata dal P. Coronelli all' illustriss. et eccellentiss. Sig. Cristino Martinelli, Partitio', Venice 1687. (Athens, Benaki Museum, 26531)*

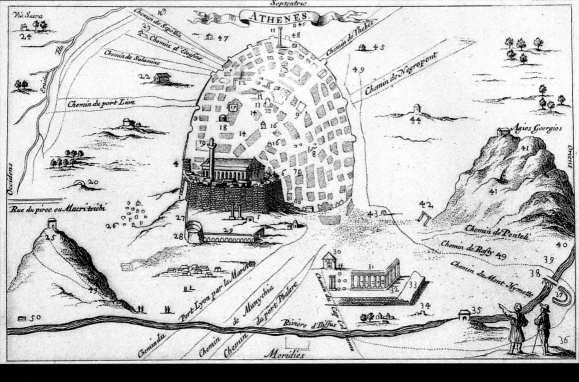

ATHENES

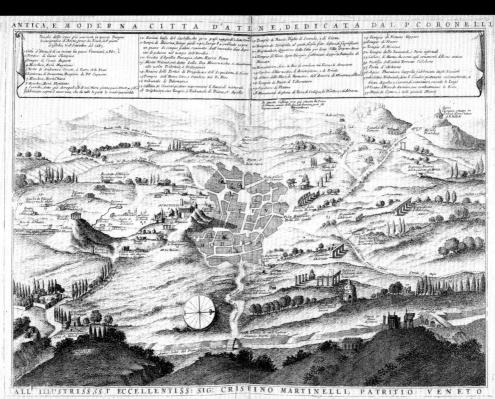

ANTICA, E MODERNA CITTA D'ATENE, DEDICATA DAL P. CORONELLI

ALL ILLUSTRISS.ST ECCELLENTISS: SIG: CRISTINO MARTINELLI, PATRITIO VENETO

ry Thomas Hope (1769-1831), an eccentric champion of the Greek Revival, sketched various views of Athens – all too few, alas – with remarkable miniaturistic skill (Fig. 15).

In the early part of the nineteenth century, when a thorough study of ancient monuments was considered an essential part of the training for an architect of the Greek Revival, serious students of architecture poured into Athens from Western Europe, eager to discover hitherto overlooked aspects of the famous classical buildings. Inevitably, architectural and archaeological research led on to official or unofficial excavations and the removal of ancient works of art from Athens, the most glaring case in point being the looting of the Parthenon reliefs and other sculptures from the Acropolis by Lord Elgin. In those days Athens was an obligatory stopping-place not only for every serious

Antiquaries and treasure-hunters

scholar but for every European traveller: 'At the period when every young man of fortune considered it an indispensable part of his education to survey the monuments of ancient art remaining in Italy, only a few desperate scholars and artists ventured to trust themselves amongst the barbarians to contemplate the ruins of Greece. But Attica at present swarms with travellers … and … a few more years may furnish the Piraeus with all the accommodations of a fashionable watering-place,' wrote Byron's travelling companion John Cam Hobhouse in 1812. Although it was the monuments that had provided the original impetus for painting pictures of Athens, by the early nineteenth century amateur artists visiting Greece were beginning to take an interest also in depicting the scenery within and around the ruins. Indeed, rapid views of the town are to be found in the sketchbooks of most of the European representatives of the Greek Revival, that is to say the architects, archaeologists, topographers and classicists who went to Athens at about that time. Among the most interesting pictorial representations of Athens from before the Greek Revolution of 1821 are the archaeological maps drawn by the French consul Louis Sébastien Fauvel (1753-1838); the engravings by the French artist François Préaux, who lived in Athens for a time at the beginning of the century, making prints for foreign visitors to take home as souvenirs; the drawings by the well-known British topographers Edward Dodwell (1777-1832) and William Gell (Fig. 10); and the drawings by the German architect Haller von Hallerstein (1774-1817), whose name is associated with the looting of sculptures from Aigina and Bassai in 1810-1811. Accurate depictions of the face of pre-Revolutionary Athens are also to be found in the work of the English artists Richard Banks Harraden (1778-1862) and William Pars (Fig. 16). The few but excellent pictures of Athens by the distinguished English historical painter Sir Charles Lock Eastlake (1793-1865) are equally true to life, as are the amateurish pictures by the English poet William Haygarth (1784-1825). Though often banal and sometimes far from accurate, the views of Athens reproduced in the countless

9. *View of Athens from Hadrian's Aqueduct, looking towards Lykabettos. Engraving, 30 x 70 cm. From J. Stuart and N. Revett, 'The Antiquities of Athens Measured and Delineated', III, London 1794. (Athens, Benaki Museum, 26526)*

10. *View of Athens in the style of Poussin, 1801. Pencil, 21.5 x 35 cm., by William Gell. (Athens, Benaki Museum, 22947)*

illustrated books published before the War of Independence are treasured by historians because, although almost all the artists concerned were amateurs, their draughtsmanship was so highly-developed that they bequeathed to posterity an invaluable collection of visual records of the Athenian scene.

'I met there many artists, English or German, drawing, measuring, endlessly and with the minute exactness of the most scrupulous commentator, those monuments, those noble creations of genius. Miserable slaves of rules, of the lightest caprice of the ancients, they write whole volumes in order to correct a mistake ... concerning the measurements of an architrave. They establish themselves in Athens for eight years in order to draw three columns ... and it is only after the efforts of many years that their sad watercolours reach the highest degree of boring perfection,' wrote the Comte Louis-Nicolas-Philippe-Auguste de Forbin in 1817. To the nineteenth-century European traveller, on whom the rediscovery of ancient Greece

A place of pilgrimage

exerted a magnetic attraction, a journey to Athens and Attica was a voyage of exploration to a country hallowed by the passage of centuries.

There can be no doubt that the landscape of Greece, where stood ruins of worldwide significance, considerably influenced the Europeans' perception of the idea of Nature. The historical development of pictorial representations of the Greek scene reflects different facets of the European attitude to Nature in conjunction with current ideologies, sensibilities and artistic conventions. The landscape of Greek history and myth – a product of aesthetic and cerebral creativity – was a spiritual landscape set against a background of transcendent space. If travellers from Europe with their sketchbooks saw the Athenian scene as a paradise of light and colour, the more scholarly perceived it as the most complete expression of the human mind and spirit. European artists of the eighteenth and nineteenth centuries, trying to depict Athens as it was while simultaneously capturing its historical impor-

11. *View of Athens from the Temple of Olympian Zeus, c. 1776-1777. Watercolour, 44 x 69 cm., by Jean-Baptiste Hilaire. (Athens, private collection)*

12. *View of Athens from the Ilissos, 1834. Oil on wood, 22 x 29.5 cm., by Johann Jacob Wolfensberger. (Private collection)*

tance and its spiritual aura, fell back on an imaginative thematic repertoire intended to convey the idea of antiquity, sometimes by re-creating the ancient world, sometimes by conjuring up romantic landscapes with a dreamy atmosphere. 'There is nothing in our visit resembling the introduction to a new circle of acquaintances; it is the revived delight of the society of long absent and beloved friends,' was the sort of remark many foreign visitors made as soon as they arrived in Greece. The *genius loci* of the Greek scene was a challenge to the artist, and consequently the historical value of this huge archive of the artist travellers' views of Athens (both originals and prints) is twofold. In the first place, of course, the pictures contain authentic evidence of various details of the city's past appearance that would otherwise be lost, given that the face of Athens has changed beyond recognition in modern times. Secondly, as works of art illustrating the artists' particular predilections, the views of Athens provide eloquent evidence concerning the aesthetic trends then current, thanks to the wide range of visual idioms represented. The artists and the buyers of their works shared the conviction that a landscape containing images of the 'far-famed city' must

be so evocative that a 'successful' specimen of the genre would be able to stimulate the imagination and reawaken the emotions kindled by the city's illustrious history. But it need hardly be said that foreign visitors to Athens, arriving there full of preconceived ideas about ancient Greece, would look in vain for the dense olive-groves of the Athenian plain or the shady garden of Plato's Academy near the Kephisos. And so, since the nineteenth-century Attic landscape seemed so alien to their notions of it and so unworthy of the ancient ruins, the travellers simply 'corrected' it and depicted it in accordance with calligraphic visual formulae.

13. The Bombardment of the Parthenon by the Venetian Army on ☞ 26th September 1687. Watercolour, 25 x 72.5 cm, by G.M. Verneda. (Athens, Benaki Museum, 23149)

14. View of Athens from Lykabettos, c. 1785. Coloured etching, 14.5 x 62.5 cm. From L.F. Cassas and J.M.S. Bence, 'Grandes vues pittoresques des principaux cités et monuments de la Grèce et de la Sicile et des Sept Collines de Rome', Paris 1813. (Athens, Benaki Museum, 23998)

15. General view of Athens from the east, c. 1790. Pen and ink, 16 x 53 cm., by Thomas Hope. (Athens, Benaki Museum, 27231)

16. View of Athens from the Hill of Philopappos, c. 1765. Watercolour on paper, 37 x 57 cm., by William Pars. (Athens, Benaki Museum, 25197)

Veduta del Borgo e del Castello di Atene al momento del esplosione di Partenone da una bomba

'The scenery in Athens demands ... our most careful study,' wrote the Scottish landscape painter Hugh William Williams – whose pictures of Greece were so popular that they earned him the sobriquet of 'Grecian Williams' – in 1817. 'When nature presents her endless effects of beauty and of grandeur, the judgement may hesitate.... Unless we are familiar with what has been discovered by her favourite sons, she will not present those electrifying truths, which flash upon the mind in studying her not only as she is, but as seen through the medium of works of genius.... The distant views of Athens claim the style of Claude; his unbroken lines, that continuity and taking up of parts, sweetly transferring them to each other, well expresses what Athens is.' He himself and most of his fellow-artists, following the current conventions, painted the Attic landscape in a soft, often misty light, in the style of the French painter Claude Lorrain (1600-1682), the most eminent specialist in classical landscapes. Intent as they were on creating pictures with an emotional and evocative atmosphere, the artists often simply ignored the physical features of the landscape before their eyes, which they would beautify, select and rearrange to suit themselves. In Williams's 'View of Athens from Philopappos Hill' (Fig. 21) the dominant element in the composition is the light, which suffuses the whole scene with golden tints, conveying a feeling of heavenly serenity and transforming the landscape into a place of momentous significance. In the 'View of the Parthenon' by William James Muller (Fig. 17) the play of light on the three-dimensional mass of the temple and the Arcadian tranquillity of the figures in the foreground work together in harmony with the other-worldly atmosphere of the seashore in the background to suggest a lost paradise. in the 'View of the Acropolis from the Pnyx' by the Swiss painter Rudolph Müller (Fig. 20) the focal point of the composition is the radiantly luminous Acropolis, while the dialogue between it and the Pnyx is the embodiment of classical perfection and of the political, artistic and intellectual ideal of ancient Greece. It is a picture that brilliantly evokes the idealized image of Greece as a land of expiation and redemption. In fact, the more one looks at nineteenth-century pictures of Greece, the more one comes across compositions with similar ruins arranged in a 'theatrical' setting and bathed in a golden glow: a visual cliché that was a standard means of calling up the Golden Age.

17. View of the Parthenon, 1838. Oil on canvas, 58.5 x 87.5 cm., by William James Muller. (Athens, private collection)

18. View of Athens from the west, 1852. Oil on canvas, 120 x 184 cm., by Edward Lear. (Museum of the City of Athens)

19. General View of Athens, 1833. Watercolour on paper, 24.5 x 39.5 cm., by Johann-Michael Wittmer. (Athens, Benaki Museum, 23991)

The nineteenth-century school of romantic landscape painting produced a corpus of inspiring images of Athens in which the artists 're-created' a setting that gratified the feeling of nostalgic longing for the classical world. The pictorial illusion of living antiquity was heightened by the type of composition that was chosen. Most views were of the panoramic type, which, in combination with the solid geometry of the landscape, creates an impression of great depth that lets the eye and the mind roam freely and thus gives the picture a touch of romantic inaccessibility as well as classical antiquity. What is more, the panoramic treatment allowed the artist to locate the significant 'ancient Greek motif' in a real environment in the most unstudied manner.

***Re-creating
the past***

In this way the ruined monuments of Athens are transformed into self-contained aesthetic entities which are integrated into an environment that is usually of dubious authenticity. Most early nineteenth-century 'views of Athens' make no claim to be anything more than a merely acceptable representation of a well-known building or monument, depicted in a setting with a suitably 'antique' atmosphere. The natural environment is often sacrificed to the desired mood, as the focal point of the composition was the recognizable

*20. View of the Acropolis from the Pnyx, 1863. Watercolour on paper, 62.5 x 87.5 cm., by Rudolph Müller. Signed.
(Athens, Benaki Museum, 25193)*

motif: this was the 'trademark' and the bait for potential buyers. After all, there could be nothing more calculated to inspire thoughts of what one had seen and read about Athens than the image of the Acropolis. A buyer of the picture would hardly care whether it was surrounded by arid hills, as in the 'View of Athens from the West' by the German Eduard

Hildebrandt (Fig. 1), or by lush greenery, as in the 'View of Athens from the Ilissos' by the Swiss artist Johann Jacob Wolfensberger (Fig. 12).

In this pictorial dream world there was no place for contemporary allusions. Yet these, in general, were the pictures of Greece that stimulated such widespread and growing interest in the fate of Greece among Western Europeans in the early decades of the nineteenth century. And these same pictures obviously made a convincing impact, for they brought volunteers flocking to support the Greek cause. The Greek Revolution, which mobilized the forces of romanticism, enriched European art with a new thematic repertoire that immediately captured the imagination inasmuch as it combined classical, heroic and religious elements. The Acropolis and other ruined ancient monuments still figured prominently in the scenery of Philhellenic pictures: now, however, they were not there to appeal to classicists and antiquarians but to hint at and emphasize the presence of the classical past, which inspired the heroism of the revolutionary leaders. In fact the rediscovery of Athens by foreign travellers with sketchbooks was responsible not only for providing us with invaluable records of the Athenian scene but also for superimposing Philhellenism in the modern sense on the Western Europeans' love of antiquity. The struggle of the Greek freedom fighters gradually shifted European interest towards the present condition of the once-glorious city and forced them to take note of the scars left by foreign occupation. In the new climate created by the revolutionary movements of the nineteenth century the coexistence of ancient monuments and minarets on the Acropolis seemed tragic rather than picturesque. In the one 'View of the Acropolis' painted by J.M.W. Turner, the eminent English artist reveals his philhellenic sentiments by quoting Byron's words, ''Tis living Greece no more' (Fig. 2). When the French classicist and painter Louis Dupré published his *Voyage à Athènes et Constantinople* (Paris, 1825), one of the most sumptuous of all nineteenth-century art books, he offered the European public images of Athens with a sprinkling of ancient monuments which alluded to the city's long history but had absolutely nothing in common with the utopian pictures of Greece painted by romantic pilgrims.

The founding of independent Greece gave rise to the first scientific attempts to depict Athens as it really was. Whereas the antiquarian interests of the eighteenth-century public had brought into being the monumental albums of art works mentioned above, we now find a panorama of the landscape, environment and inhabitants of Athens and Attica emerging from the numerous illustrated books published in King Otho's reign: these included Ferdinand Stademann's *Panorama von Athen* (Munich, 1841), Otto Magnus von Stackelberg's album entitled *La Grèce, Vues Pittoresques et Topographiques* (Paris, 1834), the collections of prints by Heinrich Hübsch (1795-1863) and Andrea Gasparini and the picturesque scenes in Théodore du Moncel's *Vues Pittoresques des Monuments d'Athènes* (Paris, 1845). At that time, naturally enough, Bavarian artists were in the majority, having answered Otho's open invitation and taken up the challenge of turning the ruined town into a capital city worthy of the glory that was Greece. The changes brought about in the early years of the

Catching up with reality

new capital of the kingdom of Greece have been vividly recorded in the work of two architects working in Athens under the patronage of Ludwig I of Bavaria, Leo von Klenze (1784-1860) and Ludwig Lange (1817-1878). Yet it is interesting to note that both of them, influenced by their sovereign's passion for ancient Greece, also produced the most stunning series of reconstruction drawings of Athens in antiquity, embodying the current state of archaeological knowledge as well as their own classicistic ideals.

In the 1820s and 1830s artists travelling to Greece gradually became less interested in creating dramatic romantic compositions with classical allusions and made greater efforts to depict the living and deeply spiritual beauty of the landscape more objectively. In his 'View of Athens from the West' (Fig. 18), Edward Lear, who as a landscapist was noted for his expressive nuances of colour, successfully 're-created' a reliable pictorial record by reproducing the lyrical atmosphere of an Athenian sunset. Although Lear is better known to English-speaking readers for his verses, he has a more serious claim to fame as probably the best nineteenth-century painter of Greek landscapes, and on his visit to Athens in 1849 he also immortalized in his pictures the now desolate olive-groves of the surrounding plain. The picturesque contrasts presented by Athens in Otho's reign inspired many foreign artists who were best known as genre painters, such as Johann-Michael Wittmer, whose 'General View of Athens' (Fig. 19) captured what was then the city's most fascinating characteristic: the chaotic assortment of monuments of different periods, which made the place look like a stage set.

'History must have its illustrators; and none of them are more useful than the actual illustrators of the time, the artists,' declares Sir Steven Runciman. The archive of pictures of Athens by foreign artists is a heritage that stirs the viewer's imagination and sends it soaring on flights of fancy through time and space. At the same time it is an invaluable tool for the functioning of historical memory, because the desecration of Athens' natural environment destroyed the harmonious balance of mass and space which had opened the eyes of early visitors to the inner relationship between the Attic landscape and its history. These pictures, though trammelled by ideological preconceptions and a codified iconographic language, nevertheless contain some elements of actual reality. They also convey a more immediate sense of the Athenian scene and cause the historian to broaden his field of study. What the art historian has to do is to break the code whereby artists visiting Greece communicated with the Attic landscape, to comment on their ideological preconceptions and to set their work in the context of the aesthetic attitudes formed by the general historical and cultural circumstances of the time.

⌘ 21. *View of Athens from the Hill of Philopappos, 1822. Oil on canvas, 62x98 cm., by Hugh William Williams. Signed.* (*Athens, private collection*)

Athens from the End of the Ancient Era to Greek Independence, exhibition catalogue, Athens
    Cultural Capital of Europe, 1985.
Das neue Hellas Griechen und Bayern zur Zeit Ludwigs I., exhibition catalogue, Bayerisches
    National Museum, Munich 1999.
Navarri, L., *Greece and the Levant: The catalogue of the H.M. Blackmer Collection*, London 1989.
Tufano-Mallouchou, F., «Περιγραφές, έρευνες και απεικονίσεις του Παρθενώνα από τον
    Κυριακό της Αγκώνας ώς τον F. Boissonas» in *Ο Παρθενώνας και η ακτινοβολία του
    στα νεώτερα χρόνια*, Athens 1994, 164-199.
Tsigakou, F.-M., *The Rediscovery of Greece*, London (Thames and Hudson) 1981.
—, *Thomas Hope (1769-1831). Pictures from 18th century Greece*, Athens 1985.
—, *Through Romantic Eyes*, Alexandria, Virginia 1991.
—, *British Images of Greece from the Benaki Museum*, Athens 1995.

NOTES ON THE ILLUSTRATIONS

1. The German painter Eduard Hildebrandt (1818-1868) toured Greece and the Levant in the 1850s.

2. This watercolour is the first of several pictures painted by J.M.W. Turner (1775-1851) on Greek
subjects inspired by Byron. The title of the painting is an abbreviated version of the line '''Tis Greece,
but living Greece no more!' from Byron's *The Giaour*.

3. Although Münster's *Cosmographia* was published nearly fifty years after the Nürnberg *Liber Chronicarum*, the people of Western Europe still remained ignorant of what Athens really looked like. In
these early 'views' the important thing is not so much the way the town is depicted as the fact that
Athens was included among the famous cities featured in books of the period. It is worth noting
that the cartouche gives two forms of the name: Athenae and Setines.

4. This first sketch map of Athens, attributed to the Capuchin friars who established a house there
in the mid seventeenth century, marks ancient monuments and locations under the names then current. It was first published in Guillet de St. Georges, *Athènes ancienne et moderne et l'état présent de
l'empire des Turcs*, Paris 1675.

5. George Wheler (1650-1723), an English naturalist, and Jacob Spon (1647-1685), a French doctor, first
met in Venice in 1675, and that same year they set off together on an eight-month tour through
Greece and Asia Minor. They spent a month in Athens studying the ancient monuments, which are
illustrated with detailed descriptions in Spon's *Voyage d'Italie, de Dalmatie, de Grèce et du Levant fait
aux années 1675 et 1676*, Lyon 1678. Wheler published his own account of their travels four years later.
His sketch map bears a strong resemblance to Spon's, the main differences being that it views the
town from the north and is less accurate.

6. In the foreground is the Marquis de Nointel with his large retinue. Jacques Carrey (1649-1726) was a pupil in Charles Lebrun's studio when Nointel asked the eminent French artist to recommend a competent painter to accompany him on a tour of the Aegean islands and Asia Minor. Nointel, in his capacity as ambassador plenipotentiary, obtained a permit for his artist to make drawings of the ancient monuments. Carrey spent the whole of December 1674 drawing the Parthenon's Ionic frieze and pediments, under the constant supervision of a janissary. His drawings were published posthumously in 1811 in an *édition de luxe* entitled *Temple de Minerve à Athènes*.

7. See No. 5.

8. Coronelli's sketch map, drawn during Morosini's siege of Athens in September 1687, is not unlike that of the Capuchins. In 1684 the Franciscan friar Vincenzo Maria Coronelli (1650-1718), the official 'cosmographer' to the Venetian Republic, brought out a series of illustrated books about the principal battlefields of the Venetian-Turkish war, which was then in progress. His work was of great importance to the subsequent development of Greek topography.

9. James Stuart and Nicholas Revett were the last people to make drawings of the architecture of the façade of Hadrian's Aqueduct. The aqueduct was demolished in 1778 by the voivode Hadji Ali Haseki so that the stones could be used in the construction of the new stretch of city wall that bears his name. Part of the inscribed architrave was built into the Mesogeia Gate.

James Stuart (1713-1788) and Nicholas Revett (1720-1804) stayed in Athens from March 1751 until the autumn of 1753. Stuart drew the general views, while Revett did the measured drawings of the ancient monuments. They returned to England in 1755. The product of their collaboration was a monumental *édition de luxe* in four volumes entitled *The Antiquities of Athens Measured and Delineated*, London 1762-1816 (the fourth volume was published after their death). Although Revett was responsible for taking detailed measurements of the buildings, which give their joint work its unique historical value, in the end it was Stuart who became a celebrity: he was known as 'Athenian Stuart'.

10. 'William Gell presents his compliments to Miss Hawkins and sends proof positive that he is not so unwise as to neglect the opportunity of getting a view à la Poussin,' wrote the artist on the back of this drawing, in a jocular reference to the mania for imitating the idealized scenes painted by Nicolas Poussin and Claude Lorrain, the two great seventeenth-century landscapists.

The archaeologist, draughtsman and topographer Sir William Gell (1774-1836) travelled in Greece and the Troad in 1801-1802, and in 1806 he explored the island of Itháki (Ithaca) thoroughly in an attempt to identify the locations mentioned by Homer. Gell's pedantic obsession with the topography of ancient sites provoked some mockery from Byron, who called him 'classic Gell' and even 'coxcomb Gell'. However, he did publish some important treatises on Greece, including *Itinerary in Greece* (London, 1819), which was a popular pocket guidebook for visitors to the Greek mainland.

11. Jean-Baptiste Hilaire (1753-1822) was in Greece in 1776-1777 as a member of Choiseul-Gouffier's expedition to the Aegean islands. Most of the illustrations in Choiseul-Gouffier's *Voyage pittoresque de la Grèce*, 3 vols., Paris 1782-1822, are based on his drawings..

12. The Swiss painter Johann Jacob Wolfensberger (1797-1850) visited Athens in 1832 and stayed there for two years.

13. Giacomo Milheau Verneda was an artillery officer in the Venetian army and took part in the siege of the Acropolis in 1687. It is a tragic irony that the Parthenon was destroyed at the dawn of the Age of Enlightenment, just when ancient Greece was about to be rediscovered by European antiquaries.

14. The French painter Louis François Cassas (1756-1827) visited Greece in about 1785-1786.

15. Thomas Hope (1769-1831), a Scottish millionaire, went to Greece twice: once from 1787 to 1795 and again in late 1799 and early 1800. In the course of his travels he produced a very fine series of drawings which he later bound together in five volumes and kept in his library. It was generally accepted by art historians that these volumes had been sold at auction in 1930 and that all trace of them had since been lost, but in 1978 I discovered them in the Benaki Museum, where they still are. The drawings in the Benaki Museum's Hope Collection are a real treasure: besides demonstrating the amazing technical skill of this self-taught artist, they provide historians with a unique series of pictorial records of the Greek landscape, architecture and traditional costumes of the late eighteenth century.

16. In 1764, at the age of twenty-two, William Pars (1742-1782) showed such promise that he was chosen by the Society of Dilettanti to accompany the archaeologist Richard Chandler on his expedition to Asia Minor, which the Society funded. Pars was one of the main contributors to the series *The Antiquities of Ionia* (1762-1881) and also contributed to the second and third volumes of *The Antiquities of Athens*.

17. William James Muller (1812-1845), one of the most original British romantic watercolourists and one of the most authentic pleinairists of his time, spent a month and a half in Greece in 1838 on his way to Egypt.

18. The well-known landscape artist and humorous poet Edward Lear (1812-1888) toured Greece in 1848-1849 and spent most of his time in Corfu from 1855 to 1864. He is generally regarded as the outstanding nineteenth-century painter of Greek landscapes, because his approach to the Greek scene goes well beyond mere admiration for antiquity and borders on authentic testimony. What makes his work as a painter of Greek landscapes so important is not just its sheer volume (about 3,000 pictures on Greek subjects) but his heightened sensitivity to the Greek light and his interest in interpreting the landscape. Lear published two illustrated travel books about Greece: *Journals of a Landscape Painter in Albania, & c.* (London, 1851) and *Views in the Seven Ionian Islands* (London, 1863).

19. The Bavarian painter Johann-Michael Wittmer (1802-1880), a protégé of King Ludwig I of Bavaria, went to Greece in 1834 with Prince Maximilian, brother of Otho, the new King of Greece.

20. Very little is known about the Swiss painter Rudolph Müller (1802-1885). It is on record that he travelled extensively in the Mediterranean countries and in 1860 settled permanently in Rome, where he painted this picture from sketches he had drawn on the spot.

21. The Scottish artist Hugh William Williams (1773-1829), who was in his day the most popular painter of Greek landscapes with an 'antique' atmosphere, went on an extensive tour of Greece in 1817. Three years later he published an illustrated travel book in two volumes entitled *Travels in Italy, Greece and the Ionian Islands* (Edinburgh, 1820), which won great critical acclaim, and in 1827-1829 he published a series of prints entitled *Select Views in Greece*.

CHAPTER XI

*From the 19th to
the 21st Century:
Metamorphoses
of the Archaeological
Landscape in Athens*

Fani Mallouchou-Tufano

2. The Kerameikos today. (Photo: S. Mavromatis, 2000)

1. The Kerameikos, 1889-1892. (Athens, National Historical Museum)

From the 19th to the 21st Century: Metamorphoses of the Archaeological Landscape in Athens

The aura of the ancient Athenian world, with all its cultural and symbolic implications as well as what remained of its magnificent physical presence, was the underlying reason for designating Athens – then in ruins after the War of Independence – as the capital of the newly independent Greek state in 1833. This parameter was strongly emphasized in the first city plans drawn up for the new capital, which included proposals for rediscovering the ancient monuments and, more particularly, for their enhancement.

In the first plan, by Stamatios Kleanthis and Eduard Schaubert, the new city was not superimposed on the old: it occupied hitherto unbuilt land north of the Acropolis and north of the medieval town, where much of the ancient heritage was preserved underground and, to a lesser extent, on the surface. In the realms of ideology and symbolism, however, the old city and the new were closely intertwined. The Acropolis (Fig. 3), the ancient monument with the greatest ideological import for the modern Greeks and the symbol of the nation's existence in the modern civilized world, was linked both visually and on the ground (by means of Athinás Street) with the royal palace, the centre of absolute earthly power and the source of all progress and development in the newly-founded state. Wide, straight roads skirting what was left of the medieval town connected the new city with the existing ancient monuments and were planned to connect it later with the whole of the ancient city – the 'city of Hadrian' as well as the 'city of Theseus'. The ancient city occupied most of the area covered by the medieval town, from the 'Theseion' to Hadrian's Library and from there to the Monument of Lysikrates: building construction was banned in the whole of this area and provision was made for compulsory purchases of properties and subsequent excavation. The antiquities thus brought to light would, after landscaping, constitute 'a museum of ancient architecture', which would be 'displayed in all its splendour to the eyes of the admirer of ancient art, to the artist and the scholar'. By walking and meditating in this archaeological park – 'a museum the like of which is not to be found anywhere else in the world' – modern Athenians, and by implication all modern Greeks, would renew the mystical bonds linking them with their glorious past; they would look up to the example of their ancestors and draw from it the self-confidence, strength and faith necessary to create an equally glorious present and future.

The emblematic significance of the Acropolis to the newly-independent state comes out even more strongly in the proposals for the enhancement of the ancient monuments which Leo von Klenze submitted to the Regency in 1834. In Klenze's view, the best way to enlist civilized Europe's interest in and sympathy for modern Greece and, in the last analysis, to secure the European countries' recognition of Greece as a full and equal member of their fraternity, was by designating the Acropolis as an archaeological site pure and simple, wiping out all trace of the other purposes for which it had been used since antiquity, clearing away the relics of centuries of barbarism, carrying out excavations and restoring the monuments, especially the Parthenon. As far as the other antiquities were concerned, Klenze's new master plan retained the zone reserved for archaeological excavations in Kleanthis and Schaubert's plan, but he adapted it slightly to make allowances for nineteenth-century reality: the site of Hadrian's Library was excluded, as it was by this time being used as the town's marketplace.

Kleanthis and Schaubert's dream of turning Athens into a modern European capital to match the ancient city's glory and beauty and uncovering the city of Theseus and Hadrian was

3. *The Olympieion, the Acropolis and Athens from the south-east. G. Rumine, 1859. (ELIA)*

dashed immediately and irrevocably by the intrusion of harsh reality; the infant Greek state had neither the funds nor the administrative machinery to put their ambitious plan into effect; the hasty and unpremeditated decision to move the capital from Náfplion to Athens in 1834 created an urgent demand for new housing; and the Athenians, motivated either by the necessity of making ends meet or by speculative greed, were far from supportive. The new city was built all over the ruins of ancient Athens, following the street plan already in existence, and in this way the ancient buildings and monuments – whether still standing and visible or buried beneath the earth – were directly involved in the process of urban development. The same factors that had led to the abandonment of the Kleanthis-Schaubert plan also prevented it from being replaced by another which proposed the construction of the new city directly on top of the city of Theseus. If this latter plan had been adopted, in all probability the antiquities would have featured prominently as focal points for holistic or partial monumental urban planning, as was being done at that time in other European cities with a long history and age-old stratification. In Athens, however, the excavation of ancient monuments and the creation of archaeological sites had perforce to proceed in the piecemeal and often haphazard fashion that had come to be the norm in the development of the city itself. Subject to these limitations, some of Kleanthis and Schaubert's ideas were retained in one form or another. One of those was the idea of excavating and laying bare the whole of ancient Athens, a dream on which generations of architects were to be nurtured and which was to surface from time to time before being partially fulfilled in the twentieth century.

The reign of King Otho was punctuated by outbursts of patriotic ardour and dreams of national regeneration and the expansion of the modern Greek state to the limits of what had once been the Byzantine Empire. Constant efforts were made to forge a national identity, in which the ancient Greek roots were strongly emphasized. In this context great importance *The first visions:* was attached to the clearance and enhancement of the Acropolis, the sym- *1833-1853* bol of the Greek nation. Here Klenze's guidelines were followed to the letter. Throughout this period huge quantities of earth and debris were removed and buildings were demolished to clear the Acropolis of most of the Byzantine, Frankish and later ruins that covered it. At the same time the materials from the demolished buildings

were used to restore and reconstruct the ancient monuments. The rebuilding of the Temple of Athena Nike in 1835-1836 was hailed in Greece and the rest of Europe as the first tangible evidence of the revival of the Greek nation. Next, in 1837-1840 and 1845-1846, the walls of the Erechtheion were largely rebuilt and its porticoes were partially restored. In 1841-1844 large sections of the Parthenon's sekos walls and some of its peristyle columns were rebuilt. In 1843-1844 the restoration of the Temple of Athena Nike was completed and in 1850 the steps up to the Propylaia were repaired to provide easier access to the Acropolis.

4. The Acropolis and Athens from the west. P. Sebah, 1872-1875. (CCAM Archives)

As a result of all this restoration work, which was done in an extempore and empirical fashion dictated by the financial resources available and the current level of archaeological expertise, the Acropolis began to take on the appearance under which it came to be recognizable all over the world. In May 1835, when an entrance charge was first imposed, it became the first archaeological site officially open to the public. The repair and restoration work was supervised by the first enthusiastic officers of the Greek Archaeological Service and the Athens Archaeological Society, Ludwig Ross, Kyriakos Pittakis and Alexandros Rizos-Rangavis. Of these, Ross was outstanding for his scientific method and Pittakis, a native of Athens, for his unflagging and wholehearted dedication to the cause of preserving the antiquities of his birthplace – a quality that made him the emblematic figure of this period.

In the lower town there was a great spate of building construction in the first twenty years after the refounding of Athens, especially in the area designated as an archaeological zone in the Kleanthis-Schaubert plan. To deal with the situation, in November 1836 the Architecture Department of the Ministry of the Interior scheduled five areas as archaeological zones, all of them containing ancient monuments that were still standing or still partly visible: the area round the ' Theseion', the area round the Monument of Lysikrates, the site of the Roman Agora, the area round the 'Prytaneion' (now identified as the so-called Diogeneion) and the part of the Agora containing the visible remains of the Stoa of Attalos and the 'Stoa of the Giants'. In these zones local modifications were made to the city plan and schedules were prepared for compulsory purchases of properties and for excavations. Even so, the ancient remains were swamped by the living city: the bazaar was re-established in the eastern half of Hadrian's Library (then known as Hadrian's Gymnasium) and in 1834-1835 an army barracks was built on top of its western half. The Roman Agora, of which the west gate and some columns of the interior peristyle were visible, was full of houses as well as the Hill School and the army bakery. The ruins of the Stoa of Attalos (then known as Ptolemy's Gymnasium) were surrounded by buildings, while the Giants and Tritons that had once adorned the façade of the Odeion of Agrippa now occupied the basements

6. *The Odeion of Herodes from the north. P. Sebah, 1872-1875. (CCAM Archives)*

5. *The Theatre of Dionysos from the south-west. P. Sebah, 1872-1875. (CCAM Archives)*

of private houses. Apart from the Acropolis, the only sites where ancient monuments were recognizable as such were the Olympieion and the Hill of the Muses, the Pnyx and the Hill of the Nymphs on the desolate and uninhabited western and southern outskirts of the city.

In those early years of Greek independence archaeologists in Greece and elsewhere were keen to clarify the topography of ancient Athens, about which very little was then known. The bodies entrusted with the country's archaeological heritage dreamed of extensive digs to locate the ancient city's civic and cultural centre, mentioned so often in the literary sources. However, the time was not ripe for systematic excavations. Occasional digs were organized by the Archaeological Society in search of the ancient Bouleuterion (near the building now identified as the Eleusinion) and the Prytaneion (near the Church of Hagios Dhimítrios Katifóris). Pittakis carried on with his small-scale excavations in search of specific buildings and monuments in various parts of the town, which he had started during the War of Independence, and he succeeded in locating the Klepsydra, the inscription carved in the rock on the Hill of the Nymphs marking the limit of the Precinct of Zeus, and the Sacred Gate in the Kerameikos district (identified at the time as the Dipylon Gate). In practice, excavations were carried out not so much by the archaeologist's spade as by the pickaxes used in the development of the modern city. When the Royal Gardens (now the National Gardens) were being laid out, a large part of the Roman extension to the ancient city was brought to light. In 1837 construction work on a private house was held up when the builders unearthed the inscribed base of the Euboulides ex-voto, still in its original position. This was an extremely important discovery which, taken in conjunction with Pausanias's description, made it possible to establish the path of the road running from the Dipylon Gate to the Agora and thus to pinpoint their exact positions. Ross was fully aware of the significance of the find and published it internationally. However, the losses far outweighed the gains. Most of the ancient ruins unearthed during the construction of the new city were destroyed, and the ancient materials were usually reused in the new buildings. All the archaeologists could do was to take the movable finds into safe keeping, either in the 'Theseion' – which was used as the Central Museum of Antiquities from 1834 onwards – or in storerooms at some of the archaeological sites. Large-scale cleaning and clearance work on other monuments outside the Acropolis did not start until the 1850s, but thereafter it continued systematically.

In the sixty years or so from the accession of George I until 1922, Athens developed at a spectacular pace in every way. The centre was densely built-up and the city started spreading out in all directions, especially from the 1880s onwards. It had its fair share of private mansions, government office buildings, public utilities and big new churches. The local railway between Athens and Piraeus was built as early as the 1860s *Topographical exploration and discoveries, 1864-1885* and the main line railway to the rest of Greece in the 1880s. Great progress was made with the urban infrastructure: roads, public transport, electricity supplies, telephones. By the time of the Asia Minor disaster in 1922 Athens had grown into a proper European city with a rich artistic and intellectual life, a cultural capital for all the Greeks living in the East and the West. One of the highlights in its history occurred in 1896, when the Olympic Games were held there and the eyes of the world were turned upon it. The gradual headway made with the organization and physical and social urbanization of Athens was matched by similar progress with the archaeological sites and monuments.

In the first two decades after the abdication of King Otho (1862) a start was made with systematic archaeological excavations – systematic in terms of continuity, if not of method. They were carried out by the Archaeological Society, which, with Stephanos Kumanudes as its Secretary, now settled down to fulfil its primary function and became, in effect, the principal institution responsible for the protection of the country's archaeological heritage. Restoration and rebuilding work was abandoned, in keeping with the more pragmatic spirit of those years. On the Acropolis, in 'Hadrian's Gymnasium', the 'Agoranomeion', the 'Stoa of the Giants' and elsewhere, the Archaeological Society and the General Ephorate of Antiquities (headed by Panayotis Efstratiades) concentrated on small-scale consolidation work using traditional methods and materials such as iron hoops and tie-rods, shores and brickwork buttresses. By this time the Greek public was more interested in the safety of the ancient monuments (especially those on the Acropolis) and the visual impression they made (especially to foreign visitors) (Fig. 4). Construction work was started on the Acropolis Museum and railings were put up in the sites with archaeological collections, the Temple of Athena Nike, the Pinakotheke in the Propylaia and some medieval cisterns on the Acropolis. The Monument of Lysikrates was tidied up in preparation for the visit of Empress Eugénie of France in 1868/69: its base was patched up and reintegrated, the grounds around it – now earmarked for redevelopment as an open square – were cleared of the ruins of the Capuchin friary and excavated, and a low wall was built round the monument (Fig. 7). A wall was also built round the Tower of the Winds, and the piece of land in front of Hadrian's Library, where there was an archaeological collection, was enclosed by a stone wall and a wooden fence. Further measures were taken to protect the antiquities by putting up temporary fences round the newly-excavated ruins on the south slope of the Acropolis and wooden sheds (to be used as watchmen's premises and storerooms) in the orchestra of the Theatre of Dionysos, in front of the Odeion of Herodes Atticus, next to the Monument of Lysikrates and in front of Hadrian's Library.

Most of the effort, however, was concentrated on topographical exploration and the rediscovery of the ancient city. Organized excavation started on the unbuilt south slope of the Acropolis. There Pittakis had already cleared the Herodeion (Fig. 6) between 1848 and 1857. From 1857 to 1867 Efstratiades, in collaboration with Stack and Ziller, removed all the accumulated earth and debris to reveal the ruins of the Theatre of Dionysos (Fig. 5) and part of the adjacent sanctuary. But it was in 1876-1879 that this area was drastically transformed, when Kumanudes conducted systematic excavations and unearthed the ruins of the Stoa of Eumenes, the Asklepieion and the nearby temples and choregic monuments. In the city centre, interest was focused on the ruins of 'Ptolemy's Gymnasium' and the 'Stoa of the Giants', where most of the later accretions were removed and the archaeological remains were extended in a rapid succession of clearance and excavation projects. Little by little, new additions were made to the

7. The Monument of Lysikrates from the south-west. P. Sebah, 1872-1875. (CCAM Archives)

Athens archaeological landscape: the Panathenaic Stadium, excavated by Ernst Ziller and Spyridon Lampros in 1868-1869; the meeting-place of the Ekklesia of the Demos (Citizens' Assembly) on the Pnyx, first explored in 1862 by Ernst Curtius; and the Kerameikos (Fig. 1), where the large number of antiquities discovered during the construction of Piraiás Street prompted the Archaeological Society to initiate systematic excavations in 1869-1870. In 1885-1886, after the destruction by fire of the central bazaar, Kumanudes excavated the site of Hadrian's Library and unearthed its eastern half; and in 1890-1891 he excavated near the Tower of the Winds, where he demolished the later buildings and so opened up much of the south-east courtyard and the east gate of the Roman Agora.

Every new excavation did a little more to fill the gaps in the archaeologists' knowledge of the topography and monuments of the ancient city. In 1862 Kumanudes found the dedicatory inscription that enabled him to identify the Stoa of Attalos. Hadrian's Library was identified in 1885, the Roman Agora (Fig. 10) in 1890. The discovery of the funerary relief of Dexileos in 1863 suggested that the area where it was found was probably the Kerameikos, and this hypothesis was confirmed in 1870 when one of the boundary stones was found *in situ*. In 1874, when Curtius correctly identified the Sacred Gate and the Dipylon, the topography of the area became much clearer.

Unfortunately, the discovery of ancient Athens proceeded at the expense of the medieval and post-medieval town. In the first decades after independence redevelopment had already led to the disappearance of many Byzantine and Post-Byzantine buildings, churches being among the first to go. Kumanudes, the last adherent of the Enlightenment, ignored the radical change of attitude towards the constant evolution of Hellenism through the ages: when he excavated an ancient monument, he deliberately removed all trace of what he saw as the centuries of decline and barbarization. He was responsible for the destruction of a large part of the Late Roman wall with its towers, the Rizókastro and Serpendzés walls and the Middle Byzantine Church of the Megáli Panagia (in Hadrian's Library) with its magnificent interior decoration.

By the end of the 1870s, as we know from contemporary photographs, the appearance of the ancient monuments in Athens had changed considerably, but the picture they presented was still idyllic, unorganized and in complete harmony with the still unspoilt natural environment. The built-up area now extended almost as far as the Olympieion and Hadrian's Arch, but those two monuments were still just beyond the edge of the city, standing on their own in a basically rural setting. Amalías Avenue ran in front of them and the Záppion Gardens were being laid out to the north (Fig. 12). Between them, a country lane led to the cafés recently built along the River Ilissos. The columns of the Olympieion, now stripped of the medieval cubicle perched on the architrave, looked as if they were growing straight out of the ground, because the krepidoma of the temple had been covered with earth when Amalías Avenue was being built in 1861-1862. The Hill of the Muses, the Pnyx and the Hill of the Nymphs were still bare of trees and houses (Fig. 8), but the Acropolis Boulevard (the modern Dhionisíou Areopayítou and Apostólou Pávlou Streets) now ran between them and the Acropolis: its construction in

8. The Hill of the Nymphs viewed from the Acropolis. P. Sebah, 1872-1875. (CCAM Archives)

9. Panoramic view of Athens from the Hill of the Nymphs, 1869-1875. (Athens, National Historical Museum)

Panoramique d'Athènes
et de la Colline des Nymphes

the early 1860s had caused considerable damage to the ancient remains unearthed by the road-builders. The public gardens to the west of the 'Theseion' had already been planted, while to the south of the temple was a rectangular terrace used for the storage of antiquities waiting to be moved to the new Archaeological Museum. In the north-west of the city the Kerameikos cemetery was beginning to be revealed: already a few early factories had sprung up nearby, but the flourishing, age-old olive-groves of the Attic plain were still only a stone's throw away (Fig. 9). Dominating the whole landscape was the Acropolis, drastically transformed by the demolition in 1875 of the 'Frankish Tower' in the Propylaia.

10. The Roman Agora in 1891. (German Archaeological Institute)

Between the late 1880s and the Asia Minor disaster of 1922 some administrative changes were made in the country's archaeological institutions. From 1885 to 1909 Panayotis Kavvadias was the leading figure on the Greek archaeological scene in his dual capacity as General Ephor of Antiquities and Secretary of the Archaeological Society. After the coup d'état of 1909 the responsibility for all archaeological administration was placed in the hands of the state-run Archaeological Service, while the function of the Archaeological Society was strictly limited to matters of scholarship and research. Kavvadias presided over an administrative and scientific reorganization of Greek archaeology and a huge quantity of archaeological work, in keeping with the prevailing national trend towards modernization, technological progress and economic growth. It was in this period that Athens grew into a proper city with a modern, European 'feel' to it. The archaeological sites and ancient monuments were directly involved in the drive to beautify and improve the city, which was sometimes prompted by decisions to hold major international events in Athens – most notably the Olympic Games in 1896, but also the 1st International Archaeological Conference in 1905. A wide-ranging, concerted programme of excavation, restoration and general tidying-up altered the appearance of the ancient ruins almost beyond recognition, making them more presentable, better organized attractions that were fitting ornaments of the urban scene.

Urban beautification, 1885-1909

The excavations carried out during these years exemplify the progress that had been made in the science of archaeology. Digs on the Acropolis, in the Kerameikos and at the centres of the Mycenaean world significantly enlarged the scope of archaeologists' knowledge and gave them a better appreciation of the creative evolution of the Greeks over the centuries. While the excavators of Athens – especially those in the Greek archaeological services – were still keenly interested in the local topography, we begin to find stratigraphical researches, especially by members of the foreign archaeological schools and institutes that had sprung up in Greece, to shed light on the evolution of the ancient city and its monuments through the ages. Foremost among the latter group was Wilhelm Dörpfeld, the Director of the German Archaeological Institute and closest associate of the Greek Archaeological Service, whose members were predominantly royalist and pro-German. In the first decade of the twentieth century a number of younger scholars with fresh ideas and methods, including Gorham Stevens, B.H. (Bert) Hill and William B. Dinsmoor, prepared the way for the influx of American archaeologists that followed soon afterwards. The achievements of archaeological research during these years were recorded in Walter Judeich's *Topographie von Athen* (1905), reissued in a revised edition in 1931, which was used as the basis for every topographical study of ancient Athens until the Second World War.

Similarly, the number of ancient monuments restored during this period reflects the Greeks' acceptance of modern technology, to which they had been converted in the last quarter of the nineteenth century. We now find qualified engineers taking an active part in restoration projects – including Nikolaos Balanos and Anastasios Orlandos, who were later to win renown as the principal restorers of ancient Greek monuments – and efforts being made to ensure that the work was done under the best possible conditions.

Ideologically, Greek archaeologists still remained deeply committed to the old classicistic tradition, even in these changing times. In excavations, the primary object was to discover and give prominence to the Classical phase of the monuments; in restorations, it was to restore them as far as possible as they were thought to have been in Classical times. As so often before and since, the thinking behind the excavation and preservation of ancient monuments in Athens at that time was closely bound up with the whole matter of Greek national aspirations. The restoration of the Acropolis monuments, begun as an emergency operation after the 1894 earthquake, developed into a campaign for the restoration of national archetypes. In 1920-1921, when Greece – after emerging victorious in the Balkans – was setting out to conquer Asia Minor, the other 'great idea' of excavating and laying bare the whole of ancient Athens resurfaced in a more ambitious form than ever.

The first step towards giving the archaeological sites an organized urban character in accordance with European standards was to remove the sheds and makeshift fences put up during the previous decade and replace them with proper gatehouses and iron railings (most of them designed by the French engineer Désiré Matton) on trim stone walls. This work was put in hand in 1889, starting with the Kerameikos and the Monument of Lysikrates, and was stepped up in preparation for the Olympic Games in 1895-1896, when railings were erected round the 'Stoa of the Giants', the façade and the excavated section of Hadrian's Library and the east side of the Theatre of Dionysos. Plans were drawn up for other monuments and the whole of the Acropolis to be railed off, and accordingly stone walls were built in 1898 round the Stoa of Attalos and in 1908-1909 round the 'Theseion' and along the stretch of the Acropolis Boulevard from the Herodeion to the Areopagus.

At the same time systematic excavation, restoration and general refurbishment projects were put in hand on all the ancient monuments in Athens with the main object of restructuring them and adapting them to the new urban environment. From the early 1880s large-scale urban development work was done in the vicinity of the Olympieion: the Záppion building was completed and its public gardens laid out and planted, and Vassilíssis Ólgas Avenue was built. The area was completely transformed between 1895 and 1905, when Anastasios Metaxas restored the gleaming marble of the Panathenaic Stadium (Fig. 13). While all this was in progress, the Archaeological Society initiated the first excavations in the Olympieion (1883-1909, with some interruptions): most of the precinct wall was laid bare and reconstructed, the propylon was discovered, the whole site was cleared of earth and debris and the architraves and krepidoma of the temple were reinforced. Even more important than the change in the temple's appearance was the transformation of the old, everyday character of the site, which was now properly organized – but also railed off – in accordance with the dictates and psychology of the modern era.

Changes were also noticeable on the hills to the south-west of the Acropolis, which were now under siege from the expanding city: some houses had already been built on the Hill of the Nymphs (Fig. 15). These and other hills in Athens, as well as the slopes of the Acropolis, were planted with trees by the Woodland Conservation Society (Filodasiki Enosis) at the turn of the century. Afforestation proved to be their salvation because, if nothing else, it prevented the extension of the built-up area to the Pnyx and the Hill of the Muses in the following years. Meanwhile excavations were begun on all the hills, and the consolidation and partial restoration of the Monument of Philopappos in 1898-1900 left it with its now familiar silhouette.

It was in this period that a new organized archaeological site came into being: the Kerameikos. Successive excavations by the Archaeological Society since the late 1860s had brought to light the Sacred Gate, the Dipylon, the Pompeion, the Themistoklean wall, numerous Classical funerary monuments and earlier burials. The interpretation of their significance was painful enough, their excavation even more so. In 1908 the Society managed to buy up the whole of the excavated area, whereupon it put a wall round the site, drained the land and built a storehouse for the finds. A major step forward was taken in 1910 when the burial precincts along the Street of the Tombs were restored as far as possible to their original state by Alfred Brückner and Balanos (Fig. 11).

On the Acropolis, work started on projects that were to transform its interior layout and appearance completely and highlight its national importance even more strongly. From 1885 to 1890 Kavvadias excavated the whole summit right down to the bedrock. The ground was then brought up to what was thought to have been the surface level in Classical times and the architectural members scattered all over were gathered into piles. In 1898 Balanos started restoring the Acropolis monuments. By 1902 he had consolidated the opisthodomos and the west front of the Parthenon. The Erechtheion was restored between 1902 and 1909, the Propylaia between 1909 and 1917. The appearance of the Erechtheion and the plateau of the Acropolis then remained unchanged for the next seventy years.

11. The Kerameikos in 1910. (German Archaeological Institute)

These arduous labours covered the whole summit of the Acropolis, its lower slopes and even some of the ground at its foot. Between 1896 and 1909 Kavvadias extended his clearance digs to the caves on the north slope and the saddle of the Areopagus. All along the south slope, from the Theatre of Dionysos to the Herodeion, minor interventions were carried out at regular intervals between 1886 and 1922 on the maintenance of the ancient ruins and the clearance of their surroundings, at first by the Archaeological Society and later by the Archaeological Service. Meanwhile excavation was started on new sites. In 1912 the Society acquired a number of houses north-east of the Theatre of Dionysos by compulsory purchase, and excavations conducted there by Panayotis Kastriotes from 1914 to 1922 revealed the ruins of the Odeion of Perikles. Between 1891 and 1897 the German Archaeological Institute under Dörpfeld excavated the west slope of the Acropolis and the south-west slope of the Areopagus, uncovering a whole residential district of the ancient city with houses, a main street, shrines, the Peisistratid aqueduct and a monumental water fountain (Fig. 15). In 1894 this area was expropriated and brought into the archaeological zone.

The archaeological activity during this period did much to restore the archetypical character of the Acropolis. At the same time, various plans were being hatched to turn the whole of the Acropolis into an emblem of the city. One aim they all had in common was to isolate it from the rest of the city and make it stand out even more conspicuously by building a grand ring road round it: construction of the road started in 1901, but it came up against an immov-

12. *The Olympieion and its surroundings in 1875. (Athens, National Historical Museum)*

able obstacle in the form of the Anafiótika, a district above the Pláka inhabited mainly by migrants from the Aegean islands.

In the lower town, drastic changes were made in the appearance of the Monument of Lysikrates: the area around it was cleared of houses and turned into an open square in 1889, and the monument itself was restored in 1892 by the French School of Archaeology. More important than this, however, were the extensive excavations carried out, especially in the Agora, which prepared the way for later developments.

In 1890-1891, when the Piraeus railway was being extended from Thissío station to Monastiráki, the Archaeological Society under Dörpfeld excavated the north side of the Agora all along the trench being dug for the railway. In 1895-1897 the excavations were extended to the east slope of the hill of Kolonos Agoraios, the north slope of the Areopagus and sections of Adhriano_ Street: these brought to light the Temple of Apollo Patroös and the Metroön (both of which were misidentified), ancient Greek and Roman houses and a stretch of the Panathenaic Way. Meanwhile, between 1895 and 1903, the rest of the Stoa of Attalos was excavated and the fabric was reinforced (Fig. 14). In 1910 Konstantinos Kourouniotes re-excavated the site of what was then thought to be the Bouleuterion, but only some sections of the Late Roman wall and the Panathenaic Way were found there. In the same year the Archaeological Society bought up and demolished some more houses in the southern half of the Roman Agora; and the excavations that followed, under Kastriotes and Alexander Philadelpheus, brought to light a good deal more of the Roman Agora near the west gate.

13. The Olympieion viewed from the Acropolis in 1910. (German Archaeological Institute)

During this period, in the prevailing mood of national pride, the ever-latent idea of excavating and laying bare the whole of ancient Athens resurfaced once again. During the Balkan Wars (1912-1913) there seemed no reason why it should not be possible to uncover the whole of the Roman Agora and Hadrian's Library and to join them both up with the Stoa of Attalos, following the example of what had been done in the Forum Romanum in Rome. Steps were taken to move the eighty-year-old barracks and the army bakery, and the Turkish *medresseh* (theological college) was demolished in 1914. The idea gathered momentum and was presented in ever more ambitious form in the successive master plans for Athens drawn up at about this time. In 1920, when national jubilation and expansionism were at their height, the Supreme Technical Council – on which Orlandos (recently returned from an educational visit to Italy) sat as adviser on archaeological matters – prepared a new plan in which provision was made for a 'Monumental Zone' reserved for excavations (modelled on the new Zona Monumentale in Rome), covering a very large area stretching from the Kerameikos to the Acropolis Boulevard and from Hadrian's Library to the east slopes of the Hill of the Muses and the Pnyx. In 1921, the centenary year of the Greek War of Independence, Philadelpheus submitted a paper to Parliament containing specific proposals for the progressive expropriation and excavation of the site of ancient Athens within three years. This dream was shattered in 1922 by the catastrophic defeat of the Greek expeditionary force in Asia Minor.

14. The Stoa of Attalos and the Acropolis in 1902. (German Archaeological Institute)

After the Asia Minor disaster of 1922 the character and appearance of Athens underwent sweeping changes. Now, for the first time, Athens could truly be called the capital of the Greek world – but now the Greek world was confined within the frontiers of Greece. Between the two World Wars we find the first evidence of the phenomena that were to become rampant after the Second World War and have a decisive bearing on the city's future: the population explosion, leading to the rapid expansion of Athens and the beginning of multi-storey building construction in the centre; the deterioration of the natural environment as the first factories went into operation in the plain of Athens; and the disappearance of prominent features of the historical landscape under the plans for the first large-scale urban development projects.

15. The west slope of the Acropolis during the excavations of 1891-1897. (German Archaeological Institute)

This process of environmental degradation directly affected the archaeological sites and ancient monuments.

One result of the severe economic recession afflicting the whole country, especially in the first ten years after the Asia Minor disaster, was that few resources were available for work on any ancient monuments except those on the Acropolis. In these hard times the 'Sacred Rock' was ideologically recharged to become a symbol of the nation's survival and recovery. The rebuilding of the north colonnade of the Parthenon started in 1923 under Balanos, and the finished project was officially opened to the public on 17th May 1930 at the celebrations held on the Acropolis to mark the centenary of the rebirth of the Greek nation. Balanos completed his restoration work on the Parthenon in 1933, leaving it in the state in which, with improved communications, it became a familiar image all over the world after the Second World War. Between 1935 and 1940 the bastion and temple of Athena Nike were restored (the latter for the second time). Meanwhile, in 1934-1935, Balanos reinforced the crumbling walls on the north slope of the Acropolis by building massive buttresses which totally altered its appearance from that side.

Between the wars: The first disfigurements

The same circumstances made the Greek archaeological services realize that they would have to give up their cherished dream of excavating the Agora themselves. In 1929 a law was passed designating the area between the Tower of the Winds and the 'Theseion' as an archaeological site reserved for excavations. The excavation rights for the western part of this zone, from the Stoa of Attalos to the 'Theseion' and from the railway line to the north-west slopes of the Acropolis and the Areopagus, were awarded to the American School of Classical Studies (Fig. 16), while the rest of it remained under the jurisdiction of the Greek archaeological authorities. In 1931 the Americans made a start on the wholesale expropriation and excavation of the Agora (Fig. 17), a process which continued until the outbreak of the war and was completed after the war, radically altering the appearance of the area. All it was possible to do in the Greek zone was to extend the site clearance and excavation work in the middle and the south-west corner of the Roman Agora and (in 1931-1932) to demolish the Othonian barracks in the south-west corner of Hadrian's Library.

Altogether a great deal of excavation was done between the wars, some of it by the Greeks but most by foreign archaeological schools, bringing to light more and more new evidence concerning the stratigraphy of the city and its monuments. On the south-east slopes of the Acropolis the remains of the Odeion of Perikles were partially uncovered between 1924 and 1932, first under Kastriotes and then under Orlandos. In the same area the Archaeological Society conducted excavations of the Theatre of Dionysos from 1923 to 1929 under Dörpfeld, Heinrich Bulle and Ernst Fiechter, which did much to clarify its successive building phases. Systematic excavation and site clearance work on the north slope of the Acropolis and at its foot, carried out in the 1930s by the American School under Oscar Broneer, revealed the Sanctuary of Aphrodite and Eros, the

16. *The Agora viewed from the Hill of the Nymphs in 1931. (American School of Classical Studies)*

17. *The Agora excavations in 1935. (American School of Classical Studies)*

Mycenaean gateway in the Acropolis wall and the underground spring, as well as the remains of dwelling-houses dating from the Neolithic to the Mycenaean period. Concurrent excavations on the Pnyx from 1930 to 1937, under Kourouniotes, Homer Thompson and Robert Scranton, shed new light on the progressive development of the meeting-place of the ancient Citizens' Assembly and uncovered the remains of other buildings and fortification works on the historic hill. And from 1927 to 1943 the Kerameikos was systematically re-excavated and re-examined, this time by the German Archaeological Institute: new discoveries included the cemeteries of the Sub-Mycenaean and Geometric periods and part of the road from the Dipylon Gate to the Academy, lined with funerary monuments. The finds were so numerous that a museum was needed to house them all, and it was built in 1936-1938. Lastly, the gymnasium of the Academy was excavated for the first time from 1930 to 1939 on the initiative of Panayotis Aristofron, a Greek of the diaspora, and some properties thereabouts were expropriated. Aristofron's dream of setting up a worldwide League of Academies and Universities and joining up the Academy site with the Kerameikos had to be postponed because of the unstable political situation.

It was in the inter-war period, when organized tourism made its first appearance in Greece, that the archaeological authorities first had to address the issues arising from the development of the ancient monuments as tourist attractions able to deal with visitors *en masse*. At the beginning of the 1930s the Archaeological Service and the newly-founded National Tourist Organization started giving urgent attention to improving the appearance of the archaeological sites in Athens, which had long been neglected and in many cases were being used as encampments for the refugees from Asia Minor. The refugee shanties on the north slope of the Acropolis and the east slope of Kolonos Agoraios were cleared away in the next few years to make way for the excavations of the American School. Between 1933 and 1937 the Greek authorities set about tidying up the Roman Agora: the refugee encampments were pulled down, the army bakery was demolished, the whole area was fenced in and the Fethiye Mosque was repaired. In 1930 and 1934-1935 fences were put up round the 'Theseion', the Monument of Philopappos and the Temple of Olympian Zeus. For the first performances of ancient Greek drama in the Odeion of Herodes Atticus, in 1936, Balanos erected tiers of wooden seats in the cavea and repaired and reinforced the arches of the façade.

These same years saw the appearance of the first eyesores to be built in and near the archaeological sites. The humble churches of Hagia Marína and Hagia Triádha on the Hill of the Nymphs and in the Kerameikos were replaced, in 1927 and 1931 respectively, by massive new churches completely out of scale with their surroundings. In 1924 the Parthenis house was built between the Acropolis and the Hill of the Muses and in 1939 construction started on the Bastias Theatre in the Koile district (west of Filopáppou Hill). In 1934 the threat to the view of the Acropolis posed by multi-storey buildings, which were springing up all over the city, prompted the government to impose height limits on buildings in the immediate vicinity of the Acropolis. The start of work on covering the River Ilissos, in 1939-1941, gave a foretaste of what was to come.

18. The Agora viewed from the Hill of the Nymphs in 1964. (American School of Classical Studies)

19. The Acropolis from the south-west in 1955. (Photo: Alison Frantz. American School of Classical Studies)

Since the end of the Second World War Athens has undergone a greater transformation than at any other period in modern times, as it has gradually developed into the great metropolis of Greece (Fig. 20). The changes have been rapid and are noticeable in every domain of life: the size and social composition of the population; the appearance of the city, with nearly all the Neoclassical buildings being replaced by impersonal apartment and office blocks; and the natural environment, which has practically disappeared beneath the chaotic and unsightly clutter of buildings of all kinds that now cover the whole plain of Attica. Once again, the archaeological sites and monuments have been drastically affected by these developments.

***Postwar period:
Development and destruction***

In the first twenty years or so after the war the changes in the archaeological landscape were a direct consequence of the large-scale infrastructure projects carried out to ease traffic congestion and improve the tourist facilities. Broad new boulevards – Vassiléos Konstantínou, Ardhitoú and Kalliróis Avenues – were built along the course of the Ilissos, and Vassilíssis Ólgas Avenue became a main thoroughfare linking that area with the city centre, and the archaeological site of the Olympieion was altered accordingly. Extensive excavations carried out round its perimeter between 1949 and 1962, with some interruptions, yielded evidence of the land uses in this neighbourhood from the Late Helladic to the Byzantine period. The excavated areas to

20. Singroú Avenue with the Hill of the Muses, the Acropolis and Likavitós in the background, in the 1950s. (Photo: Spyros Meledzis. CCAM Archives)

north and south were planted with trees and fenced in so that they were integrated with the archaeological site. Meanwhile the propylon of the sanctuary was partly restored in 1957 and parts of the temple were consolidated in 1959-1960.

The policy of encouraging and developing tourism in Greece, which was given high priority during these years, necessitated substantial alterations to the environs of the Acropolis (Fig. 19) and the monuments situated there, so as to capitalize on their money-making potential and adapt them to meet the now pressing demands of mass cultural tourism. Between 1953 and 1958 Dimitrios Pikionis landscaped the west slopes of the Acropolis and the slopes of the Hill of the Muses and the Pnyx. His remit was to provide improved facilities for mass access to the Acropolis: what he actually accomplished was to encourage a personal, peripatetic approach to the 'Sacred Rock' by re-creating the ancient paths leading up to it and providing belvederes on the nearby hills for visual and mental contemplation (Fig. 22). His work, which embodies memories of the age-old Greek tradition, defers to the monumental scale of the site and is at the same time a modern creative intervention of high quality and deep spirituality. In the course of this work the hillsides were planted with additional varieties of trees and shrubs native to Attica. Between 1948 and 1967, with some interruptions, the whole of the Herodeion was fitted with new marble seating by the Department of Restoration. In 1960 Sound and Light shows were inaugurated on the Pnyx, for which minimal alterations were required to create the seating area.

21. The Hill of the Nymphs viewed from the Acropolis. (Photo: S. Mavromatis, 2000)

At the same time the Dora Stratou Theatre was built on the Hill of the Muses. Throughout the 1960s the local Ephorate of Antiquities carried on with the work of site preparation, excavation, structural consolidation and new boundary walls and fences on the slopes of the Acropolis, with the object of enhancing the sites and making them more presentable. Among other things, a paved path up from the Agora to the Acropolis was built in 1965, following the course of the Panathenaic Way, and part of the Peripatos (the ancient promenade running round the Acropolis) was brought back into use in 1969.

But it was in the historical centre of the city that the most drastic changes took place. From 1931 to 1956, with a gap during the war, more and more properties were expropriated, over 350 households were moved elsewhere, churches were demolished and systematic excavations were carried out by the American School of Classical Studies, laying bare most of the ancient Agora. The digs went down to the level of the Classical and Hellenistic periods, exemplary records were kept at every stage of the work and the results, published systematically, shed a great deal of light on the changing layout and architectural development of the city's civic, administrative and commercial centre from the time when the Agora was first established in the Archaic period until it was destroyed in the third century A.D.

The transformation in the appearance of the Agora was completed with the reconstruction of the Stoa of Attalos for use as the Agora Museum (opened in 1956) and the landscaping of the whole site, which was planted with native Mediterranean plants (Fig. 18). The reconstruction of the Hellenistic stoa, using modern building materials and methods but incorporating the ancient remains and replicating the original design and dimensions with such modifications to the floor plan and the positioning of the doors and windows as were necessary for its new function, lasted from 1953 to 1956 and was the biggest restoration project carried out in Athens during this period. It met with a mixed response. Its critics argued that the rebuilding of the Stoa was not only a contravention of the accepted code of restoration practice but also aesthetically unpleasing, mainly because its huge bulk overwhelmed the scant remains of the other ancient buildings round about and its gleaming white walls contrasted too glaringly with those of the Hephaisteion. With the passage of time, however, the Stoa now fits in better with the rest of the Agora – thanks largely to the prolific growth of the vegetation – and visitors have become so accustomed to the sight of it that it is now an integral part of the overall picture.

The rapid transformation of Athens, the disappearance of historic features of its landscape, the progressive degradation of the environment and the declining quality of life have led to a reappraisal of the aesthetic and environmental values of the Pláka. The necessity of preserving the Pláka as the historic centre of modern Athens – which has been high on the list of priorities since the mid 1960s and is, moreover, in line with international trends – rules out the possibility of extending the archaeological zone any further. The last systematic excavations in the Pláka were carried out by the American School in the early 1970s, south-east of the Stoa of Attalos, where a few more houses were expropriated and the excavators found part of the road

22. The Hill of the Muses after being landscaped by D. Pikionis in 1953-1958, with the Acropolis in the background. (Photo: S. Mavromatis, 2000)

linking the Roman Agora with the ancient Agora. Since then the Americans have continued digging without a break, but only in the existing archaeological zone. Because of the designation of the Pláka as a listed area, the Greek Archaeological Service has been unable to extend its systematic excavations so as to uncover the whole of Hadrian's Library and the Roman Agora and to link both of them with the ancient Agora. At these sites the Archaeological Service was busy throughout the 1960s, excavating, clearing the sites, tidying up scattered architectural and sculptural fragments, doing structural consolidation work and some small-scale restoration. In the last thirty years these sites have remained more or less unchanged. Elsewhere in the Pláka the Service has concentrated on monitoring building construction to ensure conformity with the archaeological regulations.

In other parts of Athens, systematic excavation and landscaping work in the Kerameikos (Fig. 2), followed up by excellent publications, was resumed by the German Archaeological Institute in 1956. And from 1955 to 1963 the Archaeological Service excavated Plato's Academy, where more and more land was expropriated and the site was gradually opened to the public as an archaeological grove.

During this period the Archaeological Service was heavily involved in rescue excavations all over Athens. These operations are generally carried out in conditions of the utmost urgency, with very little manpower and limited resources. The excavators do their best to keep up with the hectic pace of building construction and large-scale public infrastructure works, taking the movable antiquities into safe keeping and trying to examine, record and sometimes actually to preserve the remains of the ancient city that keep coming to light. Most of the antiquities are left where they are to be buried all over again, many are demolished and a few are left visible – but only when it is possible for the land to be expropriated. In this respect, therefore, rescue excavations do not make much difference to the archaeological landscape, but they are extremely important – even though in most cases they are incompletely published – because they provide invaluable information relating to the archaeology of ancient Athens.

By the beginning of the 1970s, twenty years of excavation in postwar Athens had built up a copious store of information about the topography, urban planning and architecture of the ancient city. This was analysed and presented in book form in *Πολεοδομική Εξέλιξις των Αθηνών* [*Urban Evolution of Athens*] (1960) and *Bildlexikon zur Topographie des antiken Athen* (1971), both by John Travlos, the architectural consultant of the Agora excavations who worked closely with the Archaeological Service during those years. These two books have been the main reference works for archaeologists from the time of their publication up to the present day.

Having survived so many vicissitudes, from visions to rediscovery, urban beautification, development and destruction, by the last quarter of the twentieth century the Athens archaeological landscape had reached the stage of physical and aesthetic degradation and social alienation. Those of the monuments that survived were still standing on the sites where they had been built, but now they were unrecognizable. Pollution of the ground on which they stood was rotting their foundations, the polluted atmosphere around them was eroding and blackening their outer surfaces. More to the point, the ancient monuments represented ideas and values of no relevance – and sometimes quite incomprehensible – to a generation brought up on the world theory now prevailing. Nevertheless they were, as they had been for so long, inseparably associated with the world's image of modern Athens and had a special place in the sentiments of the modern Athenians; and they offered some of the few breathing-spaces in the concrete jungle and a ray of hope for the city's cultural and environmental rehabilitation.

After the Colonels: The challenge of the new era

This was the position at the time of the fall of the military junta in 1974, which marked the beginning of a new phase of transformation whose outcome would determine the state of the Athens archaeological landscape in the twenty-first century. In 1975 a huge new programme of conservation and restoration was put in hand on the Acropolis, together with a burst of scientific and scholarly activity unprecedented in a project of this type. The mistakes made in earlier restoration and more recent conservation work are being corrected (Fig. 24): architectural members are being repositioned in their proper places and many of the blocks of stone lying scattered on the ground are being identified and put where they belonged. These operations have a direct impact on the appearance of the Acropolis monuments and are creating a new image (Fig. 23). At the same time pedestrian walkways are being built on the Acropolis and the scattered fragments of stone are being sorted and rearranged.

23. The Erechtheion from the east, after its restoration in 1979-1987. (Photo: S. Mavromatis, 2000)

For the large-scale rescue excavations necessitated by major urban development projects in recent years, manpower and funds have been made available on a scale previously undreamed of. Previously undiscovered ancient monuments have been found, including the gymnasium of the Lykeion (Lyceum) and the polyandrion (mass grave of soldiers killed in action) in the Demosion Sema (state cemetery), providing scholars with an ever-growing body of evidence concerning the burial grounds, roads, workshops, bath-houses, ordinary homes and luxury mansions of ancient Greek and Roman Athens. Plans drawn up for keeping certain monuments visible, sometimes in creative conjunction with modern buildings, suggest that the future expansion of the archaeological landscape will bring new experiences. Another ambitious plan conceived at the end of the century, the unification of all the main archaeological sites in Athens, though hardly more than a dream as yet, does offer the hope of a fruitful symbiosis of the ancient and modern worlds, to their mutual benefit.

While the remains of ancient buildings – those scientifically recorded and reburied as well as those still standing – now give us a satisfactory picture of the exterior of ancient Athens, the movable finds from over 150 years of excavation provide the most authentic and direct evidence concerning its inner world, its social structure and everyday life, the beliefs and artistic achievements of its people. Hidden away in archaeological storerooms, the artefacts wait patiently for that inner world to be revealed and re-created in a Museum of Ancient Athens, and the resources of modern museology are particularly well suited to that purpose. Let us hope that the new century, which some have labelled 'the century of museums, information technology and virtual reality', will rise to the challenge – a challenge which is at the same time a great necessity. Then the archaeological scene in Athens will go on being transformed, as in the past, in accordance with current trends and ideas.

24. Restoration work in progress on the Acropolis in 1985. (CCAM Archives)

SELECT BIBLIOGRAPHY

Bastea, E., *The Creation of Modern Athens: Planning the Myth*, Cambridge (CUP) 2000.

Binder, J., *The Monuments and Sites of Athens, year by year, 1750-1974* (typescript).

Biris, K., «Το υπόμνημα Κλεάνθους και Σάουμπερτ για το σχέδιο των Αθηνών» in *Αθηναϊκαί Μελέται*, I, Athens 1938.

—, *Αι Αθήναι από του 19ου εις τον 20όν αιώνα*, 3rd edn., Athens 1996.

Kokkou, A., *Η μέριμνα για τις αρχαιότητες και τα πρώτα μουσεία*, Athens 1977.

Lefas, P., *Αθήνα μια πρωτεύουσα της Ευρώπης*, Athens/Yannina 1985.

Mallouchou-Tufano, F., *Η αναστήλωση των αρχαίων μνημείων στη νεώτερη Ελλάδα (1834-1939).Το έργο της Εν Αθήναις Αρχαιολογικής Εταιρείας και της Αρχαιολογικής Υπηρεσίας*, Athens 1998.

Papageorgiou-Venetas, A., *Hauptstadt Athen, ein Stadtgedanke des Klassizismus*, Munich/Berlin 1994.

—, *Athens: The Ancient Heritage and the Historic Cityscape in a Modern Metropolis*, Athens 1994.

Pausanias, *Ελλάδος Περιήγησις, Αττικά (Description of Greece: Attica)*.

Petrakos, V., *Η Εν Αθήναις Αρχαιολογική Εταιρεία, η ιστορία των 150 χρόνων της (1837-1987)*, Athens 1987.

—, «Ιδεογραφία της εν Αθήναις Αρχαιολογικής Εταιρείας», *Αρχαιολογική Εφημερίς* 126 (1987) 25-197.

Travlos, J., *Bildlexikon zur Topographie des antiken Athen*, Tübingen 1971.

—, *Πολεοδομική εξέλιξις των Αθηνων*, Athens 1960.

ABBREVIATIONS

CCAM: Committee for the Conservation of the Acropolis Monuments
ELIA: Hellenic Literary and Historical Archives Society

CHAPTER **XII**

The Antiquities
of Athens
through the Eyes of
Foreign Travellers

MARTIN KREEB

No. 9. *Ruine d'une Edifice Antique d'Athenes.*

2. *'Stoa of Hadrian' (Hadrian's Library). Pen and ink, anonymous Flemish artist. H. Omont, 'Athènes au XVIIe siècle. Dessins des sculptures du Parthénon attribués à J. Carrey et conservés à la bibliothèque nationale, accompagnés de vues et plans d'Athènes et de l'Acropole' (1898), Pl. 20.*

1. *The Monument of Thrasyllos. J. Stuart and N. Revett, 'The Antiquities of Athens', II (1787), Ch. IV, Pl. I.*

MARTIN KREEB

The Antiquities of Athens
through the Eyes of Foreign Travellers

In medieval and post-medieval times the people of Western Europe knew very little about Athens, and what they did know was muddled, at least until the seventeenth century. For example, Hartmann Schedel (1440-1514), a doctor and naturalist who moved in the humanist circles of Nürnberg (where he may have met the young Dürer), published the *Liber Chronicarum*, a chronicle of world history, in Nürnberg in 1493. In it he sets out to give his readers the fullest possible account of the then known world by describing the most famous cities and towns and illustrating his text with 1,809 woodcuts. Although the details depicted in the woodcuts are often authentic – not only for the great cities of Italy such as Venice and Rome, but also for places far distant from central Europe, such as Jerusalem and Constantinople – his picture of Athens (Fig. 3) is little more than a figment of the imagination. What is more, he uses the same woodcut several times, for instance as illustrations of Alexandria and of some towns in Austria and Prussia. Athens, the city of the ancient Greek philosophers, was not the focus of interest for travellers at that time, most of whom were either merchants or pilgrims. Schedel's description of Athens is also rather disappointing: 'Athens was once very famous in Attica. Today very little of it remains.'

Hartmann Schedel

Eighty years later, in 1573, Martinus Crusius, a German professor of Greek at Tübingen, wrote to the Constantinopolitan scholar Theodosios Zygomalas to ask him whether the famous city of Athens still existed and if so whether, as some historians maintained, it now consisted only of a few fishermen's cottages. He received two replies, one from Zygomalas and one from another scholar, Symeon Kavassilas, both confirming not only that Athens still existed but also giving him a brief description of the once illustrious city. Zygomalas said in his letter that the city still existed, but he compared it to 'the hide of a long-dead animal'. Kavassilas wrote: 'Athens was once divided into three parts. The central part, that is the Acropolis with the Temple of the Unknown God, is now inhabited entirely by Turks, and the second part by Christians. There are also people living in the third part.' The three parts used to be understood

Martinus Crusius,
Th. Zygomalas, S. Kavassilas

as being the Acropolis, the old town and the city of Hadrian, but Crusius, following Thucydides, took them to be the Asty (the city proper), the Long Walls and the port area.

Why, one may well ask, did the West know so little about Athens, and indeed about Greece generally? How was it that Pheidias, Alkamenes and Iktinos had been so completely forgotten? There are two main reasons why the topography and art of ancient Athens were virtually ignored in the early Renaissance: in the first place, Athens had already lost its geographical importance during the Byzantine period; secondly, the humanists of the early Renaissance espoused the spiritual ideals of Christianity, not the aesthetic ideals of the ancient world. Classical literature was known in the West long before classical art. In fact it was only after 1500 that Western Europeans started showing

**Athens unknown
in the West**

any interest in ancient Greek and Roman sculpture: the Belvedere Apollo (so named from its position in the papal palace in Rome) was 'discovered' in that year and the famous statue of Laokoön in 1506, and these two works sparked the first signs of interest in Graeco-Roman art.

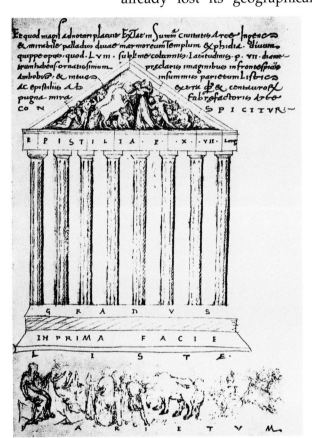

*4. The Parthenon, west front. Ciriaco
d'Ancona, Codex Hamilton 254, fol.
85r. (Berlin, National Library)*

Information about Greek antiquities reached the West only sporadically. The commonest sources of knowledge about the material remains of the ancient Greek world were journals written by Western travellers, sometimes with illustrations, which before the invention of printing were copied out by hand and circulated. As one would expect, these documents were very much in keeping with the spirit of their age. A strictly scientific approach to the subject, by modern standards, was out of the question before the early nineteenth century, because the

**Manuscript journals
by early travellers**

science of archaeology only developed with the successors of Johann Joachim Winckelmann (1717-1768), namely Christian Gottlob Heyne (1729-1812) and Karl Otfried Müller (1797-1840). That is why the few snippets of information about Athens that we have from early travellers are of great value, as they illuminate both the study of the ancient monuments and the period in which they were written.

In 1394-1395 Niccolò da Martoni, a notary, stopped off in Athens on his way to the Holy Land. He wrote a description of Athens in diary form, in Latin, part of which has

3. Athens ('Minerva'). Woodcut. (Hartmann Schedel, 'Nürnberg Chronicle', 1493, fol. 27r)

survived. On his first walk he went past the Asklepieion to 'Hadrian's Palace', as the Olympieion was then called, and the 'Palace Gate', i.e. Hadrian's Arch. From there he climbed the Acropolis, describing the Propylaia as a 'great hall' (*sala magna*). The Parthenon, according to his account, had columns in its peristyle and eighty more inside. Down the slope from the Parthenon, on the two columns above the Monument of Thrasyllos, he saw a gorgoneion which he said was there 'to protect the port by sinking enemy ships'. He also described other marvellous things, such as two springs whose water was supposed to give wisdom to any who drank it, and the colonnaded 'School of Aristotle' (perhaps the Aqueduct of Hadrian/Antoninus Pius) with traces of the original paint still to be seen on the marble. However, his journal makes no mention of various buildings and monuments known to have been visible in his time, such as the Monument of Lysikrates, the Tower of the Winds, Hadrian's Library and the 'Theseion', nor are there any illustrations.

A rare exception to the general apathy about ancient Greece in that period is Ciriaco d'Ancona (Ciriaco de' Pizzicolli, 1391-1452), a merchant whose friends included several early Renaissance scholars. Between 1425 and 1448, having already given up his business, he travelled extensively in the Mediterranean basin, gathering information about the ancient monuments of the Levant for his humanist friends. His travels took him to Egypt, Asia Minor and Greece, as well as many cities and towns in Italy. Athens he visited twice, from 7th to 22nd April 1436 and in February 1444, staying in the palace of the Acciaiuoli on the Acropolis. His interests were greatly influenced by the humanists he knew, such as Francesco Filelfo (1398-1481), Manuel Chrysoloras (1350-1415, whose niece was married to Filelfo) and Cosimo de' Medici. His papers show him to have been of a scholarly disposition: he studiously noted details for inclusion in his

5. The Parthenon, west front. Ciriaco d'Ancona, Codex Vaticanus Barberinus Latinus 4424, fol. 28v. (Rome, Vatican Library)

book *Antiquarum rerum commentaria*, recording everything he considered worth mentioning – the dates and places of his itinerary, Greek and Latin inscriptions, facts about the buildings and monuments – with rather 'naïve' drawings of anything he thought necessary.

Unfortunately, all but a few pages of Ciriaco's notes were burnt, but he had already written out some copies in a more or less abridged version, which he had sent to friends and to princes and patrons of art and literature. Some of those pages are included in the manuscript known as Codex Hamilton 254 (1442/3). Further copies of selected passages from his text and some of his drawings were made from time to time by scholars and artists such as Giuliano da Sangallo, who reproduced these excerpts in a small part of the Codex Vaticanus Barberinus Latinus 4424 (1510/1514?).

Most of the illustrations in these two manuscripts are copies of the drawings done by Ciriaco on his visits to Athens. One of them (Figs. 4-5) depicts the west façade of the Parthenon with a rough sketch of a section of the frieze below it (Hamilton 254, fol. 85r; Vat. Barb. Lat. 4424, fol. 28v). The version in Codex Hamilton 254 (Fig. 4) has the caption *Listae parietum*, which may perhaps mean 'upper edge of the walls'. In both copies the pedimental statues are depicted very inaccurately: for example, Athena is shown on her own, without Poseidon; and in Hamilton 254 the small figures are winged, like the Erotes of the Hellenistic period. In the Vatican manuscript (Fig. 5) six of the metopes are depicted

Ciriaco's illustrations

above the pediment, three on either side, making the building look like a Roman triumphal arch, and the columns have been given capitals that would be more appropriate to the Roman Composite order; in Hamilton 254, on the other hand, they are correctly shown as Doric. Both manuscripts also contain sketches of the Olympieion (Figs. 6-7), but they are copied from different originals: the one in Hamilton 254 (Fig. 6) has only seven columns in a single row, whereas the one in the Vatican manuscript (Fig. 7) also shows some of the columns in the second colonnade, i.e. at the south-east corner of the temple, as well as capitals and column bases in greater

6. *The Olympieion. Ciriaco d'Ancona, Codex Hamilton 254, fol. 87v. (Berlin, National Library)*

itals and column bases in greater detail. That page (fol. 29r) of the Vatican manuscript has an interesting assortment of sketches, including an epistyle bearing an inscription from Sparta (cf. *Inscriptiones Graecae* V 1, 378) and a composite sketch depicting a Renaissance-style version of the Clock of Andronikos of Kyrrhos (Tower of the Winds) superimposed on the Monument of Philopappos. Both of these are recognizable by their inscriptions. Today the inscriptions on the Monument of Philopappos no longer survive in their entirety, which makes Ciriaco's testimony more valuable still. The Tower of the Winds is also illustrated in Hamilton 254 (fol. 87r), but very few of the architectural features are discernible there behind the inscriptions (Fig. 8). The same is true of the sketch of the Monument of Lysikrates (Hamilton 254, fol. 88v, Fig.

7. *The Olympieion, Tower of the Winds, Monument of Philopappos. Ciriaco d'Ancona, Codex Vaticanus Barberinus Latinus 4424, fol. 29r. (Rome, Vatican Library)*

8. *The Tower of the Winds. Ciriaco d'Ancona, Codex Hamilton 254, fol. 87v. (Berlin, National Library)*

9. *The Monument of Lysikrates. Ciriaco d'Ancona, Codex Hamilton 254, fol. 88v. (Berlin, National Library)*

10. *Hadrian's Aqueduct. Ciriaco d'Ancona, Codex Hamilton 254, fol. 85v. (Berlin, National Library)*

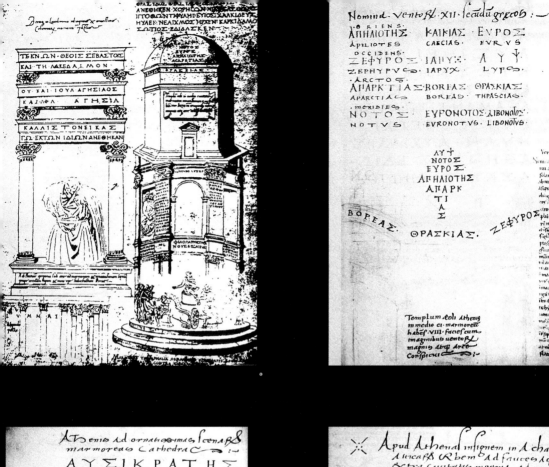

ORIENS		OCCIDENS
ΑΠΗΛΙΩΤΗΣ	ΚΑΙΚΙΑΣ	ΕΥΡΟΣ
Apiliotes	Caecias	Evrus
ΖΕΦΥΡΟΣ	ΙΑΠΥΞ	ΛΥϞ
Zephyrus	Iapyx	Lyps
ΑΠΑΡΚΤΙΑΣ	ΒΟΡΕΑΣ	ΘΡΑΣΚΙΑΣ
Aparctias	Boreas	Thrascias
ΝΟΤΟΣ	ΕΥΡΟΝΟΤΟΣ	ΛΙΒΟΝΟΤΟΣ
Notvs	Evronotus	Libonotus

ΛΥϞ
ΝΟΤΟΣ
ΕΥΡΟΣ
ΑΠΗΛΙΩΤΗΣ
ΑΠΑΡΚΤΙΑΣ

ΒΟΡΕΑΣ   ΘΡΑΣΚΙΑΣ.   ΖΕΦΥΡΟΣ

Templum æoli Athenis
in medio ci. marmoreū
habet. VIII. facieſ cum
imaginibuſ uento ß
magniſ deqᵉ Arte
Conſpicuis.

Τεκνων θεοις σεβαστος
και τη Λακεδαιμον
ου χαι Ιουλ Αγησιλαο
και Φλ Αγησια
καλλιστονεικας
Γω εκτων ιδιων ανεθηκαν

ATenis Ad ornatūimaß ſcenaß
marmoreaß Cathedra

ΑΥΣΙΚΡΑΤΗΣ
ΛΥΣΙΘΕΙΔΟΥ
ΚΙΚΥΝΝΕΥΣ
ΕΧΟΡΗΓΕΙ
ΑΚΑΜΑΝΤΙΣΠΑΔΩΝ
ΕΝΙΚΑ ΟΕΩΝ
ΗΥΛΗ ΑΥΣΙΑΔΗΣ
ΑΘΗΝΑΙΟΣ ΕΔΙΔ
ΑΣΚΕ ΕΥΑΙΝΕΤΟΣ

ΗΡΧΕ

Inbaſchinona urbe clariſſima Luſitanie.
BELLO SERTORIANO VVLNERE SVSCEPTO A KALAGVRITANO
MICIA QVEM MANV EXTEMPLO FODI AC QVIRENDE VALITVDIN
GRATIA BARCHINONAM PETII ESCVLAPIO VOTA VOVI TEMPLVM
INGRATO VT FIERET STATVI MORTE IMMATVRA ME INTERCIPIEN
ET AVALITVDINE ET ACVRA ADOLOSCENTIEM MISERABILITER DE
TVTVM VIDES

EQVITVM MAGISTER SP POMPEIA
NVS   ΑΥΣΙΚΡΑΤΗΣ

Apud Athenaſ inſignem in Achaid
Atticaß Vrbem Ad fauceſ Aqueduct
extra Ciuitatiß moenia Ad unum mil

Marmoreuſ ex duobuſ integriſ   Lapidibuſ
                        ARCVS

IMP. CAESAR. T. AELIVS

AVG. PIVS. COS. III. TR.B. POT. II. P.P. AQVAEDVCTVM INNOVIS

CONSVMMAVIT

HADRIANVS ANTONI

ATHENIS COEPTVM ADIVO HADRIANO PA

DEDICAVIT QVE

9). One drawing of particular interest is the sketch of Hadrian's Aqueduct in Codex Hamilton 254 (Fig. 10). Part of the aqueduct had already been destroyed by the seventeenth century and it was completely demolished in 1778 (part of the architrave is now in the National Gardens in Athens). Jacques Spon saw Ciriaco's sketch of the aqueduct and copied it; and Stuart and Revett used Spon's copy to make a reconstruction drawing of the monument in about 1750.

As Luigi Beschi recently noted, the evidence provided by Ciriaco is particularly important to our knowledge of ancient Athens for two reasons, firstly because he was the last European antiquary to see Athens before Greece was conquered by the Turks, and secondly because he did not go there to collect antiquities for his own or anybody else's collection. Moreover, as R. Étienne has pointed out, Ciriaco himself remarked in a letter to a friend that for our knowledge of ancient civilization the evidence provided by the buildings and inscriptions themselves is more reliable than any writer's descriptions and references. Despite his good intentions, Ciriaco sometimes misidentifies the ancient monuments: for example, he calls the Tower of the Winds the 'Temple of Aiolos'. It is also worth noting that he does not appear to have referred to Pausanias at all, perhaps because he did not have access to any manuscript of his work; but he did prepare for his journeys by reading the geographers Strabo and Ptolemy and the *Natural History* of Pliny the Elder.

For a long time after Ciriaco nothing was added to the West's knowledge of Athens or the rest of Greece: if anything, some of it was lost. In 1456 most of Greece was conquered by the Ottoman Turks and it became more and more difficult to travel to Athens. Some scholars in the West, such as the Dutchman Johan Meurs (1579-1639), tried writing about the topography of Athens without ever going there, relying on the information they could glean from Pausanias. And most of those who did actually travel as far as Greece put in at the port of Piraeus and did not even bother to cover the few miles from there to Athens. An exception was J.G. Transfeldt (1648-1685), an army officer who was taken prisoner by the Turks, escaped by jumping overboard from a ship passing close to Sounion and, after being given shelter by a family of shepherds, made his way to Athens. In the journal he sent to a Dutch friend of his, the scholar Gisbert Cuper, of which nineteen leaves survive, he recorded his impressions of Athens. No doubt his views were coloured by those of the Capuchins – since he stayed in their friary for quite some time – and of other scholars then living in Athens, including Jean Giraud, the French consul (who later became the consul of England and the Netherlands, after falling into disfavour with the French) and the physician and naturalist Jacob Spon, both of whom are discussed below; but his journal does contain some independent opinions of his own. 'The so-called Palace of Hadrian cannot possibly have been the Emperor's palace,' he wrote. 'Vitruvius's description of the Temple of Olympian Zeus fits much more closely.' Yet his correct identification failed to convince Spon, and in time it was forgotten, because Transfeldt's notes were never published. Similarly, Transfeldt read the inscription on the Monument of Lysikrates and realized that it was not a monument to Demosthenes, though he misinterpreted the inscription. In his journal he also describes Hadrian's Arch and the Tower of the Winds, which he called the 'Temple of Socrates'.

Transfeldt's arrival in Athens happened to coincide with a period when several travellers of note passed through the city within a few years of each other. The first to arrive – towards the end of 1674, more than two hundred years after Ciriaco d'Ancona – was Charles Marie François Olivier d'Angevilliers, Marquis de Nointel, who served as French ambassador to the Sublime Porte from 1670 to 1679 and was a keen collector of classical manuscripts and ancient statues, seal-stones and other artefacts. Having secured permission from the Ottoman authorities to visit the Acropolis (which was the headquarters of the Turkish garrison in Athens and therefore out of bounds to the public), Nointel sent two young artists to Athens to draw the Parthenon sculptures. One of them is commonly known as Jacques Carrey, though it is more likely that he was a young Flemish artist whose name remains unknown. The subjects of his drawings, which cover nineteen sheets of paper, include the Parthenon's pedimental statuary, metopes and Ionic frieze as well as pictures of Hadrian's Library (then known as the Stoa of Hadrian) (Fig. 2), four figures from the sculptural ornamentation of the Tower of the Winds ('the Tomb of Socrates'), the Olympieion with Hadrian's Arch ('the Emperor Hadrian's palace with its entrance gate') (Fig. 15) and a view of Athens showing Hadrian's Arch, the Olympieion, the Stadium, Ardettos Hill, etc. The reason why the 'Carrey drawings' – especially those of the Parthenon sculptures – are of such value to future generations is that they were made before the Parthenon was blown up in the bombardment of 1687: many of them provide the only evidence from which the original reliefs can be reconstructed.

*The period
around 1675*

These drawings had an eventful subsequent history. Bernard de Montfaucon (1655-1741) used some of them in his massive book *L'antiquité explorée et représentée en figures* (five volumes published in 1719 and a five-volume supplement in 1724!). No other scholars or travellers were able to use them in the eighteenth century, because they disappeared from view for a total of about eighty years. We know that they were acquired from Nointel by Michel Bégon, a collector of antiquities. Following Bégon's death in 1710 they remained in oblivion until about 1770, when, at the instigation of Antoine Chrysostôme Quatremère de Quincy (1755-1849) and other classical scholars including the Comte de Caylus, they were bought by the Bibliothèque Royale in Paris (now the Bibliothèque Nationale), where they gathered dust for another twenty years or so. The first person to make use of them after their rediscovery was Jean-Denis Barbié du Bocage, who in 1799 produced an album of illustrations for the *Voyage du jeune Anacharsis en Grèce* by Abbé Jean-Jacques Barthélemy (1716-1795), part of which was translated into Greek by Rigas Feraios. The drawings eventually became accessible to scholars when they were published in 1854 by the Comte de Laborde and again in 1898 by Henri Omont.

Jacob (or Jacques) Spon (1647-1685), a Frenchman of German descent born at Lyon, was a contemporary of Transfeldt, Giraud and Nointel. Spon went to Athens in 1675 and was the best-prepared of all Western travellers to Greece, having read not only Pausanias and the ancient Greek historians (such as Herodotos and Thucydides) but Sangallo's copy of Ciriaco's journal as well! Spon, a Protestant, studied medicine and archaeology at Montpellier and Strasbourg universities. While still a student, he met the Abbé Pecoil, Nointel's chaplain, who

11. The west pediment of the Parthenon in 1674. Engraving by Barbié du Bocage after 'Jacques Carrey'. J.J. Barthélemy, 'Voyage du jeune Anacharsis en Grèce. Atlas' (1799 and subsequent reprints), Pl. 19. It is interesting to note that the west pediment is still described here as the 'Fronton antérieur'.

gave him the manuscript of the Abbé Babin's sketchbook of Athens. This Spon edited and published under the title of *Relation de l'état présent de la ville d'Athènes, ancienne capitale de la Grèce. Avec un abregé de son histoire et de ses antichitez*, Lyon (Pascal) 1674, the main value of which is that it was the first book to contain a town plan of contemporary Athens (Fig. 12). Not long after its publication Spon headed towards Greece. His first stopping-place was Rome: there, in the Vatican Library, he read various books on the history and topography of Athens, including Sangallo's manuscript with some of Ciriaco's notes and sketches. He also met some English collectors and travellers in Rome, including George Wheler (1650-1723), who shared his passion for collecting antiquities. Spon was particularly interested in inscriptions and coins (some of which he obtained from Transfeldt, who had lived for a time in Aleppo) and Wheler in 'marbles' (some of which he subsequently gave to Oxford University). Eventually they both left Rome and travelled by way of Venice, Dalmatia, Zákinthos, Kíthira, Tínos, Delos and Alexandria Troas to Constantinople. There Spon renewed his acquaintance with the Abbé Pecoil, who gave him access to the 'Carrey drawings' of the Parthenon. In the winter of 1675-1676 Spon and Wheler arrived in Athens, where they were shown the sights by Jean Giraud (1658-*p*.1688).

Spon describes these travels in his book *Voyage d'Italie, de Dalmatie, de Grèce et du Levant fait aux années 1675 et 1676 par Jacob Spon ... et George Wheler...*, published in three volumes at Lyon in 1678. It was reprinted almost immediately, in 1679 at Amsterdam, and in 1681 it was

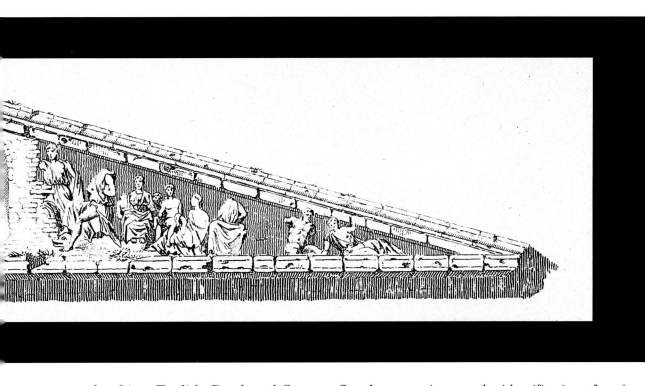

translated into English, Dutch and German. Spon's suggestions on the identification of ancient buildings and sites were in many cases more accurate than those of earlier travellers. He read the inscription on the so-called 'Lantern of Demosthenes' and realized (at the same time as Transfeldt) that it was the Monument of Lysikrates, He failed to find the inscription 'To the Unknown God' on the Parthenon, described by Kavassilas, and concluded that it was no longer extant; he also rejected the name 'Pantheon', which Zygomalas had used of the Parthenon. However, some of his conclusions were wrong: he believed that the front of the Parthenon was the west end (where the main entrance to the Christian church and the mosque was); in the west pediment he identified two of the figures in the Kekrops group as the Emperor Hadrian (whose features he claimed to recognize) and his wife Sabina; and he held that the pedimental statuary was not the work of Praxiteles, as Zygomalas maintained, but of a sculptor of the Hadrianic period.

In the preface to his book Spon makes various recommendations on methodology, pointing out that he had prepared for his journey by reading the entire work of the Dutch scholar Jan Gruter, listing countless Greek and Latin inscriptions, and had spent five whole months in Rome, visiting ancient monuments and reading in the libraries. 'Inscriptions are essential for a proper understanding and identification of monuments and sites,' he observes. By dint of epigraphical studies he identified Sólona as the ancient Amphissa and Kastrí as Delphi, among many other places. He also explains in his book that he has had the inscriptions printed in capitals, but with the words separated, noting that 'the ancients probably made mistakes when they inscribed all the words in continuous script'.

All this makes Spon a truly scientific archaeologist, one of an extremely rare breed in his

Vûe d'Athenes dont vne partie est cachée derriere la colline

La grande mosquée

Citadelle

mazures de l'Areopage

Portail du Palais d'Hadrian

Restes du Palais d'Hadrian

méridies

ATHENES

Chemin de Thebes

Chemin d'Eleusine

Chemin de Pirée, ou de P. Lione

Chemin de Medeli

Chemin de Raphti

Chemin d'Athenes

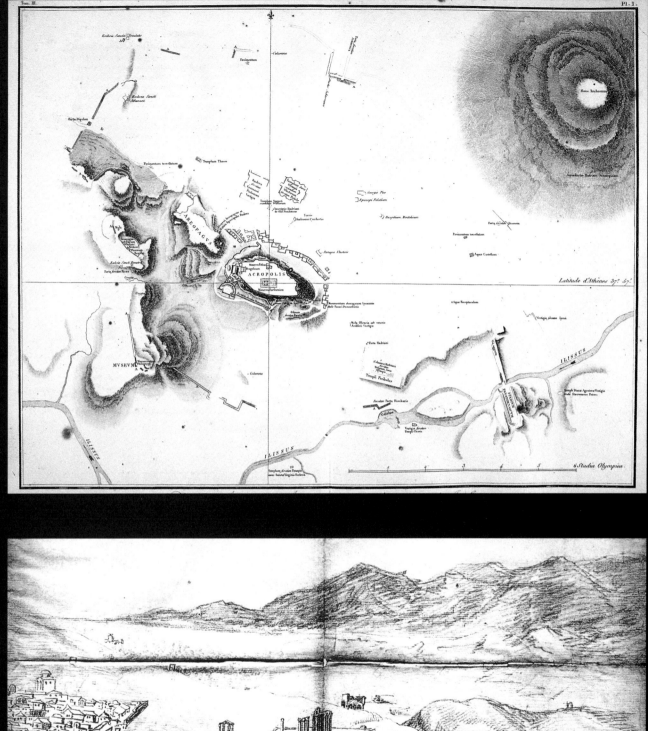

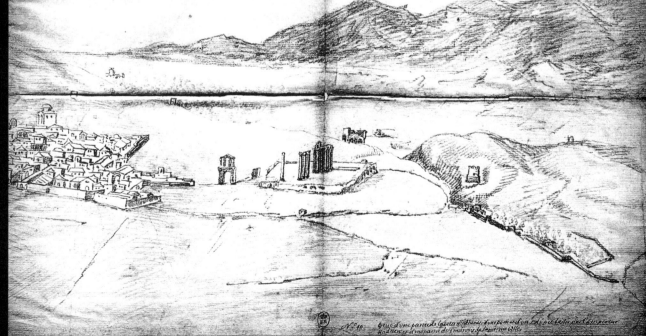

day. Thereafter anybody studying the topography and monuments of Athens and ancient Greece had to pay heed to his revolutionary interpretations of the archaeological evidence and to his drawings, which were few in number and sadly deficient in quality. His travelling companion, Wheler, also published a book about their journey in which he attempted to give his own interpretations of the monuments and sites, but without much success: for example, he thought that only the cella of the Parthenon was built in the time of Perikles, that the peristyle was added by Attalos, who decorated it with the reliefs of Gauls mentioned by Pausanias (this is Wheler's interpretation of the metopes), and that the pediments were added by Hadrian.

Almost simultaneously, in 1675, André Guillet de St. Georges (*c.* 1625-1705) published a book entitled *Athènes ancienne et nouvelle*, which was translated into English only a year later. Guillet gave descriptions of things he had not seen himself, and consequently he made many mistakes. For several years he carried on a war of words with Spon in a series of letters that both of them published, but their quarrel did nothing to clarify the question of Athenian topography. It is worth noting that Guillet identified the Ilissos Temple as the Temple of the Muses and correctly identified the Tower of the Winds and Kimon's wall. However, he was a product of the generation that attached far greater weight to ancient writings than to the monuments themselves, and he could not forgive Spon for questioning the accuracy of Strabo, Ptolemy and other writers. Incidentally, Spon read Guillet's book on his voyage out to Greece: it was only later that he realized how many shocking errors it contained. Guillet used the Capuchins' town plan of Athens in his book, but he 'embellished' it with an inventory of 181 ancient and contemporary place-names, buildings and city gates (Fig. 13), all explained in an extremely lengthy caption. Although most of his identifications are correct, some are figments of his imagination: '32. Temple of Aphrodite Ourania', '36. Temple of Hephaistos', '37. Stoa Poikile', '42. Boule of the Five Hundred, Palace of Themistokles', '137. Tomb of Plato', '147. Theatre of Regilla'.

The blowing-up of the Parthenon in the bombardment of 26th September 1687 (Fig. 16) finally awakened European interest in the illustrious building and in ancient Athens generally. Army officers present at the scene of the disaster expressed their great regret and openly wondered whether the capture of the Acropolis justified the destruction of the ancient monument that had remained more or less intact for so many centuries. A direct result of the cat-

12. Athens in 1674. J.P. Babin, 'Relation de l'état présent de la ville d'Athènes' (1674), Pl. 1 (insert). (Photo: German Archaeological Institute, Athens)

13. Plan of Athens in 1675. J. Guillet, 'Athènes ancienne et nouvelle' (1675), Pl. 1 (insert). (Photo: German Archaeological Institute, Athens)

14. Plan of the ancient monuments in Athens, ca. 1750. J. Stuart and N. Revett, 'The Antiquities of Athens', III (1794), following the preface. (From the German edition of the book)

15. 'The Emperor Hadrian's Palace with the entrance gate' (The Olympieion and Hadrian's Arch). Pen and ink, anonymous Flemish artist. H. Omont, 'Athènes au XVIIe siècle...', Pl. 23.

astrophe was that Spon's and Wheler's books were hastily reprinted and translated into many languages. The spirit of the age inspired other, less talented, writers to publish books, one of them being Francesco Fanelli, whose *Atene Attica* was published in Venice in 1707. Fanelli devotes three parts of his book to the history of Athens and does not touch on the topography until the fourth. Like Guillet, he was a teller of tall stories, and his classical learning was clearly superficial: he refers to Hadrian's Library as the 'Temple of Olympian Zeus', the Monument of Philopappos as the 'Mouseion, or Arch of Trajan'; the architects of the Parthenon he names as Stimios and Kallikranes; although he had seen the Monument of Thrasyllos and read the inscription on it, he identifies it as the 'Temple of Apollo'; the gate of Athena Archegetis he calls the 'Temple of Augustus'; he includes a drawing of the inscription associated with Hadrian's Aqueduct which is full of mistakes, both as regards the stone and in the inscription itself. The plan of Athens in his book is the best one ever printed up to that time; however, it is not by him but by Giacomo Verneda, a surveyor in the Venetian army. The key to the plan is Fanelli's, unfortunately, and not surprisingly the text and the key do not always agree: for example, the 'Arch of Trajan' mentioned in the key does not appear anywhere in the description of the Monument of Philopappos in the text.

The Society of Dilettanti was founded in London in 1733 to promote culture and travel. In England this was the age of the Grand Tour: members of the Society often gave material support and educational assistance to travellers going to ancient Greek and Roman sites, and they also travelled themselves. It is beyond question that a great contribution to the West's knowledge of ancient Athens was made by two young Englishmen, the painter James Stuart (1713-*a*.1788) and the architect Nicholas Revett (1720-1804), whose expedition to Athens was sponsored by the Dilettanti. While in Rome they published a proclamation in which they pointed out that, whereas the ancient monuments of Rome were very well-known, those of Athens were hardly known at all. They therefore proposed to make detailed drawings of them and in this way to preserve them for posterity, asserting that ***The Society*** the monuments were in immediate danger from the Turks. In recognition ***of Dilettanti*** of their initiative in this matter they were elected to the Society of Dilettanti, which made it much easier for them to press ahead with their plans. Not that they were the only travellers to Greece in this period, by any means. Richard Pococke (1704-1765) passed through Athens and spent enough time there to make detailed notes, plans and drawings of ancient buildings (*A Description of the East and Some Other Countries*, III, London 1745). Lord Charlemont went to Athens with the draughtsman Richard Dalton in 1749 and Dalton demonstrated his talent in a series of drawings of sculptures, chiefly those of the Parthenon (*A Series of Engravings, Representative Views of Places, Buildings, Antiquities in Sicily, Greece, Asia Minor and Egypt*, London 1751-1752). Julien David Le Roy (1728-1803), who had read Stuart and Revett's proclamation, published a large tome entitled *Les ruines des plus beaux monumens de la Grèce* in 1758. Without taking more than a few measurements, Le Roy managed to produce a sort of architectural 'measured drawing' which was well received, so much so that his book was translated into English only a year later and into German in 1764. He also propounded

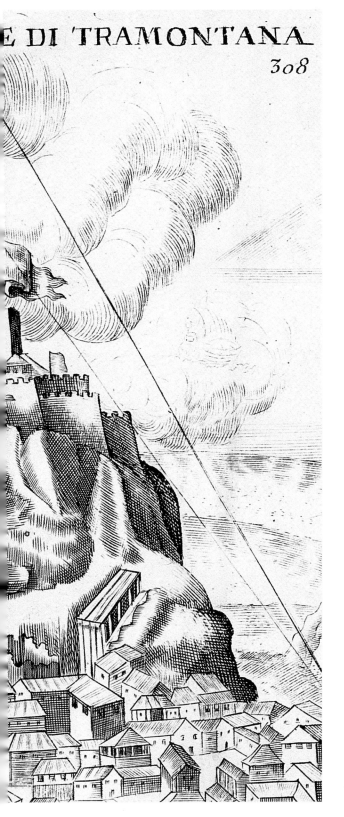

E DI TRAMONTANA

308

a theory on ancient architecture based on his measurements, most of which were in fact inaccurate. In the second edition of his book (1770) he tried to defend himself against the criticism of Stuart and Revett, but the arguments he used were feeble: for example, 'If Stuart aimed at absolute accuracy in his measurements of the monuments, that is the only merit of his book.'

Stuart and Revett spent a long time in Athens: they were there for over two years altogether, though during that time they went to other places, including Thessalonika, where they made drawings of the Portico of the Idols known as *Las Incantadas*, 'the Enchanted Ones' (*Antiquities of Athens*, III, Ch. 9), and Delos, where they studied the Stoa of Philip and drew a map of the island (*ibid.*, Ch. 10). Their aim was not merely to make measured drawings with the greatest possible precision but also to check the accuracy of earlier theories relating to proposed restorations or reconstructions, the identification of ruined buildings and the topography of ancient Athens generally. To them belongs the credit for producing the most accurate plan of the ancient ruins of Athens up to that time (Fig. 14). They made innumerable corrections to earlier identifications: for example, they rejected the identification of the Gate of Athena Archegetis as the Temple of Roma and Augustus (suggested by Spon and Wheler and again by Fanelli), preferring to call it simply 'Doric stoa'. 'The actual Temple of Roma and Augustus must have been on the Acropolis,' they say, quite correctly, referring to the relevant inscription published by Jan Gruter. They were unable to identify some buildings, such as Hadrian's Library, though they did reject its usual name of 'Temple of Olympian Zeus' be-

16. *The destruction of the Parthenon in 1687. F. Fanelli, 'Atene Attica' (1707), Pl. 1 (insert). (Photo: German Archaeological Institute, Athens)*

cause they correctly identified the Olympieion – as Transfeldt had already done – with what was known as 'Hadrian's Palace'. The cavea of the Theatre of Dionysos they recognized as the cavea of a theatre, but (since the Odeion of Herodes Atticus was then thought to be the Theatre of Dionysos) they identified it as the Odeion of Perikles. Several buildings are known to us in detail mainly from the descriptions given by Stuart and Revett: the Ilissos temple, the Ilissos bridge (Fig. 17), Hadrian's Aqueduct (for which, as we have seen, they relied on the earlier studies by Spon, who in turn had used the notes of Ciriaco d'Ancona) and the choregic monument of Thrasyllos (Fig. 1). Their exhaustive work, astonishing both for its quantity and for its accuracy, is still useful to scholars to this day. One last point worth emphasizing is that these two experts on the ancient monuments of Athens had not come to Greece for the purpose of collecting antiquities, either for themselves or on behalf of anyone else.

The publication of the five-volume *Antiquities of Athens* was fraught with difficulties. Revett pulled out of the project even before the first volume came out in 1762, leaving Stuart to edit it by himself. On Stuart's death, his widow gave the material for the second volume to William Newton, who published it in 1787. Then Newton died, and the third volume was published by Willey Reveley in 1794. The third volume, which contains the town plan of Athens and a map of Attica giving both ancient and modern place-names, covers the Hephaisteion ('Temple of Theseus'), the Olympieion, Hadrian's Arch, Hadrian's Aqueduct (demolished in 1778) and the Monument of Philopappos. It also contains a few drawings of the Ilissos bridge (with a general view of the bridge), the Panathenaic Stadium, the Pnyx ('Odeion of Regilla') and the so-called Agoranomeion in the eastern half of the Roman Forum. The fourth and fifth volumes, published by the Society of Dilettanti itself, are not concerned with the monuments of Athens.

Stuart and Revett's long stay in Athens influenced their subsequent careers. Stuart came to be known in England as 'Athenian Stuart' and designed numerous houses and mansions in the 'Grecian' style, while Revett built a church of St. Lawrence modelled on the Temple of Apollo on Delos. In the ensuing decades the 'Grecian' style, brought to public notice through their book, became ever more popular.

In the eighteenth century, museums, which until then had been the sole preserve of the aristocracy, first became accessible to the public: among them were the British Museum (1759), the Uffizi Gallery in Florence (1769), the Pio-Clementino Museum in the Vatican (1772) and the Louvre (1793). Understandably, foreign ambassadors and consuls as well as rich travellers

The first state-run museums

now wanted to enrich their respective 'national' museums. It is at about this time that we first find a foreign ambassador applying for permission to remove parts of the Parthenon's sculptural decoration with the professed object of saving them, but also, obviously, in order to take them back to his home country's biggest museum, the Louvre. Marie-Gabriel-Florent-Auguste de Choiseul Gouffier (1752-1817), a member of the prestigious Académie des Inscriptions et de Belles-lettres, was appointed French ambassador to the Porte in 1784. In 1787 he sent Louis François Sébastien Fauvel (1753-1838) to Athens to procure antiquities. With

Fauvel's help he managed to buy a relief from the Parthenon's Ionic frieze and one of the metopes (No. 10 on the south side). His collection was confiscated during the French Revolution: the frieze relief was made over to the Louvre in 1798 and the metope in 1818. Choiseul Gouffier was a collector more interested in ancient art for its own sake than for its value as an investment, and so he had in his collection a good many plaster casts of sculptures that he was interested in but had not been able to buy. Several other artists and travellers visited Athens in the latter part of the eighteenth century, but there is only room here to mention Sir Richard Worsley (b. 1751), whose drawings of the Parthenon so moved Goethe when he saw them in Rome in 1787 that he noted in his diary that they had made 'a remarkable and indelible impression' on him.

Unquestionably one of the blackest episodes in the history of ancient art occurred when

17. View of the Ilissos bridge. J. Stuart and N. Revett, 'The Antiquities of Athens', III (1794), Ch. VII, Pl. I.

Napoleon, on 10th April 1797, carried off a hundred of the most famous statues in Rome (as well as others from elsewhere in Italy) as spoils of war to found the Musée Napoléon, which was to form part of the Louvre: these ancient works of art were not returned to Italy until 1816. The statues were accompanied to France by their faithful guardian Ennio Quirino Visconti (1751-1818), who had supervised the arrangement of the antiquities in the Vatican Museum for Pope Pius VI and then saw to it that they were properly displayed in the Musée Napoléon. He also compiled a catalogue of the collection (*Musée Napoléon*, 1803).

A similar but far worse fate was soon to befall the Parthenon sculptures. In 1801 Lord Elgin, the British ambassador to the Porte, arrived in Athens and eventually succeeded in doing what Choiseul Gouffier had wanted but been unable to do, namely 'to save the

Parthenon sculptures from the risk of being vandalized by the Turks'. As we all know, this 'salvation' involved detaching a large part of the temple's sculptural ornamentation, which had remained in place since antiquity, and then transporting the booty to England. Among the other items taken away were one Caryatid and one column from the Erechtheion and parts of the sculptural ornamentation of the Temple of Athena Nike, including the frieze and the parapet slabs. One very serious consequence of this action was that it was bound to cause structural damage to the buildings, but Elgin did not let this stand between him and his goal of carrying off as many sculptures as possible. Since the metopes could not be neatly removed, he engaged stonemasons and unskilled workers to hack away the edges of the triglyphs so that they could slide the metopes out. His men also sawed off the backs of the frieze slabs to make them lighter, less bulky and more easily transportable. The removal of the spoils to England turned out eventfully. One ship sank, and divers were employed to bring the sculptures to the surface. Elgin himself was taken prisoner by the French, who made 'laudable' efforts to seize the marbles, too, before they reached England. When he eventually returned home, Elgin had to search high and low for the marbles, which had been casually dumped in warehouses.

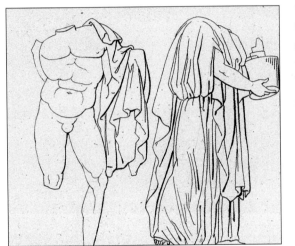

18. The Parthenon, south metope 17, after 'Jacques Carrey'. P.O. Brøndsted, 'Reisen und Untersuchungen in Griechenland', II (1830), Pl. 51 No. 17.

Since artistic taste in the West had been formed largely by the sculptures from the Cortile del Belvedere in the Vatican – notably the statues of Apollo and Laokoön, which had recently been seized by the French and brought to Paris – most connoisseurs were fairly unenthusiastic when they first saw the Parthenon marbles. For some years after their arrival in England, archaeologists and art historians wondered whether they really were so very valuable after all and the British Museum showed no interest whatsoever in buying them. One of the fiercest opponents of the proposed purchase was Richard Payne Knight (1750-1824), who maintained that the sculptures dated from Hadrian's reign. It took all the persuasive powers of Quatremère de Quincy, Visconti and several other scholars to push the Museum's Trustees to change their mind. A number of books and pamphlets on the valuation of the Parthenon marbles were published in these years, including a *Memorandum on the Subject of the Earl of Elgin's Pursuits in Greece* (1811), *Atheniensia, or Remarks on the Topography and Buildings of Athens* by William Wilkins (1816), *The Elgin Marbles, with an abridged historical and topographical account of Athens* by E.J. Burrow (1817), *Mémoires sur des ouvrages de sculpture du Parthénon* by Ennio Quirino Visconti (1818) and *Lettres écrites de Londres à Rome, et adressées à Athènes* by A.C. Quatremère de Quincy (1818).

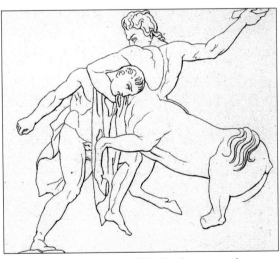

19. The Parthenon, south metope 1. P.O. Brøndsted, 'Reisen und Untersuchungen in Griechenland', II (1830), Pl. 46 No. 1.

In the end the British Museum did buy the marbles, but for much less than Elgin was expecting: he had spent at least twice as much money as he received from the Museum.

Opinion was sharply divided on the subject of the purchase, which was completed in 1816. Some rejoiced over the acquisition of such important sculptures by Britain, but there was also an immediate outcry against Elgin's act of plunder and destruction, not only on the Continent but in Britain as well. A fellow-member of the House of Lords, Lord Byron, who was to fight with the Greeks in their War of Independence, made scathingly sarcastic comments about his compatriot in a letter to a friend, and he also inveighs against Elgin in his poem *Childe Harold's Pilgrimage*. Two English artists with an interest in the ancient world, Edward Daniel Clarke and Edward Dodwell, voiced their distress and their disapproval of Elgin's actions. Another who was strongly critical was the Danish painter and early archaeologist Peter Brøndsted, as mentioned below. The author of the first handbook on archaeology, Karl Otfried Müller (1797-1840), whose early death was a sad loss, repeatedly stated that he considered Elgin's depredations illegal as well as misguided. The sculptor Antonio Canova (1757-1822), who had restored countless ancient statues, refused to touch the Parthenon marbles because of their artistic value.

The presence of the marbles in England made less of an impact than might have been expected. English artists, who Elgin hoped would be influenced by them, clung to the ideals of the Renaissance and remained unmoved by the Greek sculptures. In any case, lovers of Greece were more interested in the modern Greeks' struggle for liberation than in ancient Greek art. All in all, therefore, the influence of the Parthenon sculptures was somewhat limited. Their new owners lost no time in publishing a catalogue of them (*Description of the Collection of Ancient Marbles in the British Museum*, 11 vols., 1812-1861). The Danish artist Peter Oluf Brøndsted (1780-1842) set to work to publish a lengthy independent study of the Parthenon marbles: the second volume of his book *Reisen und Untersuchungen in Griechenland, nebst Darstellung und Erklärung vieler neuentdeckter Denkmäler griechischen Styls*, which appeared in 1830, concentrates mainly on the metopes. Working from the drawings of the destroyed metopes by the anonymous Flemish artist ('Jacques Carrey') (Fig. 18) and from his own sketches of those he had seen for himself (Fig. 19), he produced line drawings of the metopes which clearly show the influence of contemporary style. Unfortunately only these two, out of the eight volumes that Brøndsted intended to write, ever appeared in print. His criticism of Elgin's conduct and of the British Museum's decision to put the sculptures on display is damning: 'The metopes are wrongly positioned, so they are not seen at the right height,' he comments, 'The marble slab bearing the relief projects obtrusively from the wall, whereas in the Parthenon it was set flush with the triglyphs, serving as a background; and all fifteen of the metopes depict Centaurs. Consequently, anyone wishing to study the metopes seriously must definitely go to Athens. However, the building itself has been very badly damaged by all this maltreatment.'

Political and military developments in Greece affected the relations between the Greeks and foreign visitors, while at the same time changes were taking place in the science of archaeology. In 1821, the year of the outbreak of the Greek War of Independence, Colonel

William Martin Leake (1777-1860) brought out his book *The Topography of Athens*. Leake had been sent on a tour of northern Greece, the Peloponnese and Attica which occupied him from 1805 to 1810, and the fruits of his travels were published in ten volumes. *The Topography of Athens* was the first scientific topographical description of the city, as opposed to the travel journals written by earlier travellers who had touched on topographical matters. With Pausanias as his guide, Leake set out to describe as many buildings and monuments as possible. His book was translated without delay (into German in 1829) and reissued in an improved edition in 1841 (translated into German in 1844). Leake does not fit easily into any of the usual categories of antiquarians or travellers of his time: what sets him apart is perhaps his genius.

The liberation of Greece coincided with the emergence of the history of ancient art as a scientific discipline. The Istituto di Corrispondenza Archeologica was founded in Rome in 1829: it was an international institution whose stated object was to disseminate archaeological news all over the world by means of its periodical publications. For the very first issue of its Bulletin (the *Bollettino dell' Istituto*) Karl Otfried Müller wrote a paper on the Parthenon marbles. Müller also wrote the first textbook of archaeology (*Handbuch der Archäologie der Kunst*, 1830), which deals at length with the Acropolis sculptures.

The founding of the first archaeological institute

One of the Greeks' first concerns after the liberation of their country was to take good care of the antiquities and stop the looting of ancient works of art: after all, as the revolutionary hero Makriyannis wrote in his memoirs, 'That was what we fought for.' However, as Leo von Klenze (1784-1864) informs us, the members of the new ruling class – mostly Bavarian army officers – had an almost insatiable appetite for antiquities. The campaign for the preservation of the country's cultural heritage was supported by Greeks and influential foreigners alike, including Kyriakos Pittakis and Ludwig Ross, though in fact the issue had been debated at the First National Assembly in 1822 and the Senate of Eastern Continental Greece had then charged the political Ephor with responsibility for the protection of antiquities. Immediately after the War of Independence scientific excavations were put in hand, the first step being to clear the Acropolis of the Turkish houses that had been built inside the citadel. Finally, the foundation of the Athens Archaeological Society in 1837 marked a major turning-point in the history of the preservation of the city's ancient remains. From then on, priority was given to the scientific study of antiquities and systematic excavations were conducted with that object in view.

Important as the foundation of the Athens Archaeological Society was for the discipline of archaeology, it should not be forgotten that modern archaeology is also greatly indebted to the early travellers: to Ciriaco d'Ancona, Spon, Stuart and Revett and so many others who braved the hazards of a journey to Athens, often motivated only by their interest in and admiration for the city's glorious past and the monuments still standing as reminders of it. Without those travellers, much evidence would have been lost for ever.

On the history of research on the ancient monuments of Athens and the rest of Greece, see Richard Stoneman, *Land of Lost Gods: The Search for Classical Greece* (1987). On the Athenian monuments in particular see: Curt Wachsmuth, *Die Stadt Athen im Alterthum* (1874-1890), esp. I 58-90, 725-763; Ferdinand Gregorovius, *Geschichte der Stadt Athen im Mittelalter* (1889, frequently reprinted); Walter Judeich, *Topographie von Athen* (2nd edn., 1931), esp. 15-42. On travellers to Greece in general see Adolf Michaelis, *Der Parthenon* (1871), 54-106; for excerpts from the writings of Ciriaco, Babin, Guillet, Spon and others, *ibid.* 334 ff. On travellers and artists in connection with the Parthenon, see the chapters by Fani Mallouchou-Tufano and Stelios Lydakis in Panayotis Tournikiotis (ed.), *The Parthenon and its Impact in Modern Times* (1994), 162-199 and 230-257 respectively. A more general work is Max Wegner's *Land der Griechen* (3rd edn., 1955), which contains passages from the writings of various travellers as well as an almost complete list of travellers up to 1941 and their publications. A good book for general readers is Roland and Françoise Étienne, *La Grèce antique, archéologie d'une découverte* (1990), which is very readable and has an extensive bibliography. For a selection of passages by writers and travellers of this period see George Tolias, George Depastas and Voula Louvrou, *Ο πυρετός των Μαρμάρων. Μαρτυρίες για τη λεηλασία των Ελληνικών μνημείων 1800-1820* (1996); and Angeliki Kokkou deals with a related subject in her book *Η μέριμνα για τις αρχαιότητες στην Ελλάδα και τα πρώτα μουσεία* (1977). A recent work on Ciriaco and Athens is Luigi Beschi's paper 'I disegni ateniesi di Ciriaco: analisi di una tradizione' in *Ciriaco d'Ancona e la cultura antiquaria dell'Umanesimo, Atti del Convegno internazionale di studio, Ancona, 6-9 febbraio 1992* (1998), 83-102. On Spon see Roland Étienne and Jean-Claude Mossière (ed.), *Jacob Spon. Un humaniste lyonnais du XVIIe siècle* (1993); see also Martin Kreeb, 'Zur Beschreibung Athens im Reisebericht Jacob Spons von 1675/1676' in *Wissenschaft mit Enthusiasmus, Beiträge ... Klaus Fittschen gewidmet*, ed. J. Bergemann (2001), 1-26. Lastly, William St. Clair has been an active participant in the debate over the Parthenon marbles for decades now: see his book *Lord Elgin and the Marbles: The controversial history of the Parthenon sculptures* (3rd edn., 1998).

CHAPTER XIII

The Founding
of Modern Athens:
The New City Plan and
Urban Development

Manos Biris

2. The Athens Observatory on the Hill of the Nymphs, designed by Theophil von Hansen (1842): view from the Areopagus. (Romaïdis Photograph Album, late 19th cent.)

1. *Aerial photograph of Athens in 1950. (Author's own photographic archive)*

The Founding of Modern Athens:
The New City Plan
and Urban Development

When Athens was designated 'Royal Seat and Capital City' under the terms of a Royal Decree published in the *Government Gazette* of 28th September 1834 (R.D. 18/30 September 1834, Article 2), the historic city embarked on its reconstruction on the basis not of a new plan but of an existing one that had already been revised. Implementation of the original plan prepared by Stamatios Kleanthis and Eduard Schaubert, which was ratified by the Government on 29 June/11 July 1833, was suspended roughly twelve months later. In other words, the formal foundation of the capital of the newly-fledged Greek state took place in the shadow of a 'misjudgment' which could hardly be said to have augured well for the smooth regeneration of the city. Yet the very choice of Athens as the new capital in 1833, from a selection of contenders that included Náfplion, Argos, Trípolis, even Mégara and Piraeus, was itself made not on the basis of purely rationalistic – what we should today call 'technocratic' – criteria: rather, it emerged from comparisons relating to ideological and petty political considerations that were naturally also fairly parochial in character. Whilst this matter still remains to be fully elucidated, nonetheless the initiative taken by the ideologue King Ludwig I of Bavaria unquestionably acted as a catalyst with regard to the final decision. On the other hand, this design solution had been prepared some considerable time beforehand and had the backing of the advisors to the Greek 'Governor' (President), Kapodistrias. However, sensing – with his infallible political judgment – that a hasty decision by him would no doubt provoke tension during this sensitive phase of his reconstruction programme and that that would be unhelpful if not downright dangerous, the founder of the recently-liberated Greek state left the matter to be investigated by his colleagues who were better equipped to deal with the task.

Amongst these were the aforementioned architects, Stamatios Kleanthis (1799-1862) and Eduard Schaubert (1804-1860), two friends and colleagues who were both graduates of the Berlin Academy of Architecture and former students of the renowned exponent of German classical architecture, Friedrich von Schinkel. In the summer of 1830 they took up appointments as architects at Aígina, then the seat of government, and applied themselves with genuine enthusiasm to their work both on the design and construction of public buildings and on the development of an appropriate technical education for young architects.

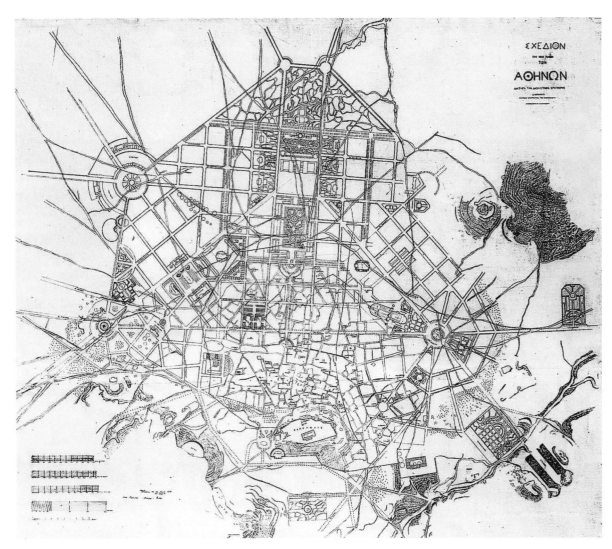

3. The Kleanthis-Schaubert plan (1833): copy made in 1836. (Author's own photographic archive)

Despite their multifarious activities on Aígina, their minds were preoccupied with nearby Athens, which they envisaged would ultimately become the country's capital. It was an idea which they tried to put across to Andreas Moustoxydis, a friend of Kapodistrias', who at first refused to be persuaded. However, a visit to Athens by the President in January 1831 suggests that the endeavours of the two architects had the desired effect, insofar as he allowed them to work there on a detailed documentation of the existing situation, a task which they carried out with the utmost care and attention in a relatively short period of time. By the spring of the following year they were already in a position to present an outline plan based on their survey, for which they finally received an official mandate in May 1832.

Commissioning the two architects to prepare the new plan for Athens made it a virtual certainty that the city would be proclaimed the new Greek capital; for all practical purposes, this was effected with the ratification of the planning proposal in question by the first ruler of the new Greek state, King Otho, on 29 June/11 July 1833. This was undoubtedly the most responsible action undertaken by Ludwig I of Bavaria's young son, who showed no particular sign of self-assurance or decision-making ability during the period of his active reign (effectively from 1835 to 1862). Actually, at the time when the plan was signed the country was ruled by a council of Regents (Armansberg, Maurer, Heideck) until Prince Otho came of age. Most historians thus agree that it was Ludwig's lively interest in the classical splendour of Athens and the direct influence exerted by the philhellene monarch on the Regency Council – and naturally on his own son – that brought about the irreversible decision to make Athens the new Greek capital.

The Kleanthis-Schaubert Plan. As already stated, the plan prepared by the two architects for the new city of Athens did not have the good fortune to be put into effect intact, even during the first stage of its implementation. Inherent weaknesses in the plan and, above all, the interests of those directly affected by it and the lack of any compensation for those who suffered damages as a result of the new layout of streets and properties, sparked off considerable indignation on the part of the Athenians and ultimately brought about the complete suspension of the plan's implementation in June, 1934.

Alternative proposals

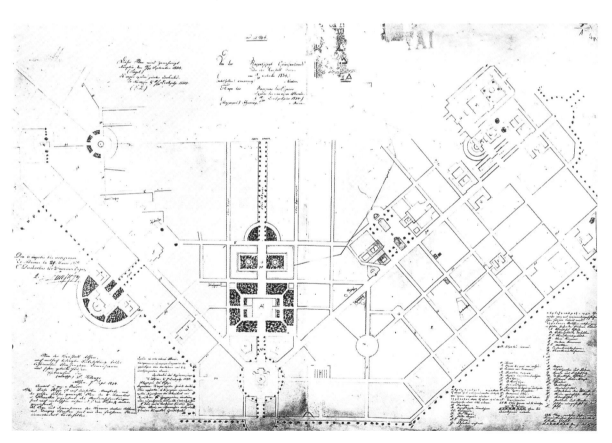

4. *Klenze's amended plan (1834): copy made in 1835. (Author's own photographic archive)*

At this point it should be explained that the houses within the town's labyrinthine system of narrow streets and alleyways, bounded by the flimsy wall built by Hadji Ali Haseki in 1778, were for the most part in woeful condition, many having been abandoned during the War of Independence (1821-1828), yet their owners' claims for compensation were substantial. The same was true of plots of land outside the town: although the departing Turks sold these tracts to the Greeks cheaply, their new owners demanded far more than the value set by the Regency, that is to say many times the price of 20 lepta per square pik [a unit of length approximately equal to 64 cm]. In addition to these problems there was also the matter of finding immediate housing for those whose homes had to be either demolished or requisitioned for use by government personnel.

The plan's basic defect – that is, the complicated network of proposed new roads within the old town – was concisely summed up a century later, in 1933, by the planning historian Kostas Biris, in the following words: 'One criticism that could be levelled at the plan devised by Kleanthis and Schaubert with regard to the street layout is that the old town was intersected by many [new] roads.'

It is a fact that the proposal put forward by the two architects covered the area lying to the north of the old town, with the main roads converging on the square in front of the Palace (roughly on the site of the present Omónia Square). From this point, Piraiós Street led away towards the south-west and Stadhíou Street towards the south-east, in precise alignment with the ancient Panathenaic Stadium. Bisecting the angle formed by these two streets, running due south from the Royal Palace to the Acropolis, was Athinás Street. Approximately thirty metres wide, this thoroughfare cut through the old town as far as Monastiráki, where it crossed Ermoú Street at right angles. The latter constituted the base of an almost isosceles triangle, encountering Stadhíou Street and Piraiós Street at two circular piazzas: Moussón Square to the east and Kékropos Square to the west. Further to the south, the area from the present-day Pandhróssou Street up as far as the Acropolis (that is, most of the Pláka district) was designated an 'archaeological site' and was consequently not to be built on. So far so good: if we disregard the present site of the Palace and the fact that the Pláka is today a densely built-up area, it might be said that the plan's basic geometry has been preserved much as it was. Unfortunately, however, this impression is a false one. What has in fact been preserved is a shadowy version of the initial plan, since the original also included the following distinctive features: (a) a network of very broad boulevards forming the basic framework of the new city centre and permitting its orderly expansion; (b) a grand main square ('Garden of the People' and commercial centre) approximately 500 metres in length and half that in width, to be located between the Royal Palace and the southern section of Athinás Street; (c) a system for the unobstructed expansion of the street plan beyond Stadhíou and Piraiós Streets, and the possibility of extending the built-up area to the north of the Palace complex.

These important features, which would have had a significant bearing on the survival of a city 'for 40,000 inhabitants', were excluded from the plan during its subsequent revision. Along with these features the plan's entire philosophical basis was also sacrificed, at least with regard to the way its authors interpreted the fundamental idea behind the new city layout in their

5. Plan of Athens in 1860 by the army engineer Emmanuel Kallerghis. (Author's own photographic archive)

memorandum: 'Although not absolutely flat, the area [proposed] for the new city is nonetheless suitable for development.... As far as the street plan is concerned, we have sought to adapt it to the lie of the land as far as possible, but without spoiling the desired symmetry, insofar as this could be achieved. In our view there were two points that required particular attention: finding the most suitable location for the Royal Palace and its official square as the city centre, and establishing as easy and direct a link between it and the present city as possible.'

Although space does not permit more detailed reference, it will be quite clear that, apart from its functional effectiveness (which sadly was later diminished), the Kleanthis-Schaubert plan was based mainly on sensitive accommodation to the historic landscape and the physical features of the terrain – but always retaining the Royal Palace as a central pivot. Adapting the two main thoroughfares of Stadhíou Street and Piraiós Street to the existing gradients was actually an ideal solution, and the slightly higher ground leading up to the Palace offered a magnificent view of the Acropolis and the broader horizons of Attica across the 'Garden of the People'. On the other hand, as already mentioned, the close proximity of old and new resulted in the disagreeable superimposition of the new street plan on the old town and an unsatisfactory outcome with regard to implementation of the plan.

The truth is that the choice of the level ground north of the Acropolis for the site of the new city was ideal for its integration in the historic landscape, and that location was therefore firmly espoused by the Court. Quite apart from this consideration, the area to the south of the Acropolis contained low ground that was marshy in wet weather and was undoubtedly less healthy. Yet it did have the major advantage of being virgin land not yet built on, and several proposals for the southward transfer of the capital's administrative centre, at least, were therefore put forward many years later.

Piraeus, too, was still completely undeveloped and had not been parcelled out into properties – a fact that prompted the Munich-born architect, Johann G. Gutensohn, to propose it unreservedly as the new capital city. However, the considerable distance between Piraeus and the 'historic landscape' of Athens raised insurmountable problems and the idea was, hardly surprisingly, stillborn.

A seemingly more innovative proposal was put forward – though not until about 1837 – by the versatile architect Lysandros Kaftandzoglou (1811-1885). His idea was that Ermoú Street should be extended eastwards for more than a kilometre as far as the banks of the River Ilissos and thereby become the city's main thoroughfare, flanked by the new streets laid out in a rectangular grid. This would have permitted not merely the protection of the historic monuments and the old town as a whole, but also their incorporation in a kind of archaeological park, an idea that Kaftandzoglou enthusiastically championed. On the other hand, the expansion of the city centre would have been difficult if not actually impossible, since (in Kaftandzoglou's plan) it was hemmed in by the two hills of Likavitós and Ardhitós.

In any event, it is easy to see that a fundamental flaw in the Kleanthis-Schaubert plan really did exist, but it is equally true that this weakness was exaggerated in relation to its undeniable advantages. In this respect some blame has to be borne by the Government, which was in an impossible predicament over granting compensation for properties to be absorbed in the new street plan (mainly in the old town) while simultaneously finding a solution to the acute housing problem and implementing the compulsory purchase orders necessary for the clearance of the archaeological site.

The order was therefore given for the plan to be suspended and in the summer of 1834 Ludwig I dispatched his own architect (and 'secret adviser'), the famous pioneer of classicism in Munich, Leo von Klenze (1784-1864), to enforce the necessary solution.

While Klenze was well versed in Greek architecture, he was at the same time a true representative of European Romanticism. The second of these two facts will probably be of more use to us than the first in enabling us to formulate an objective judgment of his proposal. For the overall conception of the Kleanthes-Schaubert plan and the accompanying memorandum by its architects are enough to convince us that they meant their proposal to strike a balance between pure ideology and discrete rationalism, based on long-range criteria.

The Klenze Plan

On the other hand, Klenze's general line of thinking is not particularly clear despite the lengthy screeds accompanying his proposal, the principal one being his 'Self-evident Observations', which he submitted to the Regency together with his comments. Indeed, the draft version of that proposal (which was ratified in September 1934, as already mentioned) contained amendments and compromises that rather undermined the purely philosophical nature of the proposals put forward by Klenze the Romantic. Thus he did not attempt a radical revision of the existing study, although in his view the best solution was for the city to be built where it would not intrude upon the classical monuments and the old town – in other words, in the area south-west of the Acropolis. In the end he opted to transfer the Palace buildings to the Kerameikos, thereby underlining a more natural integration of the main points of reference within the urban structure and (as he himself explained) doing away with the pointless symmetry and axial framework of the earlier plan. Moreover, throughout the entire complex of Royal Palace buildings Klenze accentuated the diversity of shapes and the excellent way in which it accommodated the sloping terrain by encircling the buildings with a garden stocked with Mediterranean plants – all factors that hinted at the architect's excellent abilities and authentically Romantic disposition.

On the other hand, in order to promote a sense of 'picturesqueness' (as he believed), he drastically reduced the width of the streets and abolished the magnificent boulevards; at the junction of Stadhíou and Piraiós Streets he made provision for a simple square with a church standing in the centre. It is obvious that he saw no need for any future expansion of the city and so he set its northern limit at the site of this square (to be precise, where the present-day Satovriándhou Street lies) and its eastern limit along the line followed by Panepistimíou Street, in the middle of which he placed the capital's cultural centre, a group of buildings in a semi-circular garden. He retained only that part of the new plan which lay to the west of Piraiós Street, including in this area the well laid-out Loudhovíkou Square (now Eleftherías Square), and he left the site of the archaeological excavations near the Acropolis untouched, thereby sparing the old town many of the alterations to its street plan. Thus in fact, through a kind of

6. Plan of Athens in 1908 by A. Georgiadis. (Author's own photographic archive)

7. *Plan of Athens in 1930 by Kostas Biris.* (*Author's own photographic archive*)

policy of limitation, he did succeed in reducing the negative impact resulting from implementation of the original plan.

It should be noted, however, that despite his well-reasoned opinions concerning human scale (well-reasoned in the fullest sense of the term), his respect for the historic monuments and his wish to introduce a touch of picturesque local colour, it was the abstractive and distorting nature of his interventions (such as the bend at the end of Stadhíou Street) which undermined the city's natural growth and could be said to have contributed to today's problems.

On the whole it is true to say that criticism of a city plan necessarily arises from the negative experiences which have occurred at a later date, i.e. after its implementation, and from its adaptability to developments over time. Yet the architect, too, undoubtedly has it in his power to use his foresight. Modern scholars of Athens' planning history tend towards the view that it was Lysandros Kaftandzoglou who proposed the most apposite solutions, particularly with regard to an enlarged 'archaeological park' whose presence would be an important factor in planning the city's future growth. In this matter – that is, the protection of the historic environment – Kaftandzoglou was more of a town planner, Klenze more of an archaeologist.

8. How Athens looked during Otho's reign: the Dependency of the Convent of the Holy Sepulchre (Metókhi tou Panayíou Táfou). (Author's own photographic archive. Photograph taken 1950)

The Palace Question. With Klenze's plan approved, the question of the location of the Royal Palace arose once again (even though implementation of the street plan had already begun) because of the problems emerging in the Kerameikos area. The eminent Berlin architect, Karl Friedrich von Schinkel (1781-1841), became involved in the delibera- *The Gärtner intervention* tions and in the urging of Maximilian, the heir to the Bavarian throne, he prepared a plan for the Royal Palace to be sited on the Acropolis.

We shall not dwell on this plan of Schinkel's; since it was never put into effect it is of limited historical interest. While there was virtual unanimity (apart from the views held by Schinkel's own student, Ferdinand von Quast) concerning the unrealistic nature of such a drastic intervention on the site of a unique historic monument – even the architect of the plan expressed his reservations – the audacity, sophistication and academic refinement of this grand design should not be underrated. Allied to the plan for siting the Palace on the Acropolis was a proposal by Quast for the new city to be expanded in the direction of the Hill of the Nymphs, thereby enabling the historic landscape and the town which developed under Turkish rule to be preserved intact. It was a view that had Romantic connotations and took little notice of the area's unsuitable terrain, although the configuration of the land did, in fact, provide considerable scope for protecting the monuments of ancient Athens and setting them off to advantage.

Be that as it may, it was once again Ludwig of Bavaria himself who, after an important visit to Athens that lasted from December 1835 to March 1836, made the final decision that the Palace should be transferred to its present site on the southern slopes of Likavitós with a view of the Acropolis and beyond to the Saronic Gulf.

At around that time another architect, Friedrich von Gärtner, had begun to eclipse the hitherto all-powerful Klenze in Munich, and it was he who received the order from the King to design and undertake the construction of the Palace that would be Otho's home. Work on the imposing but rather heavy-looking building that is today the Greek Parliament in Syntagma Square began in 1836 and was completed around 1842. At the same time the architect responsible for supervision of the project, whose name was Hoch, laid out the area around the Royal Palace, especially on the west side, setting the boundaries of the square in front of the Palace and the main thoroughfare that led southwards in continuation of Panepistimíou Street, that is Amalías Avenue. Hoch also devised a more realistic shape for the Royal Gardens than the large semicircle envisaged by Gärtner, and extended them southwards. Eventually, by about 1847, they stretched as far as Iródhou Attikoú Street and Vassilíssis Olgas Avenue and were planted by the landscape gardeners Schmidt and Baucaut, under the supervision of Queen Amalia.

Dismissal of the foreigners. Unhappily for the future of the Greek capital, the approval of Klenze's plan proved in reality to be a disputed settlement of the problem concerning the city plan. Furthermore, after the dismissal of the foreign architects and engineers following the bloodless coup d'état of 3rd September 1843, planning was placed in the care of the Interior Ministry's Public Works Directorate and in the hands of Greek army officers, chiefly engineers.

Otho's reign

The extremely accurate plan of the city drawn in 1836 by Stauffert on four large sheets, on a scale of 1:2,500, proves that a considerable amount of building was done in the old part of the town to the south of Adhrianoú Street, in what was supposed to be the 'archaeological excavation' zone. Because the compulsory purchase scheme proved unworkable, very few sites were eventually set aside for historical research, while in the remainder of the area work began on straightening and rationalizing the network of narrow streets in the medieval town. A similar tidying up of the street plan to the north of Adhrianoú Street was based on another highly accurate survey carried out by a Bavarian Army engineer, W. von Weiler. In making these alterations, care was taken to keep the demolition of houses down to a minimum; however, this was not the case with the little old churches in the town, which were literally obliterated so that both the building materials and the plots could be sold off – by the Government.

9. How Athens looked in the reign of George I: Filellínon Street. (Romaïdis Photograph Album, late 19th cent.) ☞

By today's standards this would be considered a criminal act, but it was not deemed to be so at that time, when antiquity was the sole yardstick in the ideology relating to the protection of ancient monuments.

To decide on the general lines of the new city, a committee composed of Army engineers and architects (L. Smolenskis, L. Kaftandzoglou, E. Manitakis, T. Komninos and T. von Hansen) was set up in 1846. A year later the committee submitted a master plan on a scale of 1:2,500, which naturally reflected all the cuts made in both the functional and communal areas of the city, as well as the many compromises reached in the siting of roads – the result of the many adventures that had dogged the original Kleanthis-Schaubert plan for fourteen years. On the other hand, practical proposals were made for the planning of the areas beyond Panepistimíou Street (Neápoli) and Piraiós Street (Metaxouryío). Approval was also given for the northward extension of Aiólou Street beyond Stadhíou Street: this was to become the start of the future Patissíon Street. The splendid 'Garden of the People', along Athinás Street, was considerably reduced in size and fragmented in this plan; in addition, the plan showed the west wing of the University, which was under construction, and the layout of the gardens round the Civic Hospital in Akadhimías Street; while at the western end of Ermoú Street, near the 'Theseion' and the Kerameikos, a number of open spaces were created and planted with trees and shrubs

10. The Athens Municipal Theatre, designed by Ernst Ziller (1873-1888). Before its demolition in 1940 it was one of the main points of reference in the city centre. (Romaïdis Photograph Album, late 19th cent.)

11. View of Athens from the Pnyx. (Romaïdis Photograph ☞ *Album, late 19th cent.)*

Rhomaïdes

in keeping with the area's archaeological surroundings. However, the plan did not include definitive proposals for the eastern end of Ermoú Street, Syntagma Square, most of the Royal Gardens and Amalías Avenue down to the curve at the intersection with Dhionisíou Areopayítou Street. Work on this sector and the northward expansion of the city plan (roughly as far as the line of Stournári Street) was carried out by another committee headed by Colonel D. Stavridis of the Corps of Engineers. The topographical plan for this area was finally approved in 1860.

Thus the picture we have today of the urban structure of Athens' 'historic centre' had more or less crystallized by the end of Otho's reign and fairly dense redevelopment had been carried out on the basis of the new street plan. Initially houses were built on the north-eastern side of the city (in Neápoli), along both sides of Piraiós Street and in the Metaxouryío district. There was also intensive construction work within the old town, as one would expect, especially along Athinás, Aiólou and Ermoú Streets. These were elegant buildings in the Neoclassical style, constructed in accordance with certain basic rules introduced by the Bavarians as early as 1836.

Various strategic positions in the new city were soon occupied by some fine public buildings: these included the University (designed by the Danish architect, Christian Hansen), the Observatory (by Theophil von Hansen), the Arsákion (by Kaftandzoglou), the Civic Hospital, the Metropolis or Cathedral (finished in 1860), the Eye Hospital, the Foundlings' Home and several others, some of which (like the Mint, the Printing-House and the Military Hospital) had

12. Extensions to the city plan following the 1922 Asia Minor disaster: aerial photograph of the refugee settlement of Néa Filadélfia (1930-1935). (Photographic archive of M. Adamis)

already been in existence for twenty to twenty-five years. Furthermore, despite the political unrest that led to the dethronement of King Otho in 1862, a certain amount of work was done to beautify the various squares and open spaces, trees were planted along the main streets (particularly during the mayoralty of I. Koniaris, 1851-1854), the First Cemetery was established and some efforts were finally made to relieve the drought problem by cleaning Hadrian's aqueduct and installing the first water mains.

The reign of George I. By the time King George I ascended the throne in 1863, the population of Athens already exceeded the figure forecast by Kleanthis and Schaubert (40,000); between 1870 and 1880 the number of inhabitants was close on 60,000 and by the turn of the century it had reached 120,000. Such rapid growth called for a more clear-cut planning framework and so in 1865 the Interior Ministry published a plan of the city (scale 1:2,000) on four sheets. These sheets formed the basis for all additions to and modifications of the city plan until near the end of the century.

*Urban Planning:
Insuperable Problems*

Two fundamental facts should be underlined at this point: firstly, that between then and about 1890 the city limits were rapidly extended until they reached from Kolonós to Ambelókipi and from Patíssia to Káto Petrálona and Kinóssaryes; and secondly, that these extensions were not made according to any 'normal' building ratio – on the con-

13. *Extensions to the city plan following the 1922 Asia Minor disaster: aerial photograph of the village of Khalándri (1930-1935).*
(Photographic archive of M. Adamis)

trary, they were extremely sparsely developed. That was because the authorities now made it their policy to include the advancing tide of illegal or unauthorized housing within city limits. Conversely, those who had built without permission put pressure on the authorities to extend the city limits so as to benefit from the public utilities provided – and of course to increase the value of their property.

At any rate, with the construction of the massive buildings of the National Technical University (the Polytechnic) and the National Archaeological Museum, the city limits were extended northwards until by about 1871 they had reached Pipínou Street. Ten years later, the settlement of Ano Patíssia was approved and linked to Athens by the 'corridor' of Patissíon Street, the total distance from Omónia Square to the end of Patissíon Street being more than four kilometres.

It has to be admitted, however, that there were also a number of purely practical factors that contributed to the construction of main roads essential to the various extensions to the city plan. For example, the existence of the suburb of Ambelókipi, the opening to the north-east created by Kifissiás Avenue and the obstacle presented by Likavitós Hill led to the creation in 1878 of the very broad thoroughfare that was Alexándhras Avenue – the brainchild of Professor I. Yenisarlis of the Surveying Department at the National Technical University. Similarly, Singroú Avenue was built approximately twenty years later when the coastal resorts had become popular with the people of Athens and the road leading south out of the city through the Makriyánni district (Falírou Street) was no longer adequate. Dhionisíou Areopayítou and Apostólou Pávlou Street, the two roads skirting the Acropolis to the south, were built long before houses began to be erected in the area. Generally speaking, the opening of the Athens-Piraeus railway in 1869 gave a considerable boost to the southward expansion of the city. Full credit must be given for the remarkable efficiency with which so many infrastructure works (laying of tramlines, surfacing of roads, installation of street lights and water mains, etc.) were carried out during the period when the new Greek capital was in its heyday, under the various governments of Harilaos Trikoupis (1882-1895, with some interruptions). The Piraeus railway was extended beyond the Theseion to Omonia Square in 1895 and was electrified in 1904. In the meantime the Attica Railways' lines to Fáliro, Kifissiá and Lávrio were also opened during the 1880s. It was not until 1908 that a substantial electric tram network began to be established in the city.

There can be no doubt that by the turn of the century Athens had blossomed into one of the finest cities in Europe. The monumental public buildings and cultural institutions were almost finished, their architecture blended harmoniously with that of the private buildings and the final result perfectly reflected the form and spirit of the local Neoclassical idiom.

This picture of striking urban beauty was only to be found in the city centre. The outlying areas continued to suffer (the population influx that took place after 1880 being a contributory factor in this respect) from the vested interests that stood to gain from the spread of the city. By

14. *View of Athens. (Photographic archive of N. Panayotopoulos)*

15. *The rapidly-changing face of Athens towards the end of the 1950s: the last two remaining houses on the north side of Ipírou Street at its junction with Trítis Septemvríou Street. A rare colour photograph from that era. (Author's own photographic archive)*

1907, almost 1,600 hectares had been added to the area covered by the original plan (Kallithéa alone accounting for 98 hectares), although the population density was extremely low.

This reckless expansion of the city became even more acute in the wake of the Asia Minor disaster in 1922, when entrepreneurs and contractors illegally developed tracts of land which would afterwards, under the beneficial legislation then in force, be incorporated in the city plan. Before that the government had considered various abortive proposals for planning reform in the centre of Athens, the details of which are beyond the scope of this work. They included a study by Pavlos Vakas in 1896 recommending the construction of a number of unobtrusive main thoroughfares, studies by the German architect Ludwig Hoffmann and A. Georgiadis (1908) involving some more radical modifications (most notably the extension of Koraï Street towards Monastiráki and the building of more monumental thoroughfares) and finally a study by the celebrated British town planner, Thomas Mawson (1914), which contained a number of rather odd planning and architectural proposals holding out extremely optimistic prospects for urban regeneration, which he set out in a remarkable series of topographic plans and axonometric drawings.

16. View of the 'Theseion' and the Acropolis in the early 1870s, showing the Vlassaroú district of Athens, later demolished in order to clear the site of the Agora for excavation. Behind what is now Apostólou Pávlou Street (in the foreground) lie the still unland-scaped grounds of the 'Theseion'. The two-storey house where the architect Kleanthis drew up the first city plan for Athens with his friend and colleague, Schaubert, may be seen at the extreme left, behind the temple. (Author's own photographic archive)

The most realistic of all these studies was one conducted by Petros Kalligas, a member of the Supreme Technical Council of State (a body of which the French planner, E. Hébrard, was also a member until 1921). Kalligas's plan, which was revised after the Asia Minor disaster (1922), contained suggestions for a complete overhaul of the planning system in the Greek capital, block by block, based on sound judgment and a realistic appreciation of the situation. Among other things, the plan recommended the establishment of an administrative centre near the Ilissos, enlargement of the archaeological zone around the Acropolis, the extension of Trítis Septemvríou Street and improvements to the railway stations. Even though it proved its worth many times over during the period of profound upheaval occasioned by the resettlement of refugees from Asia Minor, and although the question of private housing schemes – an issue not unrelated to the refugee problem – was now extremely pressing, the plan was scrapped by presidential decree in 1926.

This was the context in which the Athenian planning authorities had to contend with the problems of the twentieth century, which involved dealing with a social situation that was undergoing radical changes, facing the prospect of assimilating heterogeneous population groups into the urban structure and coming to grips with the spectre of a rapidly increasing and insatiable tendency towards over-centralization.

BIBLIOGRAPHY

Biris, K., *Τα πρώτα σχέδια των Αθηνών*, Athens 1933.
—, *Αθηναϊκαί μελέται*, I, Athens 1938, II, Athens 1939.
—, *Αι Αθήναι από του 19ου εις τον 20όν αιώνα*, Athens 1966.
Fountoulaki, O., *Stamatios Kleanthes* (dissertation), Munich 1979.
Hederer, Oswald, *Leo von Klenze*, Munich 1964.
Kaftandzoglou, L., *Περί μεταρρυθμίσεως της πόλεως των Αθηνών, γνώμαι*, Athens 1858.
Kambouroglou, D., *Μελέται και Έρευναι*, Athens 1925, 1927.
Koepp, F. (ed.), *Schauberts handschriftlicher Nachlass*, Archäologischer Anzeiger, 1890.
Kühn, M., *Schinkel und das Entwurf von Schaubert und Kleanthes fuer die Neustadt Athen*, 'Berlin
    und die Antike', II, 1979.
Michael, J., *Entwicklungsüberlegungen und -initiativen zum Stadtplan von Athen nach dessen Erhe-
    bung zur Hauptstadt Griechenlands*, Athens 1969.
Paraskevopoulos, G., *Οι Δήμαρχοι των Αθηνών (1835-1907)*, Athens 1907.
Papageorgiou-Venetas, A., *Hauptstadt Athen – ein Stadtgedanke des Klassizismus*, Munich/Berlin
    1994.
Russack, H., *Deutsche Bauen in Athen*, Berlin 1942.
Vakas, P., *Ο αρχιτέκτων του σχεδίου των Αθηνών, Στ. Κλεάνθης*, Athens 1931.

CHAPTER XIV

*The Formation
of Athenian
Neoclassicism*

GEORGIOS A. PANETSOS

2. T. Hansen, Metropolitan Cathedral (original proposal for the site finally chosen, 1842), west elevation. Pencil on paper. Vienna, Akademie der bildenden Künste. (Author's own photographic archive)

1. T. Hansen, Záppion Hall (1879-1888), the atrium. (Studio KONTOS/Photostock)

GEORGIOS A. PANETSOS

The Formation of Athenian Neoclassicism

While the ideals of Greek and Roman antiquity were being rapturously embraced by European intellectuals, Late Byzantine Hellenism – the true successor to the ancient heritage – was in the throes of succumbing to Ottoman domination. For centuries thereafter the Greek world was to experience a régime of humiliation. Under conditions of penury and prohibition, with all resources, human and material, being channelled towards the service of the overlord, there is always limited scope for the development of architectural style. The architecture of the enslaved was reduced to rudimentary building, and it was only at the large monasteries which, far away from towns and villages, retained a relatively high degree of administrative and financial autonomy, that the Byzantine architectural manner managed to survive, though with no possibility of progress or innovation.

During this period, between the fifteenth and the seventeenth century, European architecture was constantly evolving, both in terms of technique and more particularly of style, through the adoption of the classical language, which was gradually codified into a coherent yet flexible expressive system. This evolution originated in the study of Roman monuments; it seemed to have spent itself only when the classical orders were overshadowed by the plastic excesses of the baroque and later displaced by the rococo style in the eighteenth century. It was this superficially decorative version of European architecture that permeated into the East. Yirmisekiz Çelebi Mehmet Efendi, Constantinople's ambassador to Paris from 1720, was so captivated by the Louis Quinze style that when he went home he took with him detail drawings of Versailles and Marly-le-Roi, which soon swayed the tastes of the Ottoman court and were applied – with some alterations – to the Sultan's private quarters. Foreign architects were now employed with increasing frequency in Constantinople. However, Western influence was not confined to the capital, nor did it necessarily pass through the capital on its way to the provinces. By the early eighteenth century an active class of traders and shipowners from different parts of the subjugated lands had already begun to develop direct contacts with Europe.

The economic takeoff of the Greek world, which started after the Treaty of Kütchük Kainardji (1774) and continued right up to the eve of the Greek Revolution in 1821, enabled people to pursue comforts, without altering the traditional internal layout of their homes, and to spend money on decorating them in the prevailing baroque and rococo styles, which in Europe were already on the decline. However, it was the proclivity towards education and culture which accompanied the new prosperity, prompted by contact with the European Enlightenment, that created the conditions for substantial changes in attitude and approach. And it was these changes that brought about the Revolution. As far as architecture was concerned, by 1822 the Wallachian branch of the princely Phanariot family of Ghika had already acquired a genuine Neoclassical mansion in Bucharest.

Around 1800, Neoclassicism was the established idiom of early romantic expression. It fused aspects of French rationalism and British empiricism with more recent developments, such as the interest in archaeological studies inspired by the finds from Herculaneum and Pompeii, and the new definition of beauty based on J.J. Winckelmann's interpretation of classical art. However, it no longer had the liberal political connotations that the Enlightenment had attributed to the classical tradition. In architecture in particular, Neoclassicism sought a new approach in which simplicity of mass and decoration, expedient construction and respect for the nature of materials would be held up as the basic condition of *beauty*. This quest focused not on Roman but on Greek architecture, first in Sicily and later in Greece. In Greece, with the acquisition of independence, Neoclassicism momentarily regained its original political content: a state of liberty was created on the ruins of the old order, alongside the relics of *antiquity*, and a new society was born out of the community of the descendants of the ancient Greeks.

Amid the climate of romanticism, Athens – for centuries an unimportant township – now returned to prominence, thanks to the aura of its ancient heritage. Writing about Athens in

**Kleanthis
and Schaubert
in Athens**

1830 and describing the effects of the town's capture by Reshid Pasha's troops on 24th May 1827, after an eleven-month siege that resulted in its being deserted for three years (for the second time in a hundred and thirty years), J.F. Michaud had this to say: 'We strode amid heaps of debris along a path that had been cleared through the rubble, treading with every step on stones, half-collapsed walls and col-

3. Ferdinand Stademann. 'Panorama von Athen'. Munich, 1841 (detail of lithograph). View of the town from the Hill of the Nymphs, as planned in 1835. The Royal Mint, the Vouros and Afthonidis residences, the octagonal hall and the Kondostavlos House (the first royal residence in Athens on the site of the Old Parliament building) and the Royal Stables can be seen at the foot of Likavitós Hill, as well as the old town to the north and north-west of the Acropolis.

umn drums, scattered amongst the dust of the ruins…. There is neither road nor square, no garden, monastery or church … and the owls we encountered – the bird of Athena and the only resident of Athens in recent years – are now merely a symbol of the devastation….' It was to this ravaged town that Ioannis Kapodistrias came on 12th January 1831, accompanied by Stamatios Kleanthis and Gustav-Eduard Schaubert (who had been appointed as government architects in June 1830), to negotiate the handover of the Acropolis (still occupied by the Turkish garrison) to the Greek administration.

4. View of Athens from Likavitós, looking south-west. The photograph, taken around 1875, shows the royal palace (the dome of the little chapel standing out above the flat roofs, without the north portico), the Royal Pharmacy, the nearly finished Syngros House on the corner of Vassilíssis Sofías Avenue and Zalokósta Street, the houses of the Skylitsis, Koutsis and Mavromichalis families (the latter with a pediment and without the later addition of a third floor) on Amalías Avenue and the Dimitriou and Koromilas houses on Syntagma Square. The sparsely-built area in the foreground includes the present-day Pindhárou, Kriezótou, Voukourestíou, Sólonos, A. Soútsou and Akadhimías Streets. (Friedrich von Gärtner, 'Ein Architektenleben 1791-1847', Munich 1992-93)

Having first-hand knowledge of the facts at their disposal and perceiving how matters would develop, first Schaubert (who was impatient to begin a study of the Acropolis monuments immediately after the withdrawal of the Turkish garrison) and then Kleanthis, a little while later, resigned from their positions in the public service and settled in Athens. In the autumn of 1831 they embarked on a survey of the ruined town – a task which, by virtue of a government decree dated 24th May, 1832, enabled them to undertake the design of the first town plan of Athens. This fairly brief but productive collaboration united them in a way that drew a veil over the personal characteristics of two otherwise very different personalities.

Stamatios Stamatiou (1797/1802-1860), who was called Kleanthis because, like the ancient philosopher Kleanthes, he worked at night so as to be able to study during the daytime, was born at Velvendhós, near Kozáni in northern Greece. He was educated in Bucharest, arguably the most important centre of the Greek Enlightenment; he enlisted in the Sacred Company (a band of ethnic Greek volunteers raised in the Danubian principalities to fight for the liberation of Greece), fought at Dragatsani and survived, crossed over into Austrian territory, fled to Leipzig and ended up in Berlin, where he obtained the best architectural education to be had at the time under K.F. Schinkel at the Bauakademie. The straitened circumstances of his early life and his contact with active Greeks in Europe's commercial communities generated in Kleanthis an entrepreneurial spirit, a tenacity and pragmatism that frequently led him to carry out actions of a questionable nature and ultimately forced him to stop practising as an architect altogether.

Schaubert (1804-1860), on the other hand, who had also studied under Schinkel in Berlin, seems to have been a man of integrity, unassuming and with a strong sense of duty. Apart from a three-year break – the period of his collaboration with Kleanthis – he held a number of key positions in the public service between 1830 and 1843 and his contribution to developments in Athenian architecture was a decisive one. Of equal importance was his remarkably extensive work in documenting the architecture of antiquity, an achievement which failed to receive the recognition it deserved, since – with the principal exception of the restoration of the Temple of Athena Nike on the Acropolis – it was not written up in books or otherwise widely publicized.

At the time when Kleanthis and Schaubert arrived in Athens, no architects were living in the town and those who visited did not stay for long. In any case, it was impossible to gain access to the Acropolis because of the continued presence of the Turkish garrison, and living conditions were wretched. So the two architects soon began to undertake private commissions in the face of innumerable difficulties. In January 1832 Schaubert wrote to A.F. von Quast in Berlin: 'We have begun to build country villas in as urban a style as possible.... We have been commissioned to build houses for Admiral Malcolm, the Russian and Austrian consuls, several Americans and Greeks, even an Athenian, and we are trying to produce the best we can, in terms of both construction and amenities.'

These first examples of Kleanthis and Schaubert's work introduced a new residential typology to Athens. Instead of having the rooms arranged sequentially around a courtyard walled off from the street (as was the custom with traditional Athenian houses built during the Turkish occupation), they opted for the discipline of a single prismatic mass or a combination of such masses, within which the distribution of the rooms followed a hierarchical order, with no alteration to the symmetry and orderly arrangement of the elevations or the overall form. Depending on the potential of the site, some of these houses gave directly on to the garden, to verandahs or to spacious flat roofs for recreation and relaxation. This was clearly a kind of architecture that reflected the sophisticated lifestyle and modern taste of the foreigners who had settled in Athens and of Greeks returning from the diaspora. The shortage of good building materials and experienced builders in general, let alone skilled workmen with specialized knowledge of Classical decorative art, inevitably limited stylistic attributes to a minimum. The result was that attention was focused on the importance of graceful proportions and plain formal choice in a manner pleasing to the modern eye. The same constraints also dictated 'archaic' constructional features, such as the steeply sloping roof (1:2.5) and crude pediment of the Malcolm villa; however, the rapid growth of technical expertise in the years immediately following meant that these were soon dispensed with.

During the period when Kleanthis and Schaubert were erecting their first buildings in Athens after the War of Independence, and before the town was chosen as capital of the newly-fledged state, Crown Prince Maximilian of Bavaria, brother of Otto (the future King Otho of Greece), asked K.F. Schinkel, the greatest classical architect after 1800, for a theoretical definition of an 'ideal' architecture for Athens. Schinkel set out in writing the principles of an uncon-

The Athenian vision of K.F. Schinkel

strained, 'organic' kind architecture which, instead of merely reproducing familiar models, would allow a genuine 'continuation of history'. He made it clear that he was against any architecture 'in the style of the passé neo-Italian or neo-French models, in which a misunderstanding of symmetry results in such tedious affectation.' In the same text, dated 24th January 1833, Schinkel also referred to the royal palace and proposed 'as an important aid and a very basic means for achieving the goal [of an "ideal" architecture for Athens] an architectural conception in keeping with a way of life for the king based on the customs and needs of the country, and also [the] choice of a striking and attractive location for a building of this kind'; he considered that 'this should […] be the first step towards accomplishing this task.' 'The architect should thoroughly investigate the nature

5. K.F. Schinkel. The royal palace on the Acropolis (proposal of 1834), south elevation. Pen-and-ink and watercolour on paper. (Munich, Staatliche graphische Sammlung)

of the lifestyle and location and make the most of its countless advantages for the project in hand.'

These were the principles he was to apply a little later, after Athens had been designated 'capital city and seat of the monarchy' in 1833, when Maximilian and Crown Prince Friedrich-Wilhelm of Prussia, Otho's uncle, appointed Schinkel to draw up plans for a royal palace on the Acropolis. Such a proposition today would be considered sacrilegious and provoke an outcry. Until then, however, the Acropolis had been merely a military barracks where the monuments, recently looted by Lord Elgin and his imitators, stood shoulder to shoulder with buildings of no merit and were regarded as a source of construction material and marble for lime-burning. Schinkel's proposal was based on the scant archaeological facts known at that period. It was completed within a very short time and sent to King Otho in the spring of 1834. According to his design the palace would occupy the eastern part of the Acropolis, where there were no antiquities. The ruins of classical monuments, stripped clean of centuries' worth of additions, and the reconstructed statue of Athena Promachos were to figure prominently as emblematic features in the open spaces on either side of the path leading from the Propylaia to the palace. Instead of an enclosed, symmetrical mass of buildings, Schinkel proposed a closely-knit composition of low wings built around several atria – an arrangement not so very different from the urban structure of the historic centre of Athens. The plan was not, of course, based on his experience of the site – Schinkel never actually set foot in Greece – but rather on a creative render-

ing of the villas of Pompeii and Pliny's descriptions; nevertheless, he adhered faithfully to the Athenian models of the classical orders (which he knew from the publications of Stuart and Revett), while making some remarkable typological innovations. The differences in the height, area and orientation of the various wings offered variety, despite the size of the complex. The visual axes were such as to afford a succession of different views, taking full advantage of the site's potential in this respect, while colonnades, porticoes, canopies and several different types of landscaping made the most of the possibilities for outdoor living offered by the Attic climate.

On a higher level than that of the appeal to the senses, the coexistence of ancient and modern, nature and art, landscape and architecture, ruins and new buildings created an atmosphere evocative not merely of beauty, but of sublimity. Schinkel himself, in the posthumous publication

of his proposal in 1841, included both this and his design for the Schloss Orianda (a palace in the Crimea) in the domain of 'higher architecture, that which exists beyond the exigencies of everyday practice'.

As was to be expected, the idea of building the palace on the Acropolis provoked considerable dissent. Although Otho was delighted with the plan and its implicit analogy with the dawn of Athenian history — for the Acropolis was the home of Kekrops, the city's first king — his father, Ludwig

6. T. Hansen, private house on the palace square in Athens, between 1842 and 1846. Juxtaposition of the palace and the Dimitriou House showing the suggested layout of Syntagma Square, indicative of the architect's intentions. Vienna, Akademie der bildenden Künste. (Author's own photographic archive)

I of Bavaria, adamantly ruled out the possibility of any new building being put up on the Acropolis. Instead of the 'continuation of history' that Schinkel had proposed, what prevailed was the modernist concept of its objective approach. Leo von Klenze, a capable architect and astute advisor to King Ludwig, determined the fate of Schinkel's scheme by presenting it to Otho along with his own severe criticism of it. His motives would undoubtedly have included a strong desire to win this enviable commission for himself. During his few months' stay in Athens in the summer of 1834 he amended the already approved city plan, changed the location of the palace buildings and pressed for the removal from the Acropolis of remains dating from the Middle Ages or later, the restoration of the ancient monuments and the establishment of a museum. These decisions secured the conditions for the scientific study of ancient architecture; and at the same time they kept the evolution of modern Greek architecture within the academic tradition for the next ninety years or so. Although his decision has been vindicated by history, there is no denying that Schinkel's impeccably prepared plan, which

7. The royal palace (1836-1842). Design for wall decoration in Otho's study (1843). Pencil, tempera and watercolour on paper. Munich, Technical University. (Friedrich von Gärtner, 'Ein Architektenleben 1791-1847', Munich 1992-93)

expressed the undiminished relevance of the classical spirit to modern Greece in a typical manifestation of the romantic classicism then current in Europe, laid the foundations for a new kind of architecture which foreshadowed that of the twentieth century.

Klenze put forward an alternative scheme for the Hagios Athanássios district near the 'Theseion', in which he followed the principles laid down by Schinkel and replicated several of the attributes of his design, but without the cogency and coherence of the original. The new proposal, along with a third made by Ludwig Lange (which halved the floor area of the palace), was rejected. Harsh reality decreed the adoption of the most economical solutions possible.

The palace, as finally built to plans by Friedrich von Gärtner, followed totally different principles. The composite network of porticoes, atria and enclosed spaces, the integration of palace and government buildings into an urban complex and the creation of a small 'royal acropolis' on the edge of the city were replaced by a single compact edifice concealing two atria with a purely functional purpose. The design of the building conformed, *mutatis mutandis*, with the pragmatic strategy for which Kleanthis and Schaubert had opted in the years immediately preceding, in their first designs: a single architectural mass of precise proportions, with limited decoration. In the case of the palace, the design choices were characterized by vibrant tension and a singular intensity. The elementary overall form, with only some discreet modifications of the geometric shape and with no indication of its volume or depth, elevated the design of the palace to an architectural paradigm. This being so, its decoration – that is, its stylistic treatment – had to be kept to a minimum and applied only to 'key' parts of the building. Added interest was given to the formal façade facing the city by the wide portico on the west side, the balcony for ceremonial royal appearances and, above all this, the Doric pediment. The 'private' side – the side with the private apartments, overlooking the palace garden – retained the long stoa from Schinkel's original design. The eastern elevation, which at that time looked towards the open countryside, also had a small portico, while the north side of the building, facing the royal stables, was left unadorned. The entire building was crowned by a cornice embellished with marble akroteria and antefixes which, joined together in a continuous row, presaged one of the idiomatic features of later Athenian Neoclassicism.

Despite the state's limited resources and the difficulties encountered, work on the construction of the palace took only seven years, although a further five years were required to complete the magnificent interior decoration. Unfortunately, the ravages of time and successive restorations during the twentieth century to convert the building for use as the Greek Parliament have ensured that almost nothing is left of the palace's interior splendour.

If construction of the palace symbolized the foundation of the system of government and the establishment of social and cultural models, practical needs related to the organization and

The beginnings of the 'Athenian School' and Theophilos Hansen

effective operation of a modern state imposed immediate demands for offices to house the administration. In fact, the hasty transfer of the seat of the monarchy from Náfplion to Athens led to the adoption of some makeshift measures. Several government departments were accommodated in churches or mosques, in temporary rented premises or in new buildings hurriedly erected for the purpose. In 1834 the Ministry of the Interior's Committee for Building and Department of Architecture were set up to deal with the problem.

8. C. Hansen. The Othonion University (1839-1864), detail of the elevation: the so-called Propylaia. (Studio KONTOS/ Photostock)

Eduard Schaubert was appointed head of the Department, with C. Hansen, Röser and Hoffer as its first officials. While the history of the location and architectural design of the palace was still in the process of evolution, the three architects, using an austere style that included no complicated structures or expensive details, designed Athens' first public buildings: the Royal Mint was designed by the Danish architect Christian Hansen (1835), the Royal Stables by Röser (1834) and the Royal Printing House by Hoffer (1834). Several more architects were progressively added to this team, including F. Stauffert (an Austrian) and E. Laurent. Other offices

10. T. Hansen, Dimitriou House (1842-1843), elevation facing Syntagma Square. Pencil and watercolour on paper. (Vienna, Akademie der bildenden Künste)

in the public service were held by W. von Weiler, the designer of the Military Hospital, and J. Erlacher, who was active mainly in Ermoúpolis on the island of Síros.

The importance of the establishment of the Department of Architecture was not confined merely to the task of erecting a number of buildings of a high standard. Probably of greater significance is the fact that a number of talented young architects were gradually assembled there, most of them from the German states, Austria and Denmark, thus creating a cadre for the development of architectural theory and practice and the study of ancient, medieval and post-medieval Greek architecture. This nucleus was supported by a broader team composed of architects who had been attracted to Athens by the splendour of its ancient past, the desire to study the origi-

9. C. Hansen. The Othonion University (1839-1864), detail of the main entrance. Wall-paintings designed by Karl Rahl (1859) and carried out by Eduard Lebiedzky, 1888-1889. (Photo: N. Panayotopoulos, 2000)

nal buildings, an odd sense of the exotic and the employment opportunities presented by the reconstruction of a country in ruins. Some of them, such as T. Hansen and G. Lüders, settled in Athens while others, including the English architects O. Jones and J. Pennethorne, the Danish G. Bindesbøll and the Germans G. Semper and E. Metzger, stayed there for only short periods.

Isolated as they were in Greece and cut off from close contact with developments in Europe (apart from the information they gleaned from new arrivals in the country), these young architects turned to the ancient monuments, to which they now had easier access, with a new approach.

11. T. Hansen, Dimitriou House (1842-1843). A bay of the ground-floor arcade, showing the combination of red-figure and black-figure decoration. (Vienna, Akademie der bildenden Künste)

They saw them not as romantic ruins, nor even as objects for purely academic study, but as architectural examples that could provide them with models for new designs. This outlook, of course, was the outcome of detailed study – chiefly *in situ* observations, surveys and measured drawings, which were quickly turned into original publications and accurate reconstructions. Systematic study revealed to the architects some of the essential characteristics of ancient Greek architecture, such as the limited size and noticeably small scale of even the larger buildings, the precision of proportions, the clarity of detail, the unity of construction and form and of structure and style, the inherent appropriateness of departures from stereotyped convention, the restraint of decorative features, the use of colour and much more.

Within only a few years, between 1833 and 1843, this newly-acquired knowledge had transformed Athenian architecture. Architectural will now found its source in Athens, not Munich or Berlin. Early heterogeneity gave way to a more homogeneous character that would gradually be adopted as the idiom typical of nineteenth-century Athenian architecture.

The first fully-developed example of the 'Athenian School' of classicism which demonstrated all these characteristics was undoubtedly the University building (1839-1864) designed by Christian Hansen (1803-1883). The founding of the University in 1837 was accompanied by lofty hopes for national regeneration through education and culture and presented an opportunity for the spirit of the country's great benefactors – the generous patrons who endowed Athens and other Greek cities with the cultural and philanthropic institutions and public buildings that still shape their character – to be declared for the first time. Hansen's design for the University abandoned the closed spatial arrangement and adopted instead a double-T plan, in response to the requirements of an outward-looking yet well-ordered style of academic life that was to mark the beginning of a new era of freedom and intellectual prowess. The main elevation of the building, which had been conceived from the outset as an integrated work of art, a *Gesamtbaukunstwerk*, combining architecture, painting and sculpture after the manner of the ancient temple, was in itself a monument to this very idea. Erection of the statues of Rigas Feraios and Patriarch Gregory V intensified the sense of modern Hellenism's ideological self-determination as an amalgam of Western Enlightenment and the Orthodox Christian tradition, while portrayals of the Muses, the Sciences, philosophers and figures from antiquity, from Homer to St. Paul, served as reminders of its origins and principles. The building's actual two-storey structure is concealed behind its unbroken monumental elevation which, for the first time in Athens, satisfactorily defined the notion of public space in relation to the city. Two compact wings are linked by a painted stoa, broken only by a portico flanked by two monolithic Ionic columns that are almost exact replicas of the Ionic columns in the Propylaia. The stoa, besides being a representative example of ancient Greek architecture, here serves its proper functional role. The rationale of 'transitional space' that it expresses is also characteristic of other parts of the building, the supreme example being the Great Hall (Aula). Along the edge of the roof is a classical sima, the corner akroteria are in the form of sphinxes and the water-spouts are copies of the corresponding lion-heads at the corners of the Parthenon. A marble antefix, again similar to those of the Parthenon, hints at the architect's original intention of setting terracotta antefixes along the entire length of the cornice.

12. T. Hansen, the Sinaion Observatory (1842-1846), west elevation (detail). Etching. (Allgemeine Bauzeitung, 1846. Author's own photographic archive)

However, it is in the early work of Theophilos (Theophil) von Hansen (1803-1891) that the first complete examples are encountered of what thereafter became the typical architectural idiom, epitomizing the characteristics of the 'Athenian School'. Theophilos, the younger brother of Christian Hansen, arrived in Athens in October 1838. He was an expert draughtsman and had already acquired a thorough knowledge of the 'Grecian' classical vocabulary while studying at the Copenhagen Royal Academy; during this period he also came into contact, through his professors C.H. Hansen and G.F. Hetsch, with French classicism as represented by Boullée, Ledoux and Durand and the Prussian classicism of Schinkel. After graduating in 1836, he was awarded a scholarship to travel to Greece. Before leaving for Athens, Hansen visited Berlin and Munich to acquaint himself with the work of Schinkel, which impressed him, and also of Klenze and Gärtner, which disappointed him. On arrival in Athens, he worked on the Acropolis excavations under Ludwig Ross and studied both ancient and Byzantine architecture;

13. *T. Hansen. The Sinaion Observatory (1842-1846). Design for a lamp-post. Pencil and watercolour on paper. Vienna, Akademie der bildenden Künste. (Author's own photographic archive)*

he also undertook to teach architectural drawing and building construction at the newly-established School of Arts and Crafts (the predecessor of the Athens School of Fine Arts and the National Technical University) and assisted his brother with the work on Athens University.

In 1841, almost three years after Hansen's arrival in Athens, Antonios Dimitriou, a wealthy Greek merchant living in Trieste, commissioned him to design a mansion to be built almost directly opposite the palace on the site of the present Grande Bretagne Hotel in Syntagma Square.

Hansen's proposal contained evidence of Schinkel's influence alongside elements from both ancient and contemporary Athenian architecture. The arcades along the street frontages were borrowed from the Agoranomeion, while the restrained overall design, with its discreet handling of the building's general form, was inspired by the palace itself. The Dimitriou House introduced to Athens the architectural type known as the *Stadtpalais*, an imposing town house in which the complex demands of an opulent lifestyle were adapted to the spatial restrictions imposed by an urban plot in which the building adjoined those on either side. It also introduced the already complete repertoire of morphological/constructional features based on ancient Greek and Roman decoration – features that would gradually become standard characteristics of Athenian houses: cast iron railings, marble brackets, antefixes, terracotta vases and painted decorative designs. Architecture, construction and decoration were so well integrated in the Dimitriou House and the final result so admirably finished that when the building was completed in 1843, more or less at the same time as the palace, it created a great stir. Otho acclaimed it as a model on which the other buildings around the square should be based.

Early in 1842, Baron Georgios Sinas offered to fund the construction of an Observatory in Athens. As head of the Department of Architecture, Schaubert proposed that it should be built on Likavitós Hill and prepared plans in the Gothic style – a Gothic 'chapel' at the top of the hill – but his plans were rejected. Schaubert then asked T. Hansen to produce an alternative proposal. When this had been approved, Schaubert revealed who had made it and suggested that all responsibility for the project should be transferred to Hansen. It was Schaubert's honesty that brought about one of the happiest associations between patron and architect in the entire history of architecture and certainly the most important in modern Greece. The Observatory was finally located outside the city, on the Hill of the Nymphs, not far from the site of the Heliotropion, the sundial erected by the ancient astronomer Meton. Although at first glance the siting of the Observatory may seem to have no relevance to the city, the hill was nonetheless visible from the principal ancient monuments and insinuated itself into views of the plain of Athens and the Acropolis, so that the Observatory was always part of the 'network' of monuments from the outset. The cruciform plan of the building, crowned by its dome, is – despite the unequal lengths of its four arms – reminiscent of similar Renaissance buildings and a design proposed by Schinkel. In Athens, however, the reintroduction of the dome, especially one standing on a drum, was a direct reference to Attica's Byzantine architectural tradition. In both the dome and other details of the building – the pediment tympana, the lamp-posts, the akroteria – Hansen once again had the opportunity to demonstrate his exceptional capabilities.

Constitutional reforms introduced in 1843 meant that it was no longer possible for foreign employees to occupy positions in the public service. Thus within the space of a few months they had all been relieved of their duties, even those engaged in the supervision of public works. Most of these foreigners returned to their own countries. Theophilos Hansen stayed on to supervise the Observatory project, since all the expenses were being met by Simon Sinas. Once it was completed, he also left. In 1845, shortly before his departure, he spent three months studying and preparing life-size measured drawings of the Monument of Lysikrates: it is fair to say that his brilliant subsequent career in imperial Vienna was entirely founded on these studies.

The period of uncertainty and Lysandros Kaftandzoglou

The first phase of modern Athenian architecture – a period during which important achievements had been made – came to a close with the departure of the foreign architects. The rapid progress of the early years was stemmed. Although several Greek architects (such as P. Kalkos, D. Zezos and T. Vallianos) had studied abroad, the conditions for practising their profession in Athens were quite different. The majority had neither the experience nor even the talent of the best of their predecessors, nor had they studied the ancient monuments so thoroughly. The situation deteriorated even further as a result of the unfavourable way in which architecture was viewed by senior government officials, who set a precedent that has continued with only short breaks until the present day.

The study of ancient monuments by architects active in Greece at that time (with the exception of Kalkos) appears to have come to a standstill. The period of certainty it offered ended;

14. L. Kaftandzoglou, Church of Hagía Iríni (1846-1892), view of the interior. (Photo: N. Panayotopoulos, 2000)

in its place came a time of drifting in vague and confused directions, which were undoubtedly related to the new political and cultural influences on the recently-established Greek state during the 1840s, a decade that was critical for the whole of Europe.

Kleanthis, who apparently showed no interest in the study of ancient architecture, seems to have remained unaffected by Greek architectural trends and to have adhered to Schinkel's school of thought, without slavishly following the classical orders or conventional typology. Cut off, presumably, from state commissions, he took on a multitude of private projects including most of the wealthy residences of the period, in which he showed a flair for innovation by incorporating a number of unexpected features, such as the arched recess in the façade of the Wertheim House, the double external staircase leading up to the entrance to the D. and S. Soutsos House (still standing in a somewhat mutilated state on the corner of Panepistimíou Street and Koraí Street) and the two identical bands of decorative reliefs (one on each storey) replacing the frieze on the Rallis House in Klafthmónos Square.

Kleanthis's 'anti-classical' disposition was given full expression in a series of five projects involving villas and their outbuildings, which he carried out between 1840 and 1848 for Sophie de Marbois, the Duchess of Plaisance: these were Ilissia House in Vassilíssis Sofías Avenue (on the banks of the River Ilissos, then still outside the town) and the Maisonette, the Rododaphne, the Plaisance and the Tourelle at Pendéli. Influenced perhaps by the Duchess's temperament, Kleanthis deliberately turned away from the classical vocabulary, introducing some ambiguous picturesque features in the ground plans and elevations, in a rather abstract fashion that obscured their precise origins. Immediately after this he settled on the island of Paros, and some time later he appears to have abandoned the practice of architecture.

15. E. Schaubert, T. Hansen (original proposal, 1842-1846, see Pl. 2), D. Zezos (1846-1857), F. Boulanger (1857-1862) et al. 'The Metropolitan Cathedral' (1842-1862), detail. Lithograph. (Marinos P. Vretos, «Αι Νέαι Αθήναι», Paris 1861, Pl. 5)

The long period of France's strong cultural influence was officially inaugurated in 1846 with the founding of the French School in Athens. Although the French contribution to Athenian Neoclassicism has remained largely unexplored, the arrival of the Prix d'Athènes scholarship holders could be said to have set in motion the gradual process of disseminating the complex and often conflicting French architectural ideas of the period (free 'archaeological' approaches, theories regarding polychromy, new attitudes to comfort, luxury and sanitation, the introduction of mass-produced construction materials and components, the restoration, rehabilitation or reconstruction of ancient and medieval monuments in the old style, stylistic pluralism), the formal repertoire of the Second Empire and the experience gained from the implementation of Baron Haussmann's new design ideas for Paris. In 1856 French expertise, chiefly in the matter of technical infrastructure, was brought to Athens by the French Development Mission led by a French engineer named Daniel.

16. S. Kleanthis, Ilissia House (1840-1848). Detail of the south elevation facing the River Ilissos and Mount Hymettos. (J. Travlos, «Νεοκλασσική Αρχιτεκτονική στην Ελλάδα», Athens 1967, Fig. 161)

In the field of architecture, the 1840s were indubitably marked by the appearance of Lysandros Kaftandzoglou (1811-1885). The son of a wealthy Macedonian family that had settled in Constantinople, Kaftandzoglou and his brothers and sisters left for Marseille with their widowed French mother immediately after the outbreak of the Greek War of Independence in 1821. He was a brilliant student at St. Luke's Academy in Rome and while still an undergraduate took first place in the annual competition run by the Academy of Milan. In 1830 he sent Kapodistrias a design for a war memorial, and eight years later he arrived in Athens. There he submitted to King Otho a memorandum on the urban planning of Athens and staged an exhibition of his work (mainly undergraduate projects) at the Theseion, but without making much of an impact. He then left for Constantinople, perhaps stopping off at Thessaloníki and Mount Athos. In 1843 he returned to the Greek capital, where he took up the position of Director of the School of Arts and Crafts, and he was soon awarded his first commissions: the churches of Hagios Yeóryios Karítsis and Hagía Iríni.

The problem of church design in modern Greece had been tackled for the first time a few years earlier, in 1842, when plans were drawn up for a new Metropolitan Cathedral. Theophilos Hansen, their designer, had proposed a remarkable combination of Lombard, Renaissance and Byzantine morphological features to enclose a modular composition characterized by longitudinal and vertical emphasis. Klenze had restored the reputation of Byzantine architecture, both theoretically and in practice, in the Allerheiligen Church of the Munich court in 1827. 'We examine those aspects of Byzantine architecture which can be proved to contain elements of ancient conceptual and structural logic, as echoes of Greek antiquity. These elements fit in perfectly with the architectural needs of our time.' In 1842 Couchaud published his *Choix d'églises byzantines*, which was followed in 1845 by Didron's *Manuel d'iconographie chrétienne*; both of these volumes contributed to the reassessment of Byzantine architecture and art. The subsequent relocation of the cathedral from Panepistimíou Street to its present site obliged T. Hansen to make some modifications, on the basis of which the foundations of the church were laid. Immediately after this he had to leave, and responsibility for the project passed initially into the hands of D. Zezos, the creator of a debased style ineptly labelled 'Greek Byzantine', and thereafter to F. Boulanger, who dealt mainly with its decoration.

17. L. Kaftandzoglou, the National Technical University (1860-1876/79), view of the main building with its monumental outdoor staircase and entrance portico. (J. Travlos, «Νεοκλασσική Αρχιτεκτονική στην Ελλάδα», Athens 1967, Fig. 68)

Kaftandzoglou, an architect with an excellent theoretical training and a keen exploratory urge, endeavoured to combine the Byzantine tradition with contemporary international trends in church design and the Neoclassical style. The solutions he proposed to this complex problem constitute one of the most important contributions to modern Greek architecture. In the Church of Hagía Iríni, which served for several years as Metropolitan Cathedral and official Palace Church, the intricacies of Orthodox liturgy and ritual led to an unusual and complex layout consisting of a basilica (three-aisled on the ground floor, but with an unbroken roof span over the gallery) with a narthex, combined with two contiguous domed compartments of inscribed cross plan, one of which contained semicircular choir stalls at the sides and the other a broad central apse in a manner reminiscent of Palladio's Redentore Church in Venice (where similar liturgical considerations had to be taken into account). The existence of these two domes is of particular interest. One of them, invisible from the outside, has a skylight to illuminate the area in front of the sanctuary and the iconostasis, where the sacraments are performed. The other, of the same diameter, is located to the west of the first dome, at a higher level, and is visible from the outside, although it is of no great height, in accordance with the Constantinopolitan tradition; it serves the customary symbolic functions and covers the area corresponding to the choir stalls. It is interesting to note how this exceptionally plastic interior, in which the design strategy manages to preserve the scale and solemn religious atmosphere of a Byzantine church, is enclosed within an uninterrupted two-storey elevation where the classical orders are present in their entirety. At the same time, in the interior, Kaftandzoglou provided a solution to the problem raised earlier by Klenze: how the Doric order (used here in the basilica part of the church) could be crowned by a row of arches.

Despite their architectural merit, Kaftandzoglou's proposals for church design did not meet with the expected response. To begin with, he was addressing a public familiar with functional specialization and expressive complexity. Hardly any of his work was ever completed on time or conformed absolutely with his intentions, since none of his projects had the consistent and generous patronage enjoyed by T. Hansen and, later, by Ziller. This state of affairs naturally reduced any possibility of his buildings' acquiring the status of exemplars. In any case, an architect wishing to imitate Kaftandzoglou would have to be capable of understanding and handling the original models, if not to possess the exceptional talent of Kaftandzoglou himself. That talent was much in evidence in Kaftandzoglou's designs for the Arsákion (1841-1852) and, above all, the National Technical University (N.T.U., 1861-1876).

In the history of architecture, particularly that of classical (or rather classicistic) architecture, it has often happened that an architectural language goes through the process of being formed, then challenged and finally reconstituted. The most typical example of this dialectic process

The establishment of the 'Athenian School' of classicism

– which does not, of course, preclude the simultaneous survival of more than one phase of its evolution – is the transition from the Renaissance style to Mannerism, and then to the Baroque.

18. *L. Kaftandzoglou, the National Technical University (1860-1876/79), view of the atrium in the main building. (J. Travlos, «Νεοκλασσική Αρχιτεκτονική στην Ελλάδα», Athens 1967, Fig. 71)*

After the early days of modern Athenian architecture in the 1830s and the French 'challenge' of the 1850s, we find evidence of just such a reconstitution of the architectural language, with regard to both composition and form, in Athenian classicism around 1860. Certain characteristics of this reconstitution may be seen in Kaftandzoglou's N.T.U. buildings (1861-1876/79), which were funded by the national benefactors N. Stournaris and M. Tossizzas: the replacement of compact schemes by schemes consisting of interconnected wings or building complexes, which took place within the context of establishing a typological design method; the initiation of a sort of dialogue between the various wings or buildings through the introduction of different orders, through differences of scale or through suitable landscaping of outdoor areas; the exhaustive elaboration of the plan; attention to the urban 'presence' of the buildings; thorough clarification and ultimately standardization of stylistic details; and the use of 'quotations' from buildings of the past as features in their own right.

The N.T.U., a complex of monumental design and proportions, has two single-storey T-shaped buildings framing a square two-storey structure with an atrium, which is set back behind the open space between them. The side buildings are distinguished by their pycnostyle Doric colonnades, their close-set columns being set off to advantage by the dark red paintwork on the walls of the stoas. In the central building, at the top of a double staircase leading to the upper floor in accordance with the rules governing the superposition of the architectural orders, the dominant feature is a deep Ionic portico (as in the Propylaia), a copy of the North Porch of the Erechtheion.

19. T. Hansen, the Academy of Athens or Sinaia Academy (1859-1887). Longitudinal section of the assembly hall, with wall-paintings by C. Griepenkerl depicting the myth of Prometheus (1859). Detail. Pencil, tempera and water-colour on paper. Vienna, Akademie der bildenden Künste. (Author's own photographic archive)

The portico is repeated, with appropriate modifications, in the atrium. In combination with the tri-partite Great Hall it creates an unusual cruciform plan, in which one arm of the cross has been replaced by a broad apse.

It is interesting to observe how the route followed as one walks through the building repeatedly shifts away from the line of symmetry and back again – reminiscent, perhaps, of the Villa Giulia in Rome? – and ends up in the Great Hall, exactly in the middle of the apse. This was also to be the starting-point for two semicircular walks around the outside of the building, the plans for which were never put into effect.

A similar composite architectural treatment was given, two years earlier, to the Academy of Athens building (1859-1887), designed by T. Hansen. As in the case of the Observatory, the construction of the Academy was made possible by the generous donations of the Sinas family. In 1856 Simon Sinas inherited the fabulous wealth of his father, Georgios, and immediately dispatched a considerable sum to Otho to be spent on enhancing the city's appearance, finishing the Metropolitan Cathedral, building the Eye Hospital and the Amalíion Orphanage for Girls, and other such purposes. The following year he financed the building, or rather reconstruction, of the Greek Church in Vienna, a project he entrusted to Theophilos Hansen as an expert on Byzantine architecture. When approached with a request to finance the founding of an Academy in Athens, Sinas once again turned to Hansen and commissioned him not only to design the building but to find an appropriate site for it and make arrangements for its purchase.

Hansen returned to Athens in 1859 after spending thirteen years in Vienna, where his reputation was already firmly established. It was at this point that he conceived the idea of the

'Athenian Trilogy', a group of three public buildings of approximately the same size, scale and general composition, proportion and polychrome colour scheme, but avoiding the repeated use of standard elements. The University, which already existed, would stand at the centre of this 'trilogy', with the Academy to its right and a Museum on the left. The proposal was swiftly adopted as part of the plan for Athens, and was the first urban design project in modern Greece.

The design of the Academy was based on the architecture of the Acropolis. The overall conception – the close link between two versions of scale and complexity in the Ionic style, the dynamic composition, the topological relationship between the wings – and the architectural treatment of the approach and entrance to the building are directly derived from the Propylaia. The portico (in which Hansen did not merely reproduce the classical style but also attempted to replicate the colour scheme of the original, thereby establishing a characteristic feature of Athenian classicism) is an exact copy of the east side of the Erechtheion. The elevations of the low wings were modelled on the west elevation of the Erechtheion and only the two colossal columns supporting the statues of Athena and Apollo had their origins outside the Acropolis: they were inspired by the Temple of Apollo at Bassai. There is even a slight curvature of the krepidoma corresponding to that of the Parthenon.

The whole of the central section, with the entrance and the large assembly hall, is typologically a hexastyle amphiprostyle temple. Interestingly, the side windows are missing and light enters only from above, through an aperture in the roof (glass-covered, for practical reasons), in accordance with the theory published in 1847 by L. Ross.

In designing the Athens Academy, Hansen was constantly mindful of the city's 'other' Academy: that of Plato. On the basis of the plan (and as eventually constructed), the assembly hall thus had no dais but only

20. T. Hansen, the Academy of Athens (1859-1887). Detail of the pedimented portico and the statue of Athena by L. Drossis. (Studio KONTOS/Photostock)

rows of seats facing each other with ample space in between for numerous speakers, to enable a frank and unbiased quest for the essence of the matter in hand to be conducted dialectically

and not *ex cathedra*. The painted decoration depicts the myth of Prometheus, an allusion to the Temple of Prometheus that had existed in the ancient Academy. Such an approach could not fail to include what (according to ancient descriptions) was the most striking feature of the grounds of Plato's Academy: a grove of plane and olive trees. A magnificent doorway leads directly into the garden of the Academy from the assembly hall. For the first time in modern Greek architecture since Schinkel, the garden became an integral part of the architectural landscape.

The Academy of Athens is without doubt the crowning achievement of Athenian Neoclassicism – and indeed one of the finest classical buildings in the world. With a degree of success that has remained undiminished to the present day, and without making any concessions in his scrupulous adherence to the classical language, Theophilos Hansen managed not only to combine the requirements of function and appearance and to incorporate into the ancient structural logic some carefully selected structural innovations, but also – through skilful orchestration of the architecture, painting, sculpture and decoration – to create a monument to the tremendous drive for the intellectual regeneration of Hellenism during the first thirty years after independence.

The establishment of the 'Athenian School', which went hand in hand with the progress of work on the N.T.U. and the Academy, gradually weakened the French influence and led to the nationwide diffusion of the Athenian Neoclassical style.

During the 1850s, the most important commissions – ranging from the redesign of the Pírgos Vassilíssis (Château de la Reine, 1851-1854) and a redrafting of Klenze's plans for the Catholic Cathedral of Hagios Dhionísios (1855) to the Hall of the Olympics (1857), the Royal Theatre (1857) and the Parliament building (1858) – seem to have been given to F. Boulanger (1807-1875). Between 1851 and 1854, C. Garnier (1825-1898), the architect who later designed the Paris Opéra, built the Fotilas House at 23 Panepistimiou Street. Around 1870, E. Troumpe, often in collaboration with V. Poitrineau, erected a number of opulent private town houses and the Military Courthouse.

Following in the footsteps of Kalkos, Zezos and Vallianos

21. T. Hansen, the Academy of Athens (1859-1887). View of the coffered ceiling of the portico and the front door. (Studio KONTOS/Photostock)

came a whole new generation of Greek architects, for the most part graduates of the Military Academy. Grigoriadis (designer of the Theodoridis/Efklidis House at 19 Panepistimíou Street, 1864), Ioannis Sechos (architect of the K. Mourouzis House in Piraiás Street, 1868), Anastasios Theofilas (responsible for the Rikakis residence at 59 Panepistimíou Street, 1870) and Ioannis Lazarimos (who operated mainly in Piraeus) were among those who gave character to the frontages along the city's main avenues, using the grand architectural idiom of Theophilos Hansen, who had already designed a splendid villa in Attica (for Simon Sinas, on the site of the Pírgos Vassilíssis?), and Lysandros Kaftandzoglou, and carrying on the heritage of Stamatios Kleanthis. They thus created the framework for the city's monumental public buildings and made a decisive contribution to the civic splendour of Neoclassical Athens.

The symbolic rejection of French influence occurred in 1879 (although Troumpe remained active thereafter). It was in that year that T. Hansen was asked to modify Boulanger's plans (already partially implemented) for the Hall of the Olympics, called the Záppion Hall after the Zappas cousins who financed its construction in expectation of a revival of the Olympic Games.

Given the utilitarian nature of this building and the constraints that existed, Hansen was obliged to focus his attention on creating a compact suite of formal rooms based on the model of the Academy, *mutatis mutandis*. It consisted of an eight-columned Corinthian portico (thus making the Záppion Hall the first Neoclassical building to be erected in Athens in the Corinthian order), a spacious antechamber and a magnificent two-storey circular atrium. The portico contains an enlarged reproduction of Hansen's version of the capital on the Monument of Lysikrates, while the atrium is a self-contained area not encompassed by rooms but essentially independent of its surroundings – a 'room without a roof', so to speak. It is in every way an original classical composition: an Ionic colonnade supports a row of female herms topped by a denticulated entablature – again modelled on the Porch of the Maidens in the Erechtheion or on the Monument of Lysikrates – and large antefixes of a striking and flawless design, in the form of a female portrait mask.

With the building of the Záppion – T. Hansen's design for the Valliánios Library (1886) was substantially derived from his conception of the 'Trilogy' in 1859 – the formative and cre-

23. *The Syriotis House at 23, Vassilíssis Sofías Avenue, circa 1890, architect unknown. (J. Travlos, «Νεοκλασσική Αρχιτεκτονική ☞ στην Ελλάδα», Athens 1967, Fig. 182)*

24. *The Vergotis House at 39, Vassilíssis Sofías Avenue, circa 1880, architect unknown. The parapet of the ground-floor balcony is probably a later addition, circa 1895. (J. Travlos, «Νεοκλασσική Αρχιτεκτονική στην Ελλάδα», Athens 1967)*

25. *The Kondostavlos House on the corner of Akadhimías Street and Voukourestíou Street, circa 1870, architect unknown. (K.I. Biris, «Αι Αθήναι από του 19ου αιώνος εις τον 20όν», Athens 1966, 173)*

26. *S. Kleanthis, Amvrosios Rallis House, Klafthmónos Square, 1837. (K.I. Biris, «Αι Αθήναι από του 19ου αιώνος εις τον 20όν», Athens 1966, 97)*

27. *House on Koumoundhoúrou Square, circa 1875, architect unknown. (J. Travlos, «Νεοκλασσική Αρχιτεκτονική στην Ελλάδα», Athens 1966, Fig. 192)*

28. *I. Sechos, the Konstantinos Mourouzis House at 1, Piraiós Street, 1868. (J. Travlos, «Νεοκλασσική Αρχιτεκτονική στην Ελλάδα», Athens 1967, Fig. 189)*

22. *T. Hansen, Záppion Hall (1879-1888). The portico, with the statue of Evangelos Zappas by I. Kossos at the far end. (Studio KONTOS/Photostock)*

ative period of Athenian Neoclassicism came to an end. However, the classical style did not merely survive but its popularity spread, thanks mainly to Ziller, the most famous and perhaps the most popular of the architects working in Greece at that time.

Ernst Ziller (1837-1923) studied at the Royal School of Architecture in Dresden and was taken on as a draughtsman in T. Hansen's office in Vienna in 1858. He arrived in Athens two years later, as Hansen's deputy, to manage and supervise construction of the Athens Academy. Because of the country's political instability, work on the project made slow progress; after Otho's dethronement it stopped altogether and Ziller returned to Hansen's office in Vienna. It was during this period that he crystallized his own personal idiom, which was to mark him as the most important architect in Vienna in the second half of the nineteenth century. This idiom, known as the 'Hellenische Renaissance', enriched Hansen's already well-developed Hellenizing vocabulary with elements taken from the Italian Renaissance. Its complete codification and absolute internal consistency allowed it to be transferred and applied to almost any building, whatever its scale or purpose. This is precisely what Ziller did on his return to Athens in 1868.

After an extraordinarily long list of projects, many of which – including the Ilíou Mélathron (Troy House), the Athenian residence of Heinrich Schliemann (1878), the Municipal Theatre (from 1872), the Melas House, the Stathatos residence (1895) and Schliemann's tomb – are considered to be amongst the most outstanding works of architecture in Athens, Ziller in effect set the tone for virtually the whole of Greater Athens, from Piraeus and Fáliro to Kifissiá, after 1880, drawing on the Viennese style of Theophilos Hansen.

29. E. Ziller, Ilíou Mélathron, 1878. (J. Travlos, «Νεοκλασσική Αρχιτεκτονική στην Ελλάδα», Athens 1966, Fig. 170)

His lectures at the Technical University, his impeccable professionalism and his standardization and mass-production of decorative elements allowed the widespread use of this idiom as a generalized expression of Athenian, if not Greek, architecture at the end of the nineteenth century and the beginning of the twentieth.

30. E. Ziller, Ilíou Mélathron, 1878. The two-tiered arcade of the façade (detail). (ELIA [Hellenic Literary and Historical Archives Society], D. Papadimos papers)

31. *Working-class house, 45 Hagíon Asomáton Street. (J. Travlos, «Νεοκλασσική Αρχιτεκτονική στην Ελλάδα», Athens 1966, Fig. 207)*

Neoclassical architecture arrived in Athens at a time when in the rest of Europe it was preparing to give way to the miscellaneous trends of historicism and eclecticism. Its arrival (or rather its return) and its contact with the land, the Greek light and of course the monuments, once again revealed the creative core that had been cloaked by centuries of academic elaboration. At the same time it was seen as confirming the longed-for continuity of the ancient world in contemporary Greece and it met existing ideological and practical needs in a manner so satisfactory as to go beyond the realm of 'high' architecture, or at least signature architecture. The vocabulary used in the monumental buildings was adopted in buildings that were inferior in terms of their materials and more modest in intention. It then passed from this intermediate 'school' into popular architecture, that of the anonymous artisans who, having assimilated the main characteristics of the style in their own way, in practice disseminated new forms (such as terracotta antefixes, cantilevered marble balcony supports and iron balcony railings), which through constant use established themselves as typical attributes of nineteenth-century Greek urban architecture. The learned European postscript thus became a modern Greek folk myth.

BIBLIOGRAPHY

Αθηναϊκός Κλασικισμός, Athens (Municipality of Athens Cultural Centre) 1996, with fuller bibliography.

Biris, K., *Αι Αθήναι από του 19ου εις τον 20όν αιώνα*, Athens 1966 (repr. 1997).

Biris, M.G., *Μισός αιώνας Αθηναϊκής Αρχιτεκτονικής, 1875-1926*, Athens 1987.

Johannes, H., and K. Biris, *Αι Αθήναι του Κλασικισμού*, Athens 1939.

Loyer, F., *Architecture de la Grèce contemporaine* (doctoral thesis, 3rd Cycle, University of Paris, P) 1966 (mimeographed).

Mylonas, P., *Le classicisme architectural en Grèce*, Athens 1974.

The Neoclassical Athens of Pavlos Mylonas. Measured Drawings 1941-1955, Athens (Benaki Museum, Documentation Centre For Neo-Hellenic Architecture) 2000.

Νεοκλασική Πόλη και Αρχιτεκτονική (proceedings of conference held on 2-4 Dec. 1983 by the History of Architecture Workshop, Aristotelian University of Thessaloníki), Thessaloníki 1983.

Papageorgiou-Venetas, A., *Hauptstadt Athen, Ein Stadtgedanke des Klassizismus*, Munich 1994.

Papastamos, D., *Ερνέστος Τσίλλερ, προσπάθεια μονογραφίας*, Athens 1973.

Philippidis, D., *Νεοελληνική Αρχιτεκτονική*, Athens 1984.

Russack, H.H., *Deutsche Bauen in Athen*, Berlin 1942.

Skarpia-Heupel, X., *Η μορφολογία του Γερμανικού Κλασικισμού (1789-1848) και η δημιουργική αφομοίωσή του από την Ελληνική αρχιτεκτονική (1833-1897)*, Thessaloníki 1976.

Travlos, J., *Νεοκλασσική Αρχιτεκτονική στην Ελλάδα*, Athens 1967.

CHAPTER XV

*Public Interest in
Modern Architecture
in Athens
between the Wars*

PANAYOTIS TOURNIKIOTIS

2. Periklis Georgakopoulos, central kitchen and laundry building, Sotiría Sanatorium, 1937. (Author's own photographic archive)

❧ *1. Panos Tzelepis, 'Children's City' at Pendéli for the Patriotic Foundation for Social Welfare and Assistance (PIKPA), 1936-1937. (Author's own photographic archive)*

Public Interest in Modern Architecture in Athens between the Wars

The pinnacle of twentieth-century architecture manifested itself in various forms of modernism over a long period spanning several decades, but found its most consummate expression during the inter-war years. While this appraisal may seem self-evident at the turn of the millennium, it is one that acknowledges the continuation, changes and reversals in style that took place at the beginning or end of the century, trends that unquestionably had a decisive impact on both architecture itself and the philosophy on which it is based. In any case, an architectural style can still hand down masterpieces to posterity, irrespective of the way its overall performance is judged over time and above and beyond any organized concentration of innovative and new-fangled ideas. But it was the fresh outlook cultivated during that period which provided fertile ground for an encounter between the materials to hand and the prevailing social and cultural conditions, throwing into prominence a new kind of artistic and architectural creation that continues to influence most of our accomplishments, good and bad, even today. Moreover, it gave rise to the construction of the century's most outstanding buildings, the finest heritage for the future of a new age that promised so much. It is to this pinnacle of perfection that we now turn our attention as we consider the architecture of Athens in the period between the two World Wars. Since much has already been written on the subject of housing styles and private initiative in the architectural field, we shall take a look at buildings erected in the public sector – edifices which constituted shining examples of the modern approach to architectural construction, an approach that had repercussions worldwide (though these buildings may be less than familiar to many of us).

Modern architecture in Athens (indeed, in Greece as a whole) saw a tremendous upsurge at the end of the 1920s and throughout the 1930s – a trend that was expressed through social ideas and reflected the public interest. The visions of Greek architects largely mirrored (at a theoretical level, at least) the approach adopted by the great masters of Europe, as exemplified in France or Germany. As was to be expected, though, their ideas and architectural expression depended (as far as the conditions of the age allowed) on the specific socio-economic, political and cultural circumstances prevailing in Greece during that period. These conditions were very different from the situation that existed in the ruling capitalist states of central Europe. Consequently theoretical specifications – and above all the social and planning documentation of the ideas expressed by, for example, Le Corbusier and the architects who organized the celebrated International Congresses for Modern Architecture – could be seen to have only a relative bearing on what was happening in Greece. Our towns were not yet cities. Even in Athens, houses had only one or two storeys and were surrounded by a garden or courtyard, and the streets were too wide for questions relating to inadequate lighting or ventilation or insanitary housing conditions to apply. Building concentration would have to increase in order to create what for Greece would be a desirable modern city. Besides, industrial development was very limited, as was the presence of a working class, which could hardly have been described as a threat in the sense understood in other European cities. All this does not, of course, mean the situation in Athens was ideal in terms of the social welfare situation that prevailed. On the contrary, many homes failed to meet contemporary standards of hygiene, and where health and education was concerned the scope of the public welfare service was fairly limited. Given these conditions, the opportunities for implementing the social vision embodied in Modern Architecture presented themselves at two levels: on the one hand, the sudden need to provide housing for more than a million refugees following the disastrous war in Asia Minor (1918-1922), in conditions that could be likened to those surrounding the reconstruction of central Europe after the Second World War (more than 80,000 refugee homes were built in under twelve years); and on the other, the political interest in two areas of social welfare, namely education and health, which were part of a broader vision concerning *modernization* that would give Greeks a 'foothold' in Europe (more than 3,000 schools and dozens of hospitals were built in ten years).

In both cases, the public sector called for a style of architecture which would not simply deal with the problems in the most functional and technically correct way, but would at the same time reflect the most recent approaches to these issues adopted by the countries of central Europe. As a strategy, an aesthetic style and an ideology, Modern Architecture was regarded as the principal means for attaining the social vision, much of which was ideological and was encapsulated in the *modernization* of Greece. Innumerable schools, hospitals and refugee homes were thus built, under conditions that were at times enviable, without pressure from social groups or anguished complaints from architects, but rather with the guidance and goodwill of the state which was therefore on the lookout for ambitious (and largely unknown) young architects, many of whom had studied abroad. The results were often impressive and architecture in the Greek capital was widely acclaimed at the time in the context of the modernist movement. This crucial highlighting of the particular relationship between vision and reality as it manifested itself in Athens, changing the city's appearance during the critical decade of the 1930s, forms the nucleus of this article.

The total number of refugees who poured into Greece between 1917 and 1923 in the wake of the Asia Minor disaster, the Russian Revolution and the population exchange with Bulgaria after the First World War has been estimated at 1.4 million – in a country that had (at that time) only four million inhabitants. Roughly half of the refugees settled in rural and the other half in urban areas. The 500,000 or so who settled in various parts of Athens and Piraeus thereby doubled the

3. Dimitris Pikionis, junior school at Pefkákia, 1931-1932. (P. Karantinos)

population of these two conurbations and effectively united them. Twelve main and thirty-four smaller settlements were created at a distance of between one and four kilometres outside the *Refugee apartment blocks* boundaries of the already developed parts of the city. Most of the work was carried out by the Committee for the Rehabilitation of Refugees, which was set up by and run with the direct economic aid and administrative supervision of the League of Nations. Its principal goal was to build as many homes as possible at minimum expense and within the shortest possible time. The layout of the new settlements was simple and followed a geometric grid pattern with very few public open spaces, most

4. Kyriakoulis Panayotakos, junior school in Filoláou Street, 1933. (P. Karantinos)

of these taking the form of squares. The houses were all of the same design, with either one or two rooms and a lavatory. Built in the traditional manner, their sloping tiled roofs were a common characteristic. Many of these buildings still exist in the Kaisarianí and Néa Ionía districts, but it is difficult to evaluate them using the criteria of the modernist movement.

After 1930 the study and construction of buildings passed into the hands of the Ministry of Welfare, which was the agent of the Greek state. It was the first time Greek architects had concerned themselves with housing for the masses. Most of them at that time advocated the multi-storey apartment block as the new, 'civilized' housing method which would provide excellent living conditions even for the poor. Between 1933 and 1936, more than 1,000 small flats in refugee apartment blocks were designed and built in central areas of Athens and Piraeus. These blocks were a clear reflection of the quest by European modernism for cheap housing and efficient urban design techniques, such as those proposed at the 2nd and 3rd International Congresses

for Modern Architecture in 1929 and 1930 and later discussed at the 4th Congress, which was held in Athens in 1933. Each of these congresses sought to attain a minimum dwelling space through a housing type common in Europe at that period. The area of the two-roomed flats with kitchen, lavatory and storeroom ranged from 30 to 33 square metres; single-roomed flats occupied roughly 23 square metres. As a rule the apartment blocks were three storeys high, with no corridors and no lift. A single staircase served six flats and there was a communal laundry area on the top floor or in the basement. The buildings were rectangular and arranged in parallel rows, in simple L-shaped formations or along three sides of a square, depending on the site available and its orientation. They were perfectly plain, without any decorative features. The staircase windows, projecting balconies and geometric shapes revealed a clear sense of the aesthetics of the modern movement. For reasons of economy, the floor of each storey was made of reinforced concrete and supported by plastered masonry. This explains the limitation on apertures. Also for reasons of economy, no landscaping work was carried out in the open space between the buildings. Most of the refugee apartment blocks are still inhabited but they were never collectively maintained; many are deeply scarred from the violent history they saw, as the main strongholds

of the Communist forces, during the civil war (from 1944) and also as a result of the frequent patch-up jobs carried out by the residents themselves in the years that followed.

An outstanding example of one such complex is the refugee housing on Alexándhras Avenue, alongside the High Court buildings. These eight blocks, built between 1933 and 1935 by the architect Kimon Laskaris and civil engineer Dimitris Kyriakos and containing a total of 228 single- or two-roomed apartments, constitute a landmark in the modern city. They are amongst the ten buildings selected by the Greek team for the DoCoMoMo (Documentation and Conservation of buildings, sites and neighbourhoods of the Modern Movement) for the international register of Modern Architecture, but they have been corrupted in the collective consciousness of the people of Athens and now represent a memory of that tragic period of fratricide which ought to be forgotten. From time to time they are threatened with demolition by either the Ministry of the Environment, Planning and Public Works or the National Economy Ministry, both of which plan to replace them with a simple park, or with office accommodation or other questionable schemes. Yet some general maintenance, simple renovation of the interiors and appropriate landscaping of the area around the buildings would have afforded living conditions that were ideal for the crowded city centre – conditions far superior to those prevailing in the nearby private-sector, post-war apartment blocks.

This observation is even more pertinent to the complex of seven apartment blocks, containing 120 flats, built by Kimon Laskaris between 1933 and 1936. His apartments comprised two rooms, kitchen, lavatory and storeroom, all within the space of a mere 30 or 20 square metres. The buildings were arranged around a small square in what is now one of the most prestigious districts in central Athens, close to the wooded Likavitós Hill and only a short distance from the American Embassy (the work of Walter Gropius) and the new Megaron Concert Hall. A further example is the cluster of four apartment blocks at Dhourgoúti, built in 1935-36 by Kimon Laskaris and Dimitris Kyriakos. Between 1938 and 1940 three more blocks were added, bringing the total number of flats to 237. Today the buildings stand alongside a busy traffic intersection and are inhabited by immigrants; the flats are fairly run-down and provide a stark contrast to their linear continuation on Singroú Avenue, with its office blocks, shops and big hotels.

Unlike the wholly compulsory nature of the provision made by the Ministry of Welfare aimed at dealing with an urgent housing problem and trying to resolve it in the most modern way possible (within the confines of European experience) by assigning studies to young architects such as Kimon Laskaris who had just returned from Paris, the Ministry of Education drew up and carried out, as part of a politically justified modernization scheme, a huge and ambitious school-building programme throughout Greece. The programme was implemented mainly by young architects in accordance with specifications grounded on the ideological, rational and aesthetic approach of the modern movement. At the same time, and until the end of the decade, a large number of buildings designed for hospital care and social welfare were planned and erect-

5. Kimon Laskaris and Dimitris Kyriakos, refugee apartment blocks in Alexándhras Avenue, Athens, 1933. (Author's own photographic archive)

ed, with the same objective in view; but unlike the schools, little research into these constructions has so far been carried out and published. As far as both the functionality and the actual construction and appearance of the buildings are concerned, the specifications for both educational establishments and hospitals and social welfare centres largely complied with the criteria of a strict form of rationalism. The systematic spread of these structures throughout the country not only fulfilled the aims of a modern social state, but it also served to propagate the image of austere rectangular blocks concentrated in a simple geometric arrangement with large doors and windows and (more rarely) curves and free-standing pillars, in the traditional surroundings of small towns or the suburbs of

Buildings in the education, health and social welfare sectors

Athens, Piraeus and Thessaloniki. Unlike the refugee apartment blocks, which have retained their original run-down appearance, most of the schools, hospitals and social welfare buildings have undergone major alterations, given that they have to adapt to the constantly changing needs of society. New wings and additional floors have been built, further installations added and in some instances buildings have been demolished; moreover, continuous maintenance work has been carried out with obvious repercussions on the shape and design of the buildings, which were regarded more as useful 'shells' in which people's needs could be better served than as pieces of architecture, modern or otherwise.

The education reform measures introduced in 1929, coupled with the government's overall social policy during the period 1928-1932, produced immediate and impressive results in the education field. By 1933, a total of 1,809 schools had been erected throughout the country, with over 1,000 more still to be built. In order to carry out the design and execution of the immense task it had set itself, the Ministry of Education's technical department recruited members of the younger generation with a feeling for the current trends of the modern movement; only a very few 'masters' from the older generation, such as Dimitris Pikionis and Aristotelis Zachos, took part in the scheme. Many of the school build-

6. Patroklos Karantinos, school at Maroússi, 1932. (P. Karantinos)

ings in Athens attracted the attention of European architects at the 4th Congress for Modern Architecture and were publicized in leading French, German, English and Italian journals. Through references in contemporary publications, detailed records and the conscientious documenting of primary material, school buildings erected during that period were accorded the recognition they deserved, even if very few of them have actually been declared listed buildings. Some examples are appended below.

The junior school that stands amongst the pine trees on the slopes of Likavitós Hill was designed between 1931 and 1932 by Dimitris Pikionis, at that time already a professor at the School of Architecture. The clear-cut prismatic structures with their large, rectangular expanses of glass follow the slope of the hillside, while the natural surroundings in which the school is set are accentuated by means of the stone pathways linking the structures and by the extension of the classrooms on to the roofs of the buildings. However, a number of elements derived from the ancient Greek tradition, such as the stoa on the north-eastern side of the buildings, were grafted on to the general rationalism, along with some facile allusions to the building techniques of anonymous Greek architecture.

7. Nikolaos Mitsakis, junior school in Kolétti Street, 1932. (P. Karantinos)

The two junior schools designed and built in Athens by Kyriakoulis Panayotakos, on Liossíon Street (1932-33) and on Filoláou Street in 1933, received immediate recognition as examples of the style advocated by Le Corbusier (who in his enthusiasm signed his name on the white wall of the Liossíon Street school in the summer of 1933). Built in imposing but plain geometric blocks with a number of selective elements on cantilevered structures or *pilotis*, large expanses of window and a rational use of space, these schools constituted a refreshing intervention in two traditional and relatively undeveloped neighbourhoods, a typical example of the modernization to which the government aspired and the intensely austere nature of Greek modernism.

Further examples of these elements are to be found in the schools designed by Patroklos Karantinos. Erected all over the country, these buildings were endowed with the same spirit of modernism despite the wide variety in their geographic and cultural locations, ranging from alongside the Acropolis in Athens (1931) to Mytilíni (1932), from Síros to Crete and from working-class Piraeus to neo-classical Náfplion.

Nikolaos Mitsakis, on the other hand, sought to establish a balance between the strict idiom of rational modernism and the special characteristics inherent in every region's own cultural expression. He did this by imbuing the design features of the schools he built with allusions

8. Konstantinos Kitsikis, new 300-bed men's wing, Sotiría Sanatorium, 1937.
(Author's own photographic archive)

to both the classical and the popular architectural tradition. In this case, modernity has more to do with the rationale of the building's construction and efficiency than with its shape, which conforms to the austere vocabulary of the purely geometric surfaces found only in the big cities.

The 1930s saw a similar upsurge in the construction of buildings in the health and social welfare sector. Several large hospitals were erected in Athens and other cities and many smaller units sprang up around the country. Incorporating varying degrees of modernism, these functional buildings were designed by architects who were given much greater freedom in their work than those implementing the state-controlled school building programme. Sometimes the austere forms of a modern type of classicism dominated, while at others full cognizance of the basic principles, language and syntax of the modern movement prevailed. There were important developments in the last three years of that decade with the establishment of a state-controlled technical department at the Ministry of Health, which undertook a systematic effort on the lines of the school-building programme – except that it was now fascism that ruled the political scene. This fact prompted a regression to the traditional, local or Neoclassical idiom, but it also paved the way for a strict form of rationalism that in all probability reflected the Italian model.

The first example I shall refer to hovers on the threshold between school building and hospital; it is a fairly early construction, designed in 1929 and built within the first few years of the ensuing decade. The Medical School of Athens University is a real hospital and has retained this use right up to the present day. Its German-educated architect, Emmanouil Kriezis, was a professor of building technology at the School of Architecture. His work was characterized generally by a severe rationalism of function and shape, involving cylindrical and polygonal elements arranged in a linear fashion that harked back to the syntax of Neoclassical structures, and also by the

🕮 9. *Patroklos Karantinos, junior school in Kallispéri Street, 1932. (P. Karantinos)*

interesting and obvious use of reinforced concrete in assembly areas (such as the anatomy amphitheatre) and the stylistic typology of his apertures, with considerable variation.

The hospitals and sanatoria built by Ioannis Despotopoulos, whose studies included a period at the Bauhaus, were designed with more flexible perspectives and a syntactical treatment reminiscent of Alvar Aalto. When the Sotiría sanatorium was built in Athens in 1932, particular emphasis was placed on a simultaneous concern for 'aesthetics and the appropriate design and layout to meet the various needs and requirements' in a composition that had all the basic characteristics of the modern movement but underwent several transformations and modifications as a result of additions made at a later date. Just as impressive, but more austere, is the architecture of the Arkadhía sanatorium built not far from Trípolis, a town then somewhat in decline; as a result the building, now a regional hospital, has remained in its original form, with all the problems inherent in poor maintenance.

To return to the large Sotiría complex in Athens, I should like to mention four other buildings designed in 1937, during the 'fascist' period: (a) the Sotiría Nurses' Home designed by Ioannis Antoniadis, who had studied architecture in Ghent: despite the classical arrangement of shapes, the building featured several characteristics of the modern movement; (b) the new 300-bed men's ward designed by the Berlin-trained architect, Kostas Kitsikis: the most outstanding characteristics of this building were its curved functional design, its resourceful use of natural light and the way that its symmetry was informed by an unmistakably modern vocabulary; (c) the new 300-bed women's ward designed by Panayis Metaxas, who studied architecture in Dresden: the structure exhibited a predominantly linear organization with some striking semi-circular features; and finally, (d) the hospital's central kitchen and laundry complex, designed by another Dresden-trained architect, Periklis Georgakopoulos: his work demonstrated the

10. Emmanouil Kriezis, Athens University Medical School, 1929. (A. Giacumacatos)

most elaborate treatment of the design process so far, based on the principles of the modern movement and totally emancipated from any tendency for morphological or typological retrospection. All four of these buildings still exist and continue to be used as part of the Chest Hospital, but little attention is paid today to the unique quality of their architecture.

During the 1930s, further hospital units were built either with state participation or with donations from public benefactors, and competitions for their design were proclaimed nationally and internationally. As examples dating of this period, I should like to mention the Aglaía Kyriakoú Clinic for Destitute Children, designed by Ioannis Antoniadis (1934-1936), with its corner clock-tower housing the liftshafts; the Georgios Stavros and Georg Fugg Hospital on Mount Párnitha, also the work of Antoniadis (1934-1936); and the Maríka Iliádhi Maternity Hospital, designed by the Swiss architect G. Epitaux in collaboration with his German-trained colleague, Georgios Diamantopoulos (1928-1932). I would also refer to the competition for the construction of the Amalíion Orphanage for Girls at Maroússi, won in 1938 by two architects from Budapest with a design of wholly modern conception that was never actually built; and the abortive competition held in 1936 for plans for a student convalescent home, in which mainly young Greek architects took part; the selection panel was presided over by A. Orlandos.

And finally, the smaller welfare buildings, such as the works of Panos Tzelepis for the Patriotic Foundation for Social Welfare and Assistance (PIKPA), which benefits mainly children, presented some features of particular interest. This children's village, established on the Athens coast between 1936 and 1939 with a manifestly modern idiom, was demolished during the Second World War, but its replacement, built on the slopes of Mount Pendéli (1936-1937), is still in its original state. Built on three sides of a square in a style reminiscent of Bruno Taut, the complex has developed a social rationale of its own regarding the

11. Georgios Zogolopoulos, junior school in Kifissiá, 1931. (Author's own photographic archive)

organization of space in a streamlined construction that features the conspicuous use of rein-forced concrete and equally obvious stonework: the structure follows a more general modulus, from the beds down to the fine details, and seeks to merge, morphologically and symbolically, with the relatively mountainous and wooded terrain on which it is built.

Some hospital buildings, such as the University Hospital designed by Kriezis and the children's villages of Tzelepis, received international acclaim and were publicized in leading journals – because, naturally, of the interest shown by and the relationships that existed between architects – while others received no such recognition or at best were featured in Greek journals. As far as most of these buildings are concerned, there is a prevailing feeling of indifference or even contempt today, both on the part of the state and in the collective consciousness of the general public. If we look at the social welfare structures built in Greece between the wars as a whole – the apartment blocks for refugees, the schools, the hospitals – we could say that a widespread spirit of indifference and contempt prevailed. With the apartment blocks, this feeling takes the form of denial leading to the immediate danger of demolition. With the schools, there are a few exceptions pertaining to a number of broadly acclaimed buildings or ones designated as listed buildings, where the name of the architect is well known (such as Pikionis); most of them, however, have suffered from neglect and poor maintenance as a result of alterations and additions that have rendered the original design unrecognizable, although the buildings are still in use. With regard to the hospital buildings dating from this period, it is too early to speak of the cultivation of any architectural conscience or interest in these structures, even in architectural circles. The largest hospital units and those in urban areas have suffered considerable decay and undergone many alterations and additions for the sake of modernization and improved functionality, whereas many regional hospitals, whose resources are dwindling, have kept their original form but suffer from lack of maintenance.

To sum up, the influence of the modern movement was much in evidence in social welfare buildings in Greece between the wars, but nowadays there is far less awareness of the impor-tance and merit of their architectural style than there was at the time of their construction. In all probability – from a functional, structural and aesthetic point of view – these buildings embodied, at that time, a social and ideological vision of modernization which came to an inglorious end with the fascist dicta-torship and ten years of fighting that included the civil war. Nowadays they represent, more than anything else, the memory of the sufferings of that era and all the shortages and deprivation that existed in postwar Greece – miseries from which the collective consciousness of the Greek people would have liked to be delivered by the demolition of these structures at one fell swoop, thereby blazing the way to a very different and much more opti-mistic future. The façades of the refugee apartment blocks in central Athens, left unmaintained for fifty-five years and still scarred by the bullet holes sustained during the civil war, are no longer looking for some kind of curative intervention in the form of repair and conservation;

*Ineffectual
modernization*

12. *Georgios Zogolopoulos, detail of junior school in Kifissiá, 1931. (Author's own photographic archive)*

what is called for now is total demolition. It is precisely in this context that (as far as modern Greek architects are concerned, at least) the problem regarding conservation or simple mainte-nance of public buildings dating from the period between the wars arises, and also the ques-tion of returning to and delving more deeply into the most important lessons of the modern movement as it was perceived and interpreted in Greece. As for the architectural heritage of a particular place, this cannot be discounted: it may well be a dazzling one, like the dazzling

13. *Ioannis Despotopoulos, Sotiría Sanatorium, 1932. (Author's own photographic archive)*

example provided by many of the buildings referred to earlier; but the fate of this heritage, which ranges from merely fading away into obscurity to being constantly reused and rehabil-itated, is bound up with the way we seek to rebuild the past in our imagination in order to leave a legacy for the future.

BIBLIOGRAPHY

Antoniadis, I.A., «Η κλινική απόρων παίδων Αγλαΐας Κυριακού», *Τεχνικά Χρονικά*, 1 Sept. 1936, 761-767.

—, «Το επί της Πάρνηθος Νοσοκομείον Γεωργίου Σταύρου και Γεωργίου Φουγκ», *Τεχνικά Χρονικά*, 1 Oct. 1936, 900-912.

—, «Ο νέος οίκος αδελφών [της "Σωτηρίας"]», *Τεχνικά Χρονικά*, 1 Mar. 1940, 180-185.

Despotopoulos, I.G., «Το λαϊκόν σανατόριον του θεραπευτηρίου "Σωτηρίας"», *Τεχνικά Χρονικά*, 15 Sept. 1932, 902-907.

Filippidis, Dimitris, *Νεοελληνική Αρχιτεκτονική: αρχιτεκτονική θεωρία καί πράξη (1830-1980) σαν αντανάκλαση των ιδεολογικών επιλογών της νεοελληνικής κουλτούρας*, Athens (Melissa) 1984.

Georgakopoulos, P., «Το κεντρικόν κτίριον μαγειρείων και πλυντηρίων της "Σωτηρίας"», *Τεχνικά Χρονικά*, 15 June 1940, 541-545.

Giacumacatos, Andreas, and Ezio Godoli, *L'architettura delle scuole e il razionalismo in Grecia*, Florence (Modulo) 1985.

Karantinos, Patroklos (ed.), *Τα νέα σχολικά κτίρια*, Athens 1938.

Kitsikis, Kostas, «Το νέον περίπτερον 300 κλινών [της "Σωτηρίας"]», *Τεχνικά Χρονικά*, 1 Mar. 1940, 173-179.

Vassiliou, I., *Η λαϊκή κατοικία: κοινωνικές τεχνικές καί οικονομικές απόψεις – η λαϊκή κατοικία σε διάφορες ξένες χώρες και στην Ελλάδα*, Athens 1944.

SOURCES

Figs. 3, 4, 6, 7 and 9 are taken from Patroklos Karantinos (ed.), *Τα νέα σχολικά κτίρια*, and Fig. 10 from Andreas Giacumacatos and Ezio Godoli, *L'architettura delle scuole e il razionalismo in Grecia*.

CHAPTER XVI

Contemporary Architecture in Athens

DIMITRIS PHILIPPIDIS

2. Shipping offices in Aktí Miaoúli, Piraeus. (Author's own photographic archive)

✐ *1. K. Kyriakidis, T. Exarchopoulos and G. Apostolakos: Glaxo Wellcome office building, Kifissías Avenue, 1992-95. (Author's own photographic archive)*

Contemporary Architecture in Athens

You can view anything that occupies space, such as a city, in three different ways: by approaching it from the outside, first from above and then from below, and then, since the external appearance would probably be insufficient, you would have to penetrate its outer shell and see it from the inside.

Bird's eye View of a Modern City

Athens has been a 'modern' city ever since it became the new capital of independent Greece, at which time it was conceived as an ideal Neoclassical city in accordance with the most advanced planning techniques. Its modernism was summed up by Leo von Klenze when he described Athens as 'a European matter'. This state of affairs has remained unchanged throughout the one and a half centuries since then, in spite of the backsliding, procrastination and vacillation that have characterized official planning policy. The fact is that the monstrous city of Athens today, with its 4,500,000 inhabitants and its endemic problems, is as modern, alive and dynamic as ever, if not more so than ever before. And the same is true of its architecture since the Second World War.

The implied connection between urban planning and architecture is not merely superficial. Like the minute dots forming the 'grain' of a photograph, so the architecture of this conurbation reflects one or other of the features of its planning. Architecture is structurally dependent on the way in which the urban environment, the material aspect of this great city, is born and evolves. Even the architecture of the deceptively distant suburbs belongs to the city and is linked to it by indissoluble blood ties; and the same is true (unimaginable though that would have been only a few decades ago) of areas still further out from the centre, where great swathes of hillside were illegally appropriated and built upon long ago, often after the destruction of the forest by fire. Anyone who doubts this relationship has only to look out over the great plain of Athens from one of the hills in the city, such as the Acropolis or Likavitós (Lykabettos), or from one of the mountains surrounding it, such as Imitós (Hymettos) or Pendéli (Pentelikon). The extent of the 'strident sea of grey' described by so many writers can be seen in satellite photographs, which show up the numerous 'islands' formed by industrial zones, parks, cemeteries and so on (Fig. 1). The endless carpet covering the plain, furrowed all over with the dark lines of main roads (the arteries and veins carrying the city's lifeblood), is composed of focal points and nerve centres (where the concentration of shops and offices thickens the tissue) and areas of still denser texture. This is not meant to imply that the city does not have any sharp angles or 'extremities'. Just as the earth was shown on ancient maps as a finite area, with chaos beyond its outer edge, so the city too has its boundaries, forming the architectural frame that limits it at key points of its structure. Let us start our examination of the components of modern Athens by looking at these boundaries.

The continuous coastal strip has no real beginning or end. If for the sake of argument Pérama is taken as a starting-point, we have to conclude that it extends almost all the way round the peninsula of Attica, taking in the whole length of the Saronic Gulf shoreline to Sounion and then the east coast up as far as Marathon. Along this sea front, whose reflection in the water is especially striking at night, the most heterogeneous and also the most modern architecture is to be found, because the coast has been built up (initially with holiday homes, now with permanent residences) relatively recently and rapidly. Starting from the cluster of shipping offices on Aktí Miaoúli (Fig. 2) and the passenger terminal building (Fig. 3) in the port of Piraeus, the coastal strip runs round the Piraikí peninsula, past the Stadium of Peace and Friendship, along the artificial coastline of the

The sea boundary

3. Aerial view of central Athens, with the First Cemetery and the Záppion Hall in the foreground, the Acropolis and Filopáppou Hill behind. (Author's own photographic archive)

Moskháto and Néo Fáliro shoreline and on to the Fáliro Delta. Next comes a compact mass of recently-built apartment blocks along the coast road (Posidhónos Avenue) as far as Sounion, gradually thinning out as they get further from Athens. These date from the 1970s and 1980s. The only stretch where the coastline has been noticeably altered is at Fáliro, between Platía Flísvou and the shore. Interspersed with the apartment blocks are a number of hotels, here and there the continuity of the built-up area is broken by such gaps as the former Ellinikó airport and several bathing beaches, and in some places it has yet to encroach on the open countryside. The precise boundary between the city proper and the rural municipalities – not that there is any natural environment to speak of, except at Kavoúri and Vouliagméni – is now hard to define. The only real difference between them lies in the nature of the terrain and the line of the coast road, which makes room for occasional pockets of luxurious seaside villas.

The east coast of Attica has always had a less elevated social status. As in the western suburbs of Athens, most of the built-up areas started as clusters of illegally-built houses which were subsequently legalized through successive extensions of the city limits. The full extent of this semi-urban development, where much of Athens finds refuge from the stresses of the city, can best be appreciated from the deck of a ship approaching one of the east coast ports at night, when it appears as an endless expanse of orange lights. One part of this ribbon of development is the exclusive summer resort of Pórto Ráfti. Beyond Marathon Bay the architecture once again betrays the presence of the upper income groups, with larger plots of land and more spacious houses.

Set back a little from the coastal strip between Glifádha and Saronídha, like a rearguard deployed on the lower steps of the Imitós range, there are several sizable pockets of residential development, often with magnificent views over the sea. Many examples of fine architecture can be found here.

The island of Aígina, like its socially inferior neighbour Sálamis, may be considered an integral part of Athens. Here some of the most interesting holiday

4. Studio 66, D. Antonakakis and S. Antonakaki: Residence and studio, Pérdhika, Aégina, 1981 and 1990. (Author's own photographic archive)

homes have been built in recent years. The trend was initiated before the second World War, a characteristic example being the house designed for Nikos Kazantzakis by Vassilis Douras (1936-37), and has continued at a faster pace since 1970, many of the houses being designed by well-known architects (Fig. 4).

The mountains surrounding the plain of Athens, and the perimeters of the hills that emerge like islands from the sea of concrete, are the front line in the running war between the aggressive forces of building development *The mountain* – which are steadily *boundary* gaining ground up the hillsides – and defenceless nature. The main battlegrounds are the areas round abandoned quarries, which mark the present edge of the city. In some outer suburbs these old workings have been converted into open-air theatres, and in the even older quarry on Likavitós there is yet another such theatre designed by Takis Zenetos.

Northwards from the plain the city is expanding unchecked. New houses are rising apace, with or without official planning permission, many of them in the few patches of forest that remain. Some of this high-income residential development is spreading ever higher up the often steep mountainsides, offering magnificent views over the plain of Athens and the sea beyond, and more and more well-designed houses are being built on the slopes of the hills within the city (Fig. 5).

The main roads, described earlier on as 'arteries and veins', would perhaps be better compared with rivers.
There the thunderous *The arteries* roar of traffic never ceas- *and veins* es, shattering the peace and raising the stress level of everyday life. The frontages of some of these arterial roads

5. I. Liapis and I. Skroumbelos: Passenger terminal building, port of Piraeus, 1964-69. (Author's own photographic archive)

present a bewildering phantasmagoria of architectural styles, worth seeing from a fast-moving car as a succession of frames from a film. Amongst the meretricious façades lining Kifissiás, Singroú, Mesoyíon and Kifissoú Avenues some examples of good architecture stand out (Fig. 6).

The arterial roads help the city to expand outwards, but at the same time they encourage the development of local centres outside the historic city centre. Among these areas of increased density one might mention the shopping centres of Kifissiá, Glifádha and Néa Ionía.

The urban carpet covering the Athenian plain is held in place and prevented from slipping, so to speak, by a number of nail-like spikes sticking up into the sky. These are the few skyscrapers and tower blocks – very few

Focal points

in comparison with other big cities – built in the 1970s (Fig. 7).

Low-level Flights

In the crowded streets of central Athens, where the material and spiritual aspects of Greek society are evaluated every day, one can find a deliberately showy style of architecture which has been praised as it deserves, because this area is the city's 'shop window', after all. Even if what is written above gives a complete picture of the broad characteristics of modern Athenian architecture as seen from a distance, that on its own does not answer all the questions. There are more ways than this of reading an abstract representation of the great city's 'skin'. What can we expect to find as we probe deeper into its interior?

6. M. Souvatzidis: Residential and office building, 15 Yialoúrou Street, Attikó Álsos (Tourkovoúnia), 1986-93. (Author's own photographic archive)

Let us forget for the moment the basic skeleton of Athens and examine the distinctive character of the 'carpet' that covers the plain, turning it over to see how it was made, knot by knot. Now the results are more rewarding in that we start noticing some of the city's secrets, the secrets of its sufferings, of the tragedies that have been played out on this stage over the centuries and have left their mark on the buildings. The result is that real estate gradually loses its immobility and comes to life before our eyes: it is born, it falls in love, it dies. The places where the marks of this never-ending struggle are most conspicuous are the centre of Athens, the mysterious 'in-between' areas and the idyllic

The texture of the fabric

outer suburbs. The centre, because there more than anywhere else one is aware of the feeling that the whole city is a historic palimpsest, a feeling totally at odds with the concept of modernity that we are looking for. The in-between areas, because there architecture reverts to the silence of absolute anonymity: anything worth doing and saying has already been done and

7. A. Tombazis: The Dhífros residential development, Ayía Varvára, Khalándri, 1971-75. (Photographic archive of A. Tombazis)

said in the main streets. And the suburbs, because there the fabric of the city thins out and is frayed at the edges: architecture becomes a game of covert intercourse with an artificial nature.

In each case modernity is called in question and undergoes a shift of meaning and gravity. So far we have been *looking at* certain strategic points and boundaries from the outside, but now we are actually *in* some specific but equally vague place, *at* such-and-such a point, *in* such-and-such an area of the city.

The wholesale reconstruction of the centre of Athens in the 1950s and 1960s, turning it into a city of multi-storey apartment blocks and office buildings, came to an end about thirty years ago. Thereafter a start was made on the slow but steady process of restoring such old buildings as had chanced to survive. To a large extent, this return to the past offered a new version of 'modernity' in architecture, because the new could only be expressed as a contradictory reinterpretation of the old.

The desire to preserve memories was mainly confined to old neighbourhoods and was inspired by nostalgia for a lost way of life. These vague yearnings were translated into the refurbishment of certain areas of the city. Although projects of this kind occurred with increasing frequency as time went on, the

In the centre: Preserving memories

case of the Pláka district (Fig. 8) remains unique, in that it was the object of an integrated programme of restoration covering all public places, street frontages and uses.

The idea of protecting the architectural heritage was extended to cover the few, and therefore particularly valuable, open spaces in Athens. That was preceded by the brilliant landscaping of the area round the Acropolis and Filopáppou Hill by Dimitris Pikionis (Fig. 9), perhaps the best-known abroad of all modern Greek architectural projects. Quite often a renewal scheme would involve pedestrianizing a street, the first such case being a part of Voukourestíou Street (1979) and the most recent Ermoú Street (1999). In the course of these twenty years a considerable network of pedestrian precincts has been created in central Athens.

Another major initiative, launched some time later, is the project of joining archaeological sites together in an attempt to restore the ancient continuity between them and link them more closely with the city's contemporary everyday life. A first step has been made in this direction with the pedestrianization of Apostólou Pávlou and Dhionisíou Areopayítou Streets.

Two controversial examples of the redevelopment of old buildings while retaining and restoring their original shells are the work of the architect A.S. Kalligas: the city block containing the old Arsákion School (1984-92) (Fig. 10) and the Mortgage Bank building in Panepistimíou Street (1980-84). This trend was spearheaded by banks: the National Bank of Greece took over and restored the huge Melás House in Kotziá Square, the old Excelsior Hotel in Omónia Square (Fig. 11) and an old house in Thoukidhídhou Street in the Pláka, while Ergobank joined together two old buildings in Kolokotróni Street. The Athens Municipality has converted two defunct industrial plants into centres for the arts: the old gasworks (popularly known as the Gázi) in Piraiós Street (Fig. 12) and the Poulopoulos factory near the 'Theseion' (now the Melina Mercouri Cultural Centre).

Some striking examples of old buildings restored and redeveloped by private enterprise are the theatre in Kikládhon Street (K. Krokos, 1982-83), Karolos Koun's Art Theatre in the Pláka area (M. Perrakis, 1983-84), the theatre in Themistokléous Street, Exárkhia (K. Dekavallas, 1990) and the conversion of an old apartment building into a museum (K. Krokos, 1990-95).

The symbol of all this apparent postwar development is noisy Omónia Square, the hub of modern Greek life, which in 1957 was transformed by the sculptor and architect Yorgos Zongolopoulos into a bold tableau of multiple fountains.

The products of the fundamentally new style of architecture

In the centre: Building the city's new face

made possible by the huge increase in building height limits in central Athens were often disappointing, though obviously there were exceptions. Two office blocks in Akadhimías

8. The Pláka district after renovation and redevelopment, 1973-83. (Photo: N. Panayotopoulos, 2000)

Street stand out among the early works of this period, one designed by Th. Valentis and the other by E. Vourekas and P. Sakellarios. Another twenty years passed before the construction of the superb head office of the Public Power Corporation in Trítis Septemvríou Street, designed by K. Krantonellis, and two very fine bank buildings in Stadhíou Street: the Piraeus Bank by Basil Spence (Fig. 13) and the Alpha Credit Bank by N. Valsamakis. More recently we have had the office blocks designed by A. Tombazis in Vassilíssis Sofías Avenue and by Iason Rizos at the corner of Koraí and Panepistimíou Streets. Of the new hotels built in the last forty years, three have been conspicuous additions to the Athens scene: the Athens Hilton in Vassilíssis Sofías Avenue (Fig. 14), the Amalia in Amalías Avenue and the Astir Palace at the corner of Vassilíssis Sofías Avenue and Panepistimíou Street (Fig. 15).

Several important new buildings devoted to the arts and culture, including the National Gallery of Art, made their appearance in the first twenty years of the postwar reconstruction boom. Later projects in this category have included the extensions to the Benaki Museum (A.S. Kalligas) and the Byzantine Museum (M. Perrakis) and the construction of private art galleries such as the Epikentro (Ch. Papoulias) and the Visual Arts Centre (M. Souvatzidis).

All the above, however, are isolated exceptions in the vast sea of concrete apartment buildings. The rate at which these multi-storey blocks mushroomed after the Second World War, at first in the city centre and then in an ever-widening circle right out to the outer suburbs, was quite astonishing. What is less surprising is that the explosive growth of demand for housing led to a sad falling-off of quality. After an initial period of mediocre architecture, signs of a change began to appear in the work of N. Valsamakis and Takis Zenetos. There was a great boom in the construction of apartment buildings in the 1960s (Fig. 16).

The intermediate zone between the city centre and the suburbs, which is neither a 'boundary zone' nor a recognizable focal point, is a featureless wasteland occupying the empty spaces between the main structural elements in the fabric of the city. It consists

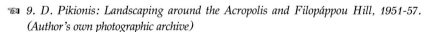

9. D. Pikionis: Landscaping around the Acropolis and Filopáppou Hill, 1951-57. (Author's own photographic archive)

10. A.S. Kalligas: Redevelopment of the Arsákion block, Panepistimíou Street, 1984-92. (Photo: N. Panayotopoulos, 2000)

11. National Bank of Greece: restoration of the former Excelsior Hotel, Omónia Square, 1976-81. (Photo: N. Panayotopoulos, 2000)

12. Athens Municipality: conversion of the old gasworks ('the Gázi'), Piraiós Street. (Photo: N. Panayotopoulos, 2000)

13. Basil Spence: Piraeus Bank, Stadhíou and Koraí Streets, 1977. (Photo: N. Panayotopoulos, 2000)

14. I. Vikelas, E. Vourekas, K. Dekavallas and S. Molfessis: Astir Hotel, Vassilíssis Sofías Avenue and Panepistimíou Street, 1977.
(Photo: N. Panayotopoulos, 2000)

of an infinite variety of architectural styles, each of a different consistency according to the history and particular conditions of each district.

Back there in the dim twilight, such undistinguished architecture is just what one might possibly expect. The likelihood of discovering public or private buildings of any architectural merit in that wilderness of working-class housing must surely be minimal, one would think, yet a few exceptions are to be   ***In the
intermediate zone***

found. One of those is the secondary school at Hagios Dhimítrios designed by Takis Zenetos (1970-76), which looks like an extraterrestrial saucer that has come to earth in an architectural desert. The overwhelming majority of the buildings in this intermediate zone are apartment blocks, though a few single-family houses survive among them.

Like sheets decorated with flowers, so the suburbs of Athens are spangled with floral motifs: we can think of them as an embroidered screen shielding the city proper. Projected on to this screen is a robust architecture, mostly postwar, all of it belonging to the private sector and defiantly opposed to anything suggestive of mass-production or standardization. Consequently the suburbs, or at least the wealthier suburbs, had the good fortune to be adorned with the most representative examples of contemporary architecture. Even the apartment blocks in the suburbs, a necessary evil when the price of land is so astronomic, are in a different class.

There are two simple reasons for this magical transformation in the suburbs: low density and the free-standing arrangement of structures. The result is that buildings are lower, have room to breathe and cease to belong to a 'façade architecture' – in fact in   ***On the screen
of the suburbs***

16. *N. Valsamakis: Apartment building, Semitélou Street, 1951-53. (Author's own photographic archive)*

15. *E. Vourekas, S. Staikos, A. Georgiadis and P. Vassiliadis: Athens Hilton Hotel, Vassilíssis Sofías Avenue, 1963. (Author's own photographic archive)*

some cases there is no street façade at all, as in the house built by N. Valsamakis for himself in Filothéi (1963). Not that the suburban zone consists of nothing but beautiful villas in large, well-kept gardens: here one also finds the 'focal points' of the city's outlying shopping centres, as well as some remnants of old villages or towns (as in Maroússi and Kifissiá). On this 'flight', therefore, we must penetrate into the hinterland of these secretive areas, these distant descendants of Western European garden cities.

17. *K. Krokos: Block of three maisonnettes, Psikhikó, 1990. (Author's own photographic archive)*

Two characteristic suburban houses are illustrated here, one by N. Valsamakis (Fig. 17) and the other by K. Krokos (Fig. 18). Of the apartment buildings and blocks of maisonnettes, some of the best are by T. and D. Biris, G. and E. Manetas and A. Tombazis (Fig. 19). In some of the suburbs the residential areas are interspersed with office blocks and ostentatious factories.

Transcendental Flights

So far we have been looking down on Athens from above, like a deus ex machina *suspended in mid-air above a gigantic model of the city. This approach, giving us a view of the city from a distance, has made it easier for us to pick out everything that is there in reality. What that actually meant, perhaps, was the 'contemporary', in other words that which is unquestionably present and vibrantly tangible. But what may lie beyond the harsh reality inseparably associated with the modern city we have seen below us?*

Into our minds come images of the 'lost' (or mutilated) architecture, all the vanished architecture that lies hidden in the bowels of the earth beneath the modern city. Nearly all of T. Zenetos's houses have been so drastically altered that his designs are visible no longer, nor do G. Zongolopoulos's fountains in Omónia Square still exist. Far worse was the outrage perpetrated on the Fix brewery in Singroú Avenue, also designed by Zenetos (1957): most of it was demolished in

18. A. Tombazis: 'Solar Village 3', a housing estate for 435 families for the Workers' Housing Board, Péfki, 1978-89. (Author's own photographic archive)

1997, leaving only a tragic relic in the heart of Athens. Many other major works of modern archi-tecture have had alterations made to them, perhaps less noticeable from the outside but no less traumatic. The category to which all these cases belong may be described as architectural masquerade. Next we should consider two more categories: the temporary and the paradoxical. Under the former heading comes the temporary structure erected for the World Athletics Championships in 1997, which stirred up a violent outcry; under the latter, the Museum of Modern Art designed by I.M. Pei, which was to have been erected in Riyíllis Street but was shelved when the remains of Aristotle's Lyceum were discovered on its intended site. And this brings us to the last category of all.

Seeing through the eyes of our imagination

There is and always will be a vast amount of unbuilt architecture: buildings that were never intended to be constructed or have been cancelled for one reason or another. Precisely because it has no material existence, this kind of architecture is not limited by the amount of land actually available in Athens: rather, its real place is in the heavens. Yet there are some visionary architects who have been bold enough to try their hand at it. Zenetos did, in his proposal (1966) for a utopian Athens suspended in mid-air like some Cloud-Cuckoo-Land. So did Ch. Papoulias when he rejected the banality of the international competition for the new Acropo-lis Museum and proposed the transcendental Erichthonion Museum (1990) deep underground in the Acropolis, in the place where the Athenians had piously buried the statues mutilated by the Persian invaders. And perhaps the same role may have been played unwittingly by those ghost buildings that won prizes in architectural competitions for Athens but were destined never to see the light of day. That intangible atmosphere must have pervaded the international proposals for Piraiós Street (which coincides with the line of the ancient Long Walls) that were shown in the 'Fragmented City' exhibition at the Athens School of Fine Arts (1997).

Great architecture on paper

BIBLIOGRAPHY

Aesopos, Yiannis, and Yorgos Simeoforidis (ed.), *Landscapes of Modernisation. Greek Architecture 1960s and 1990s*, catalogue of exhibition held in 1999 at Amsterdam, Athens (Metapolis Press).

Condaratos, Savas, and Wilfred Wang (ed.), *20th Century Architecture, Greece*, catalogue of exhi-bition organized in 1999 by the Hellenic Institute of Architecture at the DAM Museum in Frankfurt, Prestel.

Doumanis, Orestes B., *Μεταπολεμική Αρχιτεκτονική στην Ελλάδα 1945-1983*, Athens (Architek-tonika Themata) 1984.

Fessa-Emmanouil, Eleni, *Essays on Neohellenic Architecture*, Athens 2001.

Philippidis, Dimitris, *Μοντέρνα Αρχιτεκτονική στην Ελλάδα*, Athens (Melissa) 2001.

Philippidis, Dimitris, *Νεοελληνική Αρχιτεκτονική*, Athens (Melissa) 1984.

Athens Today

Nikos Vatopoulos

2. The statue of Athena by Vassos Falireas in the Pedhío Áreos park. (Photo: N. Panayotopoulos)

1. The Panathenaic Stadium. (Studio KONTOS/Photostock)

NIKOS VATOPOULOS

Athens Today

The twenty-first century finds Athens faced with perhaps the greatest challenges in its history. In the 1990s the city underwent a gradual change in its population mix, of a kind never experienced before and quite different from previous instances of population change, of which the outstanding cases were those of 1922-1923 (the mass influx of refugees from Asia Minor) and the 1950s and 1960s (urban drift). The new multicultural experience gives Athens all the hallmarks of a modern metropolis: for the first time it has tightly-knit communities of ethnic minorities, the absorption of whom into the fabric of the city is accompanied by – or perhaps causes – a new dynamic. Athens, cast in the role of the metropolis of South-Eastern Europe as early as 1989, has over the years acquired the ways of a new kind of cosmopolitanism; and that in turn, springing as it does from the very heart of the city, causes a variety of symptoms manifested in social behaviour (xenophobia, introversion) and functional restructuring (changes in the city's geography, the public transport network, and so on). These new phenomena, which go hand in hand with the new geopolitical situation in the Balkans because that is what has caused them, are demanding to make their presence felt in social, psychological, architectural and planning matters.

The Athens of the so-called 'new economy', of Economic and Monetary Union (EMU) and the 2004 Olympic Games, is first and foremost an ideological construct. The city continues to grow at its own speed, but the prevailing atmosphere and political priorities (reflecting the recent rise in Greece's geopolitical and diplomatic status in the world) cry out for a new role for it. The new Eleftherios Venizelos Airport at Spata, heralded as 'Southern Europe's new gateway to the world', symbolizes Athens' ambition of playing a leading role in the wider region of the Mediterranean basin, the Balkans and the Middle East while simultaneously taking on a subsidiary position to the major Western European capitals. The options chosen for Athens, at least in this first phase, appear to be governed by expectations of a strengthening of the local economy, and so the initial consequences have been to give greater prominence to business architecture and to ease congestion in the centre by moving much of the new building construction out to the suburbs and the main thoroughfares (Kifissías Avenue, Singroú Avenue), which epitomize the new-found prosperity. However, if Athens is to lay claim to a leading role in the wider region there will have to be some growth of the 'culture market', which many see as a necessary – indeed essential – condition for the city's coming of age in a composite international environment. Athens's emergence as the centre of the new, prosperous Greece in the post-EMU era is causing major changes both in its inhabitants' mentality and in the setting of priorities for the development of the architectural, ekistic and natural environment.

The main thrust of the improvements being undertaken in the city is pointed in two directions: first, to enhance the attractiveness of the archaeological sites (through the network promoted by the Society for the Unification of Archaeological Sites), and secondly to inject new life into the city centre, which after about twenty-five years in the doldrums is beginning to attract investors' interest once again. A common factor linking the improvement of the archaeological sites and the development of the main thoroughfares (now including Piraiós Street, Athinás Street and also Mesoyíon Avenue) exists in the new prospects for economic and tourist development, and for the enhancement of the city's image, opened up by the 2004 Olympic Games. The virtual incorporation of South-East Attica into the metropolitan area consequent

New horizons

3. Syntagma Square from near the Tomb of the Unknown Soldier, early 1980s. (Studio KONTOS/Photostock)

upon the opening of the new airport, which has assimilated the agricultural economy of the Mesóyia plain into the urban economy of the capital, is the culmination of a process of role reallocation between the rural districts of Attica and the urban districts of Athens.

In these changing conditions one can see the emergence of a new attitude to the city. Priority is being given to infrastructure projects and the provision of services to the citizen, and also to attracting private capital. As a result of these two factors it seems reasonable to conjecture that the next stage will be a gradual renewal of the fabric of the city, for one of the main problems hitherto has been the ageing of the infrastructure. Ideological attachment to the ancient world and the mythological, aesthetic and sentimental interpretation of the Attic landscape appears to be on the wane: such things are now viewed more realistically, in accordance with the dictates of the new economy. In the 1990s we have witnessed the appearance of new urban landmarks (hypermarkets on the outskirts of the city or in suburban shopping centres) and huge new exhibition centres, and the conversion of disused factories and industrial installations for other uses. These developments are symptomatic of the transformation of the city from a hybrid agglomeration of social strata to a composite whole made up of population groups which are divided laterally according to their ethnic origin, cultural

traditions, economic aspirations, social mobility and their ability (and desire) to fit into the modern society of information science and new technologies. All these changes – an avalanche of changes in recent years – are creating a functional framework for Athens as the city marches on towards a future that looks somewhat fluid but is approaching inexorably.

490

Recently there has been an internal reallocation of roles between the various districts of Athens and the suburbs. Since about 1975 the main alteration in the social, economic and ekistic structure of Athens has been the movement of whole sections of the urban population from the middle-class residential neighbourhoods of the city centre to the northern, north-eastern and southern suburbs. With the completion of this process and the dispersal of social groups over the whole of the plain of Athens, the established balance between the districts of Athens has been disturbed. Geographical and social mo-

Mobility

bility increased, and since 1990 the city centre has proved too small to cater for the increased demand for entertainment and leisure activities. Today, Athens possesses characteristics more closely related to those of international metropolitan centres. Neighbourhoods that were traditionally full of small shops, such as the Psirrí district, have been rapidly transformed into leisure centres with numerous restaurants and other places of entertainment. The Keramikós, Gázi, Metaxouryío, Rouf and Réndis districts are being given implants of urban life and mass leisure activities. The working class is being pushed ever further out to the periphery, thanks to the

4. The old gasometer at the gasworks (Gázi) after its recent conversion for use as an exhibition hall. (Studio KONTOS/Photostock)

wholesale propagation of the relatively recent homogenized model of consumer living.

The new geography of Athens is shaped by powerful social and economic imperatives, which determine and define the architectural appearance and commercial vigour of each district. For a good many years now the business centre has been moving outwards along Kifissías Avenue, with the heaviest concentration in and around Maroússi, while Maroússi itself and some of the other suburbs (Glifádha, Kifissiá, Khalándri, Néa Smírni, Néa Ionía, Peristéri, etc.) have developed into satellite towns, and the historic centre of Athens is suffering from the repercussions of these shifts.

5. The fish market in the Municipal Market (Varvákios Agorá), currently being redesigned by the architect P. Masouridis in collaboration with the 'Composition and Research' firm of architects.

The picture presented by the historic centre of Athens today falls far short of the expectations implicit in the vision of the Greek capital's new role on the world stage. However, the commercial decline of the years 1985-1995 seems to have bottomed out, with the result that the city centre has been receiving cosmetic treatment and investment, intermittently at first but with steadily increasing frequency. What is at stake for Athens, as a city with historic continuity and a great future, is, first, the reinvigoration of the vital centre – which is not coterminous with the so-called 'historic triangle' (Ermoú St. – Stadhíou St. – Athinás St.) but extends further north and includes the three parallel main thoroughfares (Stadhíou St. – Panepistimíou St. – Akadhimías St.), the Exárkhia and Kolonáki districts and Vassilíssis Sofías Avenue – and the renewal of the built-up area in the chiefly residential districts just outside that zone. Kipséli, Ghází, Zográfou, Káto Patíssia, Pangráti, Néos Kósmos, Koukáki and other parts of the city have a high building density and an appalling lack of open spaces. Moreover, many of the buildings there, built *en masse* between 1955 and 1975, are showing signs of their age to the extent that they are no longer fit for even a decent standard of living.

Quality of life

492

This has been the great problem facing Athens since then. The low quality of life available in, for example, an apartment block somewhere off Patissíon or Akharnón Street (and even in Kolonáki, *mutatis mutandis*) has contributed to the general disenchantment with the city of Athens. Whether we like it or not, the apartment block is the type of building that makes Athens the metropolis it is and defines its architectural style. A major problem with the apartment blocks built since the war is their unroofed spaces, in particular the flat roof (which no one has found any way of making less unsightly or putting to better use) and the light-wells. The cheap materials used in the construction of most apartment blocks makes these problems more acute.

6. *'The Runner' by K. Varotsos. Behind it are the recently renovated apartment blocks in Vassilíssis Sofías Avenue designed by K. Kitsikis in the late 1930s. (Photo: I. Iliadis, 2000)*

It is obvious that as time goes on the standard of the average dwelling-house in the old quarters of the city will get worse, with inevitable effects on the composition of the population and the morale of the inhabitants. This will be offset by the growth and development of the suburbs, which offer a higher standard of living, but we must remember that the city centre – the administrative, commercial and cultural centre – is the part that is expected to exemplify the current tone of the city and to demonstrate the standard of living. The atmosphere of the centre of Athens has most of the characteristics of a Mediterranean city, but in this case those characteristics often appear contradictory. Though extremely small in size, the centre of Athens has many faces. In the 'historic triangle' one can still see something of the

old character of Athens, which was closer to the Middle East than to Western Europe. Visitors are often put off by the confusion and formlessness of the urban environment. Sartre and Simone de Beauvoir, in 1937, felt very uncomfortable in this city of dreary buildings, but they were untypically critical, because some who visited Athens in the same period, such as Henry Miller, were quite won over by its dynamic energy.

Greeks have been brought up to believe that until about 1960 Athens was one of the most beautiful cities in the Mediterranean basin, if not in Europe. This is a deep-rooted belief, but it owes more to a desire to gloss over the bad name attached to the city in recent years than to objective evidence. That explains why Greeks are often surprised at the lack of evidence, or at least of sufficient evidence, to support the view that pre-war visitors found Athens a very attractive city. Most of them wrote about the beauty of the ancient monuments, various picturesque scenes that they associat-

7. *House in Vassilíssis Sofías Avenue designed by A. Metaxas for the Psychas brothers and built in 1894. It is now the French Embassy. (Studio KONTOS/Photostock)*

ed with the Near East and the lively bustle in the streets. There are no significant references to the architecture of the modern era, and it is rare to find a foreign visitor who really liked the Neoclassical houses or even the superb Neoclassical public buildings of the nineteenth century. Perhaps it is true to say that every age has its own standards for interpreting and evaluating what it sees, and the sight of Vassilíssis Sofías Avenue lined with Neoclassical buildings may well have appealed more to a visitor in 1990 (if those splendid architectural monuments had still been standing) than in 1920, when he would perhaps have been more struck by the inadequacy of the city's water supply.

What one notices most in central Athens nowadays is the chaos, rather than any of the city's architectural or other attractions. However, one would be doing the city an injustice if one failed to mention the large number of buildings which, by their stylistic variety, their monumental presence and their quality, give it its character and personality. It would be hard to find any other city that can be stylistically paired with Athens as Vienna is with Budapest and Prague, or Copenhagen with Stockholm. The impression given by Athens is of a hybrid resulting from the Mediterranean understanding of what a great conurbation should be. Historically a crossroads between the Middle East and Mediterranean Europe, Athens looks forward to the future believing in its European destiny.

Incongruities

If one looks closely at present-day Athens from a strictly architectural point of view, one notices that nineteenth- and twentieth-century buildings coexist in a manner rarely found in Europe. In the central areas it is not uncommon to find a street with frontages dating from 1880, 1920, 1935, 1958 and 1975 standing cheek by jowl. This architectural diversity is at once a virtue and a defect: a virtue because it gives one a sense of architectural – and hence aesthetic – tolerance, a defect because it shatters any conception of historic continuity and social cohesion. Yet this visual barrage of heterogeneous architectural styles is an everyday experience for the people of this city, at least in the centre and the old residential areas.

8. *The Rodokanakis house (1930) at 61, Vassilíssis Sofías Avenue, after its recent renovation. (Photo: I. Iliadis, 2000)*

Athens would stand to gain a great deal, even at the political and diplomatic level, if the authorities decided to make an asset out of what appears at first sight to be a liability. They could launch a wide-ranging programme for the restoration of buildings of all periods, even the very re-

9. *The Temple of Olympian Zeus viewed from the Záppion. (Photo: I. Iliadis, 2000)*

cent past; they could compulsorily purchase unsightly blocks in the middle of densely built-up neighbourhoods and turn them into public squares with plenty of trees and shrubs; and they could publicize this unrivalled architectural diversity as one of the city's inalienable assets. Such a course of action calls for self-confidence, which Athens lacks, and ambitious long-term planning. Athens today, for all its cacophony, still has oases of unalloyed urban beauty and still possesses an atmosphere which, if nothing else, can certainly be called interesting.

Some nineteenth-century public buildings in Athens, such as the three well-known architectural monuments by Hansen in Panepistimíou Street (the Academy of Athens, the University and the National Library), the Záppion, the Parliament building, the Old Parliament, the Archaeological Museum, the National Technical University (the 'Polytechnic') and the Eye Hospital, suggest the urban organization of a European city planned on Neoclassical principles. If Athens had kept its Neoclassical framework, it would now be in the privileged position of presenting a unique interpretation of the 'Greek Revival'. It is often said that Neoclassicism was a foreign import into Greece, alien to the local tradition. It is certainly true that some buildings, such as the Academy, could equally well be in other European cities: in fact the Parliament building in Vienna bears a strong resemblance to it, though it is architecturally inferior. But

Attic
Neoclassicism

10. Panoramic view of the Pedhío Áreos park, with the Tourkovoúnia Hills in the background at right. (Studio KONTOS/Photostock)

the point is that the Academy of Athens is one of the most nearly perfect Neoclassical buildings in the world, and it hardly matters whether or not it was a product of Greek society. What does matter is that Greek society was willing to be represented by a building of this kind and that in the long term it has taken it to its heart. What is more, on the fringe of academic Neoclassicism this style of architecture has been transplanted into the quieter streets off the main thoroughfares, and even into low-income neighbourhoods, in an outstandingly successful way. By degrees, the adoption of Neoclassical morphology, often only in the frontage of a house, has finally produced an aesthetically satisfying result. The genesis of Athenian or Attic Neoclassicism is a chapter in the history of European architecture that is often underrated in the international bibliography but is unquestionably important on several levels. There are reasons why the Athenian Neoclassical style, epitomized by the standard two-storey Athenian house, has not been given its due place in international architectural history. About eighty per cent of the houses in Athens were demolished between 1952 and 1975. Within little more than twenty years one of the noblest manifestations of modern Greek architecture was virtually wiped out, and with it was lost an important part of Greek urban culture of the period 1840-1930.

It was only natural that the disappearance of the old Athenian houses led to their being 'canonized', especially by the generations that came of age after 1960. Nowadays it is quite ex-

11. The Aígli, the historic café in the Záppion gardens. (Photo: I. Iliadis, 2000)

ceptional to see two or three Neoclassical houses standing side by side in an Athenian street. Larger aggregations of Neoclassical buildings survive only in the Pláka (where their survival is a source of dissension) and to a lesser extent in the Makriyánni, Thissío and Metaxouryío districts and off Piraiós Street on the fringes of the Psirrí and Keramikós districts. The lower end of Ermoú Street, in the Gázi neighbourhood, presents an interesting aspect of early twentieth-century Athenian architecture, but the best examples are now lost for ever. The greatest concentrations of town houses and apartment blocks were in Exárkhia and Neápoli and in and around Patissíon, Trítis Septemvríou and Akharnón Streets. These were entirely middle-class neighbourhoods until about 1960, when mass rebuilding started.

It is worth dwelling for a moment on what is called the architecture of transition, that is the transition from Neoclassicism to the Modern Movement, which fell on fertile ground in Athens, as we shall see. In formal architecture, the decline of Neoclassicism can be dated to the 1880s, when outside influences – chiefly French – started debasing pure-blooded Classicism with the grandiose Neo-Baroque and Neo-Renaissance eclecticism of the Second Empire. One example is still to be seen at No. 50, Stadhíou Street, where the once splendid Athinoyenis House remains standing in a very dilapidated state. Two other buildings in a similar style were Vouros House (at the corner of Stadhíou Street and Syntagma Square) and Skouloudis House (Syntagma Square, on the site of the King George Hotel), both now demolished; and the same ideas were apparent in the imposing Vougas House (5, Stadhíou Street) designed by Ernst Ziller, which was demolished in about 1970. Ziller, who took Greek nationality and was soon popular with

The early twentieth century

15. Anafiótika, a residential neighbourhood on the north side of the Acropolis where the first houses were built in about 1860. (Studio KONTOS/Photostock)

12. The Parliament building from Ermoú Street in the 1990s. (Studio KONTOS/Photostock)

13. The Parliament building: one of the two entrances on the south side. (Studio KONTOS/Photostock)

14. The Parliament building: the south front, showing the two entrances flanking the Doric stoa. (Studio KONTOS/Photostock)

16. Detail of the front of a house at 13, Polignótou Street, just above the Agora. (Studio KONTOS/Photostock)

17. A typical taverna in the Pláka. (Studio KONTOS/Photostock)

the local community, can perhaps be held responsible for 'undermining' ascetic Classicism by enriching it with Romantic, Pompeian and Renaissance elements. The outstanding example of Neo-Renaissance architecture in Athens is undoubtedly the Ilíou Mélathron (Schliemann's house) in Panepistimíou Street.

In spite of the attractive new stylistic trends infiltrating from the West, purely Classical houses went on being built in Athens until about 1930, but mostly in low-income neighbourhoods, where a few isolated examples can still be found today. But after 1900, and especially after the First World War, Athens was swamped with architectural experiments, most of them designed by young architects who had studied at universities in Western Europe, mainly in Germany. Although new building materials such as reinforced concrete and steel girders had been in use in Athens since the early twentieth century (the first concrete building was erected in 1907), primitive construction methods continued to be widely used, with the result that many buildings lacked the conveniences provided by the new technologies. In fact the lack of basic amenities was one of the reasons why so many notable buildings were demolished after the Second World War.

Although many of the buildings erected in the 1920s have also gone, there are still a number of fine specimens to be seen, such as the Foreign Press Association at No. 23, Akadhimías Street, designed by Vassilis Tsangris. The influx of refugees in and after 1922 led to an unprecedented building boom, and many of the surviving 'old' houses of Athens, mainly in the back streets of urban neighbourhoods, actually date from those years. It is interesting to see that Art Nouveau did not catch on in Athens as it did in other cities in Europe, perhaps because it called for more advanced technology (since it depended largely on the high performance of steel) or

18. The City Hall in Kotziá Square, during the mayoralty of D. Avramopoulos. (Studio KONTOS/Photostock)

perhaps because Athenian society was psychologically far removed from its underlying philosophy. A few Art Nouveau decorative designs (mainly plant motifs) may be spotted by an observant eye in some Athenian houses: their presence owes more to a desire for stylistic variety than an unconditional surrender to a different architectural and visual idiom.

504

Nearly all the products of the 'architectural spring' of the 1930s in Athens are still standing. The Modern Movement, introduced mainly by Greek architects who had studied in Germany, won a large following, at first among the upper middle class and later in low-income neighbourhoods as well. Apartment blocks typical of this peculiar transposition of fundamental Bauhaus principles and Art Deco aesthetics are to be found in large numbers in many parts of Athens, but especially in Kolonáki and Exárkhia. These buildings, often designed by some of the best-known and most distinguished architects of the day (such as K. Panayotakos, K. Kyriakidis, V.

The Modern Movement of the 1930s

Douras, D. Fotiadis and G. Kondoleon), revolutionized the Athenian architectural scene. At first they jarred with the prevailing morphology and scale of the city, for their high walls were out of keeping with the narrow streets – not infrequently unpaved – and often kept out the light. But they appealed to the public because of their high-quality materials, conspicuously visible in the interiors, and most of all because of their 'European' amenities such as lifts, bathrooms, water heaters and central heating. The Neoclassical house with its tiled roof, courtyard and wash-house and its lack of modern conveniences was already past history.

These apartment buildings, as well as the first modern villas in the suburbs (in Psikhikó, Ekáli, Fáliro, Glifádha and elsewhere), are now among the sights of Athens and constitute a precious architectural heritage. The short-lived springtime of Greek architecture lasted only ten years. It was rudely cut short by the outbreak of war in 1940, and by the time peace was restored – which in Greece was not until 1949 – the thread had been broken for ever. It is now a matter of top priority to compile a register of the buildings of the 1930s, which unfortunately are slowly

19. Kotziá Square, with the City Hall in the background. (Studio KONTOS/Photostock)

but surely dwindling in number, and to protect them and focus public attention on them. Even some multi-storey buildings of that period have been demolished in the centre of Athens.

In the last few years, with the absorption of the generations reared in the post-1965 architectural environment into the economically active population, a steady growth of affection for the city's recent heritage has been apparent. Whereas postwar architecture provoked strongly negative reactions until at least 1990, in the last ten years or so the attitude has been more discriminating and people have been developing a warmer feeling for the recent past. Pikionis's work on Filopáppou Hill and the Acropolis (in the 1950s) and the names of the architects Aris Konstantinidis and Takis Zenetos have been accorded general recognition. Little by little the public is getting used to the idea that the architecture of the 1950s and 1960s is not necessarily worthless and that some major buildings and other projects (both private and public), designed by good architects, have helped contemporary Greek society to

20. *The Megaron Concert Hall with its eye-catching multicoloured banners advertising current and coming events. On the right is the statue of Klytaimnestra by the sculptress Chryssa (1992). (Photo: I. Iliadis, 2000)*

regain its self-confidence. The vast metropolis that is Athens has not yet succeeded in accepting its recent past on a large scale, but it is possible to discern a trend towards accepting and giving proper respect to the good examples of recent architecture.

One of the features of the last few years has been the rampant growth of the outer suburbs owing to the saturation of the city centre. Athens is expanding in all directions, and it looks as if it will not be very long before the built-up area extends all the way to Lávrio and Sounion in the south and Rafína in the east. Athens is entering the twenty-first century with its most serious problems unsolved. Environmental and air pollution, the disposal of household and industrial waste and the shortage of parks, gardens and open spaces are real and ominous problems that exist side by side with the city's unprecedented prosperity. The countryside and the market gardens are being pushed ever further out from the centre to the north and north-west, as the whole of eastern Attica marches on towards total urbanization, and this is upsetting the ecological balance, with negative effects on the quality of everyday life. Urban hybrids and architectural forms reproducing functional chaos and the coexistence of commercial activities with private housing are springing up all over Attica. New aesthetic and social models represented in the middle-class suburbs by the new type of apartment building of postmodern form are totally distorting the scale of the suburban zone, which was still apparent until only ten or fifteen years ago in areas such as Voúla and Vrilíssia.

The urbanization of the Athens suburbs, as a natural consequence of the capital's gigantism, has created a vast conurbation whose biggest problem is its functional inefficiency. Quite apart from the incongruous architectural medley and slovenly planning, the disorderly expansion of Greater Athens is accompanied by – if it does not actually cause – far-reaching social changes in the life of both the community as a whole and its individual members. The adoption of mass consumerism as a model for living calls for the creation of counterbalances that will serve as safety valves, and eventually as a means of salvation, for many sections of the population now trapped in a psychological and social stalemate. Of course, the tendency for Athens to take the Western metropolis as a model holds out prospects of improvement as an attitude of tolerance, leading to the acceptance of deviations from a one-dimensional model, comes to be adopted as a social value in its own right.

To sum up, the explosive growth of Athens in the last fifty years has consolidated a cumulative experience of urban living previously unknown in Greece. One can only hope that the continuous redefinition of the city's real identity and the broadening of its outlook through new experiences will help to improve the quality of its inhabitants' life. That is the stake that Athens needs to win in the new century.

21. Panoramic view of Athens by night, looking towards Ambelókipi, with Athens Tower in the middle distance. (Photographic archive of N. Panayotopoulos)

Aesopos, Yannis, and Yorgos Simeoforidis (ed.), *Landscapes of Modernisation. Greek Architecture 1960s and 1990s*, Athens (Metropolis Press) 1999.

Αθήνα, κλεινόν άστυ, Athens (Miletos) 1999.

Η Αθήνα στον 20ό αιώνα. Η Αθήνα όπως δεν φαίνεται. 1940-1985, exhibition catalogue, Athens (Ministry of Culture/Architects' Association) 1985.

Biris, Kostas I., *Αι Αθήναι. Από του 19ου αιώνος εις τόν 20όν*, Athens (Melissa) 1995.

Biris, Manos, *Μισός αιώνας αθηναϊκής αρχιτεκτονικής, 1875-1925*, Athens 1987.

Fessa-Emmanouil, Eleni, «Αρχιτεκτονική επίσημη και γοήτρου στη μεταπολεμική Ελλάδα», *Θέματα Χώρου και Τεχνών* 15 (1984).

Filippidis, Dimitris, *Νεοελληνική Αρχιτεκτονική*, Athens (Melissa) 1984.

Greece: 20th-century Architecture, Deutsches Architektur-Museum/Hellenic Institute of Architecture, Prestel 1999.

Holevas, Nikos Th., *Αρχιτεκτονική του Μεσοπολέμου στα Βαλκάνια*, Athens (Filippotis) 1999.

—, *Η αρχιτεκτονική της Μετάβασης στην Αθήνα του Μεσοπολέμου*, Athens (Libro) 1999.

Kardamitsi-Adami, Maro, *Όταν κτιζόταν η Αθήνα – Δημόσια κτίρια 19ου αι.*, Athens (Libro) 1999.

INDEX

INDEX

521

ATHENS: From the Classical Period to the Present Day (5th Century B.C. – A.D. 2000) was electronically typeset by Mary Karava in G.F.S. Didot founts. Colour separations, filmsetting and stripping by COLORNET Ltd. Art editor: Panos Grigoriadis. Technical editor: Litsa Daniil. Editorial supervisor: Anna Hadjiantoniou. Dust jacket edited by Maria Poli. Printed in 2003 for KOTINOS S.A. under the supervision of M. Toumbis S.A. in an edition of 2,000 copies on Zanders Mega matt 150 gsm paper. Bookbinding by Vassilis Kypraios

KOTINOΣ